Big Money Unleashed

The Chicago Series in Law and Society

EDITED BY JOHN M. CONLEY, CHARLES EPP, AND LYNN MATHER

**Also in the series:**

*The Making of Lawyers' Careers: Inequality and Opportunity in the American Legal Profession*
by Robert L. Nelson, Ronit Dinovitzer, Bryant Garth, Joyce S. Sterling, David B. Wilkins, Meghan Dawe, and Ethan Michelson

*The Crucible of Desegregation: The Uncertain Search for Educational Equality*
by R. Shep Melnick

*Cooperation without Submission: Indigenous Jurisdictions in Native Nation-US Engagements*
by Justin B. Richland

*BigLaw: Money and Meaning in the Modern Law Firm*
by Mitt Regan and Lisa H. Rohrer

*Union by Law: Filipino American Labor Activists, Rights Radicalism, and Racial Capitalism*
by Michael W. McCann with George I. Lovell

*Speaking for the Dying: Life-and-Death Decisions in Intensive Care*
by Susan P. Shapiro

*Just Words, Third Edition: Law, Language and Power*
by John M. Conley, William M. O'Barr and Robin Conley Riner

*Islands of Sovereignty: Haitian Migration and the Borders of Empire*
by Jeffrey S. Kahn

*Building the Prison State: Race and the Politics of Mass Incarceration*
by Heather Schoenfeld

*Navigating Conflict: How Youth Handle Trouble in a High-Poverty School*
by Calvin Morrill and Michael Musheno

*The Sit-Ins: Protest and Legal Change in the Civil Rights Era*
by Christopher W. Schmidt

*Working Law: Courts, Corporations, and Symbolic Civil Rights*
by Lauren B. Edelman

*The Myth of the Litigious Society: Why We Don't Sue*
by David M. Engel

*Policing Immigrants: Local Law Enforcement on the Front Lines*
by Doris Marie Provine, Monica W. Varsanyi, Paul G. Lewis, and Scott H. Decker

*The Seductions of Quantification: Measuring Human Rights, Gender Violence, and Sex Trafficking*
by Sally Engle Merry

*Additional series titles follow index.*

# Big Money Unleashed

## The Campaign to Deregulate Election Spending

ANN SOUTHWORTH

The University of Chicago Press
Chicago and London

The University of Chicago Press, Chicago 60637
The University of Chicago Press, Ltd., London
Published 2023
Printed in the United States of America

32  31  30  29  28  27  26  25  24  23      1  2  3  4  5

ISBN-13: 978-0-226-83071-1 (cloth)
ISBN-13: 978-0-226-83073-5 (paper)
ISBN-13: 978-0-226-83072-8 (e-book)
DOI: https://doi.org/10.7208/chicago/9780226830728.001.0001

Library of Congress Cataloging-in-Publication Data

Names: Southworth, Ann, author.
Title: Big money unleashed : the campaign to deregulate election spending /
    Ann Southworth.
Other titles: Chicago series in law and society.
Description: Chicago : The University of Chicago Press, 2023. |
    Series: The Chicago series in law and society | Includes bibliographical
    references and index.
Identifiers: LCCN 2023019872 | ISBN 9780226830711 (cloth) |
    ISBN 9780226830735 (paperback) | ISBN 9780226830728 (ebook)
Subjects: LCSH: Campaign funds—Law and legislation—United States. |
    Elections—United States.
Classification: LCC JK1991 .S688 2023 | DDC 324.0973—dc23/eng/20230427
LC record available at https://lccn.loc.gov/2023019872

*To John, Amy, and Ben*

# Contents

# $peech

On January 8, 2021, one of Senator Mitch McConnell's policy advisers held a private conference call with leaders of conservative groups and Republican congressional staffers. The purpose was to discuss how to defeat legislation that would require corporations, trade associations, and nonprofit organizations that engage in election spending to publicly disclose donors who contribute more than $10,000 in an election cycle. Participants on the call acknowledged that American voters across the political spectrum favor requiring more public disclosure of big political donors. The research director for Stand Together, an advocacy group founded by billionaire Charles Koch, told those on the call that it would be "incredibly difficult" to change public opinion about the need for this measure. He also warned against responding to the argument that the legislation "stops billionaires from buying elections." He explained: "Unfortunately, we've found that that is a winning message, for both the general public and also conservatives." Rather than debate the bill, he advised Republicans to use legislative tactics to kill it.[1]

Senate Minority Leader McConnell vowed to defeat the legislation, but he also predicted that the courts would strike it down if it passed: "Hopefully political speech and the First Amendment will prevail in a more neutral format—in court . . . [F]ortunately . . . the court system over the years . . . has kept [legislators] from doing the kinds of things they are trying to do."[2]

The US Constitution does not mention money in politics, much less any right of large donors to engage in undisclosed election spending. McConnell nonetheless had reason to believe that the Supreme Court might declare the legislation unconstitutional. This book explores the developments that gave him that confidence.

\* \* \*

Most Americans, across party lines, believe that big contributors to election campaigns have more access and influence than others and that they use that power to skew public policy to their advantage.[3] Politicians ranging from Bernie Sanders[4] to Donald Trump[5] claim that the reliance by candidates and elected officials on major donors is breaking democracy. Only 20 percent of Americans say that they are satisfied with the nation's campaign finance laws.[6]

Yet legislators are limited in addressing these concerns by Supreme Court decisions holding that campaign contributions and expenditures are a form of speech protected by the Constitution and that most regulation of this type of political expression violates the First Amendment. Since the middle of the first decade of the 2000s, the Supreme Court has overturned myriad laws directed at the financing of election campaigns, and there is reason to believe that the Roberts Court will continue down this path toward invalidating constraints on campaign spending and contributions. How did the First Amendment become a major obstacle to regulating money in American politics?

The constitutional law that limits legislative action in this area is the result of a long-term process involving many players. The justices played critical roles, of course, but so did the attorneys who devised the theories necessary to support the legal doctrine, the legal-advocacy groups that pursued a litigation campaign to advance those theories, the patrons who financed these efforts, and the networks through which these actors coordinated strategy and held the Court accountable.

There was nothing inevitable about how those theories, actors, and resources came together to create new law. Nor was there anything inevitable about the constitutional doctrine that resulted.

Drawing from interviews with fifty-two lawyers who participated in key cases, as well as from public records and archival materials, this book explores the process that generated the doctrine. This book is not primarily about whether or how we should regulate money in American politics, or the competing constitutional values at stake. Nor is it about the complex body of constitutional law that governs campaign finance. Rather, it is a story of how lawyers and other key actors worked with the justices to create that law, borrowing a litigation strategy pioneered by the NAACP Legal Defense Fund to dismantle racial segregation and using it to advance a very different type of cause.

As a result of this litigation offensive, claims about the meaning of the First Amendment that were novel when introduced decades ago are now firmly embedded in constitutional law. The doctrine is a source of power for those with big money to wield in politics and for the politicians who at-tract that financial support. The judicial rulings have unleashed billions in election spending by super PACs (the popular name for what the FEC calls independent-expenditure-only political committees) and other politically ac-tive groups. Much of that spending is "dark"—meaning that the identities of large donors who seek to influence elections and elected officials through these entities are not disclosed to the public.

∗ ∗ ∗

The Supreme Court's validation of the idea that the First Amendment lim-its legislators' authority to regulate money in politics is a relatively recent phenomenon—less than fifty years old. The Court's most expansive rulings on the issue are more recent still—all products of the past two decades.

The first major decision on the topic came in *Buckley v. Valeo* (1976), aris-ing from a legal challenge to election-reform legislation adopted in the wake of the Watergate scandal.[7] The Supreme Court found that campaign finance restrictions violated the First Amendment's guarantee of free speech and as-sociation unless they served a governmental interest in preventing "corrup-tion" or "the appearance of corruption." Government could not regulate to promote political equality.[8] The Court struck down key parts of the law while leaving other pieces untouched.

For years after *Buckley*, the Supreme Court upheld campaign finance laws that could be construed as fighting corruption. But since the middle of the first decade of the 2000s, the Court has adopted a much more skep-tical stance, ruling many restrictions unconstitutional. In the most famous of these decisions, *Citizens United v. Federal Election Commission* (2010),[9] the Court held that corporations and unions have a First Amendment right to spend unlimited amounts on elections. It also found that quid pro quo corruption—trading money for political favors—is the only type of concern that the Constitution permits legislators to address through restrictions on money in politics. In this and other blockbuster decisions, the Court over-ruled precedents and repudiated the reasoning of prior cases. Reform advo-cates fear that the Court might further limit the reach of campaign finance regulation, perhaps even by striking down campaign contribution limits and disclosure requirements approved in *Buckley*.

To explain the Court's sharp deregulatory turn, election law experts fre-quently point to the retirement of Justice Sandra Day O'Connor and her re-placement by Samuel Alito in 2006.[10] Lawyers whom I interviewed agreed with this assessment. One called the replacement of Justice O'Connor with Justice Alito "cataclysmic," while another said that "what really matters is the ideology of the bench, more than anything [else]." The Supreme Court began to assume a more hostile stance toward campaign finance laws as Republican-appointed justices vetted through the conservative legal movement gained control of the Court. Justice Alito's appointment gave opponents of regulation the majority they needed. Since then, under the leadership of Chief Justice John Roberts, the Court has invalidated or severely limited nearly every campaign finance restriction it has considered.[11] Subsequent appointments of Justices Neil Gorsuch, Brett Kavanaugh, and Amy Coney Barrett have reinforced the confidence of those who want the Roberts Court's campaign finance rulings to endure and the deregulatory trend to continue.[12] In short, the justices are an important part of the story of how most campaign finance regulation has become vulnerable to constitutional challenge.[13]

But that is not the whole story, and what it leaves out should interest those who care about how constitutional law is made and remade and how conservatives have achieved significant gains through the courts in recent decades.

This account begins in the early 1970s, when a few entrepreneurial lawyers demonstrated how a policy dispute about regulating money in politics could be transformed into a constitutional battle waged through litigation. They received support from wealthy individuals of the political left and right who wanted greater freedom to use their money in elections and from politicians who wanted those individuals' financial backing. The effort gathered steam as opponents of regulation established specialized groups to challenge restrictions, recruited plaintiffs and ideologically committed lawyers, and introduced and reworked ideas to unite disparate groups and constituencies (or at least the lawyers for these groups and constituencies) around the idea that regulating campaign spending amounts to censoring political expression. The Federalist Society for Law and Public Policy Studies, a conservative and libertarian lawyer network founded in 1982, served as a site for cultivating arguments and coordinating support. Lawyers showed various types of conservatives how free-speech claims could be useful in other policy contests.[14] They tapped into legal mobilizing efforts around abortion, guns, and Tea Party activism, as well as populist mistrust of elites. The effort also attracted partial support from some civil libertarian and labor groups.

My interest in this topic grew out of my last book, *Lawyers of the Right: Professionalizing the Conservative Coalition* (2008), which examined how lawyers have contributed to the conservative revolution in American law since the 1970s. That book explored the role of lawyer networks in generating ideas necessary to change law, cultivating credibility for those ideas, pursuing law-reform campaigns modeled on those of public interest law groups of the Left, and building litigation alliances. It also considered the challenges of managing deep differences in the policy priorities of the primary constituencies of the conservative legal movement. Several "mediator" organizations—the Federalist Society and the Heritage Foundation—tried to bridge class, cultural, and ideological divisions among the lawyers for these constituencies and to mobilize the groups they led around common goals, primarily by appealing to broad themes and a shared interest in maintaining a winning coalition. While these constituencies mostly avoided direct conflict with one another in Supreme Court litigation during the period covered by my research, they generally did not actively assist one another. However, campaign finance regulation was one issue on which organizations linked with all the major constituencies of the Republican alliance joined together on the same side in litigation before the Supreme Court to argue that these regulations infringed on First Amendment rights to free speech and political association. I found it curious that groups claiming to represent the interests of social conservatives assisted in a battle that seemed likely to benefit primarily wealthy individuals and corporations, perhaps even at the expense of the more populist elements of the Republican alliance. That puzzling phenomenon was the impetus for this book.

Most scholarly and journalistic accounts of the evolution of campaign finance law do not focus on nonjudicial participants in this litigation campaign, but there are important exceptions. Robert Mutch has written two excellent books on the history of campaign finance regulation and the involvement of interest groups in legislative fights and related lawsuits.[15] His work identifies legal scholars and lawyers who crafted the First Amendment arguments that prevailed in *Buckley*, and I draw on his research in chapter 2 to piece together the early history of the litigation campaign. Gordon Silverstein's analysis of the interplay between Congress and the courts over campaign finance regulation touches on the roles of reform advocates.[16] Amanda Hollis-Brusky has documented the Federalist Society's influence on constitutional doctrine in several areas, including campaign finance, and she has identified some of the ways lawyers in this network created the intellectual capital necessary to persuade the Court to rule as it did in *Citizens United*.[17] Other scholars have provided fascinating chronicles of lawyer strategizing around *Citizens United*[18] and another important case, *McCutcheon v. Federal Election Commission* (2014), which struck down aggregate limits on the contributions an individual can give to candidates and political committees in an election cycle.[19] Mary Ziegler has written an important book on the role that the antiabortion movement played in the fight against campaign finance limits and how pro-life leaders—including James Bopp, general counsel to the National Right to Life Committee—sought to persuade social conservatives that it was a battle worth waging to gain control of the Supreme Court.[20] Wayne Batchis has examined how political alignments on campaign finance regulation have helped to flip the script on the constitutional politics of the First Amendment, as conservatives of all stripes oppose the regulation of money in politics and most liberals and progressives defend it.[21] But we do not yet have a general account of how lawyers and their organizations and patrons contributed to these developments. The topic deserves greater attention than it has received thus far because these actors have played critical roles in anchoring protection for wealth-based political influence in constitutional law.

This account draws on a variety of publicly available materials about the lawyers and organizations participating in major campaign finance decisions since the mid-1970s. For three major campaign finance cases decided by the Roberts Court—*Citizens United v. Federal Election Commission* (2010), *Arizona Free Enterprise Club's Freedom PAC v. Bennett* (2011),[22] and *McCutcheon v. Federal Election Commission* (2014)[23]—I compiled data about the alignments, missions, and financial supporters of the organizations that filed briefs, as well as biographical information about all lawyers on briefs in those cases. I also gathered all briefs filed in twelve major Supreme Court decisions on campaign finance regulation, from *Buckley* to *McCutcheon*. Using text analysis software, I analyzed the language used in these briefs and the Court's opinions to identify broad patterns in the discourse.

This book also draws from confidential interviews conducted from July 2015 through November 2017 with fifty-two lawyers who participated in major cases challenging the constitutionality of campaign finance regulations. These lawyers told me about their roles in the litigation, as well as their strategies, networks, perceptions of the stakes, and efforts to build alliances, along with many other aspects of this remarkable process of constitutional lawmaking. Their commentary supplies valuable behind-the-scenes information on topics about which other sources are entirely silent. What these lawyers recounted in interviews sheds light on how this campaign evolved and how it achieved considerable success.

All but a few of the interviewed lawyers represented parties or filed amicus curiae ("friend of the court") briefs in one or more of the three major campaign finance cases just mentioned. I interviewed lawyers on sixty-eight of the 122 briefs filed in those three cases. The opposing sides were equally represented in my sample. The interviewed lawyers represented all the major constituencies active in the litigation and all types of actors: political parties and candidates, sponsors and opponents of legislation, other elected and appointed government officials, business and trade groups, labor unions, think tanks, advocacy organizations, and scholars. I cannot say which of the parties and amici were represented by the lawyers I interviewed without compromising confidentiality, but I can say that I interviewed many of the key players. Some of the interviewed lawyers were elite appellate advocates; ten of them had handled one or more oral arguments in major campaign finance cases before the Supreme Court. Many were experienced election law experts steeped in the intricacies of campaign finance regulation through their regular navigation of those rules on behalf of candidates and party committees. They included some of the most accomplished and famous appellate advocates of our time, former members of the Federal Election Commission, and other lawyers who regularly participate at the highest levels of national debate about election law and the meaning of the First Amendment. Some lawyers interviewed for this project held considerably less substantive expertise but often no less (and frequently more) conviction about the stakes.

Those who champion the regulation of money in politics claim that their goal is reducing the outsized political influence of moneyed interests. They characterize the laws that they pursue and defend as electoral reforms. Those who challenge campaign finance regulations are skeptical about the purposes and effects of those laws, but they nevertheless frequently use the label "reformer," sometimes in scare quotes, to refer to their adversaries.[24] I therefore use the term "reformers" advisedly throughout the book to describe those who defend campaign finance regulations. I use "challengers" throughout to refer to those who seek to defeat and overturn these laws.

There were some notable differences in the overall characteristics of the reformers and challengers. The proportion of the challengers who attended the nation's top-ranked law schools was much smaller than the proportion of reformers who attended those schools, and the challengers' work locations were more geographically diverse than those of the reformers, the vast majority of whom worked in major coastal cities. Many of the challengers worked in small firms and advocacy organizations located far from major metropolitan centers. The greater diversity in the educational backgrounds and office locations of the lawyers on the challengers' side dovetails nicely with the narrative of the litigation campaign. According to that narrative, those who challenge regulation represent the interests of a broad cross section of Americans, and those who defend them protect the power of the political establishment, mainstream media, and coastal elites. One question animating this research is whether that narrative reflects the truth about whose interests and preferences this litigation campaign serves.

Part 1 of this book describes the litigation campaign. Chapter 1 situates the effort in the broad history of campaign finance legislation, the Supreme Court's changing stance toward the constitutionality of such regulation, and the broader political and social movements surrounding the Court's rulings. It explains how the modern conservative legal movement created the conditions necessary for the creation of new doctrine. Chapter 2 identifies the small group of lawyers, interest groups, and patrons who, in the 1970s and 1980s, sought to use First Amendment arguments to defeat campaign finance regulation. Entrepreneurial lawyers developed some of the arguments necessary to create new constitutional law and then took the issue to the courts, where they met resistance from advocates and groups aligned with the legislation's sponsors. The alignments of parties and amici in these early challenges were not particularly partisan. Left-leaning civil libertarians played significant roles in these cases. Chapter 3 examines how the campaign acquired a more partisan valence and how it gained momentum in the 1990s, as patrons invested in specialized expertise, strategic case selection, and evocative rhetoric. Elaborating on themes set forth in the campaign's early years, litigants characterized the controversy as a fight between elites, who sought to limit political expression, and ordinary Americans who needed greater freedom to speak about elections—notwithstanding that some of these lawsuits challenged limits on contributions and spending that far exceeded amounts that fit the budgets of most ordinary Americans. Opponents of regulation attracted new patrons and coalition partners and found elite lawyers willing to make the arguments. The Federalist Society's Free Speech and Election Law Practice Group played an important role in mobilizing and organizing the effort and bringing new advocates on board. Chapter 4 considers the lawyers, organizations, and patrons behind big wins for opponents of campaign finance regulation in the Roberts Court, focusing on three of their most significant victories. All these challenges were brought by conservative or libertarian nonprofit advocacy groups, and all featured parties and amici claiming to vindicate the First Amendment rights of regular people. Armies of interest groups and lawyers, mostly divided by political affiliation and sources of financial support, lined up on opposing sides of these cases.

Part 2 explores major themes and implications of the litigation campaign. Chapter 5 describes the litigation coalition in *Citizens United*, highlighting two aspects of this coalition that might seem strange. One is the participation of groups associated with constituencies that generally align with the Republican Party but would seem to have little direct interest in dismantling campaign finance regulation. The other is the partial support of groups ordinarily associated with liberal causes: the ACLU and the AFL-CIO. This chapter tries to explain why organizations claiming to represent constituencies that appear to be very differently situated with respect to money in politics joined together in the fight. Chapter 6 demonstrates how themes of the campaign have become entrenched in law and amplified in the commentary of the challengers. It also explores the opposing worldviews expressed by the teams of lawyers involved in these cases and how they relate to larger themes about freedom and democracy in the competing constitutional claims of the major parties. Chapter 7 examines the lawyers' commentary on the legitimacy of the campaign. The challengers offered a heroic narrative, with some of the most passionate defenses of the Court's overruling of major precedents—including decisions striking down restrictions on campaign spending by business corporations and wealthy individuals—coming from lawyers associated with the Republican Party's base and claiming to speak for people who would seem to have little to gain from these rulings. Reformers accused the Supreme Court of engaging in judicial activism and raised questions about lawyer accountability much like those directed at liberal-rights advocates in the 1960s and '70s. Chapter 8 explores what the challengers still seek to accomplish and how reformers hope to resist and reverse some of the challengers' gains. It also considers why the challengers thus far have been unable to achieve some of their most ambitious goals. The final chapter addresses what this case study tells us about the dynamics of constitutional change and the cycles of mobilization and countermobilization that produce it.

What follows is a story about the creation of constitutional doctrine that gives Mitch McConnell and other opponents of campaign finance regulation confidence that they will defeat such regulation in the courts even if legislators try to impose new restrictions on big money in American politics.

# PART ONE

# The Campaign

# The Players and Process

In *Citizens United v. Federal Election Commission* (2010), a 5–4 ruling, every justice appointed by a Republican president joined in the majority opinion finding that corporations and unions have a First Amendment right to spend unlimited amounts on elections, while every justice appointed by a Democratic president dissented.[1] *Citizens United* overruled another major case decided twenty years earlier, *Austin v. Michigan Chamber of Commerce* (1990). In *Austin*, then chief justice William Rehnquist, a Nixon appointee and a staunch conservative by the standards of the time, had joined in the majority opinion, as had two other Republican appointees. The position that these justices took in 1990 would get them laughed out of Federalist Society circles today.

How did a perspective about the meaning of the First Amendment that was entirely acceptable among conservative lawyers and judges in 1990 become anathema to Republican legal elites in 2010? Of course, the text of the Constitution had not changed. What had changed were claims about the meaning of the First Amendment—claims made by Republican Party leaders and their supporters and allies through a process that extended well beyond the Supreme Court.

✶ ✶ ✶

I will not focus here or in subsequent chapters on the details of campaign finance legislation or the Supreme Court's decisions in cases challenging those laws. But a brief description of the broad outlines of the legislative targets of the litigation campaign and the Supreme Court's changing stances provides useful background for what follows.

**The Legislative Targets.**   Legislative efforts to regulate money in elections go back more than a century. The first major federal campaign finance reform legislation passed with majorities in both houses of Congress during the The-odore Roosevelt and William Howard Taft administrations. This legislation was a response to populist anger about the increasing power of corporations and their leaders. Business money, including secret money from industrial barons in the late nineteenth and early twentieth centuries, had become a dominant force in elections. The Tillman Act, passed in 1907, prohibited corpo-rations from making campaign contributions. Congress periodically changed and added to these regulations. For example, it adopted more stringent dis-closure requirements on political committees in the 1920s, following the Tea-pot Dome scandal, which revealed a link between large campaign contributions to the Republican Party and a lease for a large oil reserve in Wyoming. In the 1940s, Congress imposed limits on federal election spending by corporations and unions.

For six decades following passage of the first campaign finance legislation, the laws were seldom enforced. The Supreme Court considered several chal-lenges to reform legislation during these years, but it mostly avoided consti-tutional questions.[2]

In the early 1970s, a period of low public trust in government following the Vietnam War, the Watergate scandal, and related social upheaval, Congress en-acted new campaign finance legislation. Like the first wave of reforms, these measures were passed by bipartisan majorities. But they also generated opposi-tion, and not only from Republicans and conservatives. Lawyers advanced the-ories, building on arguments already circulating among conservative political actors, about why the First Amendment's command that "Congress shall make no law . . . abridging the freedom of speech, or of the press" meant that legisla-tors could not regulate contributions or spending in electoral campaigns. The American Civil Liberties Union joined in advancing some of these theories.

The most recently enacted major federal campaign finance legislation, the 2002 Bipartisan Campaign Reform Act (BCRA, a.k.a. McCain-Feingold), passed with significant bipartisan support, partly as a consequence of the Enron financial scandal and despite strong opposition from Senator Mitch McConnell and other Republicans. The legislation addressed concerns about the growing impact of "soft money" contributions to the political parties—money that was not subject to existing contribution limits and prohibitions. It also addressed an increased reliance on "issue ads," which escaped the reach of existing campaign finance laws by focusing on a candidate's stance on pol-icy issues without expressly urging the candidate's election or defeat.

There are also laws in every state regulating the use of money in state and local elections. These laws, like the federal statutes, have met constitutional challenges, and some of those lawsuits have reached the US Supreme Court.

**The Supreme Court's Shifting Stance.**   Election law scholars have identified three major phases of Supreme Court rulings on the constitutionality of
campaign finance regulation.[3] During the first phase, from *Buckley* to the late
1980s, the justices issued compromise decisions, used temperate discourse in
their opinions, and aligned in ways that did not hew closely to partisan lines.
In the second phase, from 1990 through 2006, the Court mostly deferred to
legislators. However, an assertive bloc of dissenting justices, linked with a
growing and increasingly influential conservative legal movement, expressed
adamant opposition to most campaign finance regulation in this phase. A
third phase, which began with Justice Alito's appointment in 2006, resulted
in the demise of major precedents and bold new proclamations about the un-
constitutionality of most campaign finance regulation. In this phase, which
continues to this day, all Republican appointees consistently vote against
campaign finance regulation, while all Democratic appointees consistently
defend it (with rare exceptions to these patterns noted in chapter 8).

A few highlights of these three phases illustrate just how significant these
shifts have been and how they relate to changes in and around the Court.

In *Buckley v. Valeo* (1976), the Supreme Court found that campaign finance legislation adopted in the early 1970s raised concerns about free speech
and political association, but it did not invalidate the entire statute. Instead, it
struck an uneasy compromise; it invalidated the legislation's spending limits
but upheld its contribution limits, finding that the latter served a governmental interest in combating corruption or the appearance of corruption. The
Court held that Congress could limit large contributions because those contributions might lead politicians to do their bidding. But it found that spending conducted independently of candidates and their campaigns did not have
the same potential to corrupt and so could not be limited.

The Supreme Court's lengthy (295-page), split, and unsigned opinion in
*Buckley* was the work of justices who were operating under time pressure at
a very different era in the Court's history. This was an era when the goal of
finding consensus was more highly prized and more easily attained than it is
today. It was a time when justices appointed by Democratic and Republican
presidents joined together in opinions addressing topics that later became
highly contentious issues in the culture wars.[4] The justices who decided *Buckley* did not hold settled views about the constitutionality of campaign finance
regulation,[5] and their votes crossed ideological and partisan lines.

Fast forward to a case that exemplifies the Court's second phase, *Austin v.
Michigan Chamber of Commerce* (1990).[6] The Supreme Court upheld a Michigan statute prohibiting corporations from using treasury funds for independent expenditures to support or oppose candidates in elections. The Court

found that Michigan had a compelling interest in combating "the corrosive and distorting effects of immense aggregations of wealth that are accumulated with the help of the corporate form."[7] But the dissenters framed the stakes in starkly different terms. Justice Scalia characterized the regulation as an "Orwellian . . . restriction."[8] He opened his dissent with this description of its purpose and implications: "Attention all citizens. To assure the fairness of elections by preventing disproportionate expression of the views of any single powerful group, your Government has decided that the following associations of persons shall be prohibited from speaking or writing in support of any candidate."[9] Justice Kennedy's dissenting opinion called Michigan's law "repugnant to the First Amendment" and in conflict with "its central guarantee, the freedom to speak in the electoral process."[10]

As historian Robert Mutch has observed, *Austin* marked "a turning point in campaign finance cases," reflecting an "unbridgeable ideological gulf between the majority and dissenting opinions" and "incompatible premises." Mutch wrote, "The majority held to the nearly century-old premise that there is a constitutional difference in kind between corporations and people, while dissenters believed the difference was one only of degree."[11] He also commented on "a polemical tone" in the *Austin* dissents that "had not been evident in previous cases. In *Buckley*, the conservatives had derogated [the rationale for regulating campaign expenditures] by claiming that Congress sought to 'restrict' speech. The *Austin* conservatives claimed government sought the outright suppression of speech and likened it to something in George Orwell's dystopian novels. Variations of the words 'suppress,' 'censor,' 'ban,' and 'silence,' which did not appear at all in *Buckley*, popped up again and again in the *Austin* dissents."[12] Mutch observed that the split in *Austin* was "generational"; the dissenters, all Reagan appointees, were the Court's youngest and newest members.[13]

The dissenters in *Austin* expressed perspectives that were beginning to come into more direct conflict with the center-left consensus that had largely prevailed on the Court and in the legal establishment until the 1980s. The Federalist Society, the Heritage Foundation, and dozens of other conservative and libertarian groups were gaining influence. New ideas about the meaning of the First Amendment were taking shape in those institutions and in media outlets linked to them. They were not yet majority views on the Court, but they were gaining traction.

The lawsuits that followed the enactment of the BCRA exposed a deepening divide on the Court.[14] In *McConnell v. FEC* (2003),[15] the Supreme Court upheld most of the BCRA's provisions, citing the government's "strong interests in preventing corruption, and particularly its appearance."[16] But Justice

Kennedy's strongly worded dissent, in which three other conservatives joined, accused the majority of upholding laws "that suppress both spontaneous and concerted speech, leav[ing] us less free than before" and "break[ing] faith with our tradition of robust and unfettered debate."[17]

*McConnell* was the last major win for reformers; the momentum has since shifted decidedly against them. Moreover, the ideological divisions displayed in *Austin* and *McConnell* have deepened.

Fast forward again to the third phase of the Supreme Court's campaign finance rulings. Since 2006, the Court has issued a series of rulings striking down campaign finance restrictions and exposing a gaping divide in the perspectives and discourse of the majority and dissent. The justices paint starkly different pictures of the stakes, and the temperature of the disagreement is high. Conservative constitutional scholar Lillian BeVier has observed that "there is little hope for reconciliation of the competing views of the current majority and the dissenters" because "their disagreement is far more fundamental than a simple dispute about doctrine." She writes: "The problem . . . is that the justices do not reason from the same premises, either as a matter of First Amendment principle or as a matter of the empirical assumptions that drive their respective analyses. They assess the worth of political freedom differently. They entertain wildly divergent assessments of the need for legislation to 'promote democracy.' . . . Compromise on such matters is not in the cards."[18] Yale Law School dean Heather Gerken has called this clash in the justices' perspectives about campaign finance regulation "a doctrinal death match between two incompatible world views."[19]

Consider the polarized perspectives expressed by the justices in *Citizens United*. Justice Kennedy's opinion for the majority characterized campaign spending as political speech and asserted that protecting such speech, by business corporations as well as individuals, is a foundational principle enshrined in the First Amendment. His opinion manifested outrage about the BCRA's purpose: "Under our law and our tradition it seems stranger than fiction for our Government to make . . . political speech a crime. Yet this is the statute's purpose and design."[20] The Court found that corporations should not "be treated differently under the First Amendment simply because [they] are not 'natural persons.'"[21] The dissenting opinion written by Justice Stevens claimed that the Court's ruling was "profoundly misguided"[22] and "threatens to undermine the integrity of elected institutions across the Nation."[23] The dissenting opinion rejected the majority's claim that corporations hold the same right to spend money in elections as natural persons,[24] calling it "a radical departure from what had been settled First Amendment law,"[25] that the Constitution's framers had sought to protect the speech rights of "individual

Americans, not corporations."[26] Stevens referred to a long-standing distinction between individuals and corporations reflected in the Tillman Act of 1907 and *Austin*, and he described the Court's reversal on this point "a rejection of the common sense of the American people, who have recognized a need to prevent corporations from undermining self-government since the founding, and who have fought against the distinctive corrupting potential of corporate electioneering since the days of Theodore Roosevelt."[27] Stevens also sharply criticized the tone and rhetoric of the majority's opinion: "Pervading the Court's analysis is the ominous image of a 'categorical ba[n]' on corporate speech,"[28] a characterization he called "highly misleading."[29]

This schism between the majority and dissenting justices amounts to much more than disagreement over policy. Yale law professor (and former dean) Robert Post calls the divergent perspectives of the justices a "horrifying disjunction."[30] He observes that the two sides seem "to inhabit entirely different constitutional universes," reflecting "a country divided, not united,"[31] and that "the constitutional arguments slide past one another with scarcely a moment of mutual engagement."[32] The opinions reflect deep differences in worldviews and an accompanying hostility toward the other side that was entirely absent in the Court's earliest campaign finance rulings.

The divisions reflected in the opinions of the majority and dissent in *Citizens United* did not arise out of thin air. They reflect broader changes in the political landscape. The justices' views are influenced by other elites, especially those in the legal profession, the academy, and the media.[33] From the 1950s through the 1970s, most of those elites believed in a moderately active role for government. Democratic and Republican presidents once drew from the same pool of lawyers and judges when selecting Supreme Court justice nominees. After joining the bench, the justices traveled in a common elite culture and shared many basic assumptions about political and social life.[34]

But the modern conservative movement changed that. The Supreme Court began to move rightward in the years following Ronald Reagan's election, as Republican presidents used the appointments process to replace liberal and moderate justices with committed conservatives. Conservatives created their own legal establishment to counter what they viewed as the dominant liberal legal establishment. The Federalist Society emerged as a powerful networking and credentialing organization for conservative and libertarian lawyers. Robert Bork's failed nomination for a seat on the Supreme Court in 1987 marked the beginning of a new and much more politicized, partisan, and acrimonious approach to federal judicial nominations and confirmation processes.[35] The Supreme Court justices began to mingle in different worlds of polarized elites, each with its own cultural institutions and ideas about the meaning of the Constitution.[36] They began to look for approval from different "audiences,"[37] and those audiences disagreed about myriad social and political issues relevant to the questions that reached the Court.

From here forward, the focus of this book shifts from the justices to the other players in the processes that generated the landmark Supreme Court decisions. This switch will be somewhat like that involved in reversible figure-ground perception exercises featuring faces and vases, ducks and rabbits, fish and geese.[38] Like these exercises, which test a viewer's ability to relate figures to background and to bring their elements in and out of focus, the remainder of this book tries to situate the Court's current stance on the constitutionality of campaign finance regulation within the broader context in which it emerged. The justices remain in view because they are important components of the picture. But the broader context brings additional players into perspective to explain the development of constitutional doctrine and what Ken Kersch has called the "constitutional settlement," negotiated over time, about what we mean by constitutionally protected speech.[39]

* * *

The federal courts are an important arena of party competition within the American political process. Both major political parties try to use the courts to advance understandings of the Constitution that sustain electoral coalitions and promote their favored policies.[40] Electoral outcomes give the winners the power to shape the composition of the federal courts through the judicial appointments process, and those appointments facilitate the creation of constitutional doctrine reflecting the ideological and policy goals of the appointing president's political party. Substantial political science research demonstrates that the Supreme Court's jurisprudence tends, in the long run, to reflect the priorities of the dominant political alliance,[41] with a significant lag reflecting the justices' long (and increasingly lengthy) terms on the bench.[42] Past judicial appointments generally operate as a drag on the priorities of the party in power, at least until that party wins enough elections to entrench its own supporters on the Court.[43]

But shifts in electoral power and corresponding changes in judicial personnel through the appointments process are not alone sufficient to produce major constitutional change. Charles Epp's pathbreaking comparative study, *The Rights Revolution* (1998), showed that the expansion of civil rights and civil liberties during the Warren Court years required more than sympathetic judges. It also depended upon deliberate, strategic organizing by advocates, organizations, and political and financial patrons.[44] Epp coined the term "support structure" to describe these essential resources for legal mobilization and successful rights revolutions. Support structures are also sometimes called the "supply side" (ideas, legal theories, litigants, lawyers, patrons) of the process of constitutional change to distinguish them from the more commonly noticed "demand side" (courts and judges).[45]

Epp's work focused on rights revolutions from the political left, but other scholars have shown that support structures have been necessary to make new constitutional doctrine from the political right.[46] To reverse the gains made by legal liberals through the courts in the 1960s, conservatives needed to win elections and gain control over judicial appointments.[47] But they also needed to generate supply-side resources. Conservatives worked to address their disadvantages within the institutions that produce and legitimate legal ideas. Beginning in the 1970s, conservative political entrepreneurs and their patrons built new organizations and professional networks to challenge the legal establishment and the constitutional vision reflected in the Warren Court's rulings. They cultivated ideologically committed and highly credentialed lawyers to formulate arguments and lend those arguments credibility.[48] Steven Teles's work showed how this effort related to a transformed political system that has existed since the 1970s, in which the parties share control over policymaking and law with diffuse networks of activists and institutions. Party competition now takes place over a broader terrain and includes a larger set of key actors, including not only party leaders and formal party organizations but also politically aligned networks that reach into the professions, foundations, think tanks, and the media.[49]

An understanding of the political parties as extended networks of party leaders, party organizations, politicians, activists, and interest groups—sometimes referred to as "extended party" structures[50]—helps to account for how parties compete to shape constitutional doctrine in a polarized political environment. Extended party networks participate in federal judicial nomination and confirmation battles to influence the "demand side" of constitutional change.[51] This book explores how they also share in the work of developing and advancing constitutional interpretations and themes that reconcile the policy priorities of the various constituencies whose support the parties seek to attract and maintain.[52] Such appeals to abstract constitutional ideals can be useful in building and sustaining electoral coalitions and diverting attention away from conflicting elements of the parties' policy agendas.[53] Actors within extended party networks also communicate about the relevance of cases to target audiences. They file amicus briefs to inform the courts about their support for and opposition to the parties' positions. Those amicus briefs can influence judges' rulings by indicating interests that are potentially affected by and attentive to the rulings.[54]

Jack Balkin explains why this activity outside the courts matters: "To understand how American Constitutional law changes, it is not enough to consider the decisions of the courts . . . One must also consider the work of civil society organizations, political movements, and interest groups. Together, these actors shape and alter ideas of what is reasonable and unreasonable in legal argument . . . They move certain ideas about the Constitution from being considered 'off-the-wall'—that is, crazy—to being 'on-the-wall'—that is, plausible or reasonable."[55] For new ideas about the meaning of the Constitution to gain legitimacy, they "need champions in civil society, in politics, and in the legal profession who are willing to place their own reputations at risk by advocating for these ideas and attempting to persuade others of their correctness."[56] Ultimately, constitutional change through the courts requires sufficient evidence of public support to ensure that the reinterpretation of constitutional provisions will be seen as legitimate exercises of judicial power. Controversial Supreme Court decisions can set the stage for further rounds of mobilization and countermobilization by activists, interest groups, and political parties. Deeply unpopular decisions generally have electoral consequences in the long run, and they sometimes destabilize electoral coalitions.[57]

This book attends to all these ingredients of constitutional change, but it pays especially close attention to the roles of lawyers and their organizations. However eager the justices might be to revise constitutional doctrine, they cannot make law without cases to decide; lawyers must first initiate cases and shepherd them through the courts.[58] And while judges are the ultimate arbiters of the questions that come before them, they rely on advocates to supply arguments to explain, support, and defend their decisions.[59] Precedents are contestable, and their "meanings may be 'refixed'" as lawyers argue for different interpretations of constitutional provisions and cases, and as judges adopt those new interpretations.[60] Supreme Court justices sometimes send litigants cues about their willingness to consider an issue, but even the most activist justices depend on lawyers to interpret these signals and to respond through their strategic selection of cases.[61] Lawyers and their networks are especially important audiences for Supreme Court decisions because lawyers' training and professional experience equip them to assess the justices' work and hold them accountable for complying with conventions about judicial decision-making.[62]

The influence of lawyers and legal-advocacy organizations extends beyond their roles in initiating cases, supplying legal arguments, and monitoring the work of judges. Their efforts in other important arenas of constitutional contest—including legislatures, government agencies, and the media—sometimes affect judicial rulings indirectly.[63] In particular, framing, messaging, and molding public sentiment to shift the terrain on which courts decide questions may be as important for constitutional change as any arguments contained in briefs or oral advocacy.[64] Lawyers and their organizations are not the only players in these processes, but they are important players.[65] Broadening the lens still more, lawyers help party leaders, coalition elites, and judges coordinate claims and arguments about constitutional meaning. And as they shift the terrain of policy contest to their own turf—the courts—lawyers sometimes build reputations and other forms of professional and relational (and sometimes financial) capital, helping them climb professional hierarchies that tend to link lawyers at the top with the wealthiest and most powerful people and institutions.

* * *

The supply side of the effort to resist campaign finance regulation through the courts unfolded in phases that roughly mirror the three phases of the Supreme Court rulings described earlier in this chapter. In the first phase, the focus of chapter 2, entrepreneurial scholars and lawyers developed some of the ideas necessary to create new constitutional law. Individuals who sought to challenge the political party establishment teamed up with lawyers and funders to bring lawsuits based on those theories. The litigation was not particularly partisan in these early years. The conservative legal movement was just beginning to take shape, and the world of legal elites in and around the Court was not yet sorted by party. The effort acquired a more partisan valence as business groups, libertarian public interest law organizations, abortion opponents, and gun-rights activists began to challenge restrictions on their election-related activities and as the Republican Party began to identify itself with opposition to campaign finance regulation.

In the second phase of the effort, described in chapter 3, opponents of campaign finance regulation developed a more coordinated and incremental approach to fighting it, modeled on the strategy used by the NAACP Legal Defense Fund to attack racial segregation. They created specialized nonprofit organizations to lead the fight in the name of ordinary Americans. They influenced the doctrine through their selection of cases and coordination of amicus participation.[66] Challengers repackaged ideas about the meaning of the First Amendment for a lay audience, working with politicians and media figures to popularize those ideas. They developed a capacious speech frame that facilitated building a coalition to support the challenges, and they brought along some groups that would seem unlikely, at least at first glance, to benefit from unregulated spending in politics.

Chapter 4 describes the third phase of this effort, still underway. In this phase, opponents of campaign finance regulation serve up ambitious test cases to a Court that is controlled by movement conservatives and receptive to the arguments. These cases are typically brought by specialized nonprofit organizations claiming to fight for the little guy. They draw substantial amicus support from all constituencies of the GOP coalition and a few center-left groups. In this phase, challengers have achieved significant victories and overturned major precedents.

The process by which the First Amendment came to be understood as providing broad and robust protection against the regulation of money in American politics is bound up with a larger story of how conservatives and libertarians have redefined expressive freedom. Not so long ago, free-speech claims were comfortably associated with liberal attitudes and understood to conflict with conservative values. When liberals fought for the right to express controversial ideas, conservatives emphasized countervailing values to be balanced against expressive freedom.[67] But conservatives have since embraced free speech arguments as they have repurposed them to advance different policy goals. Business interests have deployed free speech arguments to challenge economic regulations, consumer protections, and compulsory union membership.[68] Religious conservatives have used free speech arguments in their shift from a defensive strategy, which sought to limit the reach of First Amendment doctrine requiring separation of church and state, toward an affirmative strategy based on arguments that the First Amendment demands greater accommodation of religion in the public sphere.[69] They have also found free speech arguments useful in resisting antidiscrimination laws.[70] In short, several threads of the Republican coalition have found common purpose in a conception of free expression that serves each of their interests.[71] This revised understanding of the First Amendment has helped the GOP build and maintain its alliance.[72] Lawyers and their organizations have facilitated these efforts to reconcile competing policy priorities into shared claims about constitutional meaning.

Through this process, First Amendment objections to campaign finance regulation have become entrenched in law and assumed in debates about whether and how to address the influence of big money in politics. The battle has been hard-fought. As Frederick Schauer has observed, competition among opposing political forces to claim the mantle of the First Amendment is "predictably fierce" because those who succeed in claiming that free speech is on their side have good reason to believe they have won the upper hand in public debate. The First Amendment, he explains, "strikes fear in the hearts of many who do not want to be seen as opposing the freedoms it enshrines."[73]

* * *

The remainder of this account draws heavily on my interviews with fifty-two lawyers who serve as key informants about the process of constitutional change that resulted in the Roberts Court's major campaign finance rulings. The interviewed lawyers represented key parties and amici in these cases. They have witnessed critical strategic decisions made behind the scenes—for example, about selecting test cases, framing issues, coordinating amicus participation, deciding which arguments to make and who would make them, and pursuing complementary strategies outside the courts. Their commentary helps to explain how the litigation coalition changed and grew, and why organizations claiming to represent the Republican base joined with business groups and Republican Party leaders, along with some civil libertarians, to assert that unregulated money in politics is an essential aspect of political speech and association. The commentary also sheds light on the lawyers' backgrounds, their incentives and aspirations, their positions in professional networks and hierarchies, and their worldviews—all of which influenced the course of this campaign. The appendix provides details about my method for selecting the lawyers to interview and the interview protocol. To encourage candor, I assured the interviewed lawyers that I would not reveal their identities. Therefore, this book uses the contents of the interviews without attributing quotations to identified individuals.

Table 1.1 summarizes some of the demographic characteristics of the interviewed lawyers. They worked in a variety of practice settings. On both sides of the litigation, there was a heavy concentration of advocates in Washington, DC. However, a higher proportion of reformers worked in major metropolitan areas on the coasts, primarily in the DC area and the Northeast, while the challengers were more geographically dispersed. Roughly the same proportion of challengers and reformers came from working-class backgrounds, but the reformers generally held much more elite educational credentials than the challengers as indicated in the ranking of the law schools they attended.[74] (As shown in table 4.1, the interviewed lawyers' practice locations and educational credentials were broadly representative of the larger pool of lawyers who participated in these cases.) All but three of the reformers identified themselves as Democrats, while most of the challengers were Republicans. On both sides, the interviewed lawyers were overwhelmingly white men.[75] Fifteen of the twenty-six lawyers on the challengers' side indicated that they regularly or sometimes participated in Federalist Society activities. None of the lawyers on the reform side participated in Federalist Society activities, but five indicated that they were active in the American Constitution Society, an organization founded in 2001 to serve as the Federalist Society's liberal counterpart. The religious backgrounds of the two sides differed as well, with

TABLE 1.1. Characteristics of interviewed lawyers

| | Challengers (N=26) | | Reformers (N=26) | |
|---|---|---|---|---|
| | # | % | # | % |
| **Employer type** | | | | |
| Private firms | 12 | 46 | 11 | 42 |
| Advocacy orgs. & think tanks | 12 | 46 | 13 | 50 |
| Academia | 2 | 8 | 2 | 8 |
| **Work location** | | | | |
| DC | 8 | 31 | 10 | 38 |
| DC suburb | 3 | 12 | 0 | 0 |
| NE | 5 | 19 | 10 | 38 |
| South | 3 | 12 | 0 | 0 |
| Midwest | 2 | 7.5 | 0 | 0 |
| Mountain | 2 | 7.5 | 2 | 8 |
| Pacific | 3 | 12 | 4 | 15 |
| **Law school tier** | | | | |
| Elite | 7 | 27 | 17 | 65 |
| Prestige | 6 | 23 | 6 | 23 |
| Regional | 8 | 31 | 3 | 12 |
| Local | 5 | 19 | 0 | 0 |
| **Party affiliation** | | | | |
| Democrat | 4 | 15 | 23 | 88 |
| Republican | 17 | 65 | 1 | 4 |
| Independent | 3 | 12 | 2 | 8 |
| Libertarian | 1 | 4 | 0 | 0 |
| Unknown | 1 | 4 | 0 | 0 |
| **Age** | | | | |
| Mean | 51 | | 57 | |
| Median | 50 | | 62 | |
| **Gender** | | | | |
| Male | 23 | 88 | 24 | 92 |
| Female | 3 | 11 | 2 | 7 |
| **Political bar assn.** | | | | |
| Federalist Society | 15 | 58 | 0 | 0 |
| ACS | 0 | 0 | 5 | 19 |
| **Religion** | | | | |
| Catholic | 10 | 38 | 2 | 8 |
| Evangelical Protestant | 4 | 15 | 0 | 0 |
| Mainline Protestant | 1 | 4 | 5 | 19 |
| Jewish | 6 | 23 | 10 | 38 |
| Other | 0 | 0 | 0 | 0 |
| Not religious | 4 | 15 | 8 | 31 |

more on the challengers' side describing themselves as Catholic or evangelical Protestant and fewer as mainline Protestant, Jewish, or not religious.[76] The
mean and median ages of reformers (57/62) were higher than those of the
challengers (51/50).

There were some notable differences among the challengers. All but one
of the lawyers for groups associated with the Republican Party's populist elements identified themselves as Catholics or evangelical Protestants, and most
had attended regional or local law schools. Their parents were less likely to
have held high status jobs than those of lawyers representing business groups,
libertarians, civil liberties organizations, and Republican leaders. Most of the
lawyers for libertarian groups described themselves as atheists or agnostics,
and half of them identified themselves as Independents.

Some of the interviewed lawyers expressed devotion to a cause—either
fighting campaign finance regulation or defending it—while others appeared
to hold more typical professional orientations. The term "cause lawyer" was
coined in the late 1990s to describe lawyers who use legal skills to pursue
ends and ideals that transcend client service, in contrast with "conventional
lawyers," who adopt a client-service and market orientation that attributes
little or no significance to whether they agree with the client's position.[77] Most
lawyers, including the lawyers involved in this campaign, fall between these
theoretical extremes. Still, the cause and conventional lawyer categories are
useful for understanding one dimension of difference among the interviewed
lawyers. Most of the lawyers working for nonprofit advocacy organizations
on both sides of this fight seemed to believe strongly in the principles they
claimed were at stake. Most of the lawyers who represented candidates, parties, and interest groups from positions in private firms appeared to be more
focused on expected consequences for their clients.[78]

I am deeply grateful for the time the interviewed lawyers gave me as I
sought to understand how campaign spending came to be treated as speech,
and regulation as censorship, in American constitutional law.

# Taking Campaign Finance Reform to Court

The legislation challenged in *Buckley v. Valeo* was the work of a coalition of reform advocates led by Common Cause, a government watchdog group.[1] Strengthened disclosure requirements in the Federal Election Campaign Act of 1971 (FECA)[2] enabled Common Cause to uncover and publicize previously undisclosed contributions by individuals and illegal corporate contributions to President Nixon's 1972 reelection campaign.[3] In 1974, in response to the Watergate break-in and subsequent investigations that exposed additional illegal contributions,[4] Congress amended the FECA to expand disclosure requirements, strengthen contribution and spending limits, institute a public financing system for presidential elections, and create the Federal Election Commission to enforce the new law. Cases challenging the constitutionality of this legislation soon followed.

This chapter identifies key players and resources behind this first phase of the litigation. Law professors and lawyers generated novel legal arguments. Candidates, third parties, and advocacy organizations brought lawsuits. Funding for the litigation came from wealthy individuals who wanted to translate their financial fortunes into political influence. The effort was small at first, but it acquired momentum as more groups and different constituencies joined the fight.

Before exploring the first phase of the litigation in greater detail, this chapter briefly describes the conservative legal movement, which began around the time of the first phase of the litigation campaign. An understanding of the conservative legal movement is necessary because it generated some of the background conditions necessary for the litigation campaign to succeed. Its history is closely intertwined with the history of campaign finance doctrine,

and its institutions are now core parts of the GOP's "extended party" structure. The work of key figures and institutions identified in the first section of
this chapter reverberates in developments described in the rest of the book.

## The Conservative Legal Movement

The conservative legal movement began in the early 1970s, primarily as a response to the expansion of civil rights and civil liberties and federal government regulation during the years when Earl Warren served as chief justice of
the Supreme Court (1953–1969) and continuing into the early years of Chief
Justice Warren Burger's tenure (1969–1986). Conservatives criticized "activist" judges and the lawyers who worked with them to accomplish liberal legal
change through the courts. Business leaders disliked the courts for permitting regulation of their commercial activities. Western landowners claimed
that judicial rulings infringed on their property rights. Southerners resented
how judges and lawyers had teamed up to dismantle segregation. Religious
conservatives were outraged by decisions finding that the Constitution protected a right to abortion and required limits on prayer in schools. These
different strands of conservatives joined in an effort to rein in judges and the
lawyers who pursued these causes.[5]

At first, conservatives engaged primarily in electoral strategies and efforts
to weaken and discredit liberal legal activism. But they began to modify their
approach as they discovered that winning elections would not necessarily
translate into power to reverse liberal legal accomplishments. To succeed,
they also needed to gain influence in the institutions that produce and legitimate ideas that shape law. Conservatives turned their attention to several influential arenas they believed were then dominated by liberal legal elites—the
judiciary, law schools, public interest law, and lawyer networks. They invested
in a broad range of activities designed to help them prevail in "the battle to
control the law."[6]

That battle entailed struggles over judicial appointments. Conservatives
fought to keep liberal jurists off the bench and to appoint their own. They also
sought to counter what they perceived as a tendency of justices appointed by
Republican presidents to "drift" left once on the Court.[7] They began to groom
reliable conservatives for the bench and to more actively patrol the nominations process. Those efforts substantially increased the proportion of federal
judges receptive to conservatives' concerns.

But reversing the gains of legal liberals during the Warren and early Burger
Court years required more than simply exerting greater control over judicial
appointments. Major change in constitutional doctrine depends on support

structures for such change, including not only those who bring the cases but also those who supply legal ideas and strategies (law professors and lawyers), and their political and financial patrons. Without those resources for legal mobilization, constitutional rights revolutions will not occur.[8]

Wealthy conservatives and their foundations began to pour money into institutions that would generate ideas and strategies necessary to wage this fight to reverse or modify the liberal-rights revolution and eventually to generate a rights revolution of their own. They invested in existing think tanks—such as the Hoover Institution and the American Enterprise Institute—and founded new ones—such as the Heritage Foundation, the Manhattan Institute, and the Cato Institute. They established dozens of advocacy organizations and media outlets. An influential memo prepared for the Scaife Foundation drew attention to the role of law schools and bar associations in shaping the legal arguments and networks that drive the development of law.[9] Conservative leaders and patrons invested in strategies to change legal education and elite lawyer networks. The law and economics movement introduced economic theory into the analysis of law and institutionalized it as a field of research in major law schools.[10] Religious conservatives created their own advocacy organizations and new "Christian worldview" law schools.[11] Through a web of institutions and professional networks, conservatives and libertarians generated arguments to advance their policy objectives and to promote the legitimacy of these ideas in the face of contrary prevailing legal doctrine. They sought to replace prevailing views about the meaning of the US Constitution and proper modes of interpretation with a different set of assumptions.

Conservative political entrepreneurs also learned that the strategies that liberal public interest law groups had pioneered could be effective weapons in fighting business regulations, challenging affirmative action, removing boundaries between church and state, and much more. Conservatives had long had effective advocates in the courts, but they began to create new advocacy groups modeled on their liberal counterparts and claiming the "public interest law" mantle.[12] Most of the first generation of conservative public interest law groups were not particularly effective. One problem was that they were transparently beholden to their financial backers and focused on the policy concerns of those donors.[13] The memo prepared for the Scaife Foundation explained that it was "critical" for the conservative movement to "seek out and find clients other than large corporations and corporate interests." It stressed the importance of ensuring that "concerns not likely to be of direct interest to wealthy donors . . . become a broader segment of the conservative public interest law movement's agenda."[14] The memo also emphasized the strategic importance of recruiting smart and ambitious young lawyers to embrace conservative causes and staff conservative public interest law firms.[15] It called on conservative public interest law groups to move beyond their largely defensive posture to develop affirmative strategies.[16]

Over time, a more proactive and strategic approach took shape. Conservative foundations invested in "second-generation" conservative public interest law organizations—groups with specialized expertise, better-developed issue agendas, and more plausible claims to represent underrepresented constituencies and/or some vision of the public good.[17] Financial patrons gave the groups' leaders greater independence to chart strategy under the leadership of ideologically committed organizational entrepreneurs.[18] Some of these organizations specialized in opposing campaign finance regulation. Since the mid-1990s, these specialized public interest law groups have served as the public face of the campaign to resist campaign finance regulation.

While "judicial activism" was a common grievance within the Republican coalition that won Ronald Reagan the presidency in 1980, conservatives became less committed to judicial deference to legislators as they acquired control over judicial appointments and established legal-advocacy groups to pursue conservative policy goals through the courts.[19] They have pursued ambitious litigation campaigns to establish (and sometimes reestablish) constitutional rights on a broad range of issues, including guns, religion, labor, land use, consumer protection, and campaign finance.[20]

One of the challenges for the Republican Party has been managing differences in the policy priorities of each of the primary constituencies of its coalition—business interests, libertarians, and social conservatives. Several "mediator" organizations have actively sought to promote cooperation, or at least minimize infighting, among these constituencies. Two of these organizations—the Federalist Society and the Heritage Foundation—have tried to create a sense of shared identity among lawyers for the various constituencies of the Republican coalition. These organization seek to bridge class, cultural, and ideological divisions and to mobilize lawyers and the groups they lead around common goals.[21]

**Originalism.**   One of the conservative legal movement's unifying projects was generating a theory of constitutional interpretation that would impede legal liberalism while also advancing the conservative movement's policy goals. The theory that emerged—"originalism"—looks to the framers' understanding of the text of the Constitution and its amendments or the original meaning of the provision at the time it was adopted. This theory holds popular appeal, promising to prevent judges from exercising arbitrary power. It also serves as a powerful vehicle for mobilizing and uniting different constituencies of the fractious conservative coalition.[22]

Critics of originalism question why we should be bound by the specific understandings of the framers, who were not representative of the nation's population even at the time of the founding and who could not have anticipated the world we now inhabit.[23] Critics also question whether the framers intended the Constitution to be interpreted according to its original meaning rather than as an enduring set of broad principles that would guide the resolution of unforeseen problems by future generations.[24] Critics also point to the difficulty of determining the framers' intent or original public meaning given the varying views and practices at the time when various constitutional provisions and amendments were adopted. They observe that the method's malleability invites selective uses of history to achieve desired results, and that the most ardent advocates of the method do not apply it faithfully and consistently.[25]

Early versions of originalism emphasized judicial restraint and served as a justification for criticizing and resisting the civil rights and civil liberties decisions of the Warren and early Burger Courts. Originalists argued that liberal judges had substituted their own ideologies for the Constitution as revealed in the document's text, structure, and history.[26] Under Attorney General Edwin Meese III, originalism became all but the official credo of the Reagan Justice Department and helped to set the stage for legal challenges by personnel of the conservative legal movement.[27] By the 1990s, with a conservative majority on the Court and conservative public interest advocacy groups eager to use litigation to attack liberal laws and policies, originalism had morphed from a theory of judicial restraint to one justifying active judicial review.[28] Some conservatives and libertarians called for recovering a "lost Constitution," or a Constitution "in exile."[29]

While conservatives of all stripes embrace originalism, they do not always agree about when judicial activism is justified to restore original understandings of the framers.[30] Some conservatives say that the justices should hesitate to overrule long-standing precedents.[31] But many conservatives favor aggressively overruling judicial decisions they deem inconsistent with the Constitution's original meaning, however well settled the contrary precedents may be. Conservatives who take this view assert that rulings to correct constitutional errors do not constitute impermissible judicial activism.[32] Some describe the reversal of long-standing precedents under the latter approach as "judicial engagement" to distinguish it from judicial activism.[33] The Roberts Court's willingness to overrule long-standing precedents has been necessary for challengers to win major victories on campaign finance regulation and other policy priorities of conservatives.

Originalism—at least as understood as a method to be applied in good faith to recover original constitutional meaning—never fit the goals of opponents of campaign finance regulation particularly well. As Robert Bork noted in a 1971 law journal article that is widely recognized as laying a foundation for originalism, "the framers seem to have had no coherent theory of free speech and appear not to have been overly concerned with the subject."[34] Bork's observation is consistent with other scholarship finding that the Founding generation held a narrow view of the Constitution's guarantee of "the freedom of speech."[35] First Amendment speech doctrine is almost entirely a product of the past half century.[36]

In the early years of the effort to resist campaign finance regulation through the courts, the constitutional arguments were not based on originalist claims. Rather, they deployed the types of constitutional argumentation more common in the 1970s, starting with the constitutional text but also referring to cases interpreting the First Amendment and analogizing from existing precedents to new circumstances. More recently, however, some challengers have offered originalist arguments to strike down campaign finance restrictions. In *Citizens United*, for example, a brief filed by Edwin Meese, Anthony Caso, and John Eastman on behalf of the Center for Constitutional Jurisprudence asserted that while "unequal distribution of wealth, concentration of media power, and negative campaigning" had existed since the founding of the republic, there was "no evidence that the First Amendment was originally understood to authorize Congress to prohibit speech related to an election based on any of these factors."[37]

Reform advocates, scholars, and liberal justices have offered some originalist claims of their own to support campaign finance regulation. They have argued that the framers feared the influence of concentrated private power and wealth and would have approved of measures necessary to prevent corruption of the political process.[38] One interviewed reformer explained why he believed the framers would have favored his side:

> That we wake up pretty much any morning, read a leading newspaper, and there it is—the X group, ten people, twenty, or one—meeting with government officials, with party officials, and they have great sway because they've contributed so much. What is that bound to say to people across the country? It's bound to say, "Well, if you're that kind of person, you're wealthy, you'll get much, much more control and influence, and I won't." And it's the "I won't" which is the greatest concern. And it's exactly what the people, the forefathers, the founders were aiming to avoid.

Reformers also emphatically denied that the founders would have envisioned that business corporations would hold a constitutional right to spend unlimited amounts on elections, as the Roberts Court held in *Citizens United*.[39]

Reformers referred to historical evidence showing that the framers believed that business corporations could be comprehensively regulated to serve the public welfare. They also emphasized historical practice—the long history of restrictions on the involvement of business corporations in the political process.

**The Federalist Society.** The Federalist Society is among the most important of the institutions created by conservatives to reverse the gains of legal liberalism. It began as a small debating society launched by law students to address what they perceived to be a disparity between the ascendance of conservative and libertarian ideas in electoral politics and their hostile reception in elite law schools. The organization received key support from officials in the Reagan administration, as well as from conservative financial patrons, who recognized that it could serve as a network linking conservatives in law schools, advocacy organizations, government, private practice, the Republican Party, and courts.

Since its founding, the Federalist Society has operated as a site for recruiting conservatives and vetting them for eventual appointment to the judiciary.[40] Among the prominent conservatives appointed to the bench during the Reagan administration were the Society's original faculty sponsors— Antonin Scalia, Ralph Winter, and Robert Bork—all of whom have played significant parts in the history of campaign finance doctrine. The Society's role in evaluating federal judicial nominees and monitoring the appointments process picked up steam following Reagan's failed nomination of Bork, then a judge on the DC Court of Appeals, to succeed Lewis Powell after his retirement from the Supreme Court in 1987. The fierce fight over Bork's nomination, which turned largely on his views about the constitutionality of restrictions on contraception and abortion, galvanized conservatives to more aggressively police the judicial nominations process and to insist that Republicans take a harder line in confirmation battles.[41] The Federalist Society network has played a critical role in screening nominees for the federal bench ever since. (As discussed in chapter 8, the network exercised unprecedented influence over judicial nominations in the Trump administration.)

Leonard Leo, co-chairman and former executive vice president of the Federalist Society, has been an especially influential figure in judicial selection and nominations processes. Before joining the Federalist Society as an employee in the early 1990s, he helped Clarence Thomas navigate his confirmation battle. Since the election of George W. Bush, Leo has periodically stepped back from his official duties at the Federalist Society to help Republican administrations choose and confirm their nominees. Working through a network of nonprofit organizations to coordinate media campaigns and other initiatives to build public support, he led the efforts to confirm Justices John Roberts, Samuel Alito, Neil Gorsuch, Brett Kavanaugh, and Amy Coney Barrett, as well as many other federal district court and court of appeals judges.[42]

In addition to serving as the de facto judicial selection advisory board for Republican administrations, the Federalist Society network has performed a variety of other important functions that have contributed toward reshaping campaign finance doctrine. It has operated as an incubator of legal arguments to advance policy goals that garner strong support from Republicans. It has fostered network ties linking disparate constituencies that have coalesced behind the Republican Party—social conservatives, libertarians, and business interests—despite deep differences in their values and policy priorities.[43] It claims to have created "a conservative and libertarian intellectual network that extends to all levels of the legal community."[44] Ties through the Federalist Society have facilitated the coordination of amicus briefs, a strategically important facet of practice before the Supreme Court.[45] The organization also links lawyers to the conservative justices and their clerks.[46]

The Federalist Society does not take official positions on public policy controversies or judicial nominations. It describes itself as a nonpartisan debate society. But it is clearly political and partisan in another sense—its indirect pursuit of the long-term legal goals of the Republican Party and its support for conservative organizational entrepreneurs whose activities are largely consistent with those of the GOP.[47] The views of Federalist Society members are not monolithic, and the decision of its founders to eschew any effort to forge consensus beyond the broad principles in its mission statement is one of the keys to its success. That strategy has helped the organization create ties and foster cooperation among the various constituencies of the conservative alliance, and it has indirectly served the Republican Party's efforts to forge and maintain a winning coalition.[48]

Originalism was not born in the Federalist Society, but the organization has played a key role in refining and legitimating this interpretive theory. Originalism has been a theme of several of its national meetings and many of its speaker panels. Its most famous proponent, Antonin Scalia, was one of the Society's original sponsors.[49]

## Legal Arguments to Support the Litigation

Free speech arguments were not central issues in hearings or congressional debates over the 1971 FECA and 1974 amendments.[50] Several witnesses and senators argued that any limit on media spending would violate the First Amendment, but there was little relevant legal precedent to support that

claim. Nobody had yet crafted those constitutional arguments. It took entrepreneurial lawyers and scholars to do that essential work.

In two influential pamphlets, Yale law professor Ralph Winter supplied
the foundational arguments used to challenge the legislation's constitutionality.[51] In the first of these publications, released by the American Enterprise
Institute (AEI) during congressional debates on the 1971 FECA, he explained
why campaigns should be free of regulation "to maintain the open political
process contemplated by the First Amendment."[52] To reach this conclusion,
Winter refashioned First Amendment doctrine that had previously applied
to political dissenters and marginalized groups to protect individuals with
substantial wealth. The critical move was to claim that "a limit on the amount
an individual may contribute to a political campaign is a limit on the amount
of political activity in which he may engage" and that "a limit on what a candidate may spend is a limit on this political speech as well as on the political
speech of those who can no longer effectively contribute money to his campaign."[53] Winter insisted that limits on campaign contributions and expenditures violate the First Amendment because neither can be "distinguished
from a law forbidding speech of over 10 minutes in public parks."[54] In response to potential objections about the unequal distribution of the resource
that facilitates this type of "speech," he wrote that money is just one of many
resources, along with free time and celebrity, that can influence elections and
are unevenly distributed in society. He conceded that money is an especially
valuable resource in political campaigns because it is easily converted into
other useful resources. Still, he insisted, if money is to be regulated to rein in
"fat cats," other valuable political resources held disproportionately by other
segments of the population also should be regulated. Singling out money for
special treatment would amount to "increas[ing] the power of some special
groups at the expense of others." It would favor those constituencies, such
as organized labor, that can exercise political influence through registration
drives and the organization of volunteers.[55] Such favoritism, he wrote, "dis-
criminates against people with little free time who must limit their campaign
activities to monetary contributions." At the same time, it "increases the political power of those who can contribute their time to the candidates they
prefer," giving "housewives, students, faculty and others with free time" what
amounts to "special privileges in the political process."[56] Winter also laid the
groundwork for challenging limitations on corporate and union contributions and expenditures. In "a short note on applying First Amendment principles to corporations and unions," he wrote that "it would seem that if persons have a constitutionally protected liberty to speak for political purposes,
they also have an associational right to pool their resources to that end."[57]

In an article published the same year, Martin Redish offered additional arguments about why campaign spending limits conflicted with the First Amendment.[58] While Winter emphasized the rights of contributors and spenders, Redish stressed societal interests. He rooted the purpose of the First Amendment in "the needs of an effective democracy"[59] and the goal of "encourag[ing] voters to receive information which will aid them in the performance of their electoral function."[60] He argued that several of the Supreme Court's recent decisions—*New York Times v. Sullivan* (limiting the right of public officials to sue for defamation),[61] *Red Lion Broadcasting v. FCC* (upholding the Federal Communications Commission's "fairness doctrine"),[62] and *Mills v. Alabama* (finding that a state statute prohibiting election-day editorials violated the First Amendment)[63]—together supported an understanding of the First Amendment "render[ing] suspect any regulations which have the effect of reducing the total amount of expression on public questions."[64] The meaning of these cases, he said, was that "the ideological marketplace of the political campaign must remain uninhibited."[65] He suggested that spending limits were based on an illegitimate concern about protecting the public from "confusing or irrational information," which was flatly inconsistent with "the theory of the 'marketplace of ideas.'"[66] He also questioned the reformers' premise that restricting election spending would promote equality among those running for office, emphasizing how resources other than money influence election outcomes.

In 1973, while Congress was considering amendments to the FECA, Winter published another pamphlet, this time with John Bolton, one of his Yale Law students. (This is the same John Bolton who later served as US ambassador to the United Nations, 2005 to 2006, and as President Trump's national security adviser from 2018 to 2019.) This paper doubled down on arguments advanced in Winter's earlier publication, asserting that when individuals are "deprived of the choice" to devote money to political purposes, "either because government limits or prohibits his using money for political purposes or takes his money in taxes and subsidizes the political activities it chooses," that individual's "freedom is impaired."[67] The pamphlet declared that money in politics performs many valuable functions that "far outweigh any harm it may do"; that many resources that can be used to influence elections are even more unevenly distributed than wealth, including volunteer services, which "are in a real sense the equivalent of money"; and that treating money differently from other types of unequally distributed resources is "wholly arbitrary." The publication emphasized the relatively affluent backgrounds of leaders of reform efforts. It also asserted that reformers' claims about the influence of money "reflect a basic and disturbing mistrust of the people," reasoning that "if campaign financing really 'distorts' legislative or executive behavior, candidates can raise its effect as an issue and the voters can respond at election time." The authors wrote that calls for campaign finance regulation reflect "the belief that the voters cannot be relied upon to perceive their own best interests" and should be "viewed with alarm."[68] Like Redish, Winter and Bolton invoked the "marketplace of ideas" metaphor that has since become ubiquitous in arguments against campaign finance regulation. The pamphlet quoted Justice Holmes's dissent in *Abrams v. United States*, which found that two Russian dissidents had violated the Espionage Act by distributing leaflets seeking to undermine the US war effort:

> When men have realized that time has upset many fighting faiths they may come to believe even more than they believe the very foundations of their own conduct that the ultimate good desired is better reached by free trade in ideas—that the best test of truth is the power of the thought to get itself accepted in the competition of the market.[69]

"If we are to have 'free trade in ideas' in the political sphere," Winter and Bolton continued, "individual citizens must be free to express whatever ideas they choose in whatever form they believe appropriate, whether or not it costs them money. There is no room for price controls in the marketplace of ideas."[70] Limiting campaign spending, they said, would be analogous to limiting "demonstrations of more than a certain number of people, or extensive voter canvassing, or too many billboards with catchy slogans."[71]

The basic arguments advanced in these publications have served ever since as key points stressed by opponents of campaign finance regulation.[72] One can see them taken up in the 1970s in editorials and op-eds in conservative journals such as *National Review* and *Human Events*.[73] These arguments also laid the foundations for the litigation campaign. The brief for the parties challenging the legislation in *Buckley* drew heavily from the reasoning in the AEI pamphlet (which is unsurprising given that Winter and Bolton were two of the brief's authors), and it cited Redish's article too.[74]

Subsequent legal challenges built upon these foundational arguments. Litigants claimed that limits on how much one can contribute to and spend on campaigns are constraints on the amount of political speech in which one can engage; that money is indistinguishable from other types of resources that influence elections and that are unequally distributed in society, such as volunteer services; and that regulating money in elections amounts to discriminating against the rich by imposing on them restrictions that do not apply to others. Those challenging campaign finance regulations also continued to advance a major theme of these early publications—that "reformers" are elites and political insiders who control the process and mistrust voters' ability to discern their own interests.

Events and publications hosted by the Federalist Society took up and expanded on these arguments in the 1980s. A 1986 student symposium on "The First Amendment: Constitutional Principles and Public Policy" opened with a lecture by Milton Friedman that linked free speech with free markets. It also included two presentations on campaign finance regulation, later published, along with Friedman's speech, as articles in one of the Federalist Society's journals, the *Harvard Journal of Law and Public Policy*.[75] In "Hands Off the Political Process," University of Virginia law professor Lillian BeVier asserted that even if the political process is "malfunctioning in terms of a utopian vision" of how it should work, "there is almost nothing that the First Amendment permits us to do about it."[76] She focused on practical reasons to view reform laws skeptically. Reform legislation has "never worked, and it never will work," she wrote. It usually serves the interests of the legislation's sponsors, enhances the power of Washington-based special interest groups at the expense of unaffiliated individuals, and makes it harder for political outsiders to challenge incumbents. Fundamentally, she explained, the problem of "undue influence" is a consequence of government that "has given itself so much to do."[77] Charles Cooper, then assistant attorney general in the Office of Legal Counsel in the Reagan administration, offered a quasi-originalist argument against campaign finance regulation in his remarks, titled "The First Amendment, Original Intent, and the Political Process." His article argued that the framers intended Congress to have very limited power to regulate elections, especially state elections, and would not have anticipated the need for the federal courts to "occup[y] themselves with determining First Amendment limitations on various exercises of this highly dubious congressional power."[78]

## Litigation Challenging the FECA and 1974 Amendments

When opponents of campaign finance regulation failed to defeat the FECA in Congress, they turned to the courts. In 1972, the ACLU and the New York Civil Liberties Union (NYCLU) successfully defended a small group of dissenters who ran into trouble when they published a two-page advertisement in the *New York Times* advocating the impeachment of President Nixon. The Nixon administration charged those who paid for the advertisement with violating the 1971 FECA by failing to file required reports and disclosures, but the Second Circuit Court of Appeals found that the law did not apply in these circumstances.[79] Next, the ACLU and NYCLU filed a lawsuit to test their own right to run a political ad criticizing the Nixon administration's opposition to court-ordered busing. A three-judge district court panel ruled that the 1971 statute did not reach the ad.[80]

**Buckley v. Valeo.**   Soon after Congress passed the 1974 amendments, a small set of parties and amici sued those responsible for enforcing the new law.[81] One of the petitioners was New York senator James Buckley, the older brother of William F. Buckley Jr., best known as the founder of the *National Review* and host of the public affairs television show "Firing Line." As Irish Catholic sons of a self-made oilman, the Buckleys were not taken seriously by the cosmopolitan elites, including many moderate Republicans.[82] James Buckley had been elected to the Senate in 1970 as the Conservative Party's candidate, and, once elected, became an outspoken advocate for outlawing abortion. He argued that his candidacy would have been impossible without financial support from a few large donors. Another party to the lawsuit was Minnesota senator Eugene McCarthy, who had failed to secure the Democratic Party nomination in 1968 and planned to run as a third-party presidential candidate in 1976. Stewart Mott, who had been McCarthy's biggest donor in the 1968 presidential primaries, also joined in the lawsuit, as did the ACLU, the NYCLU, the Libertarian Party, the American Conservative Union, the Conservative Party of the State of New York, the Mississippi Republican Party, the Conservative Victory Fund, and *Human Events*.

An interviewed lawyer who participated in the lawsuit explained the strategy:

> We put together this left-right coalition, which basically said the law systematically violates the First Amendment because it suppresses the funding of political speech; it's there to just protect the incumbents, and it freezes out all minor parties and outlier points of view because it makes it difficult, if not impossible, for them to get their message out . . . It was sort of a strange bedfellows coalition because Buckley was the conservative senator . . . and [we had] McCarthy, and then we had the ACLU on one side of the spectrum, and then most of the other groups were right-wing groups.

This lawyer characterized the litigants in *Buckley* as "a bunch of outsiders against the establishment." He added: "[The laws] had all been passed . . . with [support from] the Republicans, the Democrats, the *New York Times*, the *Washington Post*, everybody. The unions were for it because they were given a lot of benefits. The corporations were for it because they were allowed PACs for the first time." It was, he said, "the whole establishment . . . against the kooky ACLU and a couple of kooky senators."

There was nothing inevitable about the outcome in *Buckley*, as there was little relevant constitutional precedent to constrain the courts. As Gordon

Silverstein has observed, "the judges were writing on a fairly clean slate" and had several "viable frames" to choose from.[83] They could have concluded that campaign spending was conduct that facilitates political expression, not expression itself. After all, nothing in the statute prevented anyone from saying what they wanted to say. The courts could have found that the FECA limited not speech but rather the purchase of mass audiences for it. Election spending involves communication, but many types of conduct that involve communication fall entirely outside the category of constitutionally protected expressive acts, including some activities that undoubtedly involve speech. As Professor Schauer notes: " 'Speech' is what we use to enter into contracts, make wills, sell securities, warrant the quality of goods we sell, fix prices, place bets, bid at auctions, enter into conspiracies, commit blackmail, threaten, give evidence at trials, and do most of the other things that occupy our days and occupy the courts."[84] Any rule that made government regulation of all types of conduct involving communication subject to heightened First Amendment review would effectively constitutionalize huge areas of law. Deciding what falls in and outside of the category of protected "speech" is an exercise in applying analogies, drawing distinctions, and using precedents to justify those moves.[85]

The DC Circuit Court of Appeals in *Buckley* found that the challenged legislation *enhanced* First Amendment values by "broaden[ing] the choice of candidates and the opportunity to hear a variety of views."[86] It also asserted that Congress could regulate campaign finance to promote political equality: "It would be strange indeed if . . . the wealthy few could claim a constitutional guarantee to a stronger political voice than the unwealthy many because they are able to give and spend more money, and because the amounts they give and spend cannot be limited."[87] The appellate court upheld the legislation with the exception of one minor provision.[88]

When the case reached the Supreme Court, the legislation received a much chillier reception. That may have been partly because the government's lawyers offered a half-hearted defense. President Ford had only reluctantly signed the FECA amendments, and it briefly seemed possible that the Justice Department would not defend the law. After the newly appointed Republican FEC chair protested, Attorney General Edward Levi and Solicitor General Robert Bork adopted a less extreme strategy; they would file one brief defending the law and a second amicus brief expressing doubts.

Both of the government's briefs partially undercut the position advanced by legislation's supporters. The amicus brief directly questioned the constitutionality of the contribution and expenditure limits: "While facilitating the right of individuals to speak and to communicate their views to others is a goal Congress can pursue (and justifies in part the public financing provisions of FECA), it must be decided whether Congress may foster this end by inhibiting (or prohibiting) the speech of those who now speak."[89] The main brief offered a somewhat stronger defense of the statute. It rejected a simple equation of campaign spending with speech and limits on spending with censorship:

> We cannot too often stress that the legislation . . . is concerned with *money*, not speech. That is not the same thing . . . Many campaign expenditures are unrelated to speech and there are still ways of communicating that do not involve spending. But, more important, what is regulated is one of the means for communication, not speech itself. There is no censorship whatever: the candidate and his supporters may say what they like. What is more, they remain entirely free to choose their medium of communication. The law does not limit the total number of hours a candidate can speak or the number of words that can be written on his behalf. The evil aimed at is not prolixity, but the undue influence and the gross disparities resulting from unlimited spending in electoral campaigns.[90]

But the main brief also stated that "the effect of spending limits . . . must be to restrict some political speech." It characterized the spending ceiling as a "very limited restriction" and a "realistic compromise" that "trenches least on First Amendment values."[91] An internal memo to Solicitor General Bork predicted that the justices would notice these concessions: "If the only good thing we have to say about an indefensible statute is that it is 'very limited,' the Court's response should be obvious."[92]

The groups that led the legislative effort defended the statute. They argued that "our constitutional system is based on the precept that citizens of unequal wealth are entitled to an equal say in electing national leaders and urging their views on those elected after they take office."[93] Lloyd Cutler, who later served as White House counsel to Presidents Jimmy Carter and Bill Clinton, handled the oral argument for these groups. Former Watergate prosecutor Archibald Cox represented Edward Kennedy (D-MA) and Hugh Scott (R-PA), who had led the effort to enact public financing provisions in the Senate. Counsel for the petitioners were Winter, Bolton, Brice Clagett, and the ACLU's Joel Gora. The Socialist Labor Party filed an amicus brief arguing that the disclosure requirements were unconstitutional as applied to minor parties and that the standards to obtain public financing discriminated against minor parties in violation of the Constitution.[94]

The challenged legislation called for direct and speedy Supreme Court review of its constitutionality, and, as one interviewed lawyer recalled, the justices "felt an understandable need to clarify the law before the '76 election." In order to move quickly, Chief Justice Warren Burger divvied up responsibility for writing various parts of the opinion. Justice William Brennan, widely regarded as the most influential liberal to have served on the famously (and, to some, infamously) liberal Warren Court, played a major role in reconciling its components.[95]

The unsigned *Buckley* opinion was the work of justices whose votes were not always predictable based on the party of the president who appointed them. It reflected compromises and balancing of a type that was common in an era when the Court was not yet the polarized institution it is today. The opinion invalidated the legislation's spending limits but upheld its contribution limits, finding that the latter served a governmental interest in combating corruption or the appearance of corruption.[96] The Court rejected the claim that the spending restriction was justified by a governmental interest in promoting political equality, finding that justification "wholly foreign to the First Amendment."[97] It also held that candidates could use their own money without limitation to support their own campaigns.

*Buckley* sometimes is cited for the proposition that money is speech. In fact, that equation operates today as a shorthand for the position of opponents of any regulation of money in politics. The idea that campaign spending is speech is now entrenched in Supreme Court doctrine. It operates as a powerful frame in legislative deliberations and public debates, and it is pervasive in the rhetoric of challengers. But the phrase "money is speech" appeared just once in the *Buckley* opinion, in Justice White's partially *dissenting* opinion. White rejected the argument "that money is speech and that limiting the flow of money to the speaker violates the First Amendment," finding that it "proves entirely too much" because the same logic would make unconstitutional many other current laws that impose costs on communicative activities.[98] (White would have permitted limits on campaign expenditures as well as contributions.)[99] While the *Buckley* opinion did not say that "money is speech," it did endorse the notion that FECA's contribution and spending limits were an effort to "restrict the voices of people and interest groups who have money to spend" and to "mute the voices of affluent persons."[100]

Funding for the *Buckley* litigation came from the Libertarian Party, the American Conservative Union, Senator Buckley, and the New York Civil Liberties Union.[101] Charles Koch supplied some financial support for the Libertarian Party's portion of the litigation costs. His immediate interest in the case stemmed from his desire to make large contributions to the 1976 presidential campaign of Roger MacBride on the Libertarian Party ticket. Koch also wanted to persuade other wealthy conservatives to join him in challenging the Republican Party from the right.[102] He called on business leaders to recognize their "obligation to fight for the restoration of the free market and the survival of private enterprise" and to "undertake radical new efforts to overcome the prevalent anti-capitalist mentality."[103] Koch's lawyers were unsure of the legality of the large contribution that he was prepared to give MacBride's campaign, and Koch needed clarity before he would contribute. Edward H. Crane III, who was then national chair of the Libertarian Party, hired John Bolton to advise on the matter and to seek guidance from the FEC.[104] After the Supreme Court issued its ruling in *Buckley*, the FEC released an advisory opinion allowing the Libertarian Party to receive up to $25,000 per year from a single donor. In a letter to Koch updating him on these developments, Crane described the Court's validation of parts of the legislation as "a sad commentary on the status of personal liberty in this nation."[105] Several months later, Koch hired Crane to lead his family foundation, the Cato Institute, which has since become a highly influential libertarian think tank and participant in litigation challenging campaign finance regulation.[106]

In 1979, David Koch volunteered to be added to the Libertarian Party's 1980 ticket to take advantage of *Buckley*'s holding that Congress could not constitutionally prevent a candidate from donating as much as he wanted to his own election campaign. In a letter to Libertarian Party members, Koch predicted that the Libertarian Party was poised to become "a very significant force in this country—a truly effective vehicle for rolling back the coercive power of government." The letter also explained Koch's perspective on FECA's restrictions on his ability to spend on politics:

> It may turn out that the only factor preventing us from realizing our potential is that very power government has. In 1974 the Democrats and Republicans passed the Federal Election Campaign Act. It should have been entitled An Act to Preserve the Two Party Monopoly. I am fortunate enough to have the means to make a substantial contribution to our Presidential campaign. The law says I don't have that right. You, of course, know differently. I have the right to spend whatever I choose to promote what I believe. The law is, I suppose, no different in principle from thousands of other statist infringements on voluntary human action. But its ability to stifle the progress of the best hope for individual liberty in the past two centuries absolutely makes my blood boil.[107]

Ed Clark, who was the Libertarian Party's presidential candidate, recommended that Koch be selected as the VP nominee because he promised to "contribute enormous amounts of money" and because "David Koch's candidacy is a tremendous opportunity for us to expose the federal election laws as a sham, a farce, and an insult to the First Amendment and free speech."[108] The party accepted Clark's recommendation. As the Libertarian Party's 1980 vice-presidential nominee, David Koch called for abolishing all campaign spending limits.[109] He spent more than $2 million of his own money on the campaign.[110]

The Koch brothers' support for the Libertarian Party did not last, but their interest in resisting the regulation of money in politics and using their wealth to shape electoral and policy outcomes continues to this day. They, and their donor network, have supported groups challenging campaign finance regulation, and they have spent massive amounts on elections. However, the Kochs are generally cautious about publicly expressing their policy stances beyond vague and anodyne endorsements of "economic freedom" and a "free society."[111]

### Challenges to Corporate Spending Restrictions

*Buckley* addressed only the rights of individuals to spend money on politics, but several banks and their allies soon challenged a limitation on corporate spending. They objected to a Massachusetts law that prohibited corporations from making campaign contributions and expenditures on ballot measures that did not "materially affect any of the property, business or assets of the corporation."[112] When the Massachusetts legislature submitted to voters a measure authorizing an income tax on individuals, the First National Bank of Boston and several corporations announced that they would oppose the tax and use company funds to do so. The state attorney general promised to prosecute them if they proceeded with the plan, and the corporations sued, arguing that corporations should enjoy the same First Amendment speech rights as natural persons. The Supreme Judicial Court of Massachusetts rejected that argument.

When the case reached the US Supreme Court, the US Chamber of Commerce supported the challengers' position. The chamber's brief argued that the Massachusetts court decision, if permitted to stand, would "serve as a precedent to prohibit corporate free speech throughout the country" and that the case "squarely presents . . . the issue of the First Amendment rights of corporations to speak out on issues of public concern to the community in which they are located."[113] The New England Council (a group of business leaders), along with several conservative public interest law groups founded in the 1970s, also filed amicus briefs supporting the constitutional challenge.[114] The state of Montana, with its own history of corrupt influence by corporations, filed an amicus brief arguing that if there was any speech involved in this restriction on corporate spending on ballot measures, it was not ordinary political speech but rather commercial speech, which deserved less constitutional protection.[115] (Three decades later, Montana offered similar arguments to defend a century-old Montana law prohibiting corporations from making expenditures supporting or opposing candidates or political parties, but the Roberts Court found that law unconstitutional.)[116]

The Supreme Court ruled the Massachusetts law unconstitutional in *First National Bank of Boston v. Bellotti* (1978).[117] As in *Buckley*, the justices' votes did not reflect what have since become predictable partisan alignments. At various points in the justices' deliberations, it appeared that Chief Justice Warren Burger and Justices William Rehnquist and Harry Blackmun, all Nixon nominees, might be prepared to join in a majority opinion finding that corporations have no protected speech rights. But Justice Lewis Powell, another Nixon nominee, persuaded Burger and Blackmun to join in a closely divided 5–4 ruling that the Massachusetts statute was unconstitutional.[118] Justice Byron White's dissenting opinion, joined by Brennan and Marshall, argued that the majority's opinion vastly underestimated the state's interest in regulating campaign finance to check corporations' disproportionate economic power. Justice William Rehnquist's separate dissenting opinion asserted that corporations organized for commercial purposes were not entitled to all the rights of free expression enjoyed by natural persons.

Powell had hoped to persuade the justices to find that corporations have the same First Amendment rights to spend money on elections as individuals,[119] a position advocated by some of the amici.[120] He was unable to gain support for that broad proposition, but he nevertheless secured a 5–4 majority to invalidate the spending restriction by focusing on the rights of listeners to receive information, whatever the source.[121] This argument was offered in the amicus briefs of the US Chamber of Commerce and several conservative public interest law groups.[122] These briefs invoked a theory of the First Amendment advanced several years earlier in a case brought by Public Citizen, a consumer advocacy group, to challenge a Virginia law prohibiting pharmacies from advertising drug prices.[123] Public Citizen argued that the restriction harmed consumers who were deprived of information they could use to find prescription drugs at prices they could afford. The group may have intended to benefit consumers, not corporations, but it established a key precedent for the Supreme Court's ruling in *Bellotti*. Citing the Virginia pharmacy case, the opinion emphasized the societal interest in the "free flow of commercial information."[124] The Chamber of Commerce and libertarian advocacy groups have continued to build upon this precedent to expand First Amendment protection for corporate "speech."

As a concession necessary to win Justice Blackmun's vote, the opinion in *Bellotti* contains a footnote explaining that the Court did not intend to call into question long-standing restrictions on corporate spending in *candidate* elections (such as those at issue in *Citizens United*).[125] This distinction was one that the bank and its allies had invited the Court to draw.[126] Although *Bellotti*'s significance was not widely recognized at the time, it later became a key precedent upon which the Roberts Court relied in *Citizens United* to strike down limits on corporate expenditures in elections.

Justice Powell wrote the Court's opinion finding the statute unconstitutional, and in that capacity, he played a significant role in advancing the notion that corporations, like individuals, should enjoy broad speech rights.[127] But Powell's advocacy for corporate rights before joining the Court made him part of the "supply side" of this litigation campaign, too. Just months before Nixon appointed him, Powell delivered a memo to the US Chamber of Commerce asserting that the US economic system was "under broad attack" and that there was an urgent need for American business to mobilize "against those who would destroy it."[128] Powell argued that business interests faced pervasive hostility in universities, the media, and "among respectable liberals and social reformers," and that the very survival of the free enterprise system depended on the willingness of business leaders to confront their detractors. The memo urged business leaders to take a more aggressive stance "in all political arenas," but especially in the courts, which, he suggested, "may be the most important instrument for social, economic, and political change."[129] Powell identified Ralph Nader, the ACLU, public interest law firms, unions, and other such groups as "active exploiters of the judicial system" and an "activist-minded Supreme Court."[130] This memo led to the founding of the US Chamber Litigation Center, an elite litigation team that calls itself "the voice of business and free enterprise in the federal and state courts."[131] The memo also led the chamber to become more active in politics and lobbying and more partisan in its orientation.[132] Since then, the chamber has taken a more aggressive stance toward various types of regulation, including campaign finance laws.

## Abortion Opponents and Gun Rights Groups Join the Fight

Religious conservatives were not among the early opponents of campaign finance reform. Indeed, some of their organizations supported the legislation challenged in *Buckley*.[133] But the next major challenge to reach the Supreme Court grew out of the pro-life movement. Massachusetts Citizens for Life (MCFL), an organization founded to resist abortion rights, used the group's general treasury funds to distribute a flyer captioned "Everything You Need to Know to Vote Pro-Life." The FEC charged MCFL with violating the FECA's prohibition against "any corporation" using general treasury funds to finance contributions or expenditures in connection with a federal election. Lawyers for MCFL argued that the newsletter did not urge readers to vote for or against a candidate and therefore did not violate the law. This argument took advantage of language in *Buckley* suggesting that the statute applied only to express advocacy, using words such as "vote for," "vote against," "elect," and "defeat."[134] But MCFL also argued that the law would violate the First Amendment even if it applied to MCFL's newsletter. Its brief reasoned that the danger of corruption necessary to justify government regulation of political speech "does not exist . . . in the case of grassroots, nonpartisan, nonprofit issue-oriented corporations such as MCFL."[135] The brief emphasized that campaign expenditures by ideological corporations on issues of concern to their members do not "constitute the injection into the political process of vast wealth accumulated for other purposes."[136] Amicus briefs by the National Rifle Association (NRA), ACLU, and US Chamber of Commerce supported MCFL's constitutional challenge.

The Supreme Court's ruling in *Federal Election Commission v. Massachusetts Citizens for Life* (1986) accepted the challengers' argument, finding that organizations that had been formed for the purpose of promoting political ideas "do not suddenly present the specter of corruption merely by assuming the corporate form."[137] Writing for the majority, Justice Brennan found that nonprofit issue-oriented corporations that do not accept contributions from business corporations or labor unions should not be subject to corporate spending limitations for candidate elections. The dissenting opinion by Justice Rehnquist, joined by three other justices, would have upheld the application of the statute to MCFL, reasoning that the Court should defer to Congress's constitutionally sound judgment that the restriction was necessary to address concerns arising from corporate campaign spending.

This was the last of the Supreme Court's campaign finance decisions in which the division between the majority and dissent cut across ideological and partisan lines. The center-left network that had been dominant among legal elites through the mid-1980s was fragmenting. The conservative legal network, organized primarily through the Federalist Society, was growing and gaining influence. As the world of legal elites became more polarized and sorted by party, those developments influenced dynamics among the justices and their alignments in campaign finance rulings.

The participation of abortion opponents and the NRA in this challenge and others like it changed the character of the litigation campaign. It was no longer just about the rights of wealthy individuals ("fat cats") and banks to use money to exercise political influence. The effort began to attract participation from groups associated with the Republican coalition's more populist constituencies—including, eventually, Tea Partiers. The murky boundaries of the category of corporations that the Court found deserving of special treatment gave nonprofit advocacy groups reason to cooperate with business interests in the larger fight. They wanted to be able to use treasury funds, and not just segregated PACs, on election campaigns. They also wanted to be free to take money from business interests without being subject to restrictions on the use of their treasury funds. Nonprofit advocacy groups aligned with religious conservatives also began to see the broader utility of First Amendment arguments to advance causes that were more important to them than campaign finance.

In another challenge to restrictions on corporate spending—the case that resulted in the Supreme Court's ruling in *Austin v. Michigan Chamber of Commerce* (1990)[138]—it was a business-oriented nonprofit enterprise that brought the lawsuit. The Michigan Chamber of Commerce challenged a state statute prohibiting corporations from using corporate treasury funds in candidate elections for state office. The Michigan chamber was a nonprofit corporation, but three-quarters of its funding came from business corporations. It nevertheless claimed that it should qualify for an MCFL exception. Amicus support for the Michigan chamber's position came from the ACLU, several conservative public interest law organizations, and trade groups. An amicus brief joined by several advocacy groups on the political left and right argued that the FEC's interpretation of the MCFL exception was far too restrictive because it was limited to "a certain minuscule class of non-profit corporations" that accept no corporate funding.[139] Briefs filed by Common Cause[140] and the FEC[141] asserted that the MCFL exception should apply only to ideological nonprofit organizations that do not receive funds from business corporations.

The Supreme Court upheld the Michigan statute and its application to the Michigan Chamber of Commerce. It found that Michigan had a compelling interest in combating "the corrosive and distorting effects of immense aggregations of wealth that are accumulated with the help of the corporate form and that have little or no correlation to the public's support for the corporation's political ideas."[142] But the ruling drew strong dissents from Justices Scalia, Kennedy, and O'Connor. As we saw in chapter 1, the dissenters deployed exceptionally strong language, suggesting that the majority had condoned government censorship of political speech.

In the 1990s through the early years of the first decade of the 2000s, the Court continued to enforce long-standing restrictions on the use of general treasury funds (rather than separate PACs) in federal candidate elections while also expanding the reach of the corruption rationale for regulating money in politics. But the *Austin* dissents served as a strong "signal"[143] or "invitation"[144] to opponents of campaign finance regulation that three justices were prepared to reverse course by striking down campaign finance laws.[145] Movement conservatives on the Court were beginning to make their dissenting views known, and their counterparts on the "supply side"—conservative lawyers, advocacy organizations, and funders—were listening.

# Charting a Better Path

We needed a better, and a new, legal strategy . . . [modeled on] the NAACP's litigation strategy in voting rights and integration.

INTERVIEW WITH CHALLENGER

You know the wonderful campaign by the NAACP to dismantle school desegregation? That's the model. They are after dismantling all campaign finance regulation."

INTERVIEW WITH REFORMER

Following the Supreme Court's ruling in *Austin*, opponents of campaign finance regulation began to prepare for the day when a more sympathetic majority would control the Court. With Mitch McConnell in the lead, they organized a more robust, coordinated, and savvy effort to challenge restrictions. Opponents of regulation created specialized advocacy organizations that put clients claiming to fight regulation on behalf of the little guy front and center, and they attracted new sources of financial backing. They broadened the litigation coalition and found prominent lawyers to make the arguments.

## Political Patrons: Mitch McConnell and the GOP

The fight against campaign finance regulation has attracted several key political patrons since the 1970s. By far the most important of them is Kentucky senator Mitch McConnell, who has led Republican opposition to campaign finance reform legislation and has played an important role in resisting regulation through the courts. In interviews, reformers pointed again and again to McConnell's leadership. In response to my questions about the history of this effort, one advised me to "start with the Koch brothers. Start with Mitch McConnell." Another said, "McConnell has driven [it]." Other reformers described opposition to campaign finance regulation as "an article of theology" for McConnell and described him as "the lifetime leader" of opponents of regulation.

McConnell's leadership on the issue began in his first term in the US Senate in the mid-1980s, but his appreciation for the role of money in politics developed earlier. According to one news account, he told students in a political science class he taught at the University of Louisville in the 1970s that there were three things one needed to succeed in politics and build a political party: "money, money, money."[1] In 1973, as an attorney in Louisville and the chair of the Republican Party of Jefferson County, he published an opinion column in which he characterized a local campaign finance reform ordinance as "a Band-Aid on a cancer," and he called for more comprehensive and "truly effective campaign finance reform."[2] But he later explained that this expression of support for reform was about "playing for headlines" and seeking to distance himself and the local Republican Party from the Watergate scandal.[3] In his memoir, McConnell wrote that his first race for the Senate in 1984 showed him that he could not have won if he had faced limits on how much money he could raise and spend: "The only way a guy like me had a chance—a guy with no real political connections and no money, no strong political party apparatus to rely on, holding views opposed by the mainstream media and organized political groups like the labor unions—was to get around the inherent advantages of the liberal majority party by raising enough money to take my message directly to voters."[4] He attributed his "very passionate" opposition to campaign finance regulation to his commitment to the First Amendment and his willingness to fight on behalf of ordinary Americans: "The Founders had a lively fear that with the passage of time, the Constitution they labored to create would be distorted by the enemies of freedom or the ambitions of the powerful, which is exactly what I came to realize was at play in campaign finance reform initiatives."[5]

McConnell's own writings, public statements, and record suggest other motivations. His memoir shows that he viewed campaign finance regulation as a threat to the fractious Republican coalition and its fundraising strategies. He wrote that the "nagging issue of campaign finance reform" would "divide the conservative coalition that I sought to build and would also raise questions about the way we raised money to support our team."[6] Since the 1980s, the Republican coalition has included constituencies whose values and policy priorities are in significant tension with one another. The marriage has never been easy, and the conflict has grown over time, as those who claim to speak for the Republican base have tried to wrest control from the Republican establishment. Laws that stood in the way of the GOP's ability to raise and distribute money made it more difficult to hold these constituencies together.

Defeating campaign finance regulation also buoyed McConnell's own political fortunes. He is a prodigious fundraiser and is unabashed about using his fundraising prowess to exercise political influence. He has long collected large political contributions from industries that receive his political support—including coal,[7] oil and gas, and tobacco.[8] As chair of the National

Republican Senatorial Committee from 1997 through 2001, an important step in his path to the Senate's leadership ranks, he set records for raising soft money—money raised outside the FECA regulations.[9] The deregulatory effort that McConnell has led may have resulted in less control over elections by party leaders. Ultimately, it may have contributed to the radicalization of the Republican Party. But McConnell's mastery of the election money machine and his ability to use the money raised to shore up political allies has enabled him to accrue considerable political power.

McConnell has done more than any other politician to fight campaign finance legislation. In 1994, he defeated a bill proposed by Senator David Boren to regulate soft money and to provide public funding for congressional campaigns. Both houses passed versions of the bill, but McConnell organized an unusual procedural move to defeat it—a filibuster on the nomination of members of the conference committee that would resolve differences between the House and Senate bills before sending the legislation to the president. In a speech to the Heritage Foundation on "Why We Are Stopping Campaign Finance Reform," he explained that the bill's restrictions on soft money "would eliminate about a third of the money that the Republican National Committee gets."[10] He called the public funding provision an "entitlement program for politicians" and argued that "there's not much that needs to be reformed" about the existing campaign finance system. He promised to "burn 90 hours" on a filibuster of the bill and predicted that defeating a cloture motion would kill the legislative effort, because "the cavalry [was] on its way to the rescue" in the form of a Republican sweep of Congress in the 1994 election. He urged his Heritage Foundation audience to join in this "fight for the heart and soul of the country" by "help[ing] us gin up the degree of enthusiasm we need on our side" to defeat the legislation. In his memoir, he described the experience of killing this bill as "exhilarating." He was "extremely proud to have used the rules of the Senate to protect the First Amendment" and to "keep congressional elections from being taken over by the government."[11]

McConnell again led the resistance when reform efforts gained favor during John McCain's 2000 presidential campaign. The BCRA addressed concerns about the growing impact of soft-money contributions to the political parties, and it also targeted the increased use of advertisements designed to circumvent restrictions by endorsing or opposing candidates obliquely without explicitly encouraging voters to "elect" or "defeat" a candidate. Key provisions included disclosure requirements, a ban on soft money donations to the political parties, and limits on the use of corporate and union treasury funds to finance "electioneering communications," defined as "any broadcast, cable or satellite communication that clearly identified a federal candidate, airs within 30 days of a federal primary or 60 days of a federal general election and is targeted to the relevant electorate."

Several interviewed lawyers with ties to the Republican leadership explained why McCain-Feingold threatened the GOP's ability to hold its coalition together, echoing Mitch McConnell's views on the topic. One lawyer explained how the soft money that was unregulated prior to McCain-Feingold made it easier to maintain peace among the fractious elements of the party:

> The Republican Party, prior to McCain-Feingold, really was a tent, a platform, a glue that held together people who maybe didn't have a complete symmetry of opinion and belief. You had the country club Republicans who wouldn't be caught dead with a gun-toting, pro-life activist—might not even agree with them. But these were the foot soldiers. These [country club Republicans] were the people who paid for things. . . . And the Republican Party sort of held together, to some degree, because, grudgingly, whether the rich people liked the little people, or whether the little people activists liked the rich people, they needed each other, and they were all kind of under the same tent. Well, McCain-Feingold blew that up. That went away.

Soft money, this lawyer said, had enabled party committees to make grants to tax-exempt nonprofit organizations and thus to be "a source of support, and give them funding to be able to participate in the process." After McCain-Feingold, "there really was nothing for the Republican Party apparatus to [do] to keep everybody in the same boat and under that same tent. There was no way to do that anymore." A business advocate explained why he and other opponents of the legislation anticipated that McCain-Feingold would push political spending into more extreme and less accountable outlets: "The effect of the legislation would not be to limit the amount of money in politics; it would simply push money out of the mainstream political system, candidates and parties, into less transparent, less responsive, and ultimately less mediated groups."

By his own account, McConnell was "prepared to do whatever it took to kill this bill."[12] Nonetheless, the legislation passed both houses of Congress, and President George W. Bush signed it into law. In a speech at an annual event organized by Charles and David Koch, McConnell described the day of the signing as "the worst day of my political life."[13] In a signing statement, President Bush indicated that the legislation "presented serious constitutional concerns," and that he anticipated that "the courts will resolve these legitimate questions as appropriate under the law."[14] Bush thereby signaled to McConnell, the federal judiciary, and lawyers and advocacy groups that they should get to work on defeating the legislation through litigation, even as he avoided vetoing this popular bill.

In addition to leading the fight against campaign finance reform legislation since the early 1990s, McConnell has played a leading role in organizing the litigation effort and resisting FEC enforcement of existing law. In his
memoir, McConnell claims credit for assembling the litigation coalition and
team of lawyers to challenge the constitutionality of McCain-Feingold immediately after its enactment.[15] He won the role of lead plaintiff in the case
that resulted in the Supreme Court's ruling in *McConnell v. FEC* (2003). He
has also connected scholars with think tanks and funding, lent support to
new organizations, identified and sponsored Republican appointees to the
FEC, and overseen the confirmation of federal judges likely to strike down
campaign finance regulation.

McConnell's stance toward campaign finance regulation has been broadly
consistent with his party's long-standing position on the issue. The GOP has
opposed most campaign finance regulation since the first wave of reform efforts in the late nineteenth and early twentieth centuries, reflecting the common perception that unregulated money in politics benefits Republicans
more than Democrats.[16] But reform proposals still received support from a
significant subset of Republicans until early in the first decade of the 2000s.
As one interviewed reformer observed, "back in the '70s, if you go back to the
'74 FECA and the '76 FECA, those were genuinely bipartisan laws," passed
when "Congress was a very different animal . . . than it is now." Some Republican legislators supported the BCRA and defended it in the *McConnell* litigation.[17] Republican Party platforms in the 1990s and early in the first decade of
the 2000s advocated modest campaign finance reforms.[18]

But subsequent Republican platforms have extolled the virtues of unre-
strained political spending. The 2008 platform, for example, stated that "the
rights of citizenship . . . include the free-speech right to devote one's resources
to whatever cause or candidate one supports" and that Republicans opposed
"any restrictions or conditions upon those activities that would discourage
Americans from exercising their constitutional right to enter the political fray
or limit their commitment to their ideals." The 2012 platform called for the
"repeal of the remaining sections of McCain-Feingold" and opposed any attempts to "vitiate the Supreme Court's recent decisions protecting political
speech."[19] The 2016 platform stated that Republicans believe "limits on political speech serve only to protect the powerful and insulate incumbent officeholders."[20] (The Republican Party failed to adopt a new platform in 2020,
citing the reduced size of the national convention due to restrictions on gath-
ering during the COVID-19 pandemic. Instead, it simply affirmed its support
for President Trump and his administration.[21])

Most people think that unregulated political spending favors Republicans over Democrats, and the GOP's consistent stance on the issue would suggest so. Academic research on the question is less clear.[22] The following section explores the complex politics surrounding the issue.

### Democratic Party Leaders

While the Republican Party and most of its leaders have consistently opposed campaign finance regulation, the reform side has lacked a consistent major-party champion. Overall, the Democratic National Committee (DNC) and its allies have been more supportive of regulation than their GOP counterparts, perhaps reflecting their historic disadvantage vis-à-vis Republicans in attracting money from wealthy individuals and corporations.[23] The Democratic Party's platforms specifically endorsed McCain-Feingold in 1996 and 2000, and subsequent platforms have called for additional measures, including a constitutional amendment to overturn *Citizens United*.[24] The DNC has sometimes filed amicus briefs in support of campaign finance regulations.[25] But the Democratic leadership has not as dependably supported regulation as the party's official position on the issue would suggest.

Many of the reformers whom I interviewed commented on the lack of real commitment to comprehensive reform by the Democratic Party, its lawyers, its candidates, and some constituencies that are especially active in Democratic Party politics. One reformer observed that "both parties . . . have become the party of big money." Another explained that "Democrats hate us as much as Republicans; they just hate us behind the scenes because we call them out on their hypocrisy." He criticized the Democratic Party's lawyers for having been

> horrible on campaign finance issues for a long, long time. . . . The [Democratic] Party's in somewhat of a schizophrenic posture because the Democratic candidates and elected officials are all saying, "We need campaign finance reform," and their lawyers are all actively fighting against campaign finance laws, challenging and spurring deregulation of money in politics in the courts. There's a major disconnect. At least on the Republican side . . . they're singing from the same songbook. You have Republican officeholders and candidates all saying, "We don't need any of these limits, they all infringe on the First Amendment," and their lawyers are saying the same thing in court. But on the Democratic side, you have people like [naming particular lawyers] challenging campaign finance laws in court [and] showing up at the FEC and arguing for deregulation of money in politics while their clients are stumping [for reform].

The same lawyer speculated about conversations between party decision-makers and their lawyers as the cases were "percolating up." He imagined lawyers saying, "'Yeah, we should be on the side of deregulation here,' and the party's decision-makers saying, 'No, we can't do that publicly.'" Another reformer observed that the "'if you can't beat them, join them' psychology" is very much at work in the Democratic Party: "Regrettably, the Democratic Party's obviously now in a mode of trying to set this up so that they can begin using unlimited finance too."

The challengers also offered skeptical perspectives on the Democratic Party's position on campaign finance reform. A challenger asserted that while some populists within the Democratic Party, such as Bernie Sanders and perhaps Elizabeth Warren, might be principled reform advocates, most Democrats are "filthy free-riders." The same lawyer noted that Barack Obama was the first presidential candidate since Richard Nixon to reject public funding, and that Hillary Clinton also relied on major donors: "[Obama] had this super PAC; he had a (c)(4); he was raising big money. And, my God, Hillary! So, there's really no credibility on any side of this issue." He added: "The problem is that Democrats aren't opposed to big money. They're opposed to *my* big money. . . . Democrats are just not good actors on this, and they're willing to benefit as well. . . . They just don't want to take the blame." One challenger who counted himself a moderate Republican predicted that Democrats would soon hold an advantage in attracting big money: "I think if you look at the demographics, and if you look at the fact that the Republican Party has decided to give up on everyone with a graduate degree, there's no way the pot of money for the Right stays bigger than the pot of money for the Left."

These observations by the interviewed lawyers are consistent with research showing that, while Democrats historically have relied on small donors more than Republicans have, Democratic candidates and their party committees have increasingly drawn large contributions from some of the wealthiest Americans. They now attract plenty of donors in the Forbes 400—a group that was once solidly Republican.[26] Democratic candidates and party committees have made especially significant inroads in high-tech industries.[27] These individual and corporate donors do not always share the policy priorities of other interest groups that have long aligned with the Democratic Party.[28] And while some Democratic candidates in the 2018 and 2020 election cycles swore off donations from business PACs, Democrats still accepted substantial amounts from corporate PACs in those years.[29]

Some organized interests that have been especially active supporters of Democratic candidates have opposed restrictions on their political activities. One interviewed lawyer noted that "the tax-exempt community, the 501(c) community, on the progressive side, has always been a little bit leery" about campaign finance regulation. He noted, for example, that during the FEC's 2003–2004 debate over what constituted a political committee, there were "a lot of questions and criticisms raised by progressive groups on the Left. . . . And the reason is simply that once you've broadly enough defined what a political committee is, you potentially sweep up the activities of tax-exempt organizations that are active on both sides—on the Left, not just on the Right." A civil libertarian emphasized that many liberal nonprofit advocacy organizations take money from corporations: "The NAACP gets tons of corporate money, tons of corporate money, because corporations want to buy favor with civil rights groups—you know, buy off discrimination charges, and stuff like that." A reformer commented on similar ambivalence by organized labor, which "manifested itself as early as McCain-Feingold, when organized labor—which for years had been one of the leading organizing entities in the campaign finance sphere pro-reform—suddenly wound up on the other side in the *McConnell* courtroom, with the AFL-CIO lawyer arguing against one of the principal planks of McCain-Feingold." Another reformer observed that while Republicans have been especially eager to hide the fact that "they get lots of money from corporations," Democrats "get huge amounts of money from labor unions and don't want to rein in the labor unions either." Chapter 5 addresses some of the history surrounding the positions of tax-exempt groups and labor unions on campaign finance regulation. It also considers arguments that some reformers offer for treating labor unions differently from business corporations.

The greater unity among Republicans than Democrats over campaign finance regulation may reflect differences in the orientations and strategies of the two parties. Political scientists Matt Grossmann and David Hopkins have argued that Republican and Democratic parties have become fundamentally different kinds of parties.[30] The Democratic Party is more of a group coalition, drawing its strongest electoral backing from members of discrete social groups who perceive that they benefit from government policies and programs supported by the party's leaders. Party leaders emphasize delivering concrete benefits targeting its various constituencies more than achieving ideological cohesion. The Republican Party operates more as a vehicle of an ideological movement in which most members identify with abstract values of small government and American cultural traditionalism. The party's support comes less from social groups activated by identity-based interests than by members' shared sense of themselves as defenders of liberty and American values against left-wing ideas. These differences in the nature of the parties might help explain why Republicans have coalesced around the idea that campaign finance regulation cannot be squared with individual freedom, and why Democrats have tolerated greater inconsistency on the issue, as party leaders seek to assemble a policy agenda reflecting the aggregated preferences of the party's various constituencies, some of which benefit from lax rules on money in politics.

The symbolic power of free speech rhetoric and the unappealing optics of arguing against the expansion of First Amendment protection also may help explain Democratic Party leaders' failure to display consistent leadership on the issue.[31]

### The Federalist Society Free Speech and Election Law Practice Group

Following the defeat in 1995 of Congress's first attempt to enact what eventually became McCain-Feingold, the Federalist Society formed the Free Speech and Election Law Practice Group. This network brought more conservatives into the conversation and linked their varied policy concerns to themes about free speech and association. The group's first newsletter in 1996 featured an essay by Mitch McConnell describing the effort to reform campaign finance as the work of "a scandal-hungry media and self-serving politicians" and condemning "professional reformers' shameful disregard of the First Amendment."[32] The same issue of the newsletter included a column by James Bopp, criticizing the FEC's prosecution of the Christian Coalition for distributing voter guides in violation of the FECA and calling it part of "the 20-year war it has waged on the First Amendment."[33] The next issue included an essay by Bradley Smith, a professor of law at Capital University and adjunct scholar at the Cato Institute, calling it "time to deregulate American politics."[34]

Other columns published in the newsletter in its first several years linked free-speech claims to different types of concerns not directly related to election spending. Some essays highlighted how First Amendment arguments could be used to challenge claims of workplace harassment, hate speech policies on college campuses, and compulsory payment of union dues.[35] Other columns argued that the First Amendment should not be interpreted to provide protection to pornographers and violent street gangs.[36] Lawyers in large private law firms complained that federal agencies encroached on protected speech when they regulated commercial advertising, and that such regulation amounted to censoring unpopular speakers. One column argued that the Supreme Court's more lenient approach toward the regulation of advertising "encouraged bureaucrats and politicians to attack the commercial speech of politically unpopular interests—most dramatically tobacco."[37] Mitch McConnell wrote a column connecting free-speech principles to the anxieties of other constituencies within the conservative coalition: "As conservative and libertarian ideas are gaining ascendency in the marketplace of ideas, it is the left that is finding it convenient to disregard the First Amendment. Many on the left are now solicitous of restricting speech that interferes with their efforts to maintain racial preferences, perpetuate the welfare state, and increase government control over citizens."[38]

James Bopp and Brad Smith were not well known when they published their essays in the Free Speech and Election Law Practice Group newsletter in the 1990s, but they have since become prominent players in the effort to defeat campaign finance regulation. Bopp has brought more cases challenging campaign finance regulations than any other lawyer. Smith has done more than anyone since the 1970s to make the intellectual case for deregulating money in American politics.

Bopp came to the issue through his work on conservative causes. He was born in Terre Haute, Indiana, and attended Indiana University, where he headed a chapter of Young Americans for Freedom. Following his graduation from law school in Florida, he returned to Terre Haute, where he still resides. Since 1978, he has served as general counsel to the National Right to Life Committee (NRLC), and he has also represented Focus on the Family and other groups that oppose gay marriage. His interest in resisting campaign finance regulation grew out of the antiabortion movement and his role as general counsel to the National Right to Life Committee. He has filed dozens of challenges to the constitutionality of campaign finance restrictions on behalf of the NRLC and the Christian Coalition, and he has represented these and other conservative groups in myriad disputes with the FEC over their campaign activities.[39]

Most of Bopp's test cases through the early years of the first decade of the 2000s focused on advancing the rights of conservative tax-exempt advocacy organizations to engage in election activities and campaign spending. But thereafter he broadened his aims, joining an effort to completely deregulate campaign finance for business corporations and wealthy individuals as well as for ideologically driven nonprofits. He filed most of the cases that resulted in victories in the Roberts Court. Chapter 5 considers the reasons for his shift in emphasis.

Smith first came to the attention of key figures in the fight against campaign finance regulation in 1994, when he published an op-ed in the *Washington Times* arguing that the Supreme Court should strike down an Ohio statute prohibiting anonymous distribution of political campaign literature and requiring disclosure of the source of financing. The case, *McIntyre v. Ohio Elections Commission*, involved a woman who had personally distributed leaflets opposing a school district tax levy outside a middle school. In a 7–2 decision, the Court held that the Ohio statute was unconstitutional as applied in these circumstances.[40] Smith's op-ed, published before the ruling, argued that the Court should not draw the kinds of "murky distinctions" adopted in *Buckley* and its progeny. Smith asserted that the Court had created a "doctrinal nightmare" as it "sought, in vain, to set principled limits on how far the state can go in limiting campaign speech." Instead, he wrote, the Court should observe "the system of campaign speech 'regulation' favored by the Founders"—that "Congress should make no law" with respect to money in politics.[41]

Smith's op-ed prompted a phone call from David Boaz, the Cato Institute's executive vice president, indicating that Cato had been looking for somebody to write on this topic—an issue important to Cato's chair, Ed Crane. Cato commissioned Smith to write a report on campaign finance reform proposals. Smith elaborated on those arguments in a 1996 *Yale Law Journal* article titled "The Faulty Assumptions and Undemocratic Consequences of Campaign Finance Reform," writing that "reform proposals inherently favor certain political elites, support the status quo, and discourage grassroots political activity" and that "national 'reform' legislation has benefitted the wealthy at the expense of the working class."[42] Smith expanded on these views in a book, *Unfree Speech: The Folly of Campaign Finance Reform*, which argued that most campaign finance regulation is unconstitutional.[43] Smith's work caught the attention of Senator McConnell and his staff and led to invitations to testify before Congress. In 1999, then president Bill Clinton nominated Smith for an FEC post. He served in a Republican-designated seat on the FEC from 2000 through 2005.

Smith has done more than any other scholar since the 1970s to advance the legal theories that eventually prevailed in the Roberts Court. The *New York Times* has called Smith the "intellectual powerhouse" behind the campaign to deregulate campaign finance.[44] One interviewed lawyer agreed with that assessment: "Brad is kind of the godfather, right? He was the intellectual force that brought all of this about . . . If there's the king, the intellectual godfather, of the campaign finance conservative libertarian movement, it's him." Lillian BeVier, who picked up the mantle from Winter and Redish in the 1980s and advanced arguments later expanded upon by Smith, is a close second.[45]

Law review articles by BeVier, Smith, and other members of the Free Speech and Election Law Practice Group built upon arguments against campaign finance regulation first advanced by legal scholars in the 1970s and 1980s—that campaign spending is a form of constitutionally protected speech, and that attempts to regulate it constitute government censorship.[46] These lawyers also argued that corporations should be treated like associations of citizens for purposes of the First Amendment's protection of speech, notwithstanding contrary precedents.[47]

Connections among lawyers, judges, and clerks affiliated with the Federalist Society facilitated the transmission and acceptance of those arguments in the courts. Some Federalist Society members have also addressed their arguments about campaign finance regulation to the Court's broader audiences, not only through conventional outlets such as the *Wall Street Journal* and the *National Review*[48] but also through media catering to the more populist strands of the conservative alliance.

## Specialized Advocacy Groups

Bradley Smith has observed that reformers enjoyed several significant advantages in the 1990s.[49] One was specialized advocacy organizations. Reformers' specialized groups included Common Cause, which had led the reform effort since the early 1970s; the Brennan Center, founded in 1995 by New York University law professor Burt Neuborne to honor the ideals of Justice William Brennan;[50] and Democracy 21, founded in 1997 by Fred Wertheimer, who had previously served as president of Common Cause. In contrast to this formidable set of specialized groups on the reform side, Smith wrote, there was "no significant organization that was entirely or primarily dedicated" to "a skeptical approach" to campaign finance regulation.[51]

But opponents of campaign finance regulation soon remedied this disadvantage. They established several groups that focus on defending what they characterize as the constitutional rights of regular citizens against oppressive government regulations designed to silence them.

James Bopp founded the James Madison Center for Free Speech in 1997. The center describes its mission as fighting the suppression of political speech and efforts by "powerful forces in government, both state and federal, who view the First Amendment's protection of political expression as a loophole in our election laws that they must close." The organization vows to resist those who "are seeking to use government to suppress the right of citizens and citizen groups to participate in our democratic process by limiting their right to speak out about the actions of public officeholders and the position of candidates on issues and by limiting the right of citizens to join together to make their voices heard."[52] The original board included Betsy DeVos, a major GOP donor who later became President Trump's secretary of education, and Don Hodel, former secretary of the interior and president of the Christian Coalition. Senator Mitch McConnell served as honorary chairman.

Smith founded the Center for Competitive Politics in 2005, following his tenure as an FEC commissioner. Later renamed the Institute for Free Speech (IFS), the group claims to be "the only organization with a dedicated professional staff and mission seeking to promote and defend American citizens' First Amendment political speech rights."[53] Its website asserts that "it's not the big guy who is harmed by campaign finance reform . . . It's the small businessperson. It's the nonprofit organization. It's the group of citizens in the community who just see a problem in their community and decide to do something about it." IFS engages in strategic litigation, research, communications, and outreach to policymakers, including on day-to-day matters before the FEC. One interviewed challenger said that before the founding of the Center, "all you ever heard from was the reform groups. They're there all the time, on everything . . . and it *does* matter." The same lawyer explained that it was important to address the concerns of FEC commissioners when "the *Washington Post* is just bashing you and bashing your position 24/7. The *New York Times* is as well, [and] the NPR stations are [too] . . . People do begin to say, 'Is this argument even respectable?' . . . And so . . . there had to be someone out there . . . to provide them with another perspective—remind the commissioners, 'Oh yeah. There is another way to look at this.'" This lawyer believed that IFS has boosted the deregulatory cause and dealt "a bit of a blow to the reformers." David Keating, founder of SpeechNow.org and former director of the Club for Growth, became IFS's president in 2012. He describes the organization's mission as "doing for the First Amendment what the NRA did for the Second."[54]

Around the time of IFS's founding, the Institute for Justice (IJ), one of the most successful second-generation conservative public interest law groups, also launched a project to challenge campaign finance regulations. IJ, founded in 1991 with initial seed funding by Charles Koch,[55] has done more than any other organization to associate libertarian causes with the needs of ordinary Americans. Its mission—"to limit the size and scope of government power and to ensure that all Americans have the right to control their own destinies as free and responsible members of society"—is broader than those of the James Madison Center and IFS.[56] But like those more specialized organizations, IJ characterizes its opposition to campaign finance regulation as the defense of the right to free speech against political censorship: "Under the guise of reform, campaign-finance regulations protect incumbents from electoral competition and stifle political speech and association."[57] IJ's success has depended, in part, on its efforts to distance itself from immediate partisan calculations and the interests of its patrons. One interviewed lawyer attributed

IJ's initial reluctance to have "anything to do with the campaign finance area" to concerns about jeopardizing its reputation for taking principled stands. It needed to avoid representing politicians, but it found a way to get involved by focusing on how these laws "inhibit political participation and ordinary Americans speaking out." At first, this lawyer told me, IJ was just "dabbling" in the issue, but it later developed "more of an interest in campaign finance issues." The organization's website now claims that IJ has "been at the forefront of the fight against laws that hamstring the political speech of ordinary citizens and entrench political insiders." It seeks to eliminate "burdensome campaign finance laws" because "speakers and listeners should determine the value of speech, not the government."[58]

Specialized groups have led the way in advancing the themes of the campaign and chipping away at restrictions on money in politics. They have pursued an incremental litigation campaign modeled on the strategy used by the NAACP Legal Defense Fund to attack racial segregation.[59] A lawyer for one specialized group described the general strategy: "You take the low hanging fruit. You build your precedent. You go to the next one, you take the next lowest hanging fruit, you build your precedent. . . . That's what we needed to do—a series of small cases, small steps, where we can point out to the Court, 'Look, this can't be right under the First Amendment,' and then just keep building it." A lawyer for another specialized group described his organization's approach similarly: "[The organization] is always trying to find some issue that they can make actual practical incremental progress on . . . You don't go to the Court and say, 'Strike down all the bad laws at once.' It's just not going to happen. Litigation and legal change, at least in the courts, is incremental change."

These specialized groups have also pursued media strategies to complement the litigation campaign. Among the advantages that Brad Smith attributed to reformers in the 1990s was a rhetorical one.[60] Smith complained, for example, about reformers' characterization of issue ads as "sham issue ads" and *Buckley*'s express advocacy standard as a "magic words" test, thereby making the standard "sound ridiculous."[61] Lawyers for specialized groups sought to counter what they perceived as reformers' rhetorical advantage by explaining in simple terms why ordinary Americans should resist the regulation of money in politics. One such lawyer explained that, in addition to advocating in the courts, his organization argues "before the court of public opinion," helping people to understand "why these sometimes very complicated, abstruse issues in court matter." A lawyer for another specialized group explained that his organization tried to "both educate people and litigate cases" and to pursue those twin purposes "every single day."

Specialized organizations have also been more able than other groups on the challengers' side to build litigation coalitions with organizations that are not their natural political allies. A lawyer for one specialized group noted that it can be harder for "multifaceted groups, like Heritage or Cato," to "strike up alliances with people who agree with you on just one issue." Groups with broader agendas that embrace the Republican Party's position on voting requirements, voter fraud, gerrymandering, and redistricting, for example, find it "much harder . . . to forge alliances with the ACLU and the unions [and others] on campaign finance issues." That's one reason, he said, why "we pretty much stick to our knitting."

Although their activities overlap, these specialized groups do not all serve the same function within the litigation campaign. The alliances that one organization can forge are not necessarily available to the others. The James Madison Center, for example, is tied to the antiabortion movement and conflicts over gay marriage in a way that IJ and IFS are not, while IJ and IFS have tighter connections to libertarian and business networks. IJ specializes in connecting the litigation campaign to stories about how regulation harms regular people. IFS is especially active in matters before the FEC.

### New Financial Patrons

The Republican National Committee (RNC) provided funding for some of James Bopp's litigation projects,[62] but much of the money for the groups pursuing these cases has come from sources outside the Republican Party, including millionaires and billionaires who have sought to move the Republican Party rightward. Among the largest foundation contributors to the James Madison Center since its founding are the John William Pope Foundation, the Mercer Family Foundation, the Lynde and Harry Bradley Foundation, and the Dick and Betsy DeVos Family Foundation. The John William Pope Foundation is a major backer of libertarian causes, and its other grant recipients have included the John Locke Foundation, the Americans for Prosperity Foundation (a Koch-sponsored political organization), the National Taxpayers Union, and the Cato Institute.[63] The Mercer Family Foundation is based on the fortune of Renaissance Technology hedge fund manager Robert Mercer, who was also a major investor in Breitbart News.[64] Robert Mercer's daughter, Rebekah Mercer, runs the foundation, which has invested tens of millions in conservative causes. The Mercers have done little to hide their disdain for the Republican establishment and the mainstream media, and they have supported candidates who defy Wall Street on issues such as immigration and trade. The

Bradley Foundation became a significant force in conservative politics in 1985, when the Allen-Bradley Company was sold to Rockwell International for over $1.5 billion and the foundation received $290 million. The Bradley Foundation then hired Michael Joyce from the Olin Foundation to raise Bradley's profile. The foundation gives away $35 to $45 million per year, mostly to conservative causes. The DeVos multi-billion-dollar family fortune is based on the Amway direct-marketing business, launched by Richard DeVos Sr. and Jay Van Andel, who were the top independent spenders on behalf of Ronald Reagan's first presidential run.[65] In 1997, the year Betsy DeVos assisted in the James Madison Center's founding, she acknowledged that her family was the largest soft-money contributor to the GOP at the time. In an op-ed in *Roll Call*, she wrote:

> I know a little something about soft money, as my family is the largest single contributor of soft money to the national Republican Party. . . . I have decided to stop taking offense at the suggestion that we are buying influence. Now I simply concede the point. They are right. We do expect some things in return. We expect to foster a conservative governing philosophy consisting of limited government and respect for traditional American virtues. We expect a return on our investment; we expect a good and honest government. Furthermore, we expect the Republican Party to use the money to promote these policies and, yes, to win elections.[66]

The largest foundation patrons of IFS, IJ, and Cato in the decade preceding the Supreme Court's ruling in *McCutcheon* were the Robert W. Wilson Charitable Trust, the Searle Freedom Trust, the Lynde and Harry Bradley Foundation, and Dunn's Foundation for the Advancement of Right Thinking.[67] The Robert W. Wilson Charitable Trust was established in 2003 by a retired hedge-fund founder who donated most of his $500 million fortune to a variety of causes before he died in late 2013.[68] Between 2003 and 2013, the Trust gave over $1 million to IFS and $9.5 million to IJ. The Searle Freedom Trust is based on profits from Searle and Company, which created the artificial sweetener aspartame (marketed as "NutraSweet"). It gave $600k to IFS, $1.65 million to IJ, and $1.07 million to Cato. Dunn's Foundation for the Advancement of Right Thinking, established in 1994 by futures trader William A. Dunn, supports primarily free-market think tanks and advocacy groups. It gave $4.28 million to IJ, $4.1 million to Cato, and $130k to IFS. The Goldwater Institute, one of the groups that challenged Arizona's campaign finance law, received donations during the same period from Searle ($350k), Bradley ($175,000), and Mercer ($100,000). Bradley gave IFS $260,000, and the Ed

Uihlein Family Foundation, based on the Joseph Schlitz brewing fortune and run by Richard Uihlein, billionaire founder of the Uline shipping and packaging company, gave IFS $295,000 during the same period. (Richard Uihlein was the fifth-largest donor to outside spending groups in 2020.[69])

The largest foundation patrons of the primary reform organizations during the same period were the Joyce Foundation, the Pew Charitable Trusts, the Ford Foundation, and George Soros's Open Society Institute. The Joyce Foundation, based on a fortune built in the lumber industry, describes its mission as "investing in public policies and strategies to advance racial equity and economic mobility."[70] It provided substantial financial support for campaign finance reform advocacy to the Brennan Center, the Campaign Legal Center, Common Cause, and Democracy 21, as well as several state-focused organizations with similar agendas. The broad mission of the Pew Charitable Trusts, based on Sun Oil Company money, includes "invigorat[ing] civic life by encouraging democratic participation."[71] In 2005, Pew became a major funder of groups monitoring campaign finance, making substantial gifts over the next several years to the Campaign Legal Center, Democracy 21, and the Brennan Center.[72] The Ford Foundation, a longtime funder of liberal causes, was a major supporter of the Brennan Center, Americans for Campaign Reform, Common Cause, and the Campaign Legal Center.[73] The Open Society Institute, based on the fortune of hedge-fund billionaire George Soros, gave large sums to the Brennan Center, Common Cause, the League of Women Voters, and Public Campaign.[74]

Thus, much of the funding for the opposing sides of this litigation campaign came from two sets of foundations, based on the fortunes of millionaires and billionaires, and advancing different visions of America's future.

### Increased Amicus Participation

Various elements of the GOP coalition significantly stepped up their participation in challenges to campaign finance laws in the years following the Supreme Court's ruling in *Austin*. In fact, the number of amicus briefs filed on both sides of the major cases has increased substantially since then, in keeping with general trends toward increased amicus participation on both sides of divisive issues before the Supreme Court.[75] But there has been a larger increase in the number of briefs filed on the challengers' side than on the defenders' side, as shown in figure 3.1. Most of the new entrants on the challengers' side are groups claiming to speak for the GOP's populist elements.

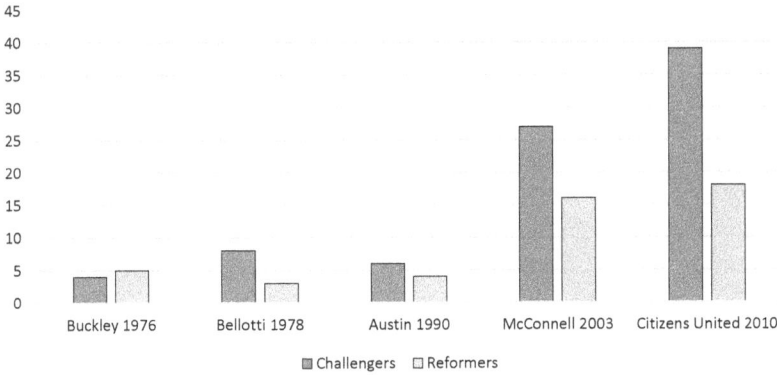

FIGURE 3.1. Tally of party and amicus briefs filed by each side in five major Supreme Court cases

## Prominent Appellate Advocates

Whether ideas are taken seriously in the courts is tied to various social conventions, including, as Jack Balkin writes, "which persons in the legal profession are willing to stand up for a particular legal argument." He explains: "In law, if not in other disciplines of thought, authority, and particularly institutional authority, counts for a lot. The more powerful and influential the people who are willing to make a legal argument, the more quickly it moves from positively loony to positively thinkable, and ultimately to something entirely consistent with 'good legal craft.'"[76] Opponents of campaign finance regulation began to find more elite members of the Supreme Court bar willing to endorse strong versions of the claim that limits on political spending constitute limits on speech.

✳ ✳ ✳

The next big showdown in the Supreme Court came in *McConnell v. FEC* (2003), the last major campaign finance victory for reformers before the Court began to reverse course. Immediately after President George W. Bush signed the BCRA, Mitch McConnell challenged the statute, as did the National Rifle Association, the ACLU, Congressman Ron Paul, the RNC, the California Democratic Party, the US Chamber of Commerce, and the National Right to Life Committee. The AFL-CIO challenged the electioneering provisions of the statute. These separate suits were eventually consolidated into one case, with Senator McConnell as lead plaintiff.

McConnell assembled an impressive team of highly credentialed lawyers to argue his case: Floyd Abrams, a premier litigator who has made his name as a proponent of First Amendment "near-absolutism";[77] Kenneth Starr, former US appellate judge, solicitor general, and Whitewater special prosecutor; and Stanford Law School dean Kathleen Sullivan. In his memoir, McConnell boasted not only about the caliber of his lawyers but also the favorable optics of having Abrams on his team: "I tapped Floyd Abrams, the most prominent—and probably the most liberal—First Amendment lawyer in America. He had represented the *New York Times* in the Pentagon Papers case, and wasn't exactly accustomed to conservatives. As I liked to say, the *New York Times* editorial page may be with McCain, but I've got their lawyer." McConnell was undoubtedly right that the professional stature of his team of lawyers lent credibility to the First Amendment arguments advanced by the challengers in *McConnell*.

Lawyers associated with the Republican Party's populist elements brought different types of professional profiles into the campaign in supporting roles. James Bopp, representing the National Right to Life Committee, was not part of the legal establishment. Nor were Herbert Titus and his co-counsel William Olson, who represented Ron Paul. Titus is a Harvard Law graduate, but he also served as the founding dean of Regent University School of Law, pursuing a vision of restoring American law to its "Biblical foundation."[78] Olson, whose website features President Ronald Reagan's "government is not the solution to our problem; government is the problem" quote, has filed over 150 amicus briefs in the Supreme Court on issues ranging from gun rights to Biblical and natural law.[79] He also served from 1993 to 2016 as legal counsel to the Free Speech Coalition, a group established in 1993 to challenge regulation of the political activities of nonprofit advocacy organizations.[80] Jay Alan Sekulow, who handled the oral argument for several individual challengers in *McConnell*, was and remains chief counsel for the American Center for Law and Justice, a legal-advocacy organization founded by Pat Robertson in 1989 to defend and advance "religious liberty, the sanctity of human life, and the two-parent, marriage-bound family."[81] (Sekulow later served as a member of President Trump's legal team and as lead outside counsel for his first impeachment trial.)

Solicitor General Theodore ("Ted") Olson and Deputy Solicitor General Paul Clement defended the legislation on behalf of the Bush administration. The sponsors of the BCRA intervened in the litigation represented by their own team of lawyers from Wilmer Cutler Pickering Hale and Dorr LLP (Lloyd Cutler's firm), with former Solicitor General Seth Waxman at the helm.

The *McConnell* litigation drew participation from many more interest groups than previous campaign finance cases to reach the Supreme Court. Most of the briefs—twenty-seven of forty-three—supported the challengers. Amici on their side included libertarian groups such as the Cato Institute, IJ, and the American Civil Rights Union—an organization founded in 1998 to serve as a conservative counterpart to the ACLU[82]—and a variety of social-conservative groups.

Amici defending the BCRA included groups that have supported campaign finance regulation since the 1970s, such as Common Cause and the League of Women Voters, as well as specialized groups formed more recently, such as the Brennan Center, Democracy 21, and the Campaign Legal Center.[83] Also defending the statute were several former ACLU leaders, who had decided that the organization's long-standing opposition to any limits on campaign spending was a mistake.[84] The Committee for Economic Development and a group of sixteen business leaders (including Warren Buffett) took the reform side, arguing that the "BCRA closes the soft money loophole through which corporations and other large contributors have been goaded into evading FECA's hard-money limits, a phenomenon that has damaged both the democratic process and the business environment."[85]

The powerful players assembled on the challenger's side, the substantial amicus support they marshaled, and the stature of some of the lawyers representing them gave the challengers reason to believe that they might prevail. An interviewed challenger who participated in both *Buckley* and *McConnell* contrasted the "kooky" outsiders team assembled for *Buckley* with the new and different type of "strange bedfellows coalition" supporting the challenge in *McConnell*. In *Buckley*, the challengers "really [were] a bunch of outsiders against the establishment, so we really felt like David and Goliath." *McConnell* was different, he said. It "was Goliath and Goliath," because on the challengers' side were "the ACLU, the AFL-CIO, the Chamber of Commerce, Mitch McConnell, the Democratic Party of California, . . . the libertarian left and right, [and] . . . the National Rifle Association," while those defending McCain-Feingold were "the good-government groups founded by billionaires."

The Supreme Court's 5–4 ruling in *McConnell v. FEC* (2003) upheld most of the BCRA's provisions, dealing a significant blow to the challengers.[86] The Court held that the requisite governmental interest "is not limited to the elimination of *quid pro quo*, cash-for-votes exchanges" but also extends to "undue influence on an officeholder's judgment, and the appearance of such influence."[87] A challenger who participated in the case recalled feeling "stunned when we lost." He was surprised because his side had assembled a formidable litigation coalition and impressive team of advocates and because they thought they had the votes on the Court to prevail. Much to the surprise and dismay of the challengers, Justice O'Connor voted to uphold the legislation.

But *McConnell* was the last major win for reformers. Thereafter, investments in organizations, strategies, and lawyer networks began to pay off for the challengers. So did the conservative legal movement's amped-up focus on judicial appointments. When President George W. Bush nominated Harriet Miers, Bush's White House counsel, to fill Justice Sandra Day O'Connor's seat after she announced her plan to retire in 2005, conservatives struck back. They insisted that Bush should have selected a candidate from the large pool of conservatives vetted through the Federalist Society network and holding judicial experience and a track record to show that they would not be "squishy" conservatives.[88] Bush eventually withdrew Miers's nomination and nominated Samuel Alito, a conservative with strong ties to the Federalist Society. He also elevated John Roberts, then a frequent Federalist Society speaker, to become chief justice following Rehnquist's retirement. Both Alito and Roberts have consistently voted to strike down campaign finance laws.[89]

The challengers were now ready to begin chipping away at rulings issued during an era when movement conservatives did not yet control the Supreme Court and when it mostly deferred to legislators. By the middle of the first decade of the 2000s, the effort to resist the regulation of money in politics was no longer one championed primarily by "kooky" outsiders. A vocal and powerful conservative legal movement was making its influence felt on and off the Court. Opponents of campaign finance regulation were now in a position to remake constitutional law to give those with the capacity to spend big money on elections greater freedom to do so.

# 4

## Winning in the Roberts Court

The Supreme Court has now . . . begun to undo some of the more extreme portions of the *McConnell* decision, [but] I think there's more work to be done.
INTERVIEW WITH LEADING CHALLENGER

We're just getting steamrolled on this side.
INTERVIEW WITH LEADING REFORMER

After Justice Alito joined the Supreme Court, challengers began to score big wins. In this third major phase of rulings, the Court has struck down restriction after restriction, in case after case, and overturned major precedents. The challengers have not (yet) achieved the goal of dismantling all regulations on money in politics, but they have made considerable progress toward that objective.

The most important element in the challengers' favor in this phase is the assumption of control of the Court by movement conservatives. In the words of one challenger, that change in the Court's composition meant that "the majority was inclined very much to listen" to opponents of regulation. They were now well positioned to "start poking holes" in the *Austin/McConnell* line of cases. But they also benefited from other types of investments highlighted in previous chapters: powerful political and financial patrons; specialized groups dedicated to dismantling the existing regulatory scheme through an incremental litigation strategy and winning public support through sympathetic media outlets; a broad litigation coalition, organized primarily through the Federalist Society; and prominent lawyers prepared to argue the deregulatory position in the Supreme Court. The last two of these developments gave the conservative justices confidence that the audiences they cared most about would approve of their rulings.

This chapter focuses on three of the most significant victories for opponents of campaign finance regulation in this third phase of the campaign—*Citizens United v. Federal Election Commission* (2010), *Arizona Free Enterprise Club v. Bennett* (2011), and *McCutcheon v. Federal Election Commission* (2014). It describes each of the cases in turn, highlighting some of the ways in which lawyers, advocacy organizations, and lawyer networks influenced the process. It also shows how polarized support structures faced off in these cases and how they characterized the outcomes.

These three cases were typical of lawsuits in the third phase in several important respects. Each was designed to make an incremental advance toward a larger goal of dismantling campaign finance regulation. All featured parties that claimed to represent the interests of regular Americans. The groups that brought the challenges combined their litigation strategies with media strategies, and they organized broad and coordinated amicus support from organizations tied to populist elements of the GOP coalition. Teams of politically aligned interest groups and advocates lined up on opposing sides. In each case, every justice nominated by a Republican president sided with the challengers, and every justice nominated by a Democratic president sided with reformers.

The three cases profiled here were not the only important victories for challengers in this third phase. For example, in *Randall v. Sorrell* (2006), a lawsuit filed by James Bopp, the Court ruled that Vermont's limits on campaign expenditures and contributions violated the First Amendment.[1] In *Federal Election Commission v. Wisconsin Right to Life* (2007), another of Bopp's lawsuits, the Court found that the BCRA's limitations on corporate electioneering communications were unconstitutional as applied to Wisconsin Right to Life's ads urging people to call their senators to tell them to oppose Russ Feingold's plan to filibuster President Bush's judicial nominees.[2] *Davis v. Federal Election Commission* (2008) struck down the "Millionaire's Amendment" to the BCRA, a provision that raised the contribution cap for individuals running against self-financed candidates.[3] In *SpeechNow.org v. Federal Election Commission* (2010), brought by the Institute for Justice, the DC Circuit Court of Appeals held that the Supreme Court's ruling in *Citizens United* required it to find that limits on contributions to "independent expenditure committees" (a.k.a. super PACs) were unconstitutional.[4] In *American Tradition Partnership Inc. v. Bullock* (2012), another case brought by Bopp, the Court struck down a century-old Montana law prohibiting corporations from making expenditures supporting or opposing candidates.[5] As we will see in chapter 8, victories for challengers continued after President Trump's Supreme Court picks—Gorsuch, Kavanaugh, and Barrett—joined the Court, giving opponents of campaign finance regulation a 6–3 supermajority.

### Citizens United v. Federal Election Commission (2010)

James Bopp and the James Madison Center filed the lawsuit that resulted in the most famous of the Roberts Court's campaign finance rulings, *Citizens*

*United v. FEC*, which held that Congress could not bar corporations from spending their treasuries on political advertising. The law had long drawn a line between political spending by corporations through their general treasuries and political spending by political action committees (PACs) funded by the corporation's individual executives and other individuals. *Citizens United* swept away that distinction. It also led directly to the DC Circuit's holding in *SpeechNow.org v. Federal Election Commission* that contributions to super PACs cannot be limited.

Bopp's client, Citizens United, was a conservative media organization with a reputation for hardball politics.[6] Since 2000, conservative activist David Bossie has served as Citizens United's president and chairman.[7] The group's stated mission is to "restore our government to citizens' control" and to do so primarily by producing "hard-hitting and influential television commercials, web advertisements, and documentaries" that help "awaken [people] to the importance of limited government, individual responsibility, free market economy, and traditional American values."[8] The organization has produced dozens of advertisements and movies on a broad range of topics that energize conservative voters.[9]

The lawsuit arose from Citizens United's plans for *Hillary: The Movie*, a critical "documentary" about Hillary Clinton, the likely Democratic presidential nominee. The group had distributed the film on DVD and in theaters, but it wanted to use treasury funds to make it available to cable subscribers. As it prepared to distribute the movie through video-on-demand and to advertise the film on TV, the organization brought a lawsuit to enjoin enforcement of the BCRA's prohibition on corporate-funded electioneering communications, as well as the statute's disclosure and disclaimer requirements.

Several of the interviewed lawyers commented on what made this a good test case for those seeking to unravel campaign finance regulation incrementally and for mobilizing the conservative base around that effort. Citizens United's immediate objective was to ensure that it could air *Hillary: The Movie* before the election despite the BCRA's electioneering communications provision. But the case also presented an opportunity for the Court to "go big" by overruling major precedents. Although Citizens United was a small nonprofit corporation, it was unclear whether it would qualify for the MCFL exception (explained in chapter 2) because it accepted contributions from business entities. The case also teed up questions about the BCRA's definition of "electioneering communications," which covered "broadcast, cable, or satellite communications" but not print and online media. Why should the BCRA's application turn on the distribution channel that Citizens United used for release of its movie? Should such movies qualify for an exemption under the clause of the

First Amendment that protects the press?[10] The case highlighted a growing disconnect between the Court's campaign finance jurisprudence and its approach to issues about regulating the Internet.[11]

Bopp had engineered a case that would raise these questions and expose tensions in the doctrine. One interviewed lawyer speculated that Bopp recognized that "there was a clash between the unfolding doctrinal logic" of campaign finance law

> and a lot of people's fundamental intuitions about what the government should be able to do . . . Because I think most people . . . have an intuitive recoil from the suggestion that if the organization in question is truly ideological in character, and it was, and . . . it's not engaged in mass broadcasting, it's prepared to make this message available to me individually—what are the stakes here exactly? And why is it that we need to treat this as something that is critical to the survival of regulatory regime? And I think . . . Jim Bopp recognized this early on.

The process of identifying good test cases and getting them before the Court in the order imagined by those who plan litigation campaigns is not always easy. One challenger told me that he had hoped that a case that his own organization had filed before *Citizens United* would reach the Court first. "We got hung up," he explained. "We couldn't get the district court to move; it just kept it and then had this long discovery period, and it just took for freaking ever." His organization's strategy was to present a narrower question on which the Court seemed more likely to rule in their favor. They would thereby create a precedent that opponents of campaign finance regulation could build upon. But *Citizens United* "leapfrogged" that case and invited a bolder response.

Several reformers expressed disappointment that the FEC had failed to see that this case was likely to make bad law. One reformer insisted that if only the FEC had reflected on how the case would "fit into our larger understanding of what the law is and how the law might develop," they could have foiled the challengers by settling the matter or resolving it through the regulatory process rather than allowing it to reach the Supreme Court. Another lawyer explained that one "could resort to sheer intellection to explain why it is that the FEC was correct to pursue [the case]." But "once you left the chamber of lawyers and . . . you were able to achieve more distance on the argument and maybe approach it the way people just walking off the street might, then all of a sudden it seemed a little bit odd that we would be having this argument at all." This was a case, he said, that "cried out for more discriminating treatment than it got" from the FEC.

Several reformers credited Fred Wertheimer, president and CEO of Democracy 21, with recognizing before most others where this case might lead: "Wertheimer had the foresight to say, 'This could be a big one,' and of course everyone said, 'No, no, the issue's not presented. [The justices] wouldn't reach out. There are a thousand ways to resolve this case without getting to the constitutional question.'" Another reformer recalled that a colleague had warned that "'this is the ultimate nightmare that you're worried about,'" but that he had responded, "'Don't worry. It can't happen. They're not going to use this case as a vehicle [to overrule major precedents].'"

Indeed, the three-judge panel that heard the claim in the trial court rejected the challenge. One member of the panel laughed out loud at Bopp's claim that *Hillary: The Movie* was an issue-oriented documentary comparable to news shows like *60 Minutes*.[12] When Bopp argued that the ads for the movie calling Clinton a "European Socialist" were issue ads, not electioneering communications, one judge on the panel asked Bopp, "What's the issue?" and Bopp responded, "That Hillary Clinton is a European Socialist." When Bopp noted that neither the movie nor the ads explicitly urged voters to vote against Clinton, Judge Lambert invoked the dismissive shorthand for the express advocacy standard that Brad Smith once cited as evidence of reformers' rhetorical advantage: "Because it doesn't use the 'magic words'?" Lambert asked sarcastically.[13]

After the Supreme Court announced that it would hear Citizens United's appeal from the lower court's ruling, Citizens United's leadership replaced Bopp with former US solicitor general Ted Olson, who had successfully defended the BCRA in *McConnell*. Olson did not initially approach the case as an opportunity to persuade the Court to find that corporations have a First Amendment right to engage in political spending. Instead, he pursued an "as applied" challenge—meaning that he argued that this particular application of the statute was unconstitutional but not that the BCRA's electioneering provision was unconstitutional in all circumstances or that there was any need to overrule major precedents.[14]

In interviews, challengers described disagreements within their side over how broadly or narrowly to frame the issues to be resolved by the Court. One challenger explained that "there's always a debate when there's any issue going before the Supreme Court . . . and you always have a group of lawyers who say, 'Oh, well, we don't want to make too sweeping an argument because we don't want to frighten the Court, so we want this to be very narrow.'" According to this lawyer, "that was the debate in *Citizens United* . . . Do we go ahead and ask for the whole enchilada? Go ahead and say, *Austin* was wrong, reverse it, set it aside, or do we try to be more narrow?" This lawyer believed that it's always best to "lay it out there, tell the whole story, tell [the justices] what you want, and then let them decide how much of the cake they are going to give you." Several challengers thought it was a mistake at the time to frame the issue as narrowly as Olson did in the first round of argument. As it turns out, Olson's narrower approach nevertheless eventually yielded the "whole enchilada"—a broad ruling that went beyond the issues presented to the Court in Olson's opening brief. A reformer with substantial Supreme Court experience marveled at how Olson "ultimately succeeded in winning the big argument without even having made it in the first instance, which is a remarkable achievement."

A dramatic exchange about book banning during the oral argument may have emboldened the Court's conservative majority to issue a broad ruling. Olson opened his oral argument by stressing that the BCRA's definition of electioneering communications would reach a small nonprofit corporation that offered interested viewers a "90-minute political documentary about a candidate for the nation's highest office." He also emphasized that the movie would be one that could be "shown in theaters, sold in DVDs, transmitted for downloading on the Internet" and its message "distributed in the form of a book" without triggering the restriction. When it was Deputy Solicitor General Malcolm Stewart's turn to argue, several of the Court's conservative justices peppered him with questions about whether Congress could have chosen to "ban" the same message delivered in the form of a book. Justice Breyer intervened to emphasize that there was no issue of banning books—only whether it would be constitutionally permissible to require Citizens United to use a separate PAC rather than corporate treasury funds.[15] But the book-banning hypothetical had already done its work in recasting the stakes of the case.

Many of the interviewed lawyers on both sides agreed that this exchange was important—if not to how the Court resolved the case, then at least to perceptions about whether the ruling was appropriate. A reformer dryly observed that "Court seemed very exercised about the possibility that the FEC was going to be banning books." A strong opponent of campaign finance regulation who attended the oral argument recalled that it was obvious that "this wasn't just an off-the-cuff question; the justices are smart enough to know where they're going with questions" and that "it was crystal clear from that moment that this case has now taken a whole different tenor, and it is possibly going to upset some foundational principles in this area." He recalled leaving the Supreme Court building and immediately calling his office to say, "'We have to do a press release immediately because this case has now just become the most significant case that anybody is aware of . . . It's going to be gigantic.'"

He also remembered that "there was suddenly joy on the side of people who were challenging the laws and concern on the side of the people who were defending them."

According to an article about the case by Jeffrey Toobin, upon learning of the majority's intention to overrule several major precedents even though the parties had not presented the issues or briefed them, Justice Souter prepared a scathing draft dissent (never released) accusing the conservatives of judicial activism.[16] The Court thereafter announced that it was relisting *Citizens United* for a new round of briefing and oral argument at the beginning of the following term on the broader questions not previously addressed by the lawyers: whether the BCRA's "electioneering communications" provision was unconstitutional and whether *Austin* and relevant parts of *McConnell* should be overruled.

Toobin's story put the justices squarely at the center of the action in expanding the stakes: "Through artful questioning, Alito, Kennedy, and Roberts had turned a fairly obscure case about campaign-finance reform into a battle over government censorship."[17] But lawyers on the challengers' side contributed to this broadening and recharacterization of the issues. In addition to Olson's obvious part—his comparison of the movie to a book in the fourth sentence of his opening argument—there is other evidence that the questions about book banning originated with the lawyers. Olson's brief argued that "the film is . . . best viewed as a rigorously researched critical biography" and "similar to the numerous critical candidate biographies found in bookstores." His brief also characterized the BCRA's prohibition on using corporate treasury funds to create the film as the "censoring of *Hillary*."[18] Bopp's brief in the lower court argued that "*Hillary* is the functional equivalent of a book" and that "if the difference in medium matters when it comes to First Amendment protection for the functional equivalent of a book," then "the government could freely engage in high-tech 'book burnings' without restriction."[19] Some of the amicus briefs also insisted that *Hillary: The Movie* was the cinematic equivalent of a book.[20] The author of one of those briefs told me that it might not be "for nothing" that Justices Alito and Kennedy both raised essentially the same question in the oral argument that he and other challengers had emphasized in their briefs: "Is this going to apply to books? Is it going to apply to other media of expression?"

Once the Court ordered reargument, lawyers on both sides understood that the stakes had changed. A reformer recalled, "Once I saw the reargument question, I realized we were in trouble." Another remembered that it had become "very clear that this was a case that was going to make some law," even though he doubted that

anybody bet that it was going to transform the law to the extent that it has. . . .
This was going to be a major case . . . It was going to go to profound questions
about political equality just as a practical effect of what the Court might hold.
But the fundamental question was: Was the Court going to do what it had
done in *Wisconsin Right to Life*, and basically find a way to trim back certain
applications of the statute? . . . Then the second question was going to be:
Could the Court conceivably go beyond this? Was the Court going to really
much more fundamentally, much more broadly, recast the terms of campaign
finance jurisprudence? . . . Surrounding all of this was the question of whether
this was the latest in what appeared to be an all-out comprehensive assault by
the Court on the reform period, that at least in its first stages began in 1974 but
certainly was supposed to have been given a shot in the arm in 2002? And did
it appear that the Court was just going to be progressively marching through
now and, in the words of Chief Justice Roberts in *Wisconsin Right to Life*, it was
going to be saying, 'Enough is enough, we've had it, we're done with this?' . . .
Was the Court going to show more and more of this very striking activist
concern with trimming back the applications of the campaign finance laws?[21]

Another lawyer remembered that it was now "evident that the full range was
in the case, and the issue was, 'Do corporations have an unlimited First Amendment right to engage in spending on political speech?'" A challenger recalled
realizing that the Court was now prepared to issue a broad ruling in their
favor and that they should seize the opportunity: "Everybody knew which
way the Court was going, and we said, 'Yes, go that way. Definitely overturn
the ban on independent expenditures!'" Another challenger recalled that his
brief had essentially argued, "You can do this; it's okay for you to [overrule
*Austin*.]"

A dramatic moment during the second round of oral argument made clear
that Chief Justice Roberts was prepared to issue a broad ruling. He reacted
strongly to an observation by Solicitor General Elena Kagan (now Justice Kagan) that the FEC had never tried to regulate books.[22] Chief Justice Roberts
responded: "But we don't put our—we don't put our First Amendment rights
in the hands of FEC bureaucrats."[23] According to one lawyer who attended
the argument, the cold transcript does not capture the emotion displayed by
Justice Roberts during this exchange. He recalled that Justice Roberts "c[ame]
out of his chair" when he declared that "we don't put our First Amendment
rights in the hands of FEC bureaucrats."[24] He interpreted the heat displayed
by Justice Roberts in that moment as "completely about *Wisconsin Right to
Life*," in which the Court had issued a narrow ruling, only to have the FEC
"gut-rip it, and reject it, and say, 'Go screw yourself.'" Another challenger said

of the solicitor general's handling of this issue that "she made a lot of good points" and "to a large extent she's right" that the FEC does not claim authority to ban the publication of books, but that the Court rightly concluded that "we nip these things in the bud precisely to protect greater speech."

The organizations on the challengers' side in *Citizens United* filed many more party and amicus briefs than did organizations on the FEC's side—thirty-nine versus eighteen. This tilt of participation in the challengers' favor reflected a significant increase since the last major confrontation over the constitutionality of the BCRA in *McConnell*. Those supporting Citizens United included Mitch McConnell, the US Chamber of Commerce, the National Rifle Association, and all the specialized groups profiled in chapter 3—the James Madison Center, IFS, and IJ. They also included other libertarian groups, such as the Pacific Legal Foundation and Cato Institute, and a variety of social-conservative organizations and groups tied to Tea Party activism. The AFL-CIO and the ACLU submitted briefs offering partial support for the constitutional challenge.

The solicitor general's office defended the challenged law. Amicus briefs taking the FEC's side included the BCRA's principal sponsors—John McCain, Russell Feingold, and former representatives Christopher Shays and Martin Meehan—as well as the Democratic National Committee (DNC) and Chris van Hollen, who served as chairman of the Democratic Congressional Campaign Committee from 2006 through 2010. Other briefs supporting the FEC's position came from the League of Women Voters, Common Cause, the Campaign Legal Center, the Brennan Center for Justice, US PIRG, Americans for Campaign Finance Reform, the Center for Political Accountability, and the Constitutional Accountability Center.[25]

Most of the groups that participated in *Citizens United* as parties and amici joined with their usual allies in electoral politics. Business, libertarian, and social-conservative groups appeared with the RNC and Mitch McConnell on one side, while liberals of various stripes sided with the Federal Election Commission and the DNC on the other. But the constituencies claimed by organizations filing briefs on the challengers' side were not all similarly situated with respect to big money in politics. Moreover, the partial support of the AFL-CIO and ACLU gave the challengers' litigation coalition a cross-partisan flavor. A closer examination of this "strange bedfellows" aspect of the challengers' litigation coalition—and whether it is truly strange—is the focus of the next chapter.

A lawyer who helped to organize amicus participation on the challengers' side said that he had observed how reformers in previous cases had effectively deployed a "phalanx of amici." The challengers needed a similar strategy—"a coordinated effort, to try to break down some of these issues for the Court, spread the field, let them see a lot of different perspectives that they're not getting—so that's what we did." Amicus coordination is always important to ensure that "you don't just have five different amici essentially repeating the arguments that are being made by the party on the merits," he explained. But *Citizens United* "was one case where we really went at it . . . We'd never before done it in that heavy-handed way." He told amici on the challengers' side:

> Look. Here's what we need. We need a brief from a bunch of academics to say, "Here's the real history of campaign finance reform." It's not the history that's in *Auto Workers*, the 1950's case where Frankfurter writes up this long bit of dicta about this glorious history of reform.[26] We need someone to say, this is a grubby business of people trying to gain political advantage over one another—people grandstanding. This isn't some heroic struggle against big money. So, we need somebody to file representing small nonprofits. We'd like a brief from former FEC commissioners talking about what it means in the actual enforcement. And we arranged that. We got lawyers to volunteer to represent those different kinds of groups and to sign onto this.

Another challenger recalled "lots of coordination" and discussion about what each group would say. His brief, for example, would "focus on not only the rights of businesses to participate in politics, to speak freely on their own" but would also attack the argument that business participation would drown out the voices of other speakers.

On the reform side, according to a leading reformer, attempts to "coordinate efforts and maintain the team" of the BCRA's defenders, which "had been pretty successful in *McConnell*," were much harder to implement in *Citizens United*. That was especially true in the second round of the litigation. The short time between the Supreme Court's call for reargument and the deadline for filing briefs led to rushed and disorganized amicus participation. One reformer recalled his dismay about having "a total of about four weeks and maybe a day or two" and that "in that amount of time we were going to be briefing an issue that had never been actually aired in that case up until that time and was really of fundamental importance beyond the field of campaign finance—the notion that, for any purposes, you can't distinguish the First Amendment rights of a business corporation from that of a human being or an ideological organization."

As expected, the Court's 5–4 ruling found that corporations have a First Amendment right to spend unlimited amounts independently to support or oppose candidates for public office, overruling *Austin*. It also invalidated the electioneering-communications provision of the BCRA, thereby partially overruling *McConnell*. The Court characterized the distinction drawn in *McConnell* and *Austin* between corporations and other types of "speakers" as a type of impermissible discrimination[27]—an argument pursued by some challengers.[28] The Court upheld the statute's disclosure requirements by an 8–1 vote, with only Justice Clarence Thomas dissenting.

The Court also articulated a narrower definition of "corruption" than the one used in prior cases, finding that the prospect that large donors and spenders will win special access to elected officials is not a problem that justifies burdening rights protected by the First Amendment. Justice Kennedy, writing for the majority, asserted that the only regulatory justification sufficient to support campaign finance regulation was preventing quid pro quo corruption—the direct exchange of money for political favors. He explained why "ingratiation and access" should not be viewed as a form of corruption that would justify government regulation, quoting his own partial dissent in *McConnell*: "Favoritism and influence are not . . . avoidable in representative politics. It is in the nature of an elected representative to favor certain policies, and, by necessary corollary, to favor the voters and contributors who support those policies. It is well understood that a substantial and legitimate reason, if not the only reason, to cast a vote for, or to make a contribution to, one candidate over another is that the candidate will respond by producing those political outcomes the supporter favors. Democracy is premised on responsiveness."[29] Kennedy also asserted that "the appearance of influence or access" flowing from expenditures on elections "will not cause the electorate to lose faith in our democracy," because "by definition an independent expenditure is political speech presented to the electorate that is not coordinated with a candidate," and because disclosure would ensure accountability.[30]

Justice Stevens's dissenting opinion rejected the argument that giving corporations First Amendment protection for election spending served the interests of "listeners" and voters. The opinion discussed at length ways in which "unregulated general treasury expenditures" on elections could "distort public debate in ways that undermine rather than advance the interest of listeners."[31] Stevens suggested that it was "only Members of this Court, not the listeners themselves, who have agitated for more corporate electioneering."[32] But this claim was not entirely true. Advocates for the Chamber of Commerce and other aligned advocacy groups had been pressing the Court to adopt this approach since the 1970s. Stevens also took strong issue with the majority's declaration that the only justification for regulating campaign expenditures is to avoid quid pro quo corruption or the appearance of quid pro quo corruption. He stated that this "crabbed view of corruption" disregarded "the fundamental demands of a democratic society" because "a democracy cannot function effectively when its constituent members believe laws are being bought and sold."[33]

In statements to the press about implications of the ruling, Bopp said that it vindicated "the ability of average citizens to participate in our democracy" and established that "our laws cannot distinguish or discriminate based on speakers."[34] In interviews, challengers offered similar assessments. In a response that was typical, a lawyer for a libertarian group told me that "having corporate speech and commercial speech added to the marketplace of ideas benefits democracy as a whole." The idea that the identity of the speaker should be irrelevant in the analysis of free speech cases is pervasive in the commentary of the interviewed challengers, as explored in chapter 6. So is the idea that the rights of "listeners" to receive information from whatever source are vindicated in broad speech rights for corporations. As one interviewed challenger put it in describing the consequences of the holding in Citizens United, "more speech just means that people are saying what they want to say, and the listeners decide how much weight they want to give that speech."

Reformers whom I interviewed painted a darker picture. They generally conceded that Citizens United has not led to massive for-profit corporate spending in elections, as some critics predicted at the time of the decision.[35] But reformers emphasized that it was never their primary concern that business corporations would pour money into election campaigns in their own names.[36] Rather, reformers worried that corporations and their owners would channel corporate money into nonprofit groups that do not disclose their donors. One explained, "What we were concerned about is that 501(c)(4) corporations like the plaintiffs, Citizens United, would be free to serve as conduits for business community money and evade disclosure, and that's exactly what has unfolded." Another reformer observed that while "you don't see business corporations doing a tremendous amount of political spending in their own names because they do not perceive that it's an effective strategy, there's still a direct effect of nonprofit corporations that receive large amounts of corporate funding engaging now directly in political speech that would not have been permissible prior to Citizens United." The Court had previously held in FEC v. Wisconsin Right to Life that the BCRA's limitations on corporate electioneering were unconstitutional as applied to issue advocacy; they were permissible only as to "express advocacy or its functional equivalent."[37] But Citizens United eliminated the need to distinguish between issue advocacy and express advocacy. What this shift means, one reformer observed, is that "the

Chamber of Commerce now no longer has to worry about whether its advocacy crosses the line."

Many reformers also worried about the long-term repercussions of *Citizens United*. One explained that *Citizens United*'s ruling "that you can't distinguish between a business corporation and a human being or an ideological organization for First Amendment purposes . . . means that entities that control vast amounts of wealth that greatly exceed those controlled by individuals in this country [could] be mobilized to exert as much force on our political system as they care to." Another reformer emphasized that the Court's ruling that all corporations, and not just MCFL organizations, can engage in election spending from corporate treasuries "opens the door for the Kochs and the billionaires of the world to do it."

One reformer spelled out what he and other reformers found particularly problematic about extending First Amendment protections for election spending to business corporations—"essentially the fact that we were going to allow corporations, where there was little accountability, where the dangers of rent-seeking were so pronounced, where the aggregation of capital was so [substantial], to gain the right to spend unlimited amounts in elections." Business corporations, these "artificial entities," should not hold this right, he said. One reason is that corporations do not represent the political views of their owners. Corporate theory generally recognizes that stockholders are poorly positioned to monitor corporate managers and that corporate managers are poorly positioned to reconcile stockholders' diverse political views. Permitting corporate political spending from general treasury funds might encourage corporate managers to engage in election spending to advance their own political preferences, or to gain unwarranted competitive advantage, or to defeat socially beneficial regulation that interferes with profitability, even if shareholders have broader concerns that would be advanced through regulation. He denied that corporations would be publicly accountable for their election spending in any meaningful sense: "Disclosure is only effective if somebody can be held accountable, and corporations, almost by their very nature, are unaccountable, or they're accountable, some in the corporate law community would say, for one thing—maximizing shareholder value. So, they always can say, 'Not my decision, it's the imperative under which I operate.' The fact that I contribute in a way that may do greater harm to society or may allow more water to be polluted—that's for the regulators to take care of,' even though all the spending is intended to impact who the regulators are."[38]

This lawyer called "fantastical" Justice Kennedy's assertion in *Citizens United* that shareholders in large, publicly traded companies have access to the procedures of corporate democracy to hold corporations responsible for their political spending. He noted that "ownership is transferred in millions and millions of shares" in minutes in some publicly traded companies, and that many people invest in mutual funds and depend on pension funds over which they have no control. Moreover, unlike PACs, through which individual corporate employees make political contributions and are identified individually, election spending by corporations entails no effective disclosure because the people who make the spending decisions are not identified.

### Arizona Free Enterprise Club v. Bennett (2011)

This case involved two separate challenges to Arizona's public financing law, the "Clean Elections Act," which was adopted through a public referendum following a series of corruption scandals. One of those scandals, "AzScam," involved the payment of cash bribes to Arizona legislators to gain their support for legalizing casino gambling. The statute created a voluntary public financing system to fund the primary and general election campaigns of candidates for state office. Candidates who chose to participate were granted an initial allocation of funds to conduct their campaign, but they received additional matching funds if a privately financed candidate's expenditures, combined with the expenditures of independent groups, exceeded the publicly financed candidate's initial state outlay.

Understanding the reason for matching-funds systems requires some attention to the history of public financing of federal elections. The Supreme Court in *Buckley* upheld a part of the 1974 amendments that provided for partial federal financing of presidential campaigns and set limits on spending by candidates as a condition of receiving public funding.[39] From the program's inception in 1976 until 1996, all candidates who ultimately prevailed took part. But in 2000 and 2004, George W. Bush opted out of the primary public funding system, and since then no major-party candidate has participated in the system. That is because the low levels of public funding and the spending limits imposed as a condition of participating prevent candidates from competing effectively against better-financed opponents. Anticipating similar "opting out" problems in state and local elections systems, some cities and states adopted supplemental funding systems with matching-funds (or "trigger funds") provisions. These systems were designed to allow participating candidates to compete effectively against privately funded candidates in competitive races while also avoiding wasteful spending in uncompetitive races. This was the type of system adopted in the Arizona statute and challenged in the *Arizona Free Enterprise Club* case.

Nonprofit advocacy organizations brought the lawsuits challenging Arizona's funding scheme. IJ filed one of the two lawsuits, and the Goldwater Institute filed the other. The petitioners in these lawsuits included several past and future candidates for Arizona state political offices who ran or planned to run privately financed campaigns. The other two petitioners were political action committees that funded such candidates. The trial court enjoined enforcement of the provision, and the Ninth Circuit reversed. The Supreme Court granted certiorari.

The challengers argued that the matching-funds provision "severely burden[ed] political speech." It did so, they said, because if candidates raised and spent amounts that the government deemed "too much money on political speech" they faced "the direct burden" on that speech in the form of government subsidies to their opponents.[40]

The challengers complemented the litigation strategy with efforts to gain favorable media coverage. In a press statement issued by IJ in advance of the Supreme Court argument, William Maurer, one of the lawyers for the petitioners, asserted that the challenged provision amounted to a "de facto limit on how much speech occurs in campaigns." This happens, he said, because if "traditionally funded candidates" decide to "speak" above the "government-set limit," their opponents, "taxpayer-financed candidates," receive additional funds. Summing up the overall speech implications of the law, he asserted that "the Clean Elections Act creates an abbreviated *Miranda* right for traditionally funded candidates: They have the right to remain silent; any speech they may undertake can and will be countered by government funding."[41] Another IJ lawyer explained that "the dirty secret of Arizona's law is that it is designed to limit speech."[42] According to Nicholas Dranias, who handled the case for the Goldwater Institute, Arizona's law amounted to telling citizens "to be quiet and let the government candidates win."[43]

Amici on the challengers' side included Mitch McConnell, IFS, Cato, former FEC commissioners, Gun Owners of America, and various Tea Party–affiliated organizations, such as the Wyoming Liberty Group and the Yankee Institute for Public Policy. They also included social-conservative groups such as the Justice and Freedom Fund, an organization founded in 1998 by James Hirsen, a law professor and author of *Tales from the Left Coast* and *Hollywood Nation*, a takedown of Hollywood celebrities and their radical politics. Amici on the government's side included the United States, various states and their "clean elections" officials, good-government groups,[44] constitutional scholars, election law scholars, former ACLU officials, and the Committee for Economic Development. Some of these amici on the reform side invoked federalism concerns, arguing that the Court should tread cautiously before striking down states' public financing schemes.[45]

In a 5–4 decision, the Supreme Court found that the matching-funds provision "substantially burden[ed] political speech" by privately financed candidates and independent expenditure groups without serving a compelling state interest. The "burden on speech" identified by the Court was that privately financed candidates and independent expenditure groups might hesitate before spending above the threshold that would trigger additional public funding for an opponent. The majority found that the real (though not stated) purpose of the matching-funds provision was "to 'level the playing field' in terms of candidate resources" and that this was not a compelling government interest.[46]

Justice Kagan's dissent, joined by Justices Ginsburg, Breyer, and Sotomayor, faulted the majority for failing to show "decent respect" for the objectives of the people of Arizona "to stop corrupt dealing—to ensure that their representatives serve the public, and not just the wealthy donors who helped put them in office."[47] The dissenters found that the matching-funds provision had addressed the difficulty of setting a public subsidy at a level that gives candidates sufficient incentive to participate in the system while also conserving public resources; Arizona had found "the Goldilocks solution—not too large, not too small, but just right."[48] The dissenters also criticized the majority for trying "to convey the impression" at "every turn" that Arizona's matching fund statute imposed a "restriction" or "burden" on political speech, when in fact, "the law has quite the opposite effect: It subsidizes and so produces *more* political speech."[49]

Following the ruling, Maurer claimed that his organization had "scored a major victory for free speech and political participation" by striking down "a bald attempt by the state to manipulate speech by forcing speakers to either trigger matching funds to their opponents, change their message, or refrain from speaking altogether."[50] In an appearance on Freedom Watch, a talk show on the Fox Business channel, Nicholas Dranias predicted that the ruling would "stop these ridiculous ideas where the government should be manipulating elections to make it level, a playing field that is fair for everyone, and skewed in favor of government-funded candidates against citizen-funded candidates." He added, "It will put a stake through the heart of that idea."[51] Another challenger, who believed that matching funds and low contribution and spending limits were key elements of a "scheme" by reformers to "coerce" candidates into participating in public financing systems, cheered the combined consequences of this ruling and *Randall v. Sorrell* (2006):[52] "In *Randall v. Sorrell*, we

strike down low limits, and then the Supreme Court strikes down these matching funds. Now what are [reformers] going to do?"

Interviewed reformers found nothing to cheer about in the *Arizona Free
Enterprise Club* decision. They disparaged the Court's treatment of the governmental interest in "leveling the playing field" for candidates in elections as
not only an insufficient justification for regulating money in politics but as an
illicit motive that was reason enough to invalidate the regulations. One reformer asserted that Arizona's attempt to "equalize the field" through the public
financing system was an important element of its strategy for enabling people
"who don't have the resources either personally, or don't appeal to moneyed
interests" to compete in elections. States and localities now must avoid any
suggestion that they seek to level the playing field even though, in another reformer's view, "that was one of the beautiful things it did." Reformers agreed
with challengers that the ruling left legislators with no choice but to either
abandon the idea of public funding or to design systems that are much more
expensive. The recent growth of spending by super PACs and dark-money
groups and the inability to respond to spending by these groups within the
context of public financing systems have added to the difficulty of designing
viable public finance systems.

### McCutcheon v. Federal Election Commission (2014)

This case challenged overall limits on total contributions an individual could
give to candidates and political committees in an election cycle, a provision
that had been upheld in *Buckley* and approved again in *McConnell*.[53] Until the
Court struck down those limits in *McCutcheon*, individuals were prohibited
from giving more than $48,600 combined to all federal candidates and from
giving more than $74,600 to all parties and political action committees com-
bined, so that there was a total aggregate individual limit of $123,200 in an
election cycle. One challenger told me that Reince Priebus, head of the RNC
at the time (and later White House chief of staff to President Trump from January through July of 2017) let it be known that he and Republican donors were
"constantly bumping up against aggregate limits" and that the limits were
"driving [Priebus] crazy." Another challenger explained why the aggregate contribution limits were a problem for the committees and for donors who were
able and willing to give more: "to max out to more than eight or nine candidates was not a huge ask for certain people" and the aggregate limit "sort of
jammed up a bunch of people who otherwise would have supported more
candidates." The limits also put the RNC in competition with the Senate and

Congressional Republican Committees. When a donor who wanted to contribute more than the aggregate limit allowed came along and eventually agreed to serve as the lead plaintiff after some cajoling, the RNC agreed to fund the lawsuit.

That donor was Shaun McCutcheon, an Alabama businessman and Republican activist. McCutcheon had met conservative election lawyer Dan Backer through conservative circles, and Backer encouraged McCutcheon to file a lawsuit against the FEC to challenge the BCRA's contribution limits. He already had contributed $1665 to each of fifteen federal candidates during the 2011–2012 election cycle, but he wanted to donate an additional $75,000 to Republican national party committees and $60,000 more to candidates. The law prohibited him from doing so; the additional contributions would cause him to exceed the aggregate individual contribution limit. One challenger explained why McCutcheon was the perfect person to bring this challenge: "Constitutional lawyers always talk about how critical it is to find the right plaintiff . . . , and Shaun was it. He's this really nice, affable guy." In press statements, McCutcheon's lawyers claimed that the challenged law had "indiscriminately restrict[ed] the rights of Americans" and taken "a sledgehammer to constitutional rights"; they asserted that "for speech to be free, it must be free from such arbitrary government restraints."[54]

James Bopp represented McCutcheon and the RNC in the three-judge district court, which granted the FEC's motion to dismiss the case. After the case reached the Supreme Court, Bopp continued to represent the RNC, but a lawyer in Paul Clement's elite appellate boutique, Bancroft LLP, handled the oral argument for McCutcheon. Amici taking McCutcheon's side included Senator Mitch McConnell, the National Republican Senatorial and Congressional Committees, libertarian organizations, and several groups espousing Tea Party goals.[55] Amici supporting the FEC's position included Democratic members of the US House of Representatives, specialized campaign finance reform groups, and many other organizations that had by now become regular participants in these cases.[56]

The challengers argued that the aggregate contribution limits "substantially burden[ed] core First Amendment rights" of individuals by limiting the number of candidates and committees to whom they can contribute the maximum amount. They also argued that the aggregate contribution limits were not "narrowly tailored" to serve an important government interest.[57]

Neither the DNC nor any other Democratic Party committees participated in *McCutcheon*. One reformer said of the failure of the Democratic Party and committees to file amicus briefs in *McCutcheon*, "There's a problem here for the party committees, which is, on the one hand, you have this Democratic

Party reform commitment . . . On the other hand, a successful outcome in *McCutcheon* on the part of the plaintiffs would have been beneficial to the parties because it would have opened up new sources of financing. So, they just kept their mouths shut."

The Supreme Court's 5–4 decision invalidated the overall contribution limits. Writing for the plurality, Chief Justice Roberts found that the limits "intrude without justification on a citizen's ability to exercise 'the most fundamental First Amendment activities.'"[58] He reiterated the definition of corruption articulated in *Citizens United*, emphasizing that "Congress may target only a specific type of corruption—'quid pro quo' corruption,"[59] defined as a "direct exchange of an official act for money."[60] He rejected the notion that government may regulate to "target the general gratitude a candidate may feel toward those who support him or his allies, or the political access such support may afford. 'Ingratiation and access . . . are not corruption.'"[61] Indeed, the opinion stated that ingratiation and access "embody a central feature of democracy—that constituents support candidates who share their beliefs and interests, and candidates who are elected can be expected to be responsive to those concerns."[62] Justice Thomas wrote a separate opinion calling for *Buckley* to be overruled and all limits on campaign contributions declared unconstitutional.

Justice Breyer's dissent, joined by Justices Kagan, Ginsburg, and Sotomayor, claimed that the majority "substitutes judges' understandings of how the political process works for the understanding of Congress." The dissent also claimed that the majority opinion "fails to recognize the difference between influence resting upon public opinion and influence bought by money alone," and "undermines, perhaps devastates, what remains of campaign finance reform." The dissent added: "Taken together with *Citizens United v. FEC*, today's decision eviscerates our Nation's campaign finance laws, leaving a remnant incapable of dealing with the grave problems of democratic legitimacy that those laws were intended to resolve."[63]

After *McCutcheon*, individuals are still bound by base contribution limits to candidates, political action committees and national party committees, but they can now give the maximum contributions to as many candidates and PACs as they like.[64] In addition, a rider attached to the omnibus appropriations bill in 2014 raised the contribution limits to party committees by allowing them to establish separate accounts for conventions, party headquarters, and legal fees, each of which could accept over $100,000 per year from individuals. The last of these items—funds for legal challenges to election outcomes—featured prominently in the 2020 presidential election, as Donald Trump's campaign filed dozens of lawsuits to challenge the election process in key states.[65] One of the interviewed Republican lawyers predicted as much, telling me that having a separate private funding mechanism for recounts and election challenges would be important "given the increasing closeness of elections and the bitterness of these fights and the shenanigans of the other side." Expenditures on election litigation have risen for both major parties since 2015.[66]

Interviewed reformers warned that the multi-million-dollar aggregate contributions that are now permitted give megadonors increased influence over electoral and policymaking processes.[67] Other reformers expressed concern about the message that these enormous aggregate contributions send to average voters given that the aggregate limits before the ruling in *McCutcheon* "were already so high, so far beyond the ability of any ordinary American to make a contribution at that level . . . The notion of having to blow them up so that one individual can now . . . literally, give millions of dollars. . . . It's saying to the average American, 'The political process is not for you. You are not big enough to swim in this ocean. It's all locked up by the people who have the most money.' It's not a healthy message for our country."

Reformers also viewed the Court's ruling in *McCutcheon* as a large and worrisome step toward eliminating contribution limits altogether. One asserted that "*McCutcheon*, while not as well known, is actually legally more dangerous than *Citizens United*" because it might spell eventual doom for all contribution limits. Another lawyer explained that the *McCutcheon* Court had crossed a line that it had previously maintained—that contribution limits are easier to defend than spending limits and are less problematic "because . . . money is being put into the pocket of the representative . . . They picked a soft target of contributions in the aggregate spending limit, which isn't the easiest thing in the world to explain. But it was a very important Rubicon to cross, I think, because once you get there, it's going to be difficult to continue to justify the individual spending limits. And the Court in the case narrowed the potential justifications for campaign finance restrictions in such a way that it's going to be impossible to justify them." He added that the Court had "basically set themselves up now so that the rest of the contribution limitations are going to be very difficult to defend." This reformer noted that the Court might "not want to drop that shoe" right away. Still, he said, "John Roberts has kind of a long view about these things," referring to the chief justice's reputation for a patient, incremental approach to changing constitutional doctrine.

Some reformers characterized the ruling in *McCutcheon* as the latest in a series of Roberts Court rulings that spelled trouble for the entire apparatus of campaign finance law. One summarized the progression this way: "*Citizens United* said, 'You can't limit the amount corporations spend on advertisements,' which has opened up a huge arena for corporations to spend huge amounts of money, mostly by donating to super PACs. . . . In the Arizona case, [the Court] made it harder for governments to set up public financing systems that would allow those who don't take big money from competing effectively. And then, probably most importantly, *McCutcheon* struck down this long-standing limit on aggregate contributions, opening the door to individuals writing huge checks up to millions of dollars to candidates and parties." Another reformer described the ruling in *McCutcheon* as part of "a concerted dismantling of campaign finance regulation, one by one, brick by brick."

Interviewed challengers agreed with reformers that *McCutcheon* eliminated a barrier to large contributions by donors capable of giving huge amounts to parties, party committees, and candidates, but they characterized this as a positive development. Several lawyers who represented groups and constituencies tied to Republican and Democratic Party leaders claimed that the decision would direct more money to the major parties, where it would be subject to more disclosure and accountability than contributions to outside groups. Lawyers with ties to the establishment's rivals within the Republican Party asserted that the decision would benefit fundraising for "outsiders" by enlarging the overall pool of contributions.

## Polarized Networks

These cases featured competing armies of interest groups and lawyers divided by political affiliation and sources of financial support.[68] The army aligned with the Supreme Court's more powerful conservative majority—the challengers—partnered with those justices to remake constitutional law. Both sides included a mix of cause lawyers and lawyers with more conventional practice orientations.

Cause lawyers were the ones who filed the cases and interacted with the media. In interviews, these lawyers described how they identified vulnerable campaign finance restrictions, found plaintiffs, framed the issues strategically, and shepherded the cases through the courts. With respect to the issues eventually litigated in *Citizens United*, for example, one lawyer recalled that he had been wondering about "what kind of lawsuit do you need to free up" independent spending and noted the "serendipity" of then being approached by a conservative who "came to see [me] to talk about almost the same thing." Lawyers involved in the challenges in *Arizona Free Enterprise Club* and *McCutcheon* recounted similar conversations with prospective litigants and party leaders about how to craft cases to change the law.

Highly credentialed lawyers with significant appellate experience were overwhelmingly the ones who handled oral arguments once the cases reached the Supreme Court. Ted Olson, counsel for Citizens United, has argued more cases before the Supreme Court than all but a handful of appellate advocates of the twenty-first century. Floyd Abrams, who handled the argument for Mitch McConnell in *Citizens United*, is widely viewed as a leading, if not the leading, litigator of First Amendment issues. Bobby Burchfield, who argued for Mitch McConnell in *McCutcheon*, headed McDermott, Will, and Emery's complex litigation practice at the time and had previously represented the RNC in *McConnell*. The US solicitor general or a deputy solicitor general, or the state counterparts in instances of challenges to state regulations, typically handled oral arguments on the government's side of these cases. Reformers' go-to choice for arguments to support the federal government's position was Seth Waxman, who served as solicitor general from 1997 to 2001 before becoming co-chair of Wilmer Hale's appellate practice. Waxman represented John McCain in *Citizens United*, and he handled the argument on behalf of the BCRA's sponsors in *McConnell*.[69]

When conflict emerged over who would handle Supreme Court arguments, appellate specialists generally prevailed over cause lawyers, presumably because their skill, experience, connections, and professional reputations made them more likely to capture the justices' votes.[70] One lawyer observed that *Citizens United* was "in many respects . . . [Bopp's] baby" until Olson took control. Another lawyer explained that the decision to replace Bopp with Olson was about "go[ing] with an attorney who had the best opportunity of winning the case," noting that Olson is "one of the ablest Supreme Court advocates there is." A similar process unfolded in *McCutcheon* when Paul Clement's appellate boutique took over once the case reached the Supreme Court. One challenger recalled that Bopp has "probably done more for campaign finance than anybody else—he's the dean of our bar essentially." But when the time came to determine who should handle the oral argument in *McCutcheon*, the RNC, which provided most of the funding for the litigation, chose the Supreme Court specialists.

Some of the lawyers who handled the oral arguments for the challengers in these cases have strong ties to the justices and/or to the polarized political and professional networks with which they are aligned. Ted Olson has been a member of the Federalist Society's Board of Visitors since its founding, and he is a regular speaker at its national conventions.[71] Bobby Burchfield was general counsel of President George H. W. Bush's reelection campaign in 1992 and represented George W. Bush during the Florida recount in 2000. Erin Murphy, then a young partner in the Bancroft LLP firm and the protégé of former solicitor general Paul Clement, handled the oral argument for Shaun

TABLE 4.1. Characteristics of lawyers on party and amicus briefs in three major cases

| | Citizens United 2010 | | Arizona Free Ent. 2011 | | McCutcheon 2014 | |
|---|---|---|---|---|---|---|
| | Challengers N=90 % | Reformers N=54 % | Challengers N=31 % | Reformers N=89 % | Challengers N=51 % | Reformers N=38 % |
| **Work location** | | | | | | |
| DC | 39 | 55 | 19 | 25 | 43 | 66 |
| DC suburb | 11 | 0 | 13 | 1 | 16 | 3 |
| Northeast | 6 | 26 | 6 | 31 | 0 | 32 |
| South | 13 | 0 | 16 | 1 | 27 | 0 |
| Midwest | 19 | 0 | 9 | 3 | 12 | 0 |
| Mountain | 3 | 7 | 19 | 9 | 0 | 0 |
| Pacific | 9 | 11 | 16 | 26 | 2 | 0 |
| **Law school tier** | | | | | | |
| Elite | 24 | 61 | 9 | 45 | 16 | 76 |
| Prestige | 26 | 26 | 13 | 30 | 33 | 18 |
| Regional | 12 | 9 | 38 | 13 | 20 | 0 |
| Local | 36 | 2 | 38 | 9 | 31 | 5 |
| **Gender** | | | | | | |
| Male | 86 | 76 | 84 | 73 | 75 | 74 |
| Female | 14 | 24 | 16 | 28 | 25 | 26 |

McCutcheon in *McCutcheon v. FEC*. Murphy clerked for Chief Justice Roberts in 2008–2009, when *Citizens United* was first argued. An interviewed lawyer explained part of the logic behind this choice: "When the chief justice is your swing vote, having somebody who knows his mind do the argument is probably not a bad thing."

Many lawyers who participated on the challenger's side of these cases share ties through the Federalist Society,[72] a key audience for the Supreme Court's conservative members. As of 2014, the year *McCutcheon v. FEC* was decided, the Federalist Society counted almost seventy thousand dues-paying members,[73] including many experienced appellate litigators well versed in ideas percolating through the Society. The role of the Federalist Society in coordinating the challengers' litigation coalition will receive more attention in the next several chapters. There is nothing comparable to the Federalist Society on the reform side. The closest analogue is the American Constitution Society, an organization founded in 2001 to serve as Federalist Society's liberal counterpart. But ACS has not yet achieved anything close to the Federalist Society's concentrated influence and reach within liberal and progressive lawyer circles.

While the profiles of the lawyers who handled the Supreme Court briefs and oral arguments for the parties on the two sides were similar, there were notable differences in the characteristics of the larger pools of lawyers involved on opposing sides in these cases. As indicated in table 4.1, a higher proportion of the challengers worked in the Midwest and South, while a greater percentage of reformers worked in DC and the Northeast. Moreover, a much lower proportion of challengers attended top-ranked law schools.[74] These differences in the characteristics of these divided armies of lawyers provide some support for the image of campaign reform champions that their detractors like to advance—that they are coastal elites who lack authentic ties to the people they claim to serve under the reform banner. The differences may also contribute to the larger narrative of the litigation campaign—that reformers are out of touch with, and perhaps even hostile to, the values and policy preferences of voters in the heartland. The next chapter takes up the question of how amicus and lawyer participation might be construed, or used, by the Court as an indication of popular support for its interpretation of the First Amendment.

## Conclusion

Since the 1970s, opponents and defenders of campaign finance regulation have been engaged in what Brad Smith has characterized as "long-term ideological warfare" over the role of money in politics.[75] The effort to resist campaign finance regulation through the courts gained steam in the 1990s as challengers organized to take advantage of the Court's increasing receptivity to their arguments. They assembled a powerful and varied set of champions who united around a shared narrative about elites, the liberal media, and their defense of the political status quo. They served up promising test cases, coordinated party and amicus participation, engaged with the media to generate support for their positions, and found skilled appellate advocates to present their positions in the Supreme Court.

With a two-thirds majority of the Court now prepared to strike down most campaign finance regulation, opponents of regulation are riding high. Lawyers on the challengers' side show no signs of letting up; they have set their sights on dismantling much of what remains of campaign finance regulation, such as disclosure requirements and contribution limits. A leading opponent of regulation confirmed the reformers' fears about the ambitions of the litigation campaign. He expressed confidence that very soon there would be "nothing left" of McCain-Feingold "but bits and pieces and remnants."

So far, the Roberts Court has rejected some of the challengers' most ambitious deregulatory goals. Still, reformers worry. One said of the gains achieved by challengers since Justice Alito's appointment, "The goal posts have moved so much, it's just remarkable." Another observed, "I think they've been emboldened by the Roberts Court to say, 'Well, let's keep going. We've managed to roll back the restrictions that we really, really didn't like, but let's keep going.'"

Reformers say that the Roberts Court's rulings and a partisan stalemate in the FEC have resulted in an almost complete breakdown of campaign finance regulation. One reformer called the Court's campaign finance rulings

> kind of a signal to the world and to the lower courts to not take these laws very seriously and to start thinking about ways to get rid of them. . . . A lot of what you've seen is people just ignoring them, in terms of setting up super PACs and using them basically as campaign arms [and thereby violating the prohibition on coordinating with campaigns]. . . . Nobody thinks any of these laws are constitutional anymore, and so they don't pay attention to them. And the FEC has gotten itself into a position where it doesn't enforce anything because the Republicans have gotten into the position of absolutism on these laws, all of it encouraged indirectly by *Citizens United*. So they don't think any of these laws should be enforced and then they won't let any of these laws be enforced, and so the whole thing has kind of unraveled, and it's going to continue to unravel, I think.

Another election law specialist agreed that "the campaign finance structure that was put into place in the early 1970s is coming unglued . . . [W]e're watching a slow-motion collapse without any real clear idea of what's going be put in its place, if anything."

# PART TWO

# Themes and Implications

# Strange Bedfellows?

Campaign finance makes for strange bedfellows. There's no doubt about it.
INTERVIEW WITH REFORMER

This chapter tries to account for the challengers' litigation alliance in *Citizens United*. Although this case is just one of the Roberts Court's blockbuster campaign finance cases, the alignments in *Citizens United* are broadly representative of the alignments in Supreme Court cases since early in the first decade of the 2000s. Two aspects of the coalition might appear "strange" at first glance. One is the participation of groups associated with constituencies that generally stand behind the Republican Party but would seem to have little direct interest in striking down all limits on election spending by corporations and wealthy individuals. The other is the involvement of groups ordinarily associated with liberal causes. We need to treat these riddles separately because they raise different types of questions with different implications.

The participation of the Republican Party and its leaders was predictable given the party's long history of resisting campaign finance regulation.[1] It is also unsurprising that other long-standing opponents of campaign finance regulation, such as the US Chamber of Commerce, took the challenger's side. But the litigation coalition also included groups with ties to more populist elements of the conservative coalition. These constituencies do not have financial resources at their command comparable to those of business interests and wealthy individuals. This difference in ability to engage in election spending would seem to put them at a disadvantage in intraparty battles for power and influence as campaign finance restrictions disappeared. Moreover, the values and policy priorities of these constituencies differ from those of many business leaders; they come from different social backgrounds, live in different places, and sometimes pursue conflicting policies. One might have expected the misalignment of priorities, resources, and values to promote divisions within the ranks of the GOP coalition, reflecting what one longtime

Republican activist described as "utter suspicion and distrust between the more moneyed interests and the grassroots" within the Republican Party. But lawyers for groups claiming to represent the party's rank and file cooperated with "moneyed interests" in the effort to accomplish a broad ruling in *Citizens United*. Not only did they project consensus about whether Citizens United should prevail in this case; they also came together around the proposition that for-profit corporations deserve the same First Amendment protection as individuals and ideologically motivated nonprofit groups.

A different kind of puzzle relates to the ACLU and the AFL-CIO, both of which took qualified positions in support of Citizen United's challenge. On many other policy issues, these organizations are fierce opponents of most of the groups that have led the fight against campaign finance regulation. The ACLU battles with Republican Party and its allies on military detention practices, domestic surveillance, abortion, LGBTQ rights, and immigration enforcement policies. But it lent partial support to the constitutional challenge in *Citizens United*. Similarly, the AFL-CIO opposes the Republican Party and the US Chamber of Commerce on myriad policy issues, including workers' rights and collective bargaining rules. It nevertheless joined in challenging the constitutionality of the BCRA's electioneering-communications provisions.

We should not necessarily be surprised that the amici filing briefs in support of Citizens United's position were not all close political allies. It is not unusual for interest groups to form litigation coalitions with politically unaligned players to advance common goals.[2] One lawyer who participated in *Citizens United* objected to what he characterized as "the overly simplistic kind of attitude that permeates" discussions about the "*Citizens United* ogres." He rejected the notion that liberal interest groups "can't possibly be on [the Republicans'] side for anything," explaining: "If you've got a common interest against a law that infringes both of your rights to do things that are very important, why [should other policy disagreements] matter?"

Still, it is important to understand what led various groups to support the challenge because their involvement may have contributed to the success of the litigation campaign. The reasons for their participation also bear on questions about accountability. Lawyers of very different social backgrounds and professional identities participated in this campaign, bringing together interest groups that do not always agree over policy behind an effort to make unlimited spending on elections a constitutional right, held by corporations as well as individuals, and to hold the Court accountable to this view of the First Amendment. Chapter 7 explores the roles and responsibilities of lawyers and advocacy organizations in this litigation campaign.

## The Challengers' Litigation Coalition

### REPUBLICAN PARTY LEADERS

GOP leaders have long resisted campaign finance regulation, but their opposition has become more uniform since the middle of the first decade of
the 2000s. The alignments in *Citizens United* were strikingly different from
those in Congress during the roll-call vote on the BCRA. The legislation
passed with nearly unanimous support from Democrats and a substantial
minority of Republicans, including, as one challenger noted, a dozen or so
"old bulls—guys like Ted Stevens and Dick Lugar from Indiana and Pete Do-
menici from New Mexico, conservative guys—they supported [the BCRA]."
The alignments were also different from those in the *McConnell* litigation, in
which many Republican co-sponsors, as well as former Republican members
of Congress, joined in four briefs defending the legislation.[3] A lawyer with
a long history of involvement in campaign finance litigation on the reform
side told me that "it was enormously important politically, and for litigation
purposes" that the BCRA was bipartisan legislation—"that you had McCain,
who's his own guy, and Feingold, who's his own guy but in a different world
from McCain, and a majority of the House and a majority of the Senate and
signed by George Bush II." This lawyer believed that bipartisan support for
the legislation "was critical" and "had an unstated impact on the Supreme
Court" in *McConnell*. But support for campaign finance regulation from Republican leaders thereafter collapsed. Several lawyers observed that Republicans who had previously backed campaign finance regulation and defended
it in the courts no longer dared to do so by the time *Citizens United* reached
the Supreme Court. They feared retaliation from Republican leaders, especially Mitch McConnell. The only Republican leaders on briefs defending
the BCRA in *Citizens United* were two of the legislation's principal sponsors,
Senator John McCain and former representative Christopher Shays.[4]

### GROUPS ALLIED WITH THE REPUBLICAN PARTY

In the first round of argument, various organizations associated with the conservative legal movement filed amici briefs supporting Citizens United's challenge. Some of these amici staked out positions reflecting their own particular
concerns. For example, the NRA invited the Court to distinguish between
different types of corporations and to find the statute unconstitutional as
applied to nonprofit advocacy corporations funded primarily by individual
members.[5] Some social-conservative groups focused their objections on the

BCRA's disclosure provisions, asserting that organizations that advocate un-popular positions were vulnerable to reprisal if they could not express their political views anonymously.[6]

But in the second round of argument, on the broader question of whether the Court should overrule *Austin* and relevant portions of *McConnell*, ad-ditional Republican-aligned groups joined Citizens United's call to abandon major precedents. Among those supporting this broader challenge were the specialized advocacy groups profiled in chapter 3—IFS, the James Madison Center for Free Speech (on behalf of seven former Republican FEC Commis-sioners), and the Institute for Justice. The US Chamber of Commerce and the Michigan Chamber of Commerce urged the Court to find that for-profit cor-porations enjoy the same campaign speech protections as natural persons.[7] The NRA again invited the Court to distinguish between nonprofit advocacy organizations and for-profit corporations, but this time it argued in the alter-native that all corporations, including for-profit corporations, were entitled to engage in unlimited spending on elections.[8] Amicus briefs filed by other groups, including some associated with the Republican base, also supported the argument that restrictions on campaign spending by *any* corporation were unconstitutional.[9]

What led these various groups to take such a strong position in favor of deregulating campaign finance and extending First Amendment protection to for-profit corporations?

**Libertarian Groups.**  The position taken by libertarian groups in *Citizens United* was consistent with their mission statements and anti-regulatory agendas. Some libertarian groups, such as the Pacific Legal Foundation, had participated in challenges to campaign finance regulations since the 1970s, while others, such as the Institute for Justice, joined the fight more recently. These libertarian organizations, old and new, share a broad stance that all campaign finance regulation is impermissible, and they do not distinguish between the rights of nonprofit advocacy and for-profit corporations. In *Bel-lotti*, the Pacific Legal Foundation filed a brief calling the Massachusetts stat-ute a "frontal assault on freedom of expression" that would "serve to isolate the business sector of the American economy from the public."[10] Its brief in *Citi-zens United* criticized the many "fine distinctions" that had emerged in the ju-risprudence around the regulation of money in politics since then, including the distinction between business corporations and advocacy groups: "The parsing and hairsplitting have rendered this area of the law a patchwork of contradictory opinions impacting political speech rights at the core of the

First Amendment."[11] It argued that "the core political speech protections of the First Amendment should be open to all equally—to the millionaire as well as to the grassroots entity that selects the corporate form to facilitate the dissemination of its message."[12] Cato and IJ took a similarly expansive view of expressive rights at issue in these cases; they urged the Supreme Court to overrule *Austin* and *McConnell* and sweep away all distinctions between types of "speakers."[13]

A lawyer for one libertarian group explained why his organization did not support distinguishing between nonprofit corporations and business corporations: "That's not the type of distinction that an organization like [ours] would draw. [This organization] is very much a champion of commercial speech as equivalent, just as important as so-called non-commercial speech. Libertarians in general view business corporations, and any business association, as a kind of reflection of the right of individuals to consensually trade with who they want and voluntarily associate with who they want. But it ultimately comes down to individual consent; so long as the individuals consent, the types of arrangements they make with others is not something the government should draw distinctions on." This lawyer added that while Ted Olson had invited the Court to distinguish between nonprofit ideological corporations and business corporations for purposes of the First Amendment analysis in *Citizens United*,[14] "within the sort of libertarian community in which I travel, that argument was not taken seriously."

For libertarian groups, then, joining in a broad attack on the restrictions challenged in *Citizens United* was not a departure. Some of these groups seek to distance themselves from the wealthy individuals and business interests that provide much of their financial backing.[15] They nevertheless support a broad deregulatory agenda, of which the campaign to deregulate money in politics is a part.

**Abortion Opponents and Other Social Conservatives.** James Bopp has filed most of the cases challenging campaign finance regulation in the Roberts Court, including restrictions on corporate spending on elections. What is the connection, if any, between campaign finance and the issues of primary concern to the abortion opponents and social conservatives he represents?

Until early in the first decade of the 2000s, Bopp's campaign finance cases focused primarily on challenging restrictions affecting ideologically motivated nonprofit groups. He handled dozens of challenges to restrictions on the election-related activities of the NRLC, the Christian Coalition, and other pro-life groups.[16] In the late 1990s, he expressed strong opposition to bills that eventually passed as the BCRA on the ground that having to use PACs rather than general treasury funds to pay for election ads would limit nonprofit pro-life organizations' ability to communicate with voters.[17] He also represented opponents of same-sex marriage in their efforts to avoid disclosing their campaign contributions and petition signatures. For example, he sought to prevent the state of Washington from releasing the names and contact information of individuals who signed a petition titled "Preserve Marriage, Protect Children." (In *Doe v. Reed* (2010), the Supreme Court ruled 8–1 that the disclosure of referendum petitions did not violate the First Amendment.)[18] But Bopp thereafter broadened his mission—to eliminate all limits on spending in elections, including restrictions on campaign spending by for-profit corporations and wealthy individuals. In an interview in 2010, he explained: "We had a 10-year plan to take all this down . . . And if we do it right, I think we can pretty well dismantle the entire regulatory regime that is called campaign finance law."[19]

If Bopp's primary allegiance was to abortion opponents and social conservatives rather than business groups or the Republican Party, one might have expected him to chart a narrower course. After all, *Massachusetts Citizens for Life* (1986)[20] held that ideological nonprofit corporations that accept minimal funding from business corporations should be treated differently from business corporations for purposes of the prohibition on spending corporate treasury funds on federal elections. That exception might well have applied to most of Bopp's clients. And in *Federal Election Commission v. Wisconsin Right to Life* (2007),[21] the Court found that the BCRA's limitations on corporate electioneering were unconstitutional as applied to Wisconsin Right to Life's ads mentioning Senator Russ Feingold.[22] One reformer called this "a huge victory" for Bopp and one that "[blew] a hole in the restrictions on sources of payment for electioneering communication ads." This holding ensured that abortion opponents could engage in issue advocacy without violating campaign finance laws.

If these rulings were sufficient to address the primary concerns of Bopp and his clients, what led him thereafter to pursue test cases that would seek to dismantle most of what remained of campaign finance laws? Why, for example, would he join in a challenge to the statute's "Millionaire's Amendment," which permitted candidates whose opponents spent more than a specified amount of their own money to accept contributions in excess of FECA limits, a provision ruled unconstitutional in *Davis v. FEC* (2008)?[23] And why would he bring a test case that would serve as a vehicle for striking down limitations on campaign expenditures by all corporations, including business corporations, in *Citizens United*?

Bopp's loss in a case he brought soon after the BCRA was enacted in 2002 provided some motivation to pursue what eventually became his broader assault on campaign finance regulation. In *Federal Election Commission v. Beaumont* (2003),[24] he represented North Carolina Right to Life in a challenge to FECA's restrictions on campaign *contributions* by corporate nonprofit advocacy groups such as NRLC. Mary Ziegler shows that Bopp believed that expanding permitted contributions to campaigns by NRLC and other pro-life groups would advance the cause of electing pro-life candidates, defeating pro-choice candidates, and eventually appointing Supreme Court justices who would overturn *Roe v. Wade*.[25] Moreover, Bopp had reason to expect that his argument for distinguishing between business corporations and nonprofits for purposes of contribution limits might prevail in the Supreme Court since it had succeeded in the courts below.[26] In retrospect, however, it seems that bringing this case might have been a miscalculation—and one that helped to nudge abortion opponents and other conservative nonprofit advocacy groups into an otherwise unlikely alliance.

Bopp's brief in *Beaumont* argued that groups such as his client "pose[d] no potential of threat to the political system," so that the governmental interest in regulating their campaign contributions was weak.[27] But the Court rejected that argument. It held that concerns about the corrupting potential underlying the ban on for-profit corporate contributions applied to nonprofit advocacy corporations too. It found that nonprofit corporations, like their for-profit counterparts, "benefit from significant state-created advantages, and may well be able to amass substantial political war chests."[28] The Court noted that "not all corporations that qualify for favorable tax treatment under Section 501(c)(4) of the Internal Revenue Code lack substantial resources" and that "the category covers some of the Nation's most politically powerful organizations, including the AARP, the National Rifle Association, and the Sierra Club."[29] Furthermore, it found that nonprofit advocacy corporations are "no less susceptible than traditional business companies to misuse as conduits for circumventing the contribution limits imposed on individuals."[30]

Bopp's loss in *Beaumont* doomed any broad argument that the justifications for regulating campaign activities by for-profit corporations did not apply to nonprofit advocacy corporations. But he did not immediately embrace the broader goal of unleashing all campaign spending. Instead, his next several Supreme Court briefs focused on the narrower interests of abortion opponents. In a case that was consolidated with ten other lawsuits in *McConnell v. FEC*, he represented the National Right to Life Committee, then US representative (and subsequent vice president) Mike Pence, and others in a challenge to the constitutionality of the BCRA's "soft money" and "electioneering" provisions,[31] and his brief emphasized how the provisions affected nonprofit ideological groups.[32] He again focused on these interests in *Wisconsin Right to Life* (2007),[33] arguing for a "grass-roots lobbying exception" to the prohibition on using corporate treasury funds to finance campaign ads.[34] (The US Chamber of Commerce argued that the nonprofit status of Wisconsin Right to Life was irrelevant.)[35] The Court's holding in that case ensured that abortion opponents could run ads that would mobilize their highly motivated and politically engaged supporters.

It was not until *Citizens United* that Bopp brought a case that would obliterate any distinction between nonprofit advocacy organizations and for-profit corporations for purposes of restrictions on campaign spending. He advised Citizens United as it developed plans to produce and air *Hillary: The Movie*, and he represented the organization in its challenge in federal district court. His primary interest was in overturning the BCRA's disclosure requirements, so that his clients could run ads without including a disclaimer indicating who paid for the communication and whether it was authorized by the candidate. But, as one reformer observed, this case was "perfectly set up to be [a] test case" for the broader proposition about the rights of for-profit corporations to engage in campaign spending, which surely was "what James Bopp envisioned when he brought the case." This lawyer noted that the architects of the case "had constructed an entity that wouldn't qualify for MCFL" because it accepted contributions from business corporations. Thus, it was "perfectly positioned to be a vehicle for overruling *Austin* and *McConnell*."

But why would Bopp have pursued such a broad test case, when he might have protected the interests of abortion opponents and other ideologically motivated groups by advancing an argument that was narrower and therefore more likely to prevail? At least part of the answer is that this approach would not have served the goal of changing the law so that ideological nonprofits would be free to take money from for-profit corporations without worrying about the consequences. When asked about the possible wisdom of urging the Court to distinguish between for-profit and nonprofit corporations in *Citizens United*, one challenger insisted that this narrower ground—which Ted Olson pursued in his brief—would not have provided adequate protection for grassroots advocacy groups. He explained:

> The argument that he made was that this is an insubstantial amount of corporate funds in this pot of money that they're using and therefore that's an exception. And of course, that harkens to *Massachusetts Citizens for Life* . . . But the problem with that—even though it was useful to a certain extent early on—is you still are subject to an investigation by the FEC. Well yeah, you can

do it, but they're going to investigate you to see whether or not your corporate funds are insubstantial. Not-for-profits can't go through FEC investigations or the threat of them. They just won't do it. They won't do the ad
if they're going be subject to second guessing by an FEC investigation on
whether or not the amount of corporate money in their account is insignifi-
cant or insubstantial.

This lawyer went on to explain why a conservative nonprofit organization
might resist having the FEC review its books: "All you have to do is look at the
DC Circuit opinion regarding National Rifle Association." He was referring
to a decision finding that the NRA had received substantial contributions
from business corporations in the 1978 and 1982 election cycles and therefore
did not qualify for the MCFL exception.[36] Driving his point home, he asserted that groups like the NRA and Citizens United have good reason to fear
government review of their funding sources: "While Hillary was in the White
House with Bill, they had one thousand FBI files illegally on their political
opponents. Now, they weren't searching through these for their birthdays to
send them a birthday card." This lawyer was referring to "Filegate," during
which Clinton White House Office of Personnel security requested FBI fold-
ers on as many as 340 people to vet holdover employees from the George W.
Bush administration. Although Ken Starr exonerated the Clintons of direct
involvement in the scandal,[37] this lawyer insisted that the incident illustrated
why "to think that any of [Citizens United's] donors would not be punished
for having funded a movie that criticized Hillary is fanciful."

Mary Ziegler points to another important motivation for Bopp to engage
in the broader fight against campaign finance regulation: he believed that
pro-life groups needed to improve their relationships within the GOP. She
notes that some party leaders concluded in the 1990s that the party's stance
on abortion had torpedoed George H. W. Bush's 1992 presidential campaign.
With the approach of the 2008 election, some Republican leaders, including possible presidential nominees Rudy Giuliani and Mitt Romney, believed
that the party had gone too far in catering to social conservatives. This shift,
they believed, had jeopardized the party's election prospects.[38] Ziegler argues
that leaders of some pro-life groups hoped that by cooperating in a more
comprehensive assault on campaign finance regulation, they would shore
up their standing within the party and gain leverage to bargain with other
Republicans for their preferred policies and judicial nominees: "If right-to-
lifers led the fight against campaign finance regulation, the anti-abortion
movement might prove its worth to a GOP establishment that was beginning
to see the abortion issue as a liability." Bopp and the NRLC's chief lobbyist

sought to persuade grassroots activists that this strategy was the best hope for overturning *Roe*. Some grassroots activists disagreed with this approach, arguing that it made abortion opponents overly dependent on the GOP.[39] Social-conservative icon Phyllis Schlafly argued that big corporations and wealthy donors would benefit more than anyone else from campaign finance deregulation.[40] Politicians of both major parties complained about the role that the NRLC played in resisting campaign finance reform.[41] But this cooperation in the effort to resist campaign finance regulation, and the increased influence that deregulation won for "outside" advocacy groups, may have helped to secure the Republican Party's laser focus on appointing new Supreme Court justices committed to overruling *Roe*. That focus, in turn, paved the way for the Court's 2022 ruling in *Dobbs v. Jackson Women's Health Organization*— holding that *Roe* was "egregiously wrong from the start."[42]

The idea that leaders of some pro-life groups joined in the broader fight against campaign finance regulation to win favor with Republican allies and to make overturning *Roe* a Republican priority is also consistent with other research on how the GOP has drawn abortion opponents and gun-rights advocates into its coalition while also retaining the support of business interests.[43] Andrew Lewis's history of the pro-life movement finds that abortion politics brought pro-lifers and evangelicals into league with other conservatives on campaign finance regulation, not because the rank and file really opposed campaign finance reform but because the partisanship of their leaders steered them toward that position.[44] It also jibes with Bopp's history as a broker for social conservatives' positions within the Republican Party. The NRLC received substantial contributions from the Republican National Committee and other Republican Party committees in the mid-1990s,[45] the same period during which the organization became increasingly supportive of Republican candidates, even when they opposed Democratic candidates with stronger antiabortion voting records.[46] While serving as vice-chairman of the RNC from 2006 through 2012, he advocated for a "Purity Resolution," which would have denied Republican Party support to any candidate who failed to affirm at least eight of ten specified principles, including opposition to "government run health care," "amnesty for illegal immigrants," "Obama's socialist agenda," abortion, and gay marriage.[47] The RNC rejected the proposal and instead adopted a resolution that simply "urge[d]" the party's leadership to support nominees who endorse the party's platform.[48] But the effort that Bopp championed, to insist that the party embrace the priorities of social conservatives, has largely succeeded in reshaping the Republican Party over the past several decades.[49]

Bopp's leadership of the cause of campaign finance deregulation also co-incided with a larger realignment of social conservatives' perspectives on the utility of the First Amendment to advance their political goals. In the period during which abortion opponents confronted restrictions on their election-related activities, they also encountered limitations on their ability to engage in demonstrations in front of abortion clinics. As Joshua Wilson has shown in his history of abortion politics, these experiences led some abortion oppo-nents to become champions of a cause that was new to them—an expansive reading of the First Amendment.[50] Christian Right leaders began to find free-speech claims useful in arguments for greater accommodation of religion in public life.[51] They made free-speech claims to protect the rights of abortion opponents to protest at clinics[52] and to resist abortion counseling require-ments.[53] First Amendment claims provided a basis for resisting the Affordable Care Act's contraception mandate,[54] limiting the reach of antidiscrimination laws,[55] and claiming access to government resources for religious schools.[56] These developments brought Christian conservatives into a complicated co-alition with civil libertarians, who defended profane speech, pornography, and flag burning, and with business groups that were advocating for broad First Amendment protections for commercial speech.

**The NRA.**   The NRA's resistance to campaign finance regulation dates to the 1980s. It has repeatedly skirmished with gun control groups and the FEC over its use of PACs and independent expenditures to campaign for and against candidates.[57] The organization's first foray into Supreme Court litigation over its election spending came in *Federal Election Commission v. Massachusetts Citizens for Life* (1986), in which it filed an amicus brief argu-ing that the challenged restriction did not apply to the group's independent expenditures and, if so construed, would violate the First Amendment.[58] In *Nixon v. Shrink Missouri Government PAC* (2000),[59] the NRA Political Vic-tory Fund joined a brief filed by Bopp on behalf of the National Right to Life PAC Fund and the National Right to Work Committee's PAC to argue that a state contribution limit of $1,075 per election violated the First Amend-ment. An FEC enforcement action against the organization and its affiliated entities for violations of the FECA brought the NRA into the courts again in *Federal Election Commission v. National Rifle Association* (2001), in which the DC Circuit Court of Appeals found that the NRA had accepted too much for-profit corporate money to qualify for the MCFL exception.[60] The NRA was one of the parties that lost in the challenge to the BCRA in *McConnell v. Federal Election Commission* (2003).

The NRA took different positions in the two rounds of argument in *Citizens United*. In the first round, it argued that the Court should distinguish business corporations from nonprofit corporations: "The voluntary donation box of a nonprofit organization must be distinguished from the cash register of a business when it comes to regulating political expression." It further argued that "for like-minded individuals lacking great wealth, pooling their donations to fund a political message is, in a real sense, the only way for them to find meaningful voice in the marketplace of ideas . . . Yet campaign-finance law continues, at least presumptively, to equate donations received by the NRA from individual supporters with the funds amassed by Exxon from shareholders and profits."[61] In the second round, however, the NRA's position better aligned with those of its Republican allies. It argued that the Court would be "amply justified" in overturning *Austin* and *McConnell*. The brief explained that those decisions "sanction[ed] an unworkable regime" and were "recent aberrations in an otherwise robust First Amendment tradition of assiduously protecting political speech and leaving it to flow free."[62]

It is difficult to account for the position that the NRA took in the second round in *Citizens United* in terms of its direct interests alone since the organization was easily distinguishable from the business corporations that were the focus of *Austin*. But its history of tangles with gun control advocates and the FEC over its election activities, and its strong partisan alignment with the Republican Party, help to explain its support for overruling *Austin*.

The NRA has long been an election spending and lobbying powerhouse. In the mid-1970s, Richard Viguerie, a pioneer in direct-mail fundraising techniques, identified gun rights as a great untapped source of political money.[63] He used those new fundraising strategies to give the NRA and his other New Right clients greater financial independence from the Republican Party and its establishment wing. The NRA and its members became more politically engaged and increasingly partisan in their orientation in the 1980s and 1990s as the Republican Party and its candidates adopted gun-rights positions in return. Since the 1990s, the NRA has made $23 million in federal campaign contributions to gun-rights supporters, with $19.3 million going to Republicans.[64] But it has injected much more money into the political process through independent expenditures.[65]

The NRA's political influence has been more a function of its ability to motivate gun owners to engage with the political process than of direct attempts to buy votes through campaign contributions.[66] It has cultivated a highly active, engaged, and powerful constituency that can be counted on to participate in elections and monitor politicians while they are in office.

Through its communications with members, it has tied gun rights to self-defense against crime and to resistance to government tyranny, and it has accused "globalist elites" such as George Soros of conspiring with liberal politicians to take away people's guns.[67] Most of the NRA's campaign spending targets the organization's own members, through advertisements appealing to their gun owner identities.[68]

The NRA substantially increased its election spending after the ruling in *Citizens United*. In 2016 alone, it spent over $54 million in federal elections.[69] The organization is widely credited with helping Donald Trump win the 2016 presidential election, having poured more than $30 million into independent expenditures supporting his bid for the White House.[70] The NRA also spent $24.4 million on the 2020 election.[71] But serious financial and legal troubles, including alleged campaign finance violations, diminished its influence in the 2020 races.[72]

**Tea Party Groups.**    The stakes for Tea Party groups in campaign finance regulation are unclear, in part because the very contours of the Tea Party movement are difficult to discern. There is no widespread consensus on what the Tea Party is or who speaks for it. It lacks any formal organization with a legitimate claim to speak for the whole. An incident often cited as the spark for the movement is CNBC reporter Rick Santelli's rant on the floor of the Chicago Mercantile Exchange in February 2009, during which he asserted that the 2008 crash was caused primarily by the irresponsible behavior of "losers"—homeowners who knowingly obtained high-risk mortgages.[73] Santelli called for a "Chicago Tea Party" to protest government intervention in the housing market.[74] During the next several years, conservative activists who agreed with Santelli's tirade founded hundreds of organizations to elect conservative Republicans to advance positions identified with the Tea Party: sharply reducing government spending and regulation; cutting taxes; repealing the Affordable Care Act (a.k.a. "Obamacare"); and closing US borders. Political scientists Theda Skocpol and Vanessa Williamson describe Tea Party activists and their supporters as people who view themselves as honest, hardworking Americans who are being taken advantage of by undeserving freeloaders. Skocpol and Williamson also show how well-funded free-market advocacy groups based in Washington, DC, supported Tea Party rallies and claimed to speak in the name of grassroots Tea Partiers.[75] Other scholars have explored the complexity of the Tea Party movement and the policy priorities of those who identify with it, but they describe various types of resentment and distrust as drivers.[76]

Some of the groups that filed amicus briefs in *Citizens United* were founded before 2009 but embrace agendas consistent with Tea Party concerns.

Organizations that fall into this broad category include American Justice Partnership, Let Freedom Ring, the Wyoming Liberty Group, the National Taxpayers Union (which organized participation in some of the Tea Party protests), DownsizeDC.org, US Border Control, and English First. These groups joined in the call to overrule *Austin* and *McConnell*.

**Cooperation within the GOP Coalition.**   The broad anti-regulatory stances taken in *Citizens United* by the National Right to Life Committee, the NRA, and other social-conservative and Tea Party–affiliated groups went beyond what was necessary to protect their own ability to engage in election spending. But those positions may have improved their relations within the GOP, which is the only major party that has taken official positions on the issues that drive the political participation of the members of these groups and the constituencies they claim to represent. Since 1992, the Republican Party platform has included language advocating a constitutional amendment outlawing abortion and supporting the appointment of judges who would overturn *Roe v. Wade*.[77] The GOP platform has included gun-rights planks since 1972,[78] but subsequent platforms have added significantly stronger statements on gun rights, as well as gay marriage, illegal immigration, and state accommodation of religion.[79] The willingness of these groups to support the maximalist position of the US Chamber of Commerce is consistent with a political science literature showing that long coalition partners attempt wherever possible to conform their positions to those of the core member with the greatest existential stake in the issue.[80] Abortion opponents, gun-rights groups, and Tea Party–affiliated organizations were enacting the "coalitional etiquette"[81] that is expected in a long coalition of intense "policy demanders."[82] These groups have their own policy priorities that are of comparable significance to them, and they expect deference from their coalition partners on those policy goals.

While none of the challengers referred to these coalition dynamics to explain the positions they took in the litigation, several reformers did so. A lawyer who has participated on the reform side for decades offered his view: "What's happened I think, is the Republicans have done a very good job of getting them on social issues." Another reformer offered his "cynical view" that "the Tea Party is just really an arm of the Republican Party, and unlimited spending by wealthy individuals and corporations can't but help the Republican Party and conservative causes." The idea that mutual interests in raising money for the party and maintaining a winning coalition explains the cooperation of populist elements in this litigation campaign is consistent with an observation by Grover Norquist, president of Americans for Tax Reform, in 2014, the year *McCutcheon* was decided: "There's no war between the Republican establishment and the Tea Party for the same reason Siamese twins who share a heart and brain do not argue much."[83] (Chapter 8 considers whether this claim is still valid.)

Some reformers expressed frustration that groups associated with populist elements aligned with the Chamber of Commerce in this litigation campaign. One commented that there is "obvious tension between the Tea Party folks and mainstream Republican folks" in that "Tea Party folks, at least initially, and to some extent still today, talk a lot about crony capitalism and are as troubled by money in politics as I am." Tea Partiers believe that House and Senate members "are all bought by big business," he added, but that has not "translat[ed] . . . into support of legislation to regulate money in politics." Arguing that Tea Partiers should be some of the strongest advocates for limits on big money because they're "ostensibly sort of anti-power and [anti] corporate," another reformer insisted that this was one area "where [populists of] the Left and the Right should be swinging together." The problem, another reformer suggested, is that the Republican base does not really understand the relationship between money in politics and other issues they care about:

> Let's take immigration. Immigration is an interesting one to me, because the conservatives, the Tea Party people, are really anti-immigration reform . . . But I don't think they understand that one of the reasons they're not getting what they want is that business doesn't want it. And that's a money and politics issue, that business relies on [undocumented immigrants]. And therefore, while the Republicans can scream and yell about people coming across the border, the truth of the matter is they know their real supporters, financial supporters, don't want a real crackdown . . . If you really wanted to deal with the issue, you go after the employers . . . People come across here because there are jobs. If you want to stop that, stop the jobs. How do you stop the jobs? You prosecute the employers. They're not going to do that, because that's where the money comes from.

This lawyer emphasized that "it's not just the Tea Party people; [many] people . . . don't understand the connection [that campaign finance] has to all their other issues." In other words, he and other reformers suggested, campaign finance operates largely in the background, not registering as relevant to the policy concerns that seem most pressing to American voters, even if it shapes electoral and policy outcomes.

Some reformers marveled at how some rank-and-file Republicans, though socially distant from those who would seem to benefit most directly from unregulated money in politics, nevertheless identify with the one percent. One reformer said, "There . . . appears to be a very large segment of . . . Tea Party Republicans who, far from being put off by rich people who are wielding power because of their vast wealth, are attracted to it." He added: "That's a very interesting phenomenon because part of the Tea Party message, of course, is that the elites have stolen the country from the common man, but they must mean different elites. It has to do with liberal elites versus rich people who speak for us ... like Ross Perot, like Donald Trump. And that they have the power to stand up to these horrible government elites and the liberal university elites and all the Northeastern liberal types, and it all gets mixed up with race and regionalism and class. It's very complicated."

Another reformer agreed that it's partly about "who they identify with," but that "it's also mixed up with other issues . . . with immigration issues, it gets mixed up with abortion rights, it gets mixed up with *all* those issues." One reformer noted that "the issue has become partisan and polarized" and "a lot of what's going on is identity politics," meaning that if "you identify as a Republican," your position on campaign finance is part of a "set of things that come along with that." Another reformer said: "You don't argue against your friends."

These reflections are consistent with research showing that the American electorate is increasingly torn by conflict rooted in identity, as voters have sorted into two parties that correspond with social, economic, and ideological cleavages. The Republican Party has built a coalition around a symbolic ideology about values and social identity that takes priority over policy preferences. Increasingly isolated and partisan collections of voters display increased mistrust and dislike for those from the other party, a phenomenon known as "affective polarization."[84] Democrats and Republicans alike tend to view the other party's members as "hypocritical, selfish, and closed-minded" and to be unwilling to socialize across party lines.[85] "Negative partisanship"—partisan behavior driven not by positive feelings toward the party one supports but by negative feelings toward the party one opposes—has driven partisans of each party to turn against each other in an escalating cycle of distrust and antipathy.[86] Pragmatic concerns that once explained policy disagreements between conservatives and liberals have been displaced by moral claims embraced with an almost religious fervor.[87]

Other research documents how these phenomena play out in particular regions. For example, Katherine Cramer's *The Politics of Resentment* shows how low-income people in rural Wisconsin feel disrespected and mistrustful toward urban liberal elites.[88] They oppose public policies designed to address political inequality because they believe that government tends to control resources for the benefit of city-dwellers at the expense of rural communities. Arlie Hochschild's *Strangers in Their Own Land*[89] offers a similar explanation for why conservative white working-class voters in Louisiana ardently defend free-market capitalism while struggling with the effects of environmental degradation caused by chemical and oil companies in their own communities. Her research identifies a potent mix of factors—cultural and financial dislocation, resentment toward coastal liberals, and perceived betrayal by the federal government—that overrides what liberals tend to see as the self-interest of voters in the heartland. Other research shows that the resentment of liberal elites is a "resource" that the Republican Party and some elected officials use to mobilize voters.[90]

Thus, the willingness of organizations associated with the Republican base to go along with the money-is-speech orthodoxy of better-resourced coalition partners is partly driven by ideology, but that ideology reflects a "coalitional bargain" worked out among politicians and leaders of highly engaged groups over time.[91] It is part of a larger, strategically constructed tapestry of ideas about limited government that helps to knit together the Republican coalition. The claim that the Constitution, properly understood, protects policies that various constituencies within the alliance care about serves as "ideological glue."[92] These political-identity and "the enemy of my enemy is my friend" logics help to explain how leaders of disparate elements of the conservative coalition, including groups claiming to represent constituencies that would seem to have less to gain, have coalesced in the fight against campaign finance regulation.

As explored in more detail in the next chapter, briefs filed by groups claiming to serve populist elements of the conservative movement served up some of the strongest warnings about the dangers of regulating money in politics. To take just one example, the Wyoming Liberty Group's brief in *Citizens United* warned that "the First Amendment struggles to survive its harshest night . . . In a Republic where the people are sovereign, the prolonged dismantlement of free speech remains a curiously persistent inclination of America's ruling elite . . . The hour grows late for this Court to end its compulsion to promulgate obscure and liberty-depriving constitutional standards."[93] The same group's brief in the second round included an entire section titled "Historic Truths: The Powerful Few Forever Seek to Silence Dissent."[94] Such apocalyptic rhetoric might not shape the justices' views, but it does provide clues about how key constituencies of the Republican coalition, or at least the lawyers for groups claiming to represent those constituencies, view the stakes and can be expected to respond to the Court's rulings.

## LIBERAL ALLIES

In addition to the many briefs filed by Republican allies in support of Citizens United's challenge, the organization also received partial support from several groups that generally side with Democrats on issues other than campaign finance regulation.

**The ACLU.**    The ACLU's brief in *Citizens United* argued that the Court should strike down the electioneering provision of the BCRA, but it took no position on whether *Austin* should be overruled.[95] The organization's stance in *Citizens United* was consistent with its opposition to most campaign finance regulation since the 1970s. Recall from chapter 2 that the involvement of the New York ACLU dates back even before *Buckley*; the organization defended sponsors of a *New York Times* advertisement advocating for the impeachment of President Richard Nixon,[96] and it litigated again to test its right to publish an ad asserting that Nixon's stand on school busing amounted to facilitating "American apartheid."[97] One reformer summarized the ACLU's position with respect to those controversies: "Look, we see some points of the other side, corruption and big money and all that, but if what you're doing is criticizing the president of the United States, and you have no apparent ties to his campaign or the opponent's campaign, you've got to be able to do that, and . . . if these laws cover that, you have to carve out a First Amendment exemption, just as we have done in defamation for public commentary about political officials." The ACLU represented Democratic senator Eugene Mc-Carthy in *Buckley* and joined in many other challenges to campaign finance regulations thereafter.

The ACLU's opposition to most campaign finance spending restrictions, beginning with *Buckley* and continuing to this day, is married to support for public funding of election campaigns and stronger disclosure requirements. The latter two positions distinguish the organization from most conservative opponents of campaign finance regulation.[98]

In *Citizens United*, the ACLU cited concerns about how the BCRA's electioneering provision would affect the organization's own ability to engage in campaign spending. Its brief stated that this provision reached broadcast ads that the organization had found to be "an important tool for promoting our ideological goals."[99] Until McCain-Feingold, one lawyer told me, the ACLU and other political-advocacy organizations like it "had been thriving on the *Buckley* decision that only express advocacy of election or defeat could be regulated. So, you could go out and run box scores, [and] say: 'These guys are horrible; these guys are ruining the environment; they're ruining civil rights; they're ruining whatever,' and have no qualms or concerns about regulation." McCain-Feingold interfered with the ACLU's ability to engage in that kind of advocacy. One civil libertarian suggested that the BCRA would have received broader support from nonprofit groups, including the ACLU, had Congress

"just gone after the business corporations." The legislation's principal sponsors had included an exemption for 501(c)(4) social welfare organizations,
so long as their funds came solely from individual contributions and were
maintained separately from corporate contributions. But an amendment by
the late Senator Wellstone eliminated that exemption for groups such as the
NRA, the Sierra Club, and similar nonprofit corporations. This challenger
told me that the Wellstone amendment reflected an assessment by its sponsors that "these nonprofits are just as bad as the big for-profit corporations,
and we've got to shut them down too." They "wanted to stifle the ACLU and
the Right to Life Committee, and the National Rifle Association," he said.
"They wanted to stifle all of them and not just General Motors."

The ACLU's stance on campaign finance is best understood as part of
a larger set of deliberations about how its issue agenda should relate to the
changing political landscape. Historians and journalists have provided excellent accounts of the organization's history,[100] and I will not recount that legacy
except to highlight how campaign finance fits into the picture. The ACLU
was founded in 1920, in the wake of Attorney General Mitchell Palmer's attempts to arrest and deport thousands of suspected radical leftists, and its
early history is tightly linked to the defense of labor activism. Laura Weinrib's
*The Taming of Free Speech* explores how the group's "radical core" in the early
twentieth century viewed the defense of free speech as a means for protecting labor activists by asserting their right to picket, boycott, and strike. These
leaders viewed civil liberties as an instrument of social change, enabling labor activists to attempt "to restructure society through the exercise of collective power."[101] But that perspective yielded to a "tamer" understanding of free
speech in the 1930s, as the ACLU constructed a broader civil-liberties coalition around a more circumscribed fight against government infringement of
"personal rights." Conservatives had initially complained about the radical
underpinnings of the ACLU's fight for free-speech rights, but those criticisms
dissipated as the organization turned from defense of aggressive labor tactics to a neutral conception of civil liberties emphasizing personal freedom
and democratic debate. By the 1930s, Weinrib explains, "civil liberties were
no longer radical." The organization advocated for freedom of expression
by employers as well as unions, believing that this approach would produce
gains for labor because ideas favoring labor interests would win out in the
marketplace of ideas.[102] But corporations hired skilled lawyers who deployed
free-speech claims to resist state control over industry. Weinrib argues that
the "liberal compromise" over the meaning of civil liberties explains how the
First Amendment became a vehicle for blocking the exercise of state power
and eventually "a potent tool for the Right."[103]

The ACLU continued to cultivate a reputation for nonpartisanship and impartial defense of civil liberties in subsequent decades, although its leaders have not always agreed on what that commitment entails. In 1940, the organization expelled a twenty-year veteran of its board for her membership in the Communist Party, but the board later rescinded her expulsion.[104] The McCarthy era revealed deep divisions between anticommunist hard-liners on the ACLU board and other board members and allies who were the targets of McCarthy's attacks.[105] The organization defended many political dissidents on the Left, including protesters in the 1960s, in cases such as *Tinker v. Des Moines*,[106] involving public school students suspended for wearing black armbands to protest the Vietnam War. But it also sometimes represented activists on the Right. In 1978, two years after the Court's decision in *Buckley*, the ACLU defended a Nazi group that sought to march through Skokie, Illinois, a heavily Jewish Chicago suburb where many Holocaust survivors lived.[107] Fast forward to 2017, when the organization's Virginia affiliate defended the right of white supremacists to hold a "Unite the Right" rally in Emancipation Park in Charlottesville to protest the removal of the statue of Robert E. Lee. Each of these episodes has generated considerable controversy within the organization, but the ACLU's leaders have maintained that the organization's politically neutral approach to civil liberties is important to the organization's credibility.

Some interviewed lawyers similarly insisted that the ACLU's position on campaign finance is critical to its reputation as a nonpartisan defender of constitutional rights and to its ability to build cross-party coalitions on other important civil liberties issues. A lawyer familiar with ACLU deliberations about the organization's stance on campaign finance regulation recalled leaders saying, in effect, "We really do have to fight this fight. It's not just about us. It's about all political speech, left, right, and center." He traced the organization's position on the issue to the absolutist First Amendment views of Justices Hugo Black and William O. Douglas: "[These justices] were in favor of speech by communists, by Nazis, by pornographers . . . , by corporations, by labor unions. They didn't want any limits, at all. And that's the theory that the ACLU bought." The same lawyer credited the ACLU's position on campaign finance with its success in convincing Mitch McConnell in 2006 to oppose a constitutional amendment to allow Congress to ban desecration of the American flag: "McConnell was one of the few Republicans who voted against outlawing flag burning, and he specifically said that 'the ACLU has convinced me that not only can you not limit campaign finance, but you can't limit flag burning.' So, it's kind of a seamless web." The organization's willingness to defend unattractive "speakers" and to align itself with conservative groups on civil liberties issues has also served some of its organizational and fundraising goals, enabling it to attract Republicans as well as Democrats as board members and contributors, even if it also sometimes cost the ACLU members and supporters too.

Some senior staff, former leaders, members, and local affiliates have strongly disagreed with the ACLU's position on campaign finance regulation. According to Samuel Walker's history of the organization, a significant minority of its board disapproved of the organization's position in *Buckley*: "Concerned about the impact of money on American politics, [they] thought that civil liberties were best protected by more stringent restrictions on campaign spending."[108] Some board members continued to press for a change in the organization's policy throughout the 1980s and 1990s, and the internal divisions continue to this day. One interviewed lawyer told me that he believed that the national organization's position on campaign finance was mistaken and out of sync with the expectations of the organization's rank-and-file membership. It reflected an outdated perspective about where the greatest threats to democracy lie. "Public law tends to reflect the last generation's mistakes," he stated; "the ACLU is still fighting McCarthy, and it still sees free speech as exceptionally weak, exceptionally vulnerable, and subject to a government that is always looking for a way to suppress it."

Beginning with *Nixon v. Shrink Missouri* (2000), several former leaders of the ACLU began filing briefs defending campaign finance regulation. In the words of one reformer, these briefs were designed to signal to the Court that "No, no, no, no, no—the ACLU is not right here; the ACLU is *wrong*." In *Citizens United*, former ACLU leaders filed a brief in support of neither party, arguing that the case should be decided in Citizens United's favor without overruling *Austin* or relevant portions of *McConnell*.[109]

In April 2010, several months after the Supreme Court's ruling in *Citizen United*, the ACLU's board slightly modified the organization's policy. Its revised statement indicates support for public financing of campaigns, narrowly drawn disclosure rules, "reasonable" limits on campaign contributions, and strict enforcement of existing bans on coordination between campaigns and super PACs, but it remains opposed to most campaign spending and contribution limitations.[110] Several lawyers interviewed for this project were active in local ACLU chapters and disapproved of the national organization's position, arguing that it still does not go far enough in addressing the need for campaign finance regulation.

**AFL-CIO.** The AFL-CIO did not participate in the first round of briefing in *Citizens United*. In the second round, it argued that the Court should find the BCRA's electioneering provision unconstitutional but that there was

no need to overrule *Austin*, which "aptly distinguished unions from corporations."[111] This brief asserted that the BCRA subjected the union to an "unworkable censorship regime" that "criminalized the AFL-CIO's use of the
broadcast medium as a legislative and policy advocacy tool."[112] It also said
that the government's interest in regulating corporate electioneering was
much more substantial than its interest in regulating union participation, and
that unions' independent expenditures should receive more favorable treatment. These were essentially the arguments that it had made previously as a
party in *McConnell*.[113]

The AFL-CIO's position on campaign finance regulation has a long and
complicated history reflecting labor's changing fortunes and political power.
Indeed, labor's role in the development of First Amendment doctrine is itself a constitutional construction tied to the history of labor activism in the
United States. The idea that labor strikes and pickets might be a form of constitutionally protected speech simply did not exist, even among labor activists, until the 1930s.[114] Arguments that labor held a First Amendment right
to spend union dues on election campaigns emerged later, in response the
efforts by conservatives to subject labor unions to restrictions on election
spending analogous to those imposed on corporations.

The first federal restrictions on campaign spending by labor unions arose
in the wake of a major wave of labor strikes following the end of World War II.
With Republicans in control of Congress for the first time since the early
1930s, Congress passed the Labor Management Relations Act of 1947, better
known as the Taft-Hartley Act. The legislation amended the 1935 National
Labor Relations Act to prohibit a variety of activities, including monetary
contributions or expenditures by unions in connection with federal elections.
It thereby aligned restrictions on unions' election spending with the Tillman
Act's restrictions on corporations' election spending.

Following passage of Taft-Hartley, unions began to raise money for use
in elections by soliciting contributions to their political action committees
(PACs). In 1968, a federal grand jury in St. Louis indicted Pipefitters Local 562—whose president, Lawrence Callanan, was a convicted felon with
mob ties—for making illegal campaign contributions through its PAC. The
indictment included a charge suggesting that it was illegal for union of-
ficers to solicit PAC contributions from union members and then decide
which candidates would receive the funds. The union was convicted, and
the Eighth Circuit Court of Appeals affirmed the decision.[115] The Supreme
Court ruled against the government, finding that Taft-Hartley's restrictions
did not apply to separate funds raised through voluntary contributions to the
union's PAC.[116]

The AFL-CIO eventually joined the bipartisan coalition behind the FECA, but only after the act was amended to clearly permit unions and corporations to use general treasury funds to establish, administer, and solicit contributions to their PACs.[117] Some conservative members of Congress had sought an amendment that would have targeted labor unions' political activity. But the AFL-CIO worked with moderate Republican members to explicitly permit corporations and unions to use general treasury funds for "the establishment, administration, and solicitation of contributions to a separate, segregated fund to be utilized for political purposes." That amendment became part of the FECA legislation that passed in 1972 and was signed by President Nixon that year.[118]

When revelations about campaign finance violations in connection with the Watergate scandal led Congress to enact further reforms in the 1974 amendments to FECA, AFL-CIO counsel Laurence Stephen Gold played an important role in convincing labor Democrats to support the legislative effort. One interviewed reformer explained that labor had "legitimate worries" that led them to insist on certain provisions as conditions for their support for the law. Among those conditions were that labor and corporate interests would be treated similarly and that the FEC would have exclusive jurisdiction to enforce the law. A challenger who participated in some of those negotiations recalled that "back in the 1970s, labor was very much on board with these restrictions." He attributed labor's support for reform at the time to the fact that "this was still the last part of the heyday of organized labor and its influence in Washington" and that organized labor was confident that it could influence the process to ensure that the reform laws would not impair labor's considerable power. A reformer likewise emphasized the greater power of labor vis-à-vis business interests during the era in which it had supported these amendments: "If you go back to FECA, the mid-1970s, Congress worked very hard—it's somewhat quaint now—to balance labor and corporate America."

But when it came to reform efforts in the late 1990s, the AFL-CIO resisted. The shift in the union's position corresponded with a change in lawyers representing the union. Laurence Stephen Gold represented the AFL-CIO in negotiations over the 1974 amendments to the FECA and in subsequent court cases, and he supported some types of campaign finance regulations that served the union's goals thereafter. But, in the words of one business advocate, the AFL-CIO's position "changed a little bit" after a different lawyer with the same first and last name, Laurence E. Gold, took over as general counsel to the AFL-CIO in 1996. Laurence E. Gold objected to provisions in the BCRA that limited ads by unions and businesses thirty days before a primary or sixty days before a general election. He called these restrictions "an attempt by incumbents to silence . . . groups that criticize them or put pressure on them to vote on certain matters."[119] One challenger explained that the AFL-CIO now "saw the danger of having prohibitions and restrictions that would be implemented by an agency that was really not accountable to anybody, and they recognized the wisdom of preserving certain rights, even if it meant that it would also apply to the business community or other groups that they might not align with." Several reformers agreed that the AFL-CIO's opposition to the BCRA reflected a reasonable concern about how campaign finance regulations could be enforced selectively to limit unions' ability to influence elections. They pointed to incidents dating back to the era that produced Taft-Hartley, but they also cited more recent examples. For example, the FEC received complaints by the National Republican Senatorial Committee, the National Republican Congressional Committee, and an independent PAC chaired by Oliver North against the AFL-CIO and affiliated unions for alleged violations of the FECA in connection with the 1996 election. After a three-year formal investigation, the FEC dismissed the complaints.[120]

Some of the interviewed lawyers pointed out that labor groups, like many other political actors, tend to view campaign finance regulation opportunistically—embracing restrictions that impede the power of their opponents and resisting those that limit their own. A lawyer for a trade group said that "the union leadership obviously wants whatever opportunities they can find that advantage them, and they want to deny any opportunities that they think advantage the other side." One reformer agreed that AFL-CIO leaders "didn't like anything that restricted their ability to spend the money the way they wanted to spend it." Explaining why "labor was always lined up with big money corporations in its opposition to campaign finance reforms of various kinds" going back to *Buckley*, another reformer said, "I think that's because they were active politically and used union member dues to fund political activities and were afraid they'd lose their clout if they lost their ability to spend." For many years, the political power of corporations and the political power of unions were sufficiently similar that unions "felt like . . . we see our lot in the same position as corporations and so we're going to be on their side." The electioneering-communications provisions of the BCRA were problematic for the AFL-CIO, another lawyer said, because "using broadcast communications, targeting particular members of Congress on issues" had been "a very active part of what the AFL-CIO's advocacy had been." This lawyer explained that concern about these restrictions led the union's lawyers to urge the Court in *Citizens United* to "put the coup de grâce, if you will, on that provision," which had been weakened in the *Wisconsin Right to Life* case three years earlier; "[the AFL-CIO] wanted them to go all the way."

Although many reformers understood why the AFL-CIO resisted some of the BCRA's restrictions on union activity, some nevertheless questioned the wisdom of filing an amicus brief in support of Citizens United's broad claims. They argued that it was imprudent to cooperate in this challenge because unions would be unable to compete in the long run with the spending that the ruling would, and did, unleash. One reformer said, "I think the idea that *Citizens United* was somehow equal, that it somehow assisted labor as much as corporate America, is just wrong. I think it's just factually wrong. It's just wrong by many, many orders of magnitude about the amount of money we're talking about." Commenting on the AFL-CIO's position on *Citizens United*, another lawyer explained that "what you had for years [but no longer] was a kind of parity between the corporations and labor—we both have our PACs, we both have our ways of doing things, and we'll stay out of each [other's way]." Another reformer insisted that the AFL-CIO's position was "shortsighted" because "ultimately, in a free for all, labor's not going to win against corporate money. There's no way; they just don't have the money." Another reformer went beyond criticizing the wisdom of the union's strategy to accusing it of hypocrisy, pointing out that the union had issued a press release "slamming the Court" for its ruling in *Citizens United* on the ground that it "further tilted the playing field in favor of the one percent against the ninety-nine percent"[121] without acknowledging that "they got exactly what they asked for" by filing a brief "urging deregulation." The AFL-CIO's policy statement in 2012 called for reversing the ruling in *Citizens United* and even indicated possible support for a narrowly drawn constitutional amendment to achieve that result.[122]

Some reformers offered reasons why labor *should* be treated differently from corporations for purposes of campaign finance regulation and why the Court should have drawn a distinction between corporate and union expenditures. One said, "When labor gives, it really does represent a broad base of contributions because they're not getting large contributions. They're just funneling large numbers of contributions into a single contribution, so there's a difference there." Another observed that union leadership's relationship with its members "is very democratic," even though, he added, "at times, like in a lot of democratic systems, there's a lot of instances where it's been corrupt."

Several reformers also commented on what they saw as the Supreme Court's contradictory approaches to the problem of collective versus individual speech rights in the corporate and union contexts. One observed that "the Roberts Court has made all these [rulings] that make it easier for corporations to spend money [on politics] and at the same time you've seen this series of First Amendment cases that have been striking pretty big blows to organized labor."

In *Janus v. AFSME* (2018)[123] it held that public employees who chose not to join a union cannot be required to help pay for collective bargaining. Justice Alito, writing for a 5–4 majority in *Janus*, found that forcing union members to finance union bargaining activity violated their First Amendment rights. One reformer suggested that rulings such as *Janus*, sitting side by side with *Citizens United*, reflect a "fictional" view that corporate managers are more accountable to shareholders ("or anybody other than . . . a self-perpetuating board") than union leaders are to their members. This lawyer predicted that the Roberts Court's reliance on the First Amendment to restrict unions' ability to finance union bargaining while also expanding the scope of First Amendment protection for campaign spending would result in great long-term disadvantage for labor: "The AFL-CIO would love to have two months of the profits of Exxon. . . . and they're going to find out . . . Corporations are going to be free and . . . [unions] are going to be totally hampered."

## Coordinating Through Lawyer Networks

The breadth of the challengers' litigation coalition may have contributed to the broad ruling in *Citizens United*. Some social science research suggests that positions taken by ideologically heterogeneous coalitions may be more likely to prevail than those made by homogeneous ones.[124] Just as a large *number* of amicus briefs might sometimes serve as a "crude barometer of public opinion on an issue,"[125] the Supreme Court might interpret the variety of constituencies represented in party and amicus briefs as a signal of broad public support for a position.[126] Support from a varied coalition is also useful to the Court's efforts "to shape public opinion"[127] by showing that it is responsive to the demands of a broad range of constituencies and is not predictably siding with particular interests.

In *Federal Election Commission v. Wisconsin Right to Life, Inc.* (2007), the majority opinion noted the apparent heterogeneity of organizations on the challengers' side as an indication of the importance of the issue to these constituencies.[128] Whether the diversity of amici actually influenced the outcome in that case, or instead merely supplied the Court with information used after the fact to justify its decision, the equally diverse but even larger coalition assembled in *Citizens United* might have functioned similarly. Some support for that view lies in the majority opinion's reference to the number of amici as evidence that the Court had received all the input it needed to decide the constitutional issues "according to law."[129]

A lawyer who helped to coordinate amicus participation on the challengers' side in *Citizens United* told me that he believed that "how we handled the amici was very effective and really helped." As evidence of its impact, he noted that the Court's opinion "cited the raw number of amici; they cited a number of the particular briefs; they cited, for example, the former FEC commissioner's brief a couple of times; they cited the scholars' brief in talking about the history." All these claims are true. The majority opinion referred to the fifty-four amicus briefs filed in the case as evidence of its thorough consideration of the issues.[130] It cited an amicus brief by campaign finance scholars to support the claim that *Austin* had relied on a "flawed historical account of campaign finance laws" contained in a previous case.[131] It cited the amicus brief of seven former chairmen of the FEC to support the proposition that campaign finance regulations have become exceedingly complex.[132] It referred to a brief by the US Chamber of Commerce for the proposition that *Austin* "permits the Government to ban the political speech of millions of associations of citizens," most of which "are small corporations without large amounts of wealth."[133] The majority opinion also emphasized the burden that the regulations impose on small nonprofits such as *Citizens United*—a theme not only of Olson's brief but also of several amicus briefs. The narrowed definition of corruption adopted by the Court—only quid pro quo corruption (the exchange of money for political favors)—was one strongly advocated by Olson's brief, as well as the brief submitted by the US Chamber of Commerce.[134]

While lawyers for business groups might not accept all arguments advanced by lawyers for the Republican base or the anti-elitist sentiments underlying them, they welcome the litigation outcomes that this coalition has produced. A lawyer for a trade group noted that "the business community . . . is not all that interested as a general proposition" in the issue of campaign finance regulation; campaign finance "is kind of interesting but it's not a priority . . . to the extent that they like to spend money, they will do so for lobbying which they increasingly recognize as important because the government is so big and so intrusive, they've got to protect themselves." He nevertheless acknowledged that the alliance between business advocates and groups associated with other elements of the Republican coalition has yielded litigation results that his clients favored: "The cause elements are driven much more ideologically [than the business interests], and thank goodness for that. Sometimes they're like Don Quixote but the rest of the time they accomplish a lot of very good things in preserving freedom of speech and liberties." What this lawyer did not say was that lobbying and campaign finance sometimes operate in tandem and reinforce the influence of each.[135] An interviewed libertarian acknowledged the relationship: "Lobbying is far, far more of a force in really impacting what the law looks like at the end of the day, but campaign contributions are a kind of ticket to the ball. You don't get to talk to these guys or have any involvement in it if you're not on the campaign roster of donors."

The ACLU's involvement may also have been useful to the challengers' position. A civil libertarian noted that in the litigation, as in legislative battles over the BCRA, "Senator McConnell was always putting his arm around the ACLU. 'See—They're with me, okay?' "[136] While none of the interviewed lawyers claimed that the ACLU's position had actually influenced the justices' votes, several suggested that the ACLU's presence had influenced perceptions about the legitimacy of the Court's rulings. One reformer said that the Supreme Court's position on the doctrine might have happened "with or without the ACLU," but that the ACLU's participation in the case "allowed everybody to think that maybe this isn't just a coup by the powerful—maybe this is a principled defense of an important American value, and this is the way it's got to be if we're going to have free speech." Another said of the organization's involvement, "They're this very well-respected voice. You have these absolutely outrageous opinions. To the extent that the ACLU is partly endorsing, or endorsing some of it, that makes it easier to say . . . this is a legitimate understanding of the First Amendment." Other reformers said that the ACLU's involvement "gives [the Court] nice cover" and helps with the "optics" of the Roberts Court's campaign finance decisions. According to another, "having the ACLU on board is something that conservatives like to tout."

Lawyers on both sides of this litigation asserted that lawyer networks helped to facilitate cooperation within the challengers' coalition. The group of lawyers who are highly active in challenging campaign finance regulations is small. Many of the lawyers know each other and keep each other informed about developments and opportunities to cooperate. "It's not a very big bar, the campaign finance bar," one libertarian noted. "The groups that are really interested in campaign finance [on the challengers' side] are fairly few," another observed: "Jim Bopp is probably the biggest most well-known person, and then there's Brad Smith, Steve Hoersting . . . There are a handful of others. There are people at Cato; Ilya Shapiro has done some work on this and Trevor Burrus. Hans von Spakovsky at Heritage. Ted Olson was involved every once in a while . . . But in terms of the people who are ideologically interested in this . . . God, there is a pretty small group, and among the ideological groups, it's really small."[137]

Another challenger indicated that amicus participation in these cases is driven in large part by "the personal relationships of the lawyers." Commenting on the how differently situated groups within the GOP coalition were able to find common ground in *Citizens United*, one reformer speculated that it was "because it was the whole same group of lawyers." He explained: "You take somebody like Jim Bopp, he was on the RNC. Who was the [Chamber of Commerce's] chief counsel? It was [Steven] Law [who was] former chief of staff to Mitch McConnell. Who created Crossroads GPS? It was Steven Law." The chairman of Crossroads GPS was Bobby Burchfield, who represented Mitch McConnell in *Citizens United*. One reformer said of the lawyers who are coordinating this litigation campaign, "They're very much part of the McConnell [team]."

While the number of lawyers charting the litigation strategy may be small, these lawyers are active in larger networks that enable them to recruit broad amicus participation. One opponent of campaign finance regulation confirmed the importance of the Federalist Society as a site for mobilizing amicus participation in *Citizens United* and other major Supreme Court cases: "It's our group, where we network. It's a very valuable function the Society performs." Nineteen of the organizations that filed briefs in support of Citizens United's challenge had at least one lawyer with ties to the Federalist Society on the brief, lending some support to the notion that the network facilitated cooperation in the case.[138] The Federalist Society also provides links between the lawyers and the Supreme Court's conservatives. Four of the justices in the majority in *Citizens United*—Alito, Thomas, Roberts, and Scalia—have spoken at Federalist Society national conventions, and Scalia, Thomas, and Alito had/have long-standing ties to the organization.

## Conclusion

The alignments of groups and constituencies in *Citizens United* and other recent challenges to campaign finance regulation are indeed strange at first glance. But they seem much less strange, or only superficially strange, after taking into account the history of the participating groups, the political context in which the campaign unfolded, and the lawyer networks that facilitated cooperation. Even if this context makes the litigation coalition understandable, however, it remains puzzling in terms of the differing stakes for the participating groups. Some of the clients and constituencies have much more money to wield in politics than others and therefore seem more likely to benefit from the case outcomes. Resources tend to flow to the most powerful members of the litigation coalition and the elite lawyers who serve them. It is an unequal coalition even if it is not entirely strange.

# Different Constitutional Universes

The intent [of campaign finance law] really is to silence conservative voices.
INTERVIEW WITH CHALLENGER

I don't think the government has any business telling people what they can say, when they can say it, how they can say it, at what times, and in what volumes, wearing what color hat, and hopping on which leg . . . How about we just go with free speech?
INTERVIEW WITH CHALLENGER

The Roberts Court [is] giving us the Anatole France First Amendment, which means that the First Amendment in its majestic impartiality allows gigantic corporations and ordinary citizens alike to spend as much as they want electing their preferred candidates to office. And that's the vision of equality and of the First Amendment that we're left with. It is a completely sterile and formalistic view of rights and how they play out in our democracy, and it leaves people who don't have money, don't have immense aggregations of wealth that they can spend on politics . . . with less of a voice, and it leaves us with a system where . . . the strength of your voice depends on the size of your wallet. That's not what democracy is supposed to look like.
INTERVIEW WITH REFORMER

We have lost our way when it comes to analysis of campaign finance. We view it solely via the lens of the First Amendment, and we only look at the purported free-speech rights of the donor class, not the rest of the population, or 99 percent who don't participate in making contributions or expenditures in the political process and can't afford to . . . And that part of the population has, in our view, First Amendment rights and the right not to have their voices drowned out.
INTERVIEW WITH REFORMER

Frames and discourse are bound up with advocates' strategies, goals, and world views, and they are integral to the diffusion, competition, and institutionalization of ideas that drive the development of law. This chapter demonstrates how arguments and themes advanced in the early stages of the litigation have become entrenched and amplified in law and in the challengers' objections to regulating money in politics. Those frames have been useful in mobilizing the challengers' litigation coalition, and they have mostly prevailed in the courts. Reformers have struggled to find an alternative frame that passes muster with the Court's conservatives.

Chapter 1 highlighted a deep divide in the perspectives of the justices on the Roberts Court. This chapter shows that lawyers, advocacy organizations, and their patrons also project radically different perspectives. The differences go well beyond disagreements over policy. Just as the justices now seem to occupy "entirely different constitutional universes," reflecting "a country divided,"[1] the same is true of the lawyers who argue before them. As one challenger observed about the perspectives of the advocates in these cases, "there's this amazing dichotomy between these two worldviews."

The challengers characterized campaign spending as speech and regulation as censorship. Reformers acknowledged that regulating money in politics raises First Amendment concerns, but they claimed that regulation is required to protect competing and equally foundational constitutional values, including some found in the First Amendment itself. Lawyers for advocacy organizations generally expressed stronger views and used sharper rhetoric than did election law experts and appellate specialists working in private firms on behalf of candidates and parties. The latter category of lawyers typically offered more nuanced perspectives about what hangs in the balance, and some of them indicated doubts about what they viewed as the simplistic characterization of the issues by some lawyers employed by advocacy organizations. One said, "There's more consensus" among the DC election law experts, "which drives the grassroots crazy, on both sides."

The broad perspective that opponents of regulation have embraced, advanced, and rallied around is reflected in this statement by their longtime leader, Senator Mitch McConnell, in his memoir:

> Underneath my liberal colleagues' efforts to regulate political speech through campaign finance reform measures was the great, untested premise that the collision of private interests with politics is somehow inherently corrupting. But what they weren't (and still aren't) able to understand is that the opposite is true. A government that spends multi-trillions of dollars a year is big enough to take away everything we've got. In the face of something so powerful, of course the public would want to elect somebody they agree with, to influence the course of legislation. To the maximum extent possible, the government needs to stay out of the way of that process, allowing everyone who wants to speak—politicians included—to do so as loudly as possible. Despite the argument offered by the Left, limiting a candidate's speech does not level the playing field, it does the opposite. Like trying to place a rock on Jell-O, pushing down on one type of speech just raises that speech elsewhere, allowing someone else to control the discourse—the press, the billionaire, the special interests, the incumbent.[2]

McConnell's statement includes all the primary themes advanced by opponents of campaign finance regulation since the 1970s. It places speech and the interests of ordinary people in opposition to overreaching government and those who seek to stifle political expression.

## Frames, Discourse, and Constitutional Change

Policy advocates of all types employ conceptual frames and discourse to influence outcomes. A vast literature across disciplines explores how frames and discourse shape how individuals, institutions, movement activists, and policymakers make sense of events, define problems, and respond to them.[3] This literature helps to explain why social, political, and economic actors compete over the description of issues in the policy domain.[4] Rights frames sometimes promote collective action that is otherwise difficult to mobilize.[5] Abstract appeals to broad constitutional ideals can help political parties build and sustain electoral coalitions.[6]

Frames and discourse also influence the success of the political movements to which litigation campaigns are attached,[7] and they sometimes shape judicial outcomes indirectly by mobilizing popular support for particular readings of the Constitution.[8] Building on Murray Edelman's work on the role of symbols in politics,[9] Ken Kersch has observed that the conservative movement has been particularly attentive to "the power of constitution-talk."[10] He argues that constitutional narratives have been "the chief thematic touchstone of the modern conservative movement"[11] and that its claims of fidelity to the Constitution have helped to unify and motivate philosophically diverse elements.[12] Calvin TerBeek's research shows how different strands of conservatives have used ideas about the original meaning of the Constitution to build a political coalition around a shared cause—resisting liberal elites.[13] The strategic deployment of constitutional frames helps to explain how various constituencies of the Republican coalition, once generally hostile to free-speech claims, have come to embrace the First Amendment as they have renegotiated and reconstituted what qualifies as legally protected speech and association.[14]

Lawyers are active players in framing activity.[15] They often serve as influential "normative entrepreneurs" who disseminate new ideas that "shape the meaning of law."[16] Lawyers' training may make them especially well suited for this kind of work. What we call legal reasoning or "thinking like a lawyer" involves the skillful use of analogies and distinctions and the ability to manipulate conceptual frames and metaphors.[17] Courts have proven to be sensitive and responsive to how lawyers frame issues,[18] and frames advanced by lawyers influence decision-making in other policy arenas as well.[19] Once taken up by judges and incorporated into legal doctrine, those frames powerfully shape "our political imagination" through shared ideas about legitimate and illegitimate arrangements and understandings.[20]

Campaign finance law is full of evidence of the operation of frames and metaphors and disputes over their relevance and application. Most obviously, metaphor underlies the notion that spending unlimited amounts of money to sway an election is a form of constitutionally protected speech and that regulating such spending activity is a form of speech suppression. As we saw in chapter 2, this idea was relatively new when lawyers introduced it in the early 1970s.

Other metaphors operating in campaign finance law include the "free trade in ideas" concept advanced by Justice Oliver Wendell Holmes Jr.,[21] elaborated by Justice William O. Douglas as the "marketplace of ideas,"[22] and applied to campaign finance regulation by legal scholars and then by the Supreme Court in the 1970s.[23] It imagines ideas as commodities that are bought, sold, and traded in a competitive market.[24] The marketplace-of-ideas metaphor continues to shape the development of the doctrine, as lawyers and judges argue about the boundaries of permissible regulation. In *Citizens United*, for example, the Court found that its prior ruling in *Austin* "interfere[d] with the 'open marketplace' of ideas protected by the First Amendment,"[25] while the dissenting opinion argued that the prohibition on corporate spending on elections had instead protected "the integrity of the marketplace of political ideas."[26]

Metaphor is also at work in *Citizens United*'s holding that corporations are entitled to the same First Amendment protections as natural persons to spend unlimited amounts of money on elections. The Court found that denying corporations that right would constitute impermissible "viewpoint discrimination" based on the speaker's identity—government favoritism toward "certain preferred speakers."[27] (This argument links to claims made by Christian Right advocates that government actors engage in viewpoint discrimination when they fund secular speech but not religious speech.[28]) The dissenting opinion in *Citizens United* rejected the analogy, noting a variety of contexts in which laws differentiate between the speech rights of different types of speakers (students, prisoners, foreigners, soldiers, etc.). Dissenters accused the majority of advancing an extravagant critique of identity-based distinctions "without ever explaining why corporate identity demands the same treatment as individual identity."[29]

In *Arizona Free Enterprise Club v. Bennett*, the majority asserted that a governmental interest in "leveling the playing field" provided no justification for Arizona's public finance scheme because "campaigning for office is not a game" but rather "a critically important form of speech."[30] Justice Kagan's dissent modified the metaphor to reach the opposite conclusion. She argued that the Arizona legislature had responded to a political scandal involving "near-routine purchase of legislators' votes" with a statute designed to "sever political candidates' dependence on large contributors." Asserting that the law provided for "less corruption, more speech" and promoted "robust campaigns leading to the election of representatives not beholden to the few, but accountable to the many," she wrote that "the people of Arizona . . . deserve the chance to reform their electoral system so as to attain that most American of goals." She concluded: "Truly, democracy is not a game."[31]

Wrangling over the use and operation of frames and metaphor is also evident in the briefs filed in these cases and in the commentary of the interviewed lawyers. The competing frames reflected in these sources correspond with what other scholars have described as the divergent constitutional vocabularies of the major parties.[32] Some of what lawyers told me in interviews demonstrates how the lawyers use these frames strategically as they seek to shape policymaking in the courts. That is not to suggest that these actors do not believe in the positions they take and the conceptual categories they use. I am prepared to accept that they do believe in them. It is nevertheless important to consider the deeper logics that these patterns of discourse express and the strategic purposes they serve.[33]

### An "Unbridgeable Ideological Gulf"

Recall from chapter 1 that Robert Mutch identified what he called a "turning point in campaign finance cases"—the emergence of an "unbridgeable ideological gulf" between the majority and dissenting opinions in *Austin*. He observed that the dissents by Justices Scalia and Kennedy "took on a polemical tone that had not been evident in previous cases" and that they adopted rhetoric implying that regulators sought "the outright suppression of speech."[34] Mutch noted an increase in language suggesting that the challenged legislation would not just regulate money in politics but would "ban," "suppress," "silence," and "censor" speech itself.

Mutch did not attempt to document these claims, but I have done so by pulling simple word counts from raw text files of the opinions.[35] Those word counts confirm Mutch's assertion that there was an uptick in *Austin* in the use of language characterizing campaign finance regulation as a form of government censorship. The dissenters in *Austin* used forms of "censor," "ban," "suppress," "silence," and "chill" thirty-two times, while those words appeared

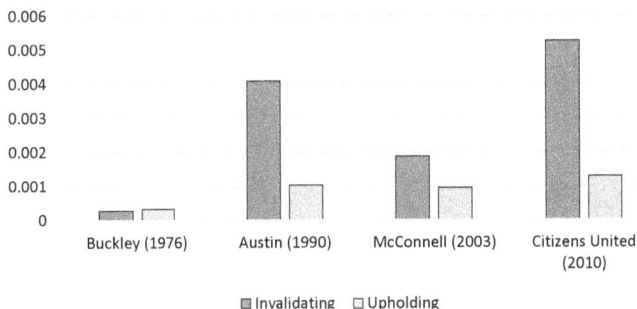

FIGURE 6.1. Frequency of use of variations of "ban," "chill," "suppress," "silence," and "censor" in opinions in four major Supreme Court cases, as a proportion of the words used by each side

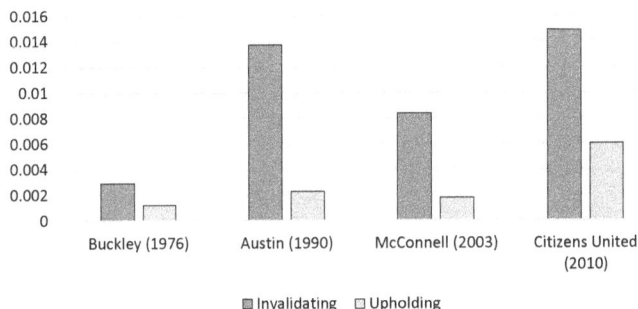

FIGURE 6.2. Frequency of use of variations of "speech," "speak," and "speaker" in opinions in four major Supreme Court cases, as a proportion of the words used by each side

only three times in the portions of *Buckley* that invalidated the contribution limits. In *McConnell*, the dissenting opinions by Justices Scalia, Thomas, Kennedy, and Rehnquist used those words forty-nine times. In *Citizens United*, Justice Kennedy's majority opinion and Justice Scalia's concurrence used them ninety times.

Figures 6.1 and 6.2 show the frequency of the use of censorship and speech language in the opinions across major cases, including *Buckley, Austin, McConnell,* and *Citizens United.* These figures distinguish between opinions that would uphold the challenged campaign finance restrictions and those that would strike them down.[36] The bars in the figures indicate the rate of use of these words—their frequency as a proportion of total words in the opinions for that "side" (either to uphold or to invalidate the challenged restriction). Figure 6.1 shows the frequency of use of forms of "ban," "chill," "suppress," "silence," and "censor" as a proportion of words used by each side. Figure 6.2 shows the frequency of use of forms of "speech," "speak," and "speaker" in

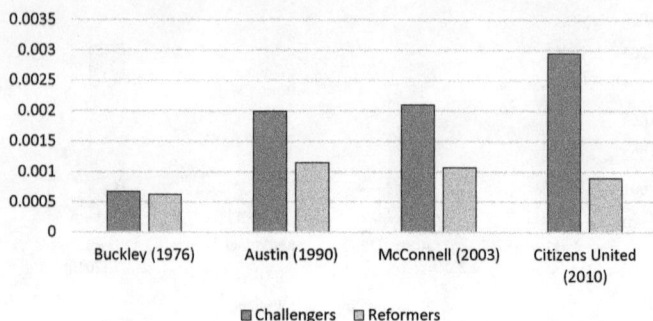

FIGURE 6.3. Frequency of use of variations of "ban," "chill," "suppress," "silence," and "censor" in party and amicus briefs in four major Supreme Court cases, as a proportion of the words used by each side

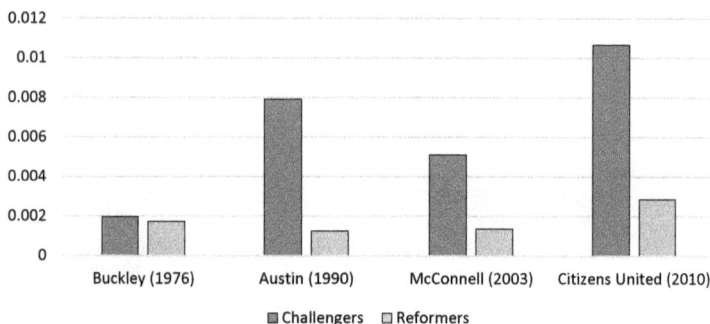

FIGURE 6.4. Frequency of use of variations of "speech," "speak," and "speaker" in party and amicus briefs in four major Supreme Court cases, as a proportion of the words used by each side

the same four rulings. The increased use of those words coincides with the conservative justices' fuller embrace of the idea that campaign spending not only facilitates political expression but *is* speech, and that restrictions on such spending constitute a form of censorship.

A similar analysis of the use of key words in party and amicus briefs in the same four cases sheds light on the competing frames deployed by lawyers and advocacy groups. Figure 6.3 shows the frequency in the appearance of forms of "ban," "chill," "suppress," "silence," and "censor" as a proportion of all words in the briefs for each side.

Using the same method to trace the use of other key words in briefs in these cases, figures 6.4 and 6.5 suggest that the challengers have leaned into the argument that campaign finance regulation interferes with "speech," "freedom," and "liberty." Some of the most strongly worded versions of these themes came from groups associated with the Republican base. One such brief filed in *Citizens United* warned of creeping government power and censorship and a quiescent public's failure to notice: "Since the enactment of the Tillman Act in 1907, Americans have witnessed the progressive decay of their security to speak their minds freely about contested political controversies ... Americans have not always been cognizant of their eroding liberties."[37] The petitioner's brief in the Arizona matching-funds case darkly insisted that "a fork in the road taken by our Republic . . . approaches yet again. Fiscally-engineered censorship must not stand."[38]

Applying the same type of analysis to the party and amicus briefs on the reformers' side, figure 6.6 suggests that reformers emphasized the language of "equality" in their briefs in *Buckley* but that they significantly downplayed that frame in subsequent cases. That change likely reflected a strategic choice to respond to the *Buckley* Court's emphatic rejection of the argument that an interest in promoting political equality would justify regulating money in politics.[39] This kind of analysis also shows that reformers have used forms of

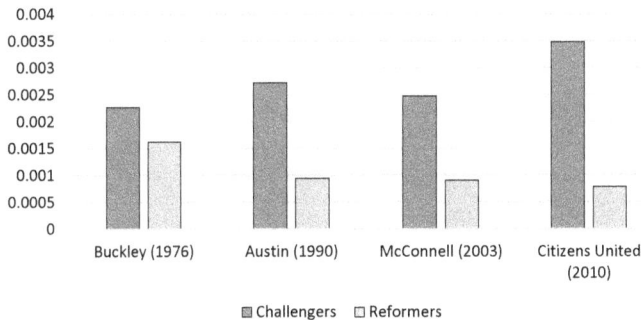

FIGURE 6.5. Frequency of use of "freedom" and "liberty" in party and amicus briefs in four major Supreme Court cases, as a proportion of the words used by each side

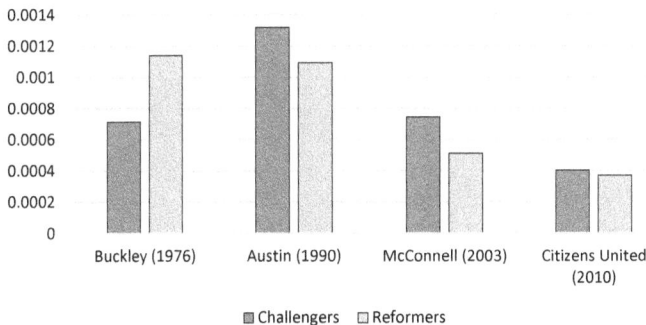

FIGURE 6.6. Frequency of use of "equal" and "equality" in party and amicus briefs in four major Supreme Court cases, as a proportion of the words used by each side

"influence," "integrity," and "democracy" more often than challengers have. However, it reveals no simple, powerful, emotive frame to rival the speech/ freedom/liberty frame relied on by opponents of regulation.

These analyses provide further evidence of how the claim that the Constitution protects campaign spending because it is speech has become assumed and embedded in law. They also suggest a relationship, though not necessarily a causal one, between the discourse of the justices and the language used by lawyers.[40]

In the interviews, the challengers and reformers used differing frames to describe their perspectives on the stakes of the campaign finance cases. In broad strokes, the challengers equated money in politics with speech and liberty, and campaign finance restrictions with censorship and repression. They expressed skepticism about government and deep mistrust of liberal elites. The reformers envisioned an essential and positive role for government in promoting fair elections, democracy, and political equality. They worried about the consequences of allowing wealthy individuals and institutions to translate economic power into political power. In the context of litigation, reformers needed to shoehorn their concerns into the corruption framework established by the Supreme Court's rulings and to steer clear of political equality arguments.[41] But in interviews, where they were free of the constraints of the doctrine and the need to disguise their true concerns, political equality was the dominant theme. Reformers conveyed deep frustration with the limitations of existing doctrine and emphasized the need for new theories and revised application of the metaphors to better protect the political process.

At a very crude level, these differences are captured in simple counts of the words used by the lawyers in interviews. The challengers used variations of "speech," "speak," or "speaking" almost twice as often as the reformers (429 versus 242), and they used "liberty" and "freedom" four times as frequently (79 versus 26). Reformers used "equal" and "equality" almost five times as often as challengers (88 versus 16) and "democracy" six times as often (114 versus 19).

These differences in discourse were all the more noteworthy in light of the substantial agreement among the interviewed lawyers about the direct consequences of the Roberts Court's campaign finance rulings. They did not offer "alternative facts" about the direct effects.[42] They mostly agreed, for example, that *Citizens United* had not generated a flood of direct corporate spending on elections; that the Court's finding that independent spending cannot be limited by Congress has given largely unregulated super PACs and lightly regulated 501(c) organizations a dominant role in elections; and that most of the money contributed thus far to super PACs has come from wealthy individuals, who have long been legally permitted to make unlimited independent expenditures in connection with elections under the *Buckley* framework.[43] But challengers and reformers offered very different perspectives about the broader consequences and implications of these rulings.

## The Challengers' Discourse

Challengers portrayed themselves as champions of free speech, with the simplest declarations coming from lawyers associated with conservative advocacy organizations and think tanks. Their commentary included frequent references to government censoring, restricting, controlling, silencing, limiting, and sanctioning speakers. An advocate for social-conservative groups stated that "to limit money in politics is simply to limit communication or limit speech. It's very simple and very straightforward, and very true. And there's simply no refutation of that . . . If you're limiting money, you're limiting speech." A lawyer employed by a libertarian think tank said of the stakes in *Citizens United*: "This is an issue of free speech versus government control and ultimately censorship. [The case was about] whether government can restrict or control what people are able to say about politics." A lawyer with ties to gun-rights and Tea Party groups described campaign finance regulations in one blue state this way: "You can't say a word. You can't even think about saying anything, or spending a dime, without being subject to egregious, oppressive, burdensome regulation." The same lawyer asserted that the holding in *Citizens United* "has freed people—organizations like the NRA, or other issue organizations—to be able to speak on behalf of their members at election time without fear of being sanctioned or fined." A lawyer who has represented Republican Party leaders in several campaign finance cases described the BCRA as "the most sweeping effort to limit public discourse since the Alien and Sedition Act." Challengers used similar speech-and-liberty language to describe the implications of the laws challenged in *Arizona Free Enterprise Club v. Bennett* and *McCutcheon v. FEC*.

The challengers' commentary was full of allusions to the government as an invader and tyrant. A lawyer with ties to the Tea Party movement said that "you have lobbying, and you have political contributions at the magnitude you do because government is invading every asset and corner of our lives . . . So, the conservative solution to money in politics is the free solution. Get government out of our lives and out of businesses, and you will radically reduce the amount of money in the political system." A lawyer for a think tank offered a view that was typical of interviewed libertarians: "If access and influence are a problem, they are a problem because of the size and scope of government. What we're concerned about is the government is going to hand out favors that it shouldn't be handing out, or it's going to be doling out punishment to people who should not be punished." Another libertarian called arguments about money in politics a "distraction" because "we need to get to the fundamental question, 'What should our government do?'"—to which his answer was that it should do very little.

Echoing arguments offered by Ralph Winter in the 1970s, some challengers stressed how political actors can use regulation cynically for strategic political advantage. A lawyer for a trade group asserted that the "accommodations and compromises" made as part of the legislative process to regulate campaign finance "jigger the system . . . usually to the perceived benefit or detriment of certain participants." A lawyer for one of the specialized groups on the challengers' side explained that "when you watch what happens at the FEC, you can't help but recognize that the vast majority of complaints have nothing to do with corruption or access . . . They have to do with 'this will hinder my opponent in this race.' That's what these things are primarily used for." A lawyer who specialized in work for Republican candidates and party committees described what lies "behind the constitutional arguments" on both sides: Republicans sometimes say, " 'Oh, this benefits us. Let's keep it the way it is,' " while Democrats advocate for rulings that benefit them: "And both sides seem to want to look toward God and say, 'Isn't this the right thing for mankind?' "

Some challengers agreed with reformers that there is an important role for government in enforcing campaign finance disclosure requirements. One such lawyer explained that "the public has the right to know, and that's relevant to their exercising the right to vote, and to the public debate—who is supporting you." But many of the cause lawyers asserted that disclosure is *all* that is required to ensure the integrity of the process because disclosure gives voters all they need to get the government they deserve.[44]

Several lawyers argued that there is *no* role whatsoever for government regulation of money in politics. One libertarian advocated giving campaign contributions the same constitutional protection as expenditures and lifting all other campaign finance restrictions: we "should criminalize bribery, purchasing of favors, that sort of thing, and that's it." Another lawyer characterized the concession that other challengers make for disclosure requirements as an unnecessary "compromise." A third libertarian asserted that anyone lawfully within the United States, whether a citizen or not, should be allowed to freely spend money and make contributions in US elections because "campaigns are just public debates, and people should be allowed to freely engage in persuasion in those debates." He called the Supreme Court's summary affirmance of the lower court ruling in *Bluman v. Federal Election Commission*, rejecting a First Amendment challenge to the ban on foreign campaign finance activity in US elections, "absolutely appalling." In response to my question about what role government should have in regulating money in politics, another lawyer with strong Tea Party ties responded, "What is hard to understand about the first five words of the First Amendment: 'Congress shall make no law'? I mean, I don't think the government should have a role." This bold "plain meaning" claim sits uneasily with an observation by Robert Bork in his famous 1971 law review article on originalism discussed in chapter 2. Bork argued that reading the First Amendment as an absolute prohibition on any governmental restraint on any form of verbal communication "is, of course, impossible." He added that "laymen may perhaps be forgiven for thinking that the literal words of the amendment command complete absence of governmental inhibition upon verbal activity, but what can one say of lawyers who believe any such thing?"[45]

The challengers' commentary in interviews incorporated many of the metaphors, analogies, and arguments first used in the campaign finance context in the early 1970s, including frequent references to the marketplace of ideas.[46] Challengers also frequently invoked arguments made in Ralph Winter's AEI pamphlets about the equivalence of money and other types of resources that people use to influence elections and that are unequally distributed in society, such as organizing skills and celebrity.[47]

Cause lawyers on the challengers' side suggested that campaign finance regulations reflected an effort by liberals to stifle conservative dissent. One said: "I don't really understand the arguments against [*Citizens United*]. I don't understand what they're afraid of. They're not getting shouted down . . . They're the ones that have the dominant social positions . . . So, for any of these people on the Left to say, 'Oh we're getting shouted down by the billionaires.' You're not getting shouted down by the billionaires; you're shouting down everyone else!" A lawyer with ties to Tea Party–affiliated groups characterized campaign finance laws as "an entire regulatory apparatus that is bent upon silencing certain voices."

Reprising Winter's argument about the liberal bias of reformers and those who control the media, challengers disparaged campaign finance rules that allow media companies to use corporate dollars to publish editorials that influence elections but prevent other types of corporations (before *Citizens United*) from using their corporate treasuries to do the same. Explaining his suspicions about reformers' motivations, an opponent of regulation asked, "Why don't they want to limit the media? Is it because the media is liberals? . . . Is that why?" Another lawyer who described himself as a "Republican with a libertarian bent" asserted that any system of campaign finance regulation that gives the media special protection is problematic:

> The government . . . should not reduce access to freedom of speech for anybody. And it should not be trying to measure influence . . . If you're going to do that game, okay, so what restrictions are you going to place on the *New York Times*? What restrictions are you then going to place on NBC? And what restrictions are you going to place on CBS? Because they're the ones having the influence, much more than anybody else in our society. So, when the people are talking about access and influence, those are the folks—if you're not talking about them, you're not making any sense if that's what you're saying you're concerned about.

He explained that he has "a big problem with the state of America's media" because it "tends to be . . . controlled primarily by the Democrat Party."

Some challengers mocked those who complain about spending by "outside" groups and the attitude reflected in the very use of this label. One characterized it this way: "So we shouldn't speak, only the candidates, this is their election. We just sit and listen." Another challenger ventured that this term conveyed a perspective about who should control elections: "To call a citizen an 'outsider' in self-government is absurd, it's an oxymoron," because it demonstrates "that the person who's calling a citizen an outsider has a whole different form of government in mind." He emphasized that citizens should control government so that it works for them, not for government bureaucrats: "Our form of government is self-government where citizens are deciding between themselves who is to temporarily be their representative to exercise limited governmental authority."

When I indicated that I wanted to better understand why there was not more resentment about the advantage that wealthy and powerful interests within the GOP might hold in intraparty struggles based on their greater financial resources, another lawyer who described himself as "an outsider" responded: "There's a *lot* of resentment about it. We in the grassroots base—there's enormous discomfort with what is perceived as the Republican political establishment that is very well funded and does the bidding of and is perceived to do the bidding of well-funded special interests." But he told me that he and others like him put their faith in their voting power, rather than regulation, to wage that fight, which he called "part of this broader establishment versus grassroots battle that's going on in the conservative movement."[48]

This lawyer argued that the Freedom Caucus crowd does not need campaign finance reform to win its battle with the Republican establishment: "People who live and espouse our values, who are uncorruptible, are being attacked

by those that are probably not corrupted or corruptible but . . . they're not seen
as responsive to the population . . . The solution to that problem is not regulations on money; it's voting." Referring to the 2016 presidential race, he observed
that "the base [didn't] like Jeb Bush" and that they used information about campaign contributions he received from wealthy donors as one of the reasons to
reject him in favor of candidates who better represented their priorities:

> The grassroots conservative audience . . . see[s] this, and because it's trans-
> parent, it's reported, they look at it and say "You know what? This guy is not
> for me. He's beholden." They'll say, "I see where this money is coming from.
> I don't like it, and I'm going to vote for somebody else." . . . That is exactly
> the purpose of transparency, and so that I think is fantastic. They'll look at
> Ted Cruz, who raised about half as much, but they see him raising that from
> small-dollar donors and obviously the Mercers or whoever else the big mon-
> ey's coming from, and they say, "Well, you know what? I don't know if I like
> Rand Paul or Ted Cruz or Scott Walker, but I definitely don't like Jeb Bush."

(Chapter 8 discusses the interviewed lawyers' competing perspectives about
the factual basis for this lawyer's confidence in the transparency of money in
politics.)

When pressed on whether a different type of concern might justify campaign finance regulation—that big donors might exert outsized influence on
the positions that candidates take once elected—this lawyer acknowledged
that this possibility might be a reason to worry. But he saw this issue less as a
problem about big money in politics and more as one "about cronyism—that
tends to be the bigger concern." When asked about how big money in politics
might relate to cronyism, he asserted that the constituencies he represents see
access and influence as a feature of the political system but not necessarily
a problem, paraphrasing Justice Roberts's opinion in *McCutcheon*:[49] "It's not
that [the Republican grassroots] don't think that access is okay. So, *they* just
want that access. Good for them. Everybody should be able to have as much
access, as much constitutionally protected, non-corrupting ingratiation and
access as they can afford. I'm a very big believer in that."

This comment seemed to go to the heart of one of the puzzles of my research: why the Republican base would support unlimited money in politics when doing so would seem to put them at a disadvantage in intraparty
struggles over policy. So I pressed on:

SOUTHWORTH: So, the point about crony capitalism. You're saying, God
bless you if you can get more—if you've got the money to spend, to get
more access and influence . . .

LAWYER: Constitutionally protected non-corrupting ingratiation and access.
SOUTHWORTH: So, that means?
LAWYER: It's a very specific term.
SOUTHWORTH: I want to understand that better. So, it means?
LAWYER: It means the Supreme Court has said you have a constitutional right to make contributions to candidates with which you are comfortable. That it's entirely reasonable that you, as a donor, will acquire—you'll gain ingratiation. They'll be grateful to you. And, you'll have access to talk to them. That's it. It's constitutionally protected, non-corrupting ingratiation and access.
SOUTHWORTH: Right. . . . But you approve . . . ?
LAWYER: Look, I mean . . . Like it or lump it, this is the system that we have. And, the Supreme Court has said that you're entitled to constitutionally protected non-corrupting ingratiation and access. That's law. And I agree with it. And conveniently enough, it's a law. If I didn't agree with it, it's still the law. And, if I agree with it and they rule the other way, well, I'm in the wrong, because that's the law. So, I tend to . . . But I really, even when I disagree, this is the system in which we live. And, if you want to change it, that's what our constitutional amendments are for.
SOUTHWORTH: But it's partly law you helped create. Right?
LAWYER: Yeah, I know . . .

This exchange seemed to suggest that Justice Roberts's assertion in *McCutcheon* that "ingratiation and access . . . are not corruption"[50] featured prominently in this lawyer's own account of the policy implications of the ruling. It also suggested that he was comfortable with the role that the challengers have played in winning the Supreme Court's approval of the idea that influence and access acquired through spending on elections is not a problem justifying regulation. He believed that those who would regulate money in politics inevitably harm those they purport to protect. He also disparaged what he saw as the patronizing attitude of those who support campaign finance regulation: "Clearly, you're dumb, you're voting the way of the last TV ad you saw. We have to stop this; we have to protect you from these bad ideas."

Another lawyer with strong ties to Tea Party candidates and populist groups expressed a similar suspicion of those who would regulate money in politics to protect the average voter. This lawyer said that "99.9 percent" of people who support campaign finance regulation "are Democrats who think that business is bad, and their job is to protect the little people" without recognizing that "it's the little people who get harmed because you have these oppressive regulatory regimes, and little people can't participate." This lawyer continued: "If you're wealthy, you can pretty much do what you want. But if you're not wealthy and you want to pool your resources with like-minded others, good luck to you. Good luck to you being able to do it without hiring somebody like me."

Some challengers characterized efforts to regulate contributions and expenditures as evidence of a failure to understand the importance of elections and politics. One said: "I don't know why you'd want to [get money out of politics]. It's really important to the governance of our local, state, and federal government. I'd much rather people be spending their money and their time on those issues than buying more potato chips or other things." The observation that Americans spend more on potato chips and other frivolous consumer items than they do on elections, and the argument that this failure to spend more on politics reflects misplaced priorities, has been circulating since at least the mid-1990s. It appears to have originated with, or to have been amplified by, leaders of the deregulatory effort. In a 1995 Cato publication, Brad Smith wrote, "Total direct campaign spending for all local, state, and federal elections, including Congress, over the same period can be reasonably estimated at between $1.5 billion and $2.0 billion, or somewhere between $7.50 and $10 per eligible voter. . . . By comparison, Americans spent two to three times as much money in 1994 alone on the purchase of potato chips."[51] In 1997, another Cato publication noted that "as a society, we spend more on potato chips, Barbie dolls, yogurt and a host of other commodities than we do on politics. While many of us may like Barbie dolls and potato chips more than we like politics, only politics has control over every aspect of our lives."[52] Around the same time, a letter to the *Washington Post* complained about Senator Mitch McConnell's "favorite parallel" between the amounts Americans spend on electoral campaigns and the sums they spend on potato chips.[53] McConnell has invoked the potato chip comparison frequently in subsequent public comments.[54]

Some challengers doubted whether it is even possible to regulate campaign finance, reprising Winter and Bolton's argument in the 1970s that "truly effective" limits on campaign spending are "not feasible"[55] and Lillian BeVier's assertion in the 1980s that campaign finance regulation has "never worked, and it never will work."[56] One libertarian asserted that "you're never going to get money out of politics." A lawyer for several candidates and party committees said that the Supreme Court's rulings "are important in that they reset the rules" but that "realistically I think that money finds a way whatever the rules are." Another challenger reported that he shares some of the reformers' concerns but nevertheless believes that "in the end . . . efforts to regulate do not work"—that "these laws [don't] really make a difference" and "just gum up the works." Endorsing what some have called the "hydraulic" theory of campaign finance,[57] a libertarian asserted that "when you clamp down on money in one place, it tends to pop up someplace else." (This argument is essentially the same as Mitch McConnell's rock-on-Jell-O analogy, quoted earlier in this chapter.)

Many challengers characterized their opponents in the fight over campaign finance regulation, and the Left in general, as weak defenders of speech and the Constitution. One said, "We're reaching a point now where I can say, the Democrat Party and the Left—they're against all the Bill of Rights. They're really not in favor of freedom of speech these days, and they're not in favor of the First Amendment, the Second Amendment, the Fifth Amendment, the Tenth Amendment, the Ninth Amendment. Which ones are they still in favor of?" The same lawyer asserted that the Left "[doesn't] want businesses to be able to say anything about how you regulate them or what you take away from them, how you tax them, and they don't want their participation in economic policy debates at all." Even the ACLU, he said, had become weak on the Bill of Rights:

> They pick and choose, based on the politics of the situation. So in some periods of time, they're in favor of extreme versions of freedom of speech, such as applying the concept to nude dancing, and things like that . . . pornography. And other times, when the politics turned against freedom of speech, they seemed to go with the politics. And then, the Second Amendment, they were not really in favor of the Second Amendment. They didn't seem to ever really be in favor of freedom on that issue. And property rights, they were not really interested in defending. They weren't in favor of freedom on those issues.

The same lawyer indicated that the Left, unlike the Right, waffles about whether to prioritize equality or speech: "This idea that there's a conflict between equality and freedom of speech . . . That's an issue on the Left. That's not an issue anywhere on the Right." Another asserted that as "the influence of ACLU liberals has waned in the Democratic Party," liberals have become "much more totalitarian in their approach to speech, and now they're running all over the country trying to shut up everybody that doesn't think exactly like they think and talk exactly like they talk." The same lawyer raised campus speech and "this micro-aggression thing" as evidence of liberals' lack of commitment to free speech. He questioned my sanity—asking, "Are you crazy?"—for teaching in a public university, given "all these speech codes, and micro-aggressions, and . . . people being brought up on charges for correcting [students' failure to] compl[y] with standard English."

Several civil libertarians on the challengers' side commented on what they characterized as a retreat by liberals from free-speech principles, but they also indicated some discomfort in finding themselves in league with conservatives on the issue of campaign finance regulation. One recalled wistfully a time when he believed there was "complete alignment between general liberal views about American society and who the good guys and the bad guys were, in terms of presidents and the like, and First Amendment principles." He regretted that among liberals, there were just a "few hardy souls" who shared his views.

The most heated rhetoric about the perils of government regulation of money in politics came from lawyers representing nonprofit advocacy groups associated with the Republican base, while lawyers who handled campaign finance cases on behalf of paying clients and those who handled the oral arguments generally used milder language and offered more nuanced perspectives about the competing stakes.[58] Essential differences in perspective contributed to "tension between the grassroots and the institutional players on both sides," one DC-based election law expert explained: "The grassroots really just does see the republic falling, and just does not care about the details on both sides and just wants to have a knockdown, nuclear exchange on this . . . The people who do this day in and day out see the complexities, understand what's at stake, and that you can't have a nuclear exchange and expect anything good to come of it, and that if you do have one and win, it's completely ephemeral because no one's going to consider it legitimate in the long run." The same lawyer complained about "demagoguery on both sides."

## The Reformers' Discourse

There was no simple word or phrase that summed up the reformers' position in a way comparable to how speech serves as a shorthand for the challengers' position. In their briefs, reformers focused on concerns about corruption, as defined by the Roberts Court in *Citizens United* to include only quid pro quo corruption—the trading of cash for votes—because that is the only justification for government regulation of money in politics now accepted by the Court.[59] But in interviews, where they were free from the constraints of existing doctrine, reformers spoke more expansively about what they believed was necessary to protect American democracy. They described the quid pro quo definition of corruption as ridiculously narrow. As one reformer put it, "the idea that you need quid pro quo exchange, quid pro quo corruption, in order to justify campaign finance laws is absurd, because no one has to say anything in this process . . . and no one does." Reformers referred to a broader conception of corruption—systemic corruption—that includes special access to policymakers and influence over policymaking by major donors. They also talked about political equality—a rationale for regulating that the Supreme Court rejected in *Buckley* and again in *Citizens United* and *McCutcheon*. This ideal, several noted, was a constitutional value that the Court's recent decision in *Shelby County v. Holder* (2013) undercut when it struck down a provision of the Voting Rights Act of 1965 designed to ensure that state and local governments did not adopt laws and policies that would deny black Americans an equal right to vote.[60]

The reformers characterized American democracy and elections as vulnerable systems requiring protection from those who would harm or co-opt or undermine them. They agreed with the Roberts Court that one of the threats that government must guard against is quid pro quo corruption. But they insisted that other such threats include efforts by wealthy individuals and corporations to translate economic power into political power through election spending and efforts to preserve and build upon their advantages through the actions and acquiescence of beholden politicians. In a comment that was typical, one reformer said, "Government has the principal responsibility of safeguarding our democracy and preventing it from being turned into a plutocracy."

Some reformers explicitly endorsed the political-equality rationale that the Court has rejected as a justification for campaign finance regulation. One said, "I think it is not only the government's role; I think it's the government's *duty* to intervene, to try to retain some rough sense of political equality in the country." Several reformers linked voting rights and campaign finance. "One of the fundamental tenets of democracy is one person, one vote," one said, "and I don't consider that to be strictly limited to one person only being able to cast one ballot in the ballot box. I consider the effectiveness of a vote to be much broader than that, and what we have today is a system in which the wealthy really run the show around elections." Another reformer recalled an inspiring speech by a civil rights activist who said [paraphrasing], " 'We have fought and died for the right to vote, but what good is that right if we do not have candidates to vote for?' " This lawyer insisted that "getting private money out of politics is the unfinished business of the voting rights movement" and essential for protecting "the political equality principles that are embedded in the promise of one person, one vote." Taking direct aim at doctrine going back to *Buckley*, another reformer said: "The Supreme Court has really pushed hard on this idea that equality is not a legitimate concern when it comes to campaign finance . . . even though I think most people would probably disagree with that."

Reformers also uniformly rejected the notion that business corporations should hold the same First Amendment rights as individual persons. This comment was typical:

> I think that government can appropriately . . . limit participation in politics to human beings. . . . I don't think that needs to include entities that are created for economic purposes to amass wealth as participants in a market economy. I don't think they need to be privileged with the ability to deploy that as if they were flesh and blood people, or even coalitions or membership groups of flesh and blood people. I think that the idea that a corporation that is organized to be in business is, for First Amendment purposes, indistinguishable from a human being is not correct. And I think one area where it's legitimate to treat them differently is in political participation.

"Yes, corporations deserve some constitutional protections," another reformer said. "But there are reasons governments can regulate their speech in ways that they can't regulate individual speech." Government regulated election spending by corporations "for decades and decades and decades" before *Citizens United* because such spending "was not viewed as consistent with basic democracy." Calling the notion that commercial corporations should have the right to spend unlimited amounts in elections "extreme" and "dangerous to the republic," another reformer said that the idea that "the very selection process that determines who shall govern in America [could be] influenced by these artificial creatures that we actually set up, we are supposed to control, not the other way around" feels "very much like a Frankenstein-type movie; we created these artificial creatures, and now they were coming in and dominating our very democratic process and destroying our government."

Some reformers suggested that effective messaging by conservative advocacy groups explained how they had managed to enlist groups associated with the GOP grassroots in a broader assault on campaign finance regulation. One said that mistrust of government "gets inflamed by these conservative groups that are very good at packaging the message that it's government [overreach] . . . 'You better keep them away from my guns, keep them away from my speech.'" The same lawyer said that some voters do not see how campaign finance relates to their everyday lives except that they know that they "want the First Amendment right to say whatever I want to say." He wished that he could convince them that campaign finance reform posed no threat to core speech rights and that the mechanisms of political influence used by moneyed interests bear little similarity to the types of political expression available to the average voter. He wanted to explain that "nobody's trying to take away your right to stand on a street corner and scream and do all that" but that such forms of individual citizen speech are "not going to get [you] a commercial at the Super Bowl" and other types of influence that big money can buy: "All your screaming and yelling about an issue, or discussing, or debating, or going to town hall meetings [does not matter] . . . The reason that you don't get a real debate is because, frankly, corporate lobbyists generally don't feel the need to go to those meetings because that's not where the decisions are being made." Another reformer agreed that "it's the distrust of government that really underlies so much of it," explaining: "It's like, . . . 'This is our last bastion of freedom here, our ability to participate in politics and to speak using our money and our contributions . . . If you allow any regulation of it, it's going to be abused—it's going be used to suppress speech.'" One reformer asserted that this anti-government sentiment explained why some lawyers and groups claiming to represent the base joined in arguing that business corporations should enjoy First Amendment rights to engage in unlimited campaign spending: "The MCFL exception was for nonprofits, and so why did you have to extend that to all corporations? Why isn't that sufficient? . . . because that's *government*."

When reformers spoke of the stakes of these cases, some modified the speech metaphor to emphasize the need to ensure that the voices of ordinary citizens are heard. Commenting on the argument made by privately financed candidates in the Arizona case—that free-speech principles prevented the government from providing matching funds to those who participate in a voluntary public financing system—one reformer said, "Yeah, you have a right to speak. You don't have the right to be the *only* speaker . . . the only voice out there." Another reformer insisted that public financing systems like Arizona's resulted in more speech, not less: "Public financing is a way to ensure that candidates who are supported by a broad cross section of the community have a chance to get their message out."

Several reformers insisted that some of the challengers and the Supreme Court's conservatives embraced an excessively narrow and misleading interpretation of the First Amendment. One explained:

> I've always thought that the First Amendment serves a larger purpose in preserving our democracy than simply guaranteeing free speech for everybody . . . I think it also was intended to serve as a sort of fundamental building block of the democratic process. And so, I'm not a First Amendment absolutist who believes that any government regulation of speech, even through the proxy of money, is necessarily inconsistent with First Amendment values. If in fact there's enough of a demonstration that government regulation is needed in order to maintain a democratic structure, that certain voices don't

overwhelm other voices and don't discourage participation . . . I think that that can constitute a compelling interest to allow the government to regulate . . . in a modest way and limited fashion.

Another lawyer emphasized that "the First Amendment is found on both sides of the equation, so you can't say that the Court is pro–First Amendment and the Court's critics are anti–First Amendment."[61] A reformer disapproved of "the tendency to apply the First Amendment as a literal statement that you take out of context, and you sort of give an open-ended pass to anybody who's purportedly speaking . . . That's not necessarily the way that our Constitution was designed to work. It was a total document, and that document is supposed to preserve democratic integrity. And if the speech is out of control, and of course calling money speech is a huge step, but if it's out of control, then that's not consistent with the Constitution taken as a whole." He called this "a huge point," adding: "There are people who follow literally words written on a page . . . It may not be all deliberate, but they don't understand the context, and if you don't . . . if you do that, you get the wrong answer sometimes."

On the reformers' side, as on the challengers' side, there were differences in professional orientations and rhetoric. But the range was narrower on the reform side, perhaps reflecting the greater similarity in these lawyers' professional training and backgrounds.[62] Reformers in private practice generally offered more moderate views and used more temperate rhetoric than those in advocacy organizations, although some of the most passionate criticism of the Roberts Court's rulings came from a lawyer in private practice who had spent time in government on the enforcement side. Several lawyers in advocacy organizations on the reform side acknowledged the serious First Amendment implications of regulating campaign finance. One such reformer described the relationship between money and speech as "complicated." He explained: "I don't think the money is speech thing is all that simple. I actually think that Stevens, who says, 'Money is property, it's not speech'—I actually think that's an over-simplification."[63] He added, however, that "the idea that if you have more money in society, you get more speech, that can't be right. That's *not* complicated. I know that's wrong, and now the hard part is figuring out what exactly is the right relationship and how you define it." Another reformer said that he recognized that there are "lots of problems" with regulating campaign finance and that there are "no simple answers to such things as where do you divide the line on speech—what's political speech, what's not?" But he felt sure that in a representative democracy, "government should be able to regulate, within limits, the money used in politics."

## Polarized Constitutional Discourse

Differences in the discourse used by reformers and challengers reflect their immersion in different sets of legal elites with differing claims about the meaning of the Constitution. (Recall from chapter 1 that fifteen of the twenty-six interviewed challengers described themselves as active in the Federalist Society.) The differences in the discourse used by reformers and challengers also reflect a larger phenomenon in American politics—how Republicans and conservatives have developed a distinctive constitutional vocabulary since the 1970s and have claimed to care more about the Constitution than liberals and Democrats do. Some legal scholars have argued that the two parties have developed "fundamentally different" constitutional agendas since the end of the Warren Court in 1969,[64] and that the parties have become "more *constitutionally* coherent and distinct over the past several decades."[65] Over the same period, social scientists have traced how conservative jurists and intellectuals have embraced and redefined (some say, "coopt[ed]")[66] the protection of expressive rights. Using computational text analysis to investigate the ideological and partisan structure of constitutional discourse outside the courts, Pozen, Talley, and Nyarko have provided empirical support for some of these claims.[67] Their analyses demonstrate that constitutional discourse has become increasingly polarized over the past four decades and that conservatives have driven much of the increase. They argue that the conservative movement's embrace of constitutional discourse and its development of a distinctive partisan rhetoric about the meaning of the Constitution explains how they have come to "own" not only terms associated with originalism and the framers but also particular constitutional provisions, including the First Amendment.[68]

The polarization of constitutional discourse is obviously linked to related phenomena already discussed: the increased polarization of electoral constituencies and political parties and their elites.[69] Some scholars have suggested that the fact that Republicans/conservatives and Democrats/liberals speak different constitutional languages may contribute to the problem of interparty hostility.[70] The commentary of the interviewed lawyers shows evidence of their immersion in polarized networks of activists who champion different visions of the First Amendment, and it reveals considerable friction between opposing sides.[71]

The full set of lawyers who filed amicus or party briefs in *Citizens United* and *McCutcheon* was politically sorted; the overwhelming majority on the challengers' side made political contributions exclusively or primarily to Republicans, while those on the reform side strongly favored Democrats.[72] The

same was true of the interviewed lawyers; just four of the challengers identified as Democrats, and just one reformer called himself a Republican.[73] I
did not ask the lawyers about whether partisan motivations influenced their
advocacy, but several interviewed lawyers addressed the point. Several libertarians emphasized their groups' independence from the major parties. One
explained that it was very important to his organization's success to "keep
an arm's length relationship with politicians and politics" since its "forte is
representing individual Americans in challenging government regulations,
not helping the Republicans, the Democrats or anybody else." But several
lawyers thought that partisan social identity contributed to the alignments
of some organizations in these cases. One reformer attributed the position
of groups associated with the Republican base not only to their "receiving
support from . . . moneyed networks" but also to how "the issue has become
partisan and polarized." Another reformer said that the alignments are "very
much just a matter of people want[ing] to support their side." A challenger
agreed that "there is a sort of political battle component" to disagreements
over campaign finance regulation, with "the two major parties aligning on
different sides . . . it's just something culturally in the country; without even
thinking about the issues, people feel like they know which side they're on
based on what party they belong to."

Some interviewed cause lawyers displayed mistrust toward lawyers and
constituencies on the other side of these cases. One reformer described the
worldview he ascribed to some of the challengers as "absurd." He added:
"Something that I may perceive as being a reasonable effort to force somebody to come clean and disclose, limit in some manner, the conservatives
generally see as big bad government coming in and stifling speech, and it's
like everything is really viewed through that lens." Another reformer commented on why Tea Party voters, whose message is that "elites have stolen the
country from the common man," nevertheless voted for Donald Trump, a
rich guy who has used his wealth to exercise political influence. He attributed
the phenomenon to a "weird, paranoid" perspective that "a lot of them have"
and that Trump has exploited. Still another reformer said of the willingness
of the Republican base to support the deregulation of money in politics that
"some of [these people] . . . are so stupid, are such dupes. They believe [in
deregulation] because that's what they've been told to believe." Referring to
the current Republican leadership, another lawyer said that he had done bipartisan work on campaign finance "until these jokers came along."

Some challengers expressed similar suspicion about reformers and the
constituencies with which they are associated. One lawyer for several Tea
Party–affiliated groups observed that "there's an element on the Left that

doesn't want to hear from anybody that disagrees with them. It's like, 'Shut them down!' . . . And why are we using this term 'liberals' when they're really not liberal at all on anything except spending other people's money?" Another challenger said of reformers, "They're like Chicken Little. If anybody would ever take the time to categorize their arguments prior to a ruling and their predictions of doom and gloom prior to a ruling, and then assess what happens after the ruling, you would find how ridiculous these people really are." Another challenger told me he was "pissed off" about reformers' criticism of the Roberts Court's campaign finance rulings because they wrongly lead Americans to believe that a "Republican Court" is consistently siding with corporate America. (He indicated that he was "also pissed off" about climate activists because "there's [no] proof to climate change up or down.") A lawyer with Tea Party ties insisted that the primary interest groups that support the Democratic Party "are the Stepford wives in terms of their ideological beliefs." The same lawyer pointed out the hypocrisy of Democrats who take big money from their own supporters and give them influence in party deliberations while criticizing Republicans for doing so: "[Liberals who object to the influence of wealthy conservatives] don't say to Stephen Bing . . . 'No, we can't take all your big bucks.' They don't say that to Tom Steyer. No; Stephen Bing is invited into the Democratic Senate caucus to speak. I'm thinking, 'Where's the *New York Times* raging about that?' There is such a double standard. It is *such* a double standard!"[74]

Several DC-based election law experts complained that cause lawyers on both sides tend to simplify their opponents' views. They suggested that the debates typically are too crude to be meaningful, with activists on opposing sides talking past each other. One challenger asserted that issues that "are really complicated" and require careful balancing of competing concerns "tend to be reduced to slogans and little snippets of 'reform' or 'freedom' or 'liberty.' " He continued: "All of those values are implicated here, but how it's all implemented and how it operates is complex." Another lawyer complained that "these issues tend to get played out in the public in very broad strokes and just sloganeering . . . [For example], either you're for disclosure, or you're for secret billionaires controlling the country." A challenger who described himself as a moderate Republican ("there's like seven of us left") spoke of the difficulty of ensuring that campaign finance regulations are "predictable and understood and not subject to political gamesmanship" in a "political environment where everyone's just screaming at each other." He insisted that "there are appropriate places for the government to act, but they need to act with care" and that "what's so frustrating about this debate and the conversations around these cases is that there aren't very many people trying to act with care, either in the debate or the litigation, or in Congress, or anywhere else." The national debate on campaign finance is "insipid and stupid on both sides," he asserted: "It's just dark money this, dark money that, First Amendment this, First Amendment that. It's not a conversation."

A few flattering assessments by reformers of their opponents' advocacy and vice versa suggested grudging respect among some of the lawyers on opposing sides of these cases. That appeared to be true more often of lawyers who already were, or aspired to be, part of the legal elite—as evidenced by their educational and professional credentials and/or their experience arguing matters before the Supreme Court. But the generally hostile tone of some of the interviewed cause lawyers' comments about their opponents left me wondering about whether these lawyers were themselves contributors to the negative partisanship and polarization reflected in the late stages of this litigation campaign.

### Commentary on the Function of Frames and Discourse in Constitutional Politics

In response to questions about their strategies, the interviewed lawyers revealed their appreciation for the power of frames and discourse. Challengers offered fewer reflections about how frames and discourse operate in campaign finance advocacy, law, and the public imagination than reformers did, but they clearly understood their importance. One challenger recalled that "the story" his side told in *Buckley* was "that this law systematically violated the First Amendment and also was an incumbent protection." A libertarian commented on how his group approached the "tall order" of persuading the Court in *Citizens United* to find a corporate First Amendment right to engage in unlimited spending in electoral campaigns: "The argument we tried to ultimately make was, 'Look, this is an issue of free speech versus government control and ultimately censorship.' It's not really an issue of corporations versus people. That's a false distinction, or a false way to look at it, because corporations are made up of and controlled by people . . . It's an issue of freedom of speech versus censorship, or freedom of speech versus government control."

Another challenger discussed the importance of providing sympathetic examples to illustrate their claims, "as good advocates do." He noted that the justices do the same in their opinions; in *Citizens United*, "the dissent's talking about Exxon," while "the majority and Scalia's concurrence [are] talking about mom-and-pop businesses and stuff, right?" A libertarian explained that "the thing that is very important" in all of these cases "is that we be able to explain in a simple narrative fashion what the case is about in a way that everyone can understand." In *SpeechNow v. FEC*, he and others "worked really hard to cut through [complicated factual issues] and keep a simple narrative about what the case was about, which is just Americans getting together and talking to the public about political issues." Another libertarian who participated in the Arizona case said, "We did a very good job of explaining in terms that people could basically understand" that the case involved "government putting its finger on the scales." This lawyer added: "We worked really hard to try to find a way to explain it in a way that you could connect to the individual clients in the case: here's how this actually impacts these people, and by extension, if you wanted to get involved in politics, it would also impact you, and it's bad and unfair, unjust." Another challenger emphasized that litigation success and failure often "depends on how you frame the argument." He explained the strategy in *McCutcheon* for undermining the claim that aggregate contribution limits deterred quid pro quo corruption: "It's pretty hard to argue that if you give the maximum contribution to twelve candidates or fifteen candidates, it's okay, but if you give to candidate sixteen suddenly that's a big problem."

Other opponents of regulation seemed less self-conscious and/or forthcoming about how frames, metaphor, and narrative operate in the doctrine and their own thinking and advocacy. Several challengers offered bewildering displays of mixed metaphorical thinking while commenting on the stakes of the Arizona matching funds case. One said:

> Every person should have the right to speak out about our government without the government coming in and diluting your speech. . . . If I as an individual want to speak out against a candidate, the government shouldn't come in and pour money into that candidate's coffers to respond to my speech. If that candidate wants to go out and ask somebody else to raise money, that's a totally different issue. That's what freedom is all about. But to have the government come in and put its thumb on the scales to try and level the playing field, that to me stands in stark contrast to everything the First Amendment stands for.

Another expressed his views about the First Amendment implications this way: "Some of the campaign reform groups and other First Amendment advocates [suggest] that the First Amendment imposes almost an obligation on the government to limit speech so that the speech of the powerful does not drown out the speech of the not powerful. In other words, leveling the play-ing field by lowering the volume of debate."

Many reformers were eager to comment on how strategic framing has advanced the campaign to resist campaign finance regulation. One said that "framing has been hugely important, *hugely* important" in accounting for why some civil liberties groups have joined in the fight. He argued that "the McCarthy experience" has "shaped this generation and the generations af-ter" and has fueled "mistrust over any government regulatory power at all, but certainly government regulatory power over communication." That, in turn, "led to a framing of this as a white hat/black hat problem, where the speaker always wore the white hat, and the regulator always wore the black hat." Another reformer explained how the speech frame has evolved to make regulation seem more problematic. He asserted that "the debate early on" was "much more of this is money a *proxy* for speech thing . . . And then conser-vatives were making a little headway, but not that much headway." But later conservatives became much more successful in reframing the issue—"that it's not just a question of money; it's a question of our ability to criticize, our abil-ity to speak out." This shift, he believed, helped challengers gain momentum because it shaped how "people perceive things." A reformer who participated in the Arizona case recalled, "When I framed the issue in terms of thinking about how to do an effective public funding program," the other side coun-tered that "you're chilling our speech, because if I speak, if I spend money, then my opponent gets to spend more money, and so, I'm not going to spend money." This lawyer tried to recast the candidate's decision to spend money as "a strategic choice," but that framing failed to persuade the Supreme Court.

Reformers discussed how particular metaphors and applications of those metaphors have become embedded in campaign finance doctrine. One law-yer rejected the analogy drawn in *Buckley* between expenditures in elections and gas in cars. The opinion for the Court stated that "a restriction on the amount of money a person or group can spend on political communication during a campaign necessarily reduces the quantity of expression by restrict-ing the number of issues discussed, the depth of their exploration, and the size of the audience reached." A footnote to that statement read, "Being free to engage in unlimited political expression subject to a ceiling on expendi-tures is like being free to drive an automobile as far and as often as one de-sires on a single tank of gasoline."[75] This reformer explained why he found that analogy inapt: "Elections are not a drive in the country; they're a race, and [so] the analogy [is] all wrong. . . . The question is not how much gas is in the tank, but how much gas is in both tanks, because you want to have a race, and a race in which only one guy has gas in the tank is a race . . . that no one will watch." Returning to the campaign context, he indicated that the consequence of vast differences in financial resources is that "it's not a meaningful contest."

Several reformers commented on problems with how the marketplace-of-ideas metaphor operates in campaign finance doctrine.[76] Their briefs used the marketplace-of-ideas metaphor but argued that markets require regulation to ensure fair competition, and they made similar points in interviews. One said that the marketplace-of-ideas metaphor is "powerful" but that "the question is . . . as with any marketplace, is there no role for regulation within that marketplace?" Another mused that "there is no real, unregulated marketplace of free ideas, right? . . . You're not going to compete with folks with millions of dollars [who can] buy the instrumentalities to get their opinions across if you're a guy standing on the street corner." Another observed that "like in capitalism, you can't leave it—the use of money in politics—unfettered because it just leads to real abuses." The assumption that markets generally require regulation to function properly is not one shared by all challengers, some of whom appeared to believe in completely unregulated political and economic markets.

Reformers also complained about the Supreme Court's finding in *Arizona Free Enterprise Club v. Bennett* that government could not legitimately seek to "level the playing field" through public funding schemes. One said, "It's just shocking to me that fair play is actually an illegitimate reason for a law." Commenting on the divergence between the Court's perspective and the general public's understanding of the meaning and moral valence of this metaphor, he added: "When I talk to laypeople about this area of law and what it means, they're shocked at the idea that, in the eyes of the Supreme Court, a level playing field is a metaphor for unfairness, whereas in common parlance, a level playing field is the ultimate metaphor for what is desirable and equal and fair in the way of treating people. . . . I didn't read comic books very much, but in Superman, wasn't there some parallel universe, Bizarro World, where everything was backwards?" This lawyer was referring to Htrae ("Earth" spelled backward), better known as Bizarro World, a backward world created by a deformed clone of Superman known as Bizarro.[77]

Several reformers decried the consequences of the larger tapestry of current First Amendment doctrine of which campaign finance law is just a part. One reformer argued that the First Amendment had become "a weapon that corporations are using against government regulation that is not aimed really at free expression." He continued: "The First Amendment is almost like the

New Lochnerism, and if a corporation can take a regulatory regime and pin-point aspects of it that it claims either compel it to speak or limit its speech, those are the places that pressure is being exerted through litigation." This lawyer was referring to the Supreme Court's 1905 ruling in *Lochner v. New York* and other decisions during the early twentieth century, in which the Supreme Court relied on the Fourteenth Amendment to defeat laws regulating business interests.[78] Another lawyer regretted that civil liberties advocates had failed to anticipate that "in some deep and troubling sense, the modern First Amendment" would become "locked in as a shibboleth and a kind of inflexible ban on any kind of government regulation—the early twenty-first-century equivalent of the substantive due-process jurisprudence of the early twentieth century—and it's the same people making the arguments and the same social class benefiting from it."[79] In other words, these reformers suggest, the First Amendment has become a resource that wealthy interests can deploy to preserve their advantages.

While challengers successfully rally around the premise that campaign contributions and expenditures are core political speech protected by the First Amendment, reformers struggle to find a shared "alternative frame"[80] that fits current doctrine. The keywords that arose most frequently in the reformers' responses to my questions about the stakes of campaign finance litigation—democracy, equality, voice, and integrity—do not add up to a winning legal theory given the Supreme Court's recent precedents and current composition. The Court has foreclosed many of the obvious alternative constitutional theories that might support regulation. One reformer explained the dilemma:

> One of the fundamental problems that we are facing on the reform side is that, especially under the Roberts Court, but also before that, starting with *Buckley v. Valeo*, the Court has essentially ruled out some of the most compelling justifications for regulating campaign finance and namely the promotion of political equality and equal voice in the process, and instead has recognized only essentially the deterrence of corruption or the appearance of corruption as legitimate bases for regulation. The Roberts Court, in particular, has so narrowed and eviscerated the meaning of corruption that it almost no longer provides any platform to stand on in terms of justifying regulation of money in politics. And that narrow corruption frame, in my view, doesn't speak to the deepest values that we need to talk about in defending the regulation of money in politics.

Gordon Silverstein has likened the interplay of the Court and reform advocates to a game of *Scrabble* in which "room to maneuver on the *Scrabble* board" has become impossibly tight.[81] The Court's precedents leave few remaining available "moves" for reformers.

Several reformers discussed efforts underway to "redefine what the constitutional rationale should be for upholding campaign finance laws." One lawyer expressed interest in developing a theory advanced by Larry Lessig and Zephyr Teachout[82] about systemic corruption—a view that "takes this from a transactional nature to the concept of corruption of our democracy and corruption of our political system." Under this rationale, it's "not simply a question of whether the money can corrupt an office holder; it's a question of whether it small-c corrupts and undermines the integrity of the political system, of the government, and, of course, it does." This lawyer explained that he prefers this rationale to some others under consideration because corruption as a basis for regulating money in politics "is an idea that has been around for decades" and "so using that as an umbrella I find very appealing, building on existing concepts."

Other reformers asserted that the corruption frame is too confining, even when reconceived as systemic corruption. One insisted that "we need a new jurisprudence that allows us to voice the goals of political equality and equal voice beyond just the interest in deterring corruption." Another explained that "from a framing point of view," it's problematic to push for a progressive agenda in which government plays an important role while also arguing that systemic corruption of politicians is a pervasive problem. Reformers need to shift the conversation to "voice and equality," he argued: "The problem is that my voice is drowned out by the billionaires . . . and that I don't come to the political table as an equal." This reformer argued that the "voice and equality" frame also meshes well with a focus on voting rights: "The beautiful thing about the voice, equal voice and equal access to the political process frames, is that it is the flipside of equal access to the ballot, right? . . . It is a fight that we've been fighting for fifty years or a hundred years. It is something that matches up very nicely, and can speak, I think, more effectively to our allies and communities of color who need to be a strong part of the coalition. Corruption doesn't speak to those folks."

The same lawyer was wary about substituting the "integrity" frame offered by Robert Post:[83] "If you go to the integrity route, one thing I worry about is that what's the flipside, what's the analogy of integrity in the voting rights space? It's voter ID and fighting fraud. That's the language that they use on the Right to say, 'Oh, we need to protect the integrity [of elections].'" Therefore, he added, "I don't think that's the best frame."[84] He believed that preferable frames "are about voice and power" and "not about clean governance, not about anti-corruption, and less about the integrity of our democracy." His preferred approach "buys into the speech frame a little bit" but flips it to say, "But what kind of voice do I have over the decisions that affect my life, and should I be drowned out and should that be equal?"

Several reformers suggested that the challenge was even more fundamental. One said:

> We really need to reexamine the whole idea that money is speech. People like [Harvard Law Professor] Larry Tribe . . . get really mad when you say that: "That's an oversimplification, that's a bumper sticker . . ." But the truth is that *has* been kind of the guiding star for the Supreme Court since *Buckley*—is that money is speech and that that's the end of the analysis. And I think they've got to go back to looking at, "Yes, money can *facilitate* speech, just like loudspeakers can facilitate speech or newspaper delivery trucks facilitate speech," but we don't just say you can't regulate newspaper delivery trucks, because they are speech. That's kind of what we do with money. I think that's just totally wrongheaded.

Another reformer said, "The first fundamental mistake was the notion that speech equals money, and . . . it's the problem with Holmes in the first place. If you come up with a really terrific metaphor or a terrific analogy, it obscures analysis." Observing that "the concept of political equality was certainly viable in the early days," when the DC Circuit Court of Appeals embraced it in *Buckley*, one reformer said, "I think it's something that we need to revive." Another reformer grumbled that "in the current box" created by the Supreme Court, "the moment you mention the word 'equality' it's declared unconstitutional."

Developing a new jurisprudence to support campaign finance regulation was a priority for reformers, not because they believed that new theories would sway the Roberts Court, but because such theories might help them gain traction when they eventually face a more receptive Court. One reformer explained: "We know that the new jurisprudence isn't going to pass the [current] Supreme Court, but you want to get the arguments ready in case the Court changes, or when the Court changes." Another emphasized that "theories, and arguments that are set forth in dissenting opinions, sometimes in the future become the majority opinions. So we think it's important to participate in these cases even when we're losing so long as we're impacting the thinking of dissenting justices, who may one day find themselves in the majority. They will be arguments familiar to them, that they will continue to embrace, and maybe pull along a new colleague or two, and become the majority opinion."

One reformer said that a political-equality rationale is "certainly not re-flected right now in the precedent as a viable basis for sustaining campaign fi-nance laws," but he wants to "inject it back into the discussion so that a future Supreme Court . . . might start saying this is a basis for upholding." Another thought that "the strategic question is, what can be done to be ready with a constitutional rationale that a new Court with a different makeup could adopt and that you could use to help them adopt it?" Acknowledging that it might be as long as "ten or fifteen years" before that new Court is in place, an-other reformer insisted that "the only responsible thing to do" now "is to put ourselves in a better position when the next window of opportunity opens . . . And that's mostly about building the intellectual case and the factual case." He added: "Unfortunately, we have time that we didn't expect to have to do that." The goal, another said, is to "plant the seeds for a future Court to be able to use in writing a different kind of majority opinion."

## Conclusion

The conservative movement's success in building a strong and broad coalition to oppose campaign finance regulation is partly a function of their success in wielding frames and discourse about the meaning of the First Amendment. This chapter shows that lawyers on opposing sides of campaign finance cases deploy different constitutional vocabularies and express different worldviews, reflecting their immersion in polarized networks of elites.[85] It also demon-strates that the arguments advanced to challenge campaign finance regula-tion in the 1970s remain key themes for lawyers involved in litigation be-fore the Roberts Court. But those arguments are expressed today in balder terms, with lawyers for advocacy groups that claim to represent the interests of ordinary Americans using some of the strongest rhetoric. Lawyers for pro-life and gun-rights groups and other organizations claiming to represent the populist elements of the GOP coalition may not like the political influence of wealthy finance- and tech-industry leaders, but they come together with lib-ertarians, civil libertarians, business interests, and Republican Party leaders around the claim that campaign finance regulation violates speech rights and transgresses individual liberty. A broad and resonant freedom-and-liberty frame helps the architects of the challengers' litigation campaign summon this support without needing to explain exactly how broad campaign finance deregulation serves the interests of the GOP's populist elements.

Reformers struggle to generate a powerful and simple alternative frame that does not run headlong into existing constitutional doctrine and the set-tled positions of the Roberts Court majority. They had much to say about the importance of upping their game in this contest, even if they do not yet agree on a plan. Some are trying to use originalism and other arguments about the meaning of the Constitution to show how the regulation of money in politics would advance constitutional values.[86] As described in chapter 8, some reformers are pursuing an "incrementalist approach" by pursuing legislative reforms that operate within the framework that the Court has established since *Citizens United*, while others are pursuing alternative strategies that seek to upend that framework. Meanwhile, the challengers appear to enjoy a sense that they and the constituencies they represent now "own" the First Amendment.

# 7

# Issues of Accountability

The [Court's conservatives] seem hell-bent on dismantling, bit by bit, the campaign finance system that has been in existence and served us pretty well since *Buckley*.
INTERVIEW WITH REFORMER

[James Bopp has] an argument that he pushes and pushes and pushes and resonates with the segment of the judiciary that happens to be in the majority now and with the segment of the population that's increasingly taking control over state legislatures and Congress. . . . I don't think it's one that the population as a whole agrees with.
INTERVIEW WITH REFORMER

Preceding chapters showed how lawyers seeking to reshape constitutional law governing the regulation of money in politics borrowed and improved upon litigation-based law-reform strategies pioneered by civil rights and civil liberties lawyers. But the law-reform litigation campaigns pursued by lawyers in the Warren and early Burger Court years generated substantial criticism, mostly but not exclusively from the political right. Critics argued that unelected judges and activist lawyers were exercising powers that properly belonged to the elected branches.[1] Some critics claimed that judges and lawyers were proclaiming rights not found in the Constitution, using illegitimate methods of interpretation and reasoning.[2] They also raised questions about whether the advocates who brought the cases truly represented the clients and constituencies on whose behalf they claimed to speak and whether they should be permitted to make law affecting people whose interests were not adequately represented in the litigation.[3]

As the composition of the federal judiciary has changed to include more judges drawn from and vetted by Federalist Society and Heritage Foundation networks, and as conservatives have created a field of legal-advocacy organizations to pursue their goals through the courts, liberals and conservatives have largely swapped roles in these debates. Now liberals and progressives are more often the ones crying foul as it has become abundantly clear that, in the words of constitutional scholar Sanford Levinson, "the Warren Court has left the building."[4]

The interviewed lawyers' commentary reflects these dynamics. Reformers accused the conservative justices of defying norms about their proper function—norms of impartiality, independence, and law-based decision-making. Some reformers insisted that the justices had violated their own professed obedience to constitutional text and history. They also questioned the accountability of some of the lawyers and leaders of this litigation campaign, suggesting that there was a gap between positions taken in the litigation and the preferences of the constituencies they claimed to represent.

Challengers asserted that the justices had complied with judicial norms, and they defended their own roles in this litigation campaign. Some challengers appeared eager to show me that they deserved credit for helping to change the law, but they avoided suggesting that they and/or the justices were engaging in the kind of activism that had made the Warren Court's rulings the unifying grievance of the conservative legal movement. They were instead part of an admirable enterprise in which advocates helped right-thinking justices read the Constitution correctly to protect rights properly found there—not one in which lawyers and judges manufactured law.

What follows is a tour of the interviewed lawyers' commentary on the judicial role and the roles of lawyers and advocacy groups. I emphasize what these lawyers said about *Citizens United* because that is the case by now most familiar to readers, but the same patterns appeared in their accounts of the other major cases in which they participated. I invite readers to review the commentary with an eye toward what it reveals about how these lawyers think history should remember the campaign.

## The Judicial Role

Justice John Roberts famously endorsed an exceptionally (and many would say absurdly) strong version of expectations about the judicial role in opening remarks during his confirmation hearings: "Judges are like umpires. Umpires don't make the rules; they apply them ... [As a Supreme Court justice] I will remember that it's my job to call balls and strikes and not to pitch or bat."[5]

Most knowledgeable observers of the Supreme Court agree that the umpire metaphor bears little resemblance to how the Court actually resolves—or can reasonably be expected to resolve—most constitutional claims. While the text of the Constitution yields clear answers to some constitutional questions, such as how old the president must be,[6] it rarely does so with respect to constitutional questions that reach the Court, which typically involve the Constitution's more open-ended provisions. Nor does the application of existing precedents reliably answer those questions in the way suggested by the "calling balls and strikes" metaphor.

More-realistic expectations about the judicial role situate it within broader political dynamics in and around the Court. I will not try here to summarize the extensive literature on judicial behavior since the primary focus of this book is on the nonjudicial contributors to constitutional change through the courts. Suffice it to say for purposes of this chapter that substantial research shows that Supreme Court justices are responsive to signals from other political actors and broader audiences, including those responsible for their appointment. Lifetime tenure partially insulates the justices from political pressure, but that insulation is limited. In a comprehensive examination of all Supreme Court cases from 1789 through 2018 involving constitutional challenges to legislation, Keith Whittington found that "the justices have proved themselves to be the allies of political coalition leaders" in patrolling the boundaries of legislative authority—both in upholding laws and striking them down.[7] A large body of empirical evidence shows that conflicts between the Supreme Court and other branches eventually resolve to bring constitutional law into alignment with the constitutional understandings and policy agenda of the dominant political coalition.[8]

The Supreme Court's legitimacy nevertheless depends upon public confidence that the justices are not just "politicians in robes." The justices have an institutional interest in preserving the authority of the Court, and therefore they tend to be attentive to expectations about proper judicial behavior. The norms that the justices are expected to obey include ideas about judicial restraint, incremental decision-making, adherence to precedent, appropriate interpretive methods, and deference to lower court fact-finding.[9] The justices are also expected to resist direct political pressure and partisan favoritism. These norms help explain why Whittington's research found that in the broad sweep of history the justices generally have operated as the allies of political leaders but "not their servants."[10] A Court that defies norms of judicial behavior risks undermining the institution's legitimacy in the eyes of the public.[11]

In the past several decades, the justices' views of the Constitution and their approaches to interpreting it have become more closely intertwined with the political ideology of the party of the appointing president. As discussed in chapter 1, this tendency has been especially true on the Republican side. As the conservative movement has taken control of the Republican Party and more vigilantly monitored the process to prevent the appointment of "squishy" conservatives,[12] the connection between the GOP and the constitutional vision of aligned justices has tightened.[13] When the justices vote in accordance with those constitutional philosophies, their votes are fairly seen as political even if they are not deliberately partisan.[14] Theories about acceptable modes of constitutional interpretation and judicial review unsurprisingly reflect the parties' changing positions in political cycles.[15] As parties gain control of the Supreme Court, they tend to support active judicial review, while the opposing party tends to preach judicial restraint.[16] Still, those interpretive philosophies are supposed to reflect the consistent "high politics" of "ideological policymaking" rather than the "low politics" of "partisan favoritism."[17]

Lawyers who participate in major constitutional battles do not all have the same stake in protecting the Supreme Court's institutional authority. Winners generally have a greater interest in portraying the justices in the majority as principled interpreters of the Constitution, while losers typically have more to gain by characterizing the process as one that reflects the partisan political context in which the deliberations occur.

True to expectations, most of the interviewed reformers described the conservative justices as activist partners in the deregulatory effort described in previous chapters, while challengers offered more-positive assessments. Some reformers cited partisan motivations and departures from the interpretive methods that are supposed to shield the justices from allegations of judicial activism. They criticized the justices for selective and flawed resorts to history in support of the supposedly neutral application of originalist methods. Challengers downplayed the coalition politics surrounding the cases and defended the notion that the Roberts Court's campaign finance rulings stand apart from politics. They insisted that the Court was only doing what was necessary to vindicate constitutional rights.

A closer look at the commentary about the Court's ruling and reasoning in *Citizens United* provides some texture to these generalizations. Reformers emphatically denied that the Court in *Citizens United* had displayed the kind of independence, impartiality, and role modesty suggested by Justice Roberts's umpire metaphor. Not all of them were bothered that Citizens United prevailed in its challenge. Indeed, several of them indicated that they would not have been troubled if the Supreme Court had ruled in Citizens United's favor on narrower grounds. But reformers generally disapproved of the Court's decision to expand the questions to be decided well beyond those raised by the challengers and without an adequate factual record.[18] One reformer grumbled that "the Supreme Court majority won the case that *they* brought." Another reformer characterized *Citizens United* as an instance in which the Court had signaled to the challengers, "Bring us a case because we want to set the country right."

Reformers expressed deep skepticism about the reasoning by which the Court arrived at the narrowed quid pro quo definition of corruption adopted in *Citizens United*. One claimed that "they did it . . . in a completely lawless way, untethered to the precedent and untethered to the facts." Previous cases, he said, had "clearly and unequivocally" indicated that the government's interest went beyond just preventing quid pro quo corruption: "They talked about undue influence and access. They didn't just talk about quid pro quo corruption. It's just a lie. But once you write it once with five votes, there it is—it's the law of the land!" Another reformer asserted that the Court "ridiculously narrowed the definition of corruption . . . without batting an eye or explaining it . . . claim[ing] that it was simply following *Buckley*," even though "*Buckley* goes out of its way to make clear that it's not talking about just plain quid pro quo corruption."

Reformers also insisted that the holding in *Citizens United* that business corporations should enjoy a First Amendment right to spend money on election ads cannot be defended as the product of originalist methods of constitutional interpretation. One lawyer claimed that reformers were the ones hewing more closely to the Constitution's text and history, which recognizes "this fundamental divide between living, breathing persons who the Declaration tells us were created and given inalienable human rights, and corporations who were created to power the economy but with a recognition that they would be subject to regulation to ensure that they didn't abuse their special privileges." The Roberts Court had "abandon[ed] this key difference that's at the core of the Constitution," he insisted; "I don't think there's anyone on the other side who credibly makes a text and history argument on their behalf." This argument was essentially the one that Justice Stevens made in his dissenting opinion in *Citizens United*, in which he noted that the Court had made "only a perfunctory attempt to ground its analysis in the principles or understandings of those who drafted and ratified the [First] Amendment." He added, "Perhaps that is because there is not a scintilla of evidence to support the notion that anyone believed it would preclude regulatory distinctions based on the corporate form. To the extent that the Framers' views are discernible and relevant to the disposition of this case, they would appear to cut strongly against the majority's position."[19]

Reformers decried what they characterized as the Supreme Court's cavalier attitude about overruling major precedents. They generally agreed with Justice Stevens's dissenting opinion, which asserted that "the only relevant thing that has changed since *Austin* and *McConnell* is the composition of this Court."[20] One reformer described *Citizens United* as an example of a decision that "start[s] with people wanting to repeal the provisions and then working backwards," without bothering to provide a sound rationale "for why they're abandoning positions that have existed for long periods of time or why they are knocking out a policy that has existed in the country for more than a hundred years, as in the case of the ban on corporate expenditures." This lawyer described the ruling as evidence of the willingness of the Roberts Court "to drive far outside the lane to achieve its deregulatory mission."

Another reformer asserted that the Court's broad ruling demonstrated that the Court is "fairly selective about when judicial humility is a virtue." Referring to Justice Roberts's comparison of judges to umpires, he added, "That's just an umpire making calls? That's an umpire calling for a whole new game!" Another reformer attributed the outcome to bald political favoritism: "An unlimited money system favors the Republicans, and that to me is the real answer to why *Citizens United* was decided the way it was decided." Only one reformer expressed any sympathy for conservatives' impulse to run with the opportunity to change the law in this area now that the tables have turned: "I can't criticize them too heavily for it. When we had the five votes in the Warren Court, we did this all the time—all the time. The Court would take the bit in its teeth and go, and . . . [once conservatives] had five votes, they decided they would strike while they had those five votes."

Reformers also mocked the majority's assertion in *Citizens United* (and later in *McCutcheon*) that "access and influence," which the Court described as "responsiveness," is a necessary feature of democracy. One referred to "this very astonishing notion that it's not corruption if, as a result of an office holder's gratitude for your having given them a lot of money, you have preferential access to that office holder over other citizens." He continued:

> In the view of the majority, it's not just that that's not corruption; that is an actual positive good. That's the way the system is supposed to work. The politicians are supposed to be responsive to their supporters. Now I'd certainly agree with that if by supporter you mean somebody who voted for you. It's obvious that politicians are going to reflect agreement with the coalitions of voters who put them in office. But what the Court is using supporters for in these opinions is not the people who elected you; it's the people who *financed* you. And so, this is another one of the things that people who are not lawyers and who are not so closely following this are amazed to learn; that the Court thinks that it is not only right, but good, for politicians to pay more attention to people who give them money than they pay to other citizens.

Reformers claimed that the Court's characterization of the relationship between financial support for politicians and influence over policy reflects a fundamental misunderstanding of how democracy should work and that it is based on a flawed historical claim about its pedigree.[21] One reformer attributed the ruling and reasoning to the Court's sympathy for the idea that the "rights of the wealthy" should not be restricted.

The challengers offered predictably favorable accounts of the Court's behavior. They applauded the decision to "go big" by overruling major precedents in these cases. Many pointed to the exchange about book banning during the first oral argument in *Citizens United* (described in chapter 4) as clear evidence of the need for bold action to protect constitutional rights. One lawyer referred to "stunned silence in the Court" following this exchange, leading the justices who were already prepared to rule for Citizens United to think, "My God; if we're in the business of banning books, there's something very serious going on here, and we ought to go to the core of it." This lawyer asserted that the majority must have decided that "[there's] nothing left to do but to overturn" contrary precedents. Another opponent of regulation emphasized that "it simply cannot be forgotten that the government's position in *Citizens United* was that it could ban a documentary movie about a political candidate during an election year." He speculated that Justice Roberts must have confronted the question, "Is there some narrow way of doing this?" and carefully considered "technical workarounds" before deciding, "No, he didn't feel institutionally that it was appropriate to give this tiny, little carve-out for this group" when the government was asserting sweeping power to ban books. A business advocate characterized *Austin*, one of the major precedents overruled in *Citizens United*, as "an outlier in the First Amendment jurisprudence" in which the Rehnquist Court had relied on a regulatory justification that "seemed to be just completely made up." An advocate for Tea Party–aligned groups explained that the Court "finally understood" that it needed to "remedy this bad decision."

Challengers also defended the majority's definition of corruption and its finding that corporations hold a First Amendment right to spend on election ads. One lawyer with ties to the Republican Party leadership complained that "the bounds of the term 'corruption'" in the years between *Buckley* and *Citizens United* "had gotten scarily out of control—that it could mean almost anything associated with money in politics." Some challengers asserted that distinguishing corporations from other "speakers" for purposes of campaign finance regulation amounted to a type of constitutionally impermissible discrimination (reprising the argument made by Ralph Winter in the early 1970s).

Challengers described how they strategized to get cases to a Court that was ready to reverse course after Justice Alito's arrival, and how they jockeyed among themselves to get there first. One described his frustration with the slow progress of a lawsuit that his organization had filed before the one that resulted in one of the Roberts Court's major campaign finance rulings. His case had been "languishing" for years in the courts below; "We were trying to find a creative way to get it out from under a judge who had no interest in ever deciding it." While his organization was working "to get it moving again," another organization filed a different lawsuit in which his own group eventually intervened and "brought [their] clients along." That served the challengers' overall strategy, which was to "get a case to the Supreme Court that would allow the Roberts Court to issue a favorable ruling." Another opponent of regulation described a case that his organization brought in order to take a "halfway step" toward the more ambitious deregulatory goal achieved in another of the Court's major rulings. But his organization "just barely got beat to the Supreme Court" by James Bopp, who brought the more ambitious test case. The lawyer who lost the race to the Supreme Court conceded that Bopp had been "proven right" and that he had been "proven wrong" by the Court's willingness to strike down the restriction in one clean sweep.

Reformers typically asserted that they never stood a chance given the majority's views about campaign finance regulation. One told me that he doubted that his brief had any effect on the Court in *Citizens United* because "there were five justices with pretty firm views on this issue." "There was no stopping" the majority, another said, "once they decided they were going to take on the broader constitutional question." He explained: "Given these ideological divisions on the Court, you pretty much know how it's going to come out at the beginning of the case, and you have to do what you can to try to alter that result, but it's largely a futile effort." Another reformer worried that his brief might have encouraged the Court to issue a broad (and, in his view, terrible) ruling by demonstrating convincingly that major precedents foreclosed the Court from ruling in Citizens United's favor without overruling those precedents: "We really flung down the gauntlet to the chief justice on the idea of judicial modesty, and he doesn't seem to have cared."

## The Roles of Lawyers and Advocacy Groups

The lawyers who led liberal-rights campaigns waged during the Warren Court years drew criticism from the political right and left. From the Right, as described in chapter 2, various critics questioned advocates' use of the courts to accomplish what they could not accomplish through the elected branches.[22] Southern states asserted that the NAACP's litigation tactics and its methods for finding clients violated professional ethical standards.[23] Christian Right leaders chided ACLU lawyers for using the legal system to "turn wrongs into rights."[24] Lewis Powell's memo to the US Chamber of Commerce complained that Ralph Nader, ACLU lawyers, and public interest law firms were "active exploiters of the judicial system" and an "activist-minded Supreme Court."[25]

Liberal-rights advocates also drew criticism from the Left, much of it focusing on lawyer accountability to clients and the broader constituencies they claimed to serve. Harvard law professor Derrick Bell famously questioned the conduct of some NAACP lawyers in connection with the campaign to achieve racial equity in public schools. He asserted that the lawyers' "single-minded commitment" to maximum school desegregation led them to disregard the wishes of some black parents who placed a higher priority on improving educational opportunities for their children.[26] Critics raised similar questions about lawyer accountability to clients and constituencies in campaigns for abortion rights and marriage equality.[27]

In the literature about accountability in social movements, questions about lawyer accountability are sometimes intertwined with questions about strategy. Social scientists have argued that professional self-interest and hubris often lead lawyers to emphasize litigation and to divert resources away from strategies likely to produce more fundamental social change.[28] A literature on "movement lawyering" calls on lawyers to work closely with organizers and to defer to goals identified by others. It emphasizes mobilizing law from the bottom up, rather than trying to achieve social change through law reform from the top down.[29] The most optimistic of these accounts imagine lawyers who seek to collaborate with social movements rather than lead them. They contemplate sophisticated, democratically led organizations that can monitor lawyers and hold them accountable.[30] Some scholars argue that accountability issues for lawyers linked with broad-based law-reform campaigns are best understood as general questions about responsible leadership for lawyers and nonlawyers alike.[31]

The bar's rules of professional conduct deal with issues of lawyer accountability in litigation campaigns only obliquely. They require lawyers to abide by clients' decisions about the objectives of the representation and to consult with them about the means to pursue those objectives.[32] They prohibit lawyers from representing conflicting interests; lawyers may not represent a client when such a representation would be "materially limited by the lawyer's responsibilities to . . . a third person or by a personal interest of the lawyer."[33] Lawyers may not permit a person who pays a lawyer to provide services for another to direct the lawyer's professional judgment in providing those services.[34] The rules provide that when the client is an organization, the lawyer should treat the entity as the client.[35]

But the ethics rules are silent on many of the broader questions of lawyer accountability that arise in law-reform campaigns. For example, they do not consider issues that arise whenever lawyers seek to represent groups with poorly defined decision-making processes, or loose coalitions in which power among the different groups within the coalition is unequal. In these situations, it can be difficult to decide who speaks for the group or coalition, and it can be hard to reconcile the competing claims and interests of differ-ently situated members.[36] The rules do not address whether lawyers should consider how the precedential impact of lawsuits will affect groups of people who are not represented, or not adequately represented, in the litigation.[37] Nor do they address lawyers' duties with respect to the development of law that may not be felt immediately but will have a lasting impact on future generations.[38]

The existing literature on how lawyers should handle these broader issues of accountability focuses primarily on efforts to advance liberal and progres-sive causes.[39] But with a conservative supermajority now in control of the Court, and with a flourishing conservative legal movement pursuing ambi-tious litigation campaigns on a host of policy issues,[40] these question deserve more attention than they have received thus far as they relate to campaigns led by lawyers of the political right.

Some of the interviewed lawyers' commentary suggests the potential rel-evance of these questions to the campaign to deregulate money in American politics. Some reformers asserted that lawyers and advocacy groups had taken advantage of people's ignorance about the actual repercussions of the litiga-tion outcomes to advance their own ideological goals or the strategic interests of GOP leaders. Reformers also questioned whether the First Amendment jurisprudence that challengers have developed and the litigation coalition they have constructed serve the interests of all coalition partners equally well. Beyond that, they argued that the process by which this campaign created new law on money in politics has led to profoundly undemocratic results.

Several reformers expressed skepticism about whether Bopp's campaign finance work actually serves the interests of social conservatives or, more generally, regular people of modest means, as the website of his advocacy organization, the James Madison Center for Free Speech, suggests.[41] The reformer who credited James Bopp with "shap[ing] the whole movement" for deregulation also insisted that Bopp's position is not one that grassroots conservatives support "to the extent they pay attention to it."[42] Another re-former noted that Bopp "is a social conservative" but was "also on the RNC," implying that the latter role might have inclined him to seek to accommodate the priorities of Republican coalition partners.[43] Another reformer scoffed at Bopp's portrayal of himself as a nonpartisan defender of the expressive rights of ordinary people: "Bopp knows exactly what he's doing [in fighting for the deregulation of campaign spending]. . . . Well, you do have George Soros, and you do have [Tom] Steyer, but the fact is that the overwhelming amount of money goes to right-wing—extreme right-wing—groups, and everyone knows that." Another said, "I see Jim Bopp as aligned with deregulatory interests of big business" even though "I don't think Jim Bopp sees himself that way, or at least, that's not his public persona; his public persona is champion of the First Amendment and the little guy's right to participate in politics without having to hire a lawyer."

As explored in previous chapters and, in more detail, in Ziegler's book, the decision by Bopp and the NRLC to pursue a broad assault on campaign finance regulation was controversial among abortion opponents and other social conservatives. John McCain, an abortion opponent, accused the NRLC and its leaders of being "increasingly less interested in the abortion cause than they were . . . in the pursuit of political power for its own sake."[44] Other pro-life politicians and activists were skeptical about whether the NRLC's focus on campaign finance deregulation served the pro-life cause.

Interviewed reformers suggested that the speech-and-liberty frame that challengers have constructed to assemble a litigation coalition has enabled them to recruit participation by Tea Party–affiliated groups that are only dimly aware of how the litigation campaign relates to the interests of their members. One said, "I think the idea that 'money is speech' and 'keep the government's hands off my speech' has become something that helps identify you on the Right, and so it's hard to break through, even though that isn't serving their interests in any way. And actually, if you sat down with them, person to person, and said, 'Does it really make sense?' many of them would say, 'No, that's crazy; in fact, that's what we're fighting *against*.'"

Some reformers stated or insinuated that Republican leaders and wealthy donors have manipulated and bought support from the GOP base and/or the leaders and lawyers who claim to represent them. According to this criticism, Republican voters tend to take their cues on issues from party elites, who have invested heavily in the message that political spending is an essential element of individual expression and freedom. Several reformers noted that substantial financial support for Tea Party groups has come from wealthy individuals and foundations, making it, as one reformer said, "a little hard to tell" what is "the authentic Tea Party." He explained: "It does seem like at least part of what's happened to the Tea Party is that they've been co-opted by very wealthy conservatives, as Americans for Prosperity and Crossroads GPS-type networks . . . That's where their bread is buttered."[45] A reformer who served in a senior position in the Reagan administration but has since found himself at odds with the Republican Party's position on campaign finance regulation said that he believed that "Tea Party people—[including] a lot of good people with real convictions . . . have been totally snowed; they've been totally manipulated by people who know much better [and] know exactly what they're doing" and realize that "if you dismantle [campaign finance regulations], huge amounts of money will control elections." Another reformer similarly claimed that "Tea Party folks," including some who have been elected to Congress, "have been co-opted by the mainstream Republican opposition to campaign finance reform." This reformer added: "I don't know if it's been super explicit, or how it's really happened, but it seems like the Tea Party base is still concerned about crony capitalism, and Tea Party members of Congress either just don't have the juice to do anything about it or have been co-opted into the mainstream Republican opposition to campaign finance reform." Commenting on the rise in super PAC spending since *Citizens United*, one reformer asked rhetorically, "Do Tea Party people have much in common with any of the major funders of the super PACs? Which major funder of a super PAC would you say is a Tea Partier? . . . We have a hedge fund manager. We have people like the Koch brothers. We have [Sheldon] Adelson. . . . These aren't Tea Partiers!" These reformers claimed that the outside funding that *Citizens United* and *SpeechNow* unleashed has done little to promote the interests of the Republican base and may, in fact, disserve them, while allowing wealthy donors to use populist energy to achieve their own deregulatory objectives.

Some reformers also argued that the ACLU's position on campaign finance regulation, set by a board consisting primarily of lawyers, puts the organization in conflict with the preferences of some of its members. One reformer acknowledged that the ACLU "get[s] a lot of strength from being known for" its "free speech marketplace of ideas stuff," but some reformers were deeply skeptical about the organization's stance on campaign finance regulation. One said, "I understand where they're coming from. I just think . . . they're missing the larger picture of what this has done to democracy, which really ought to be as much their concern [as] some absolutist position on what the First Amendment means." Two reformers said that they were once ACLU members but quit over the organization's position on campaign finance regulation. One thought it significant that the national ACLU does not highlight its position on campaign finance in its fundraising appeals or on its website: "They never say . . . 'Among the issues we're fighting for you, for our civil liberties, is the right for you to spend money on elections.' . . . And they never say that because they know that their rank-and-file supporters would be up in arms if they actually really knew that the ACLU has been on the wrong side of this issue for forty years."

Several reformers also questioned the accountability of some union lawyers and leaders. As noted in chapter 5, the AFL-CIO joined in a challenge to the BCRA's electioneering-communications provisions in *McConnell* and again in *Citizens United*.[46] One reformer asserted that the union's position was "antithetical" to the interests of its members because "if you look at the soft money that was being shut down, [more than] 90 percent of the Republican Party's soft money was coming from business, and more than 90 percent of the Democrats' soft money was coming from business; labor was a minuscule player in this." Another reformer criticized the position taken by the AFL-CIO in *Citizens United* but argued that organized labor had "been walking hand in hand with conservative Republicans seeking deregulation of money in politics for decades. It's nothing new." The same lawyer claimed that, to the extent that the rank-and-file membership, and the organizing staff of the union, care about the role of money in politics, "they're all like, 'Campaign finance reform. End dark money. Reverse *Citizens United!*'" And, yet, he said, "their lawyers show up at the FEC and file briefs in court . . . seeking deregulation, and they have [done so] for decades." He asserted that there's a "disconnect between their lawyers and the rank and file."

Several reformers even doubted whether business interests are well served by the US Chamber of Commerce and its lawyers, who have long fought for the right of business corporations to spend freely in elections. One lawyer insisted that many business leaders welcome campaign finance regulation because they do not want to be pressured by politicians for donations that are inconsistent with their fiduciary obligations. A brief filed in *Citizens United* by the Committee for Economic Development, a nonprofit business-policy organization led by business executives, sought to counter the notion that corporations "want more leeway to spend money on political campaigns." To the contrary, it said, "the business leaders who serve as CED's trustees believe that a decision striking down the ban on corporate electioneering expenditures would severely harm corporate interests." The brief continued: "It would expose corporations to corrupt shakedowns for political money. Corporations would face intense pressure to provide indirect financial support for candidates to attract the attention of, and avoid retribution from, elected officials. Corporate electioneering would harm public confidence in business, fueling the perception that large corporations secure unfair advantages by purchasing political influence. Yet each corporation would be helpless to get out of the political game, fearful of losing out in the economic marketplace to competitors that were willing to play ball."[47]

One reformer said that without regulation of corporate spending on campaigns, businesses "have to pay to play because if they don't and their competitor does, they'll perceive themselves to be at a disadvantage; they view it as coercive." He noted that this explanation was the one offered by the CEO of American Airlines in 1973 in the Watergate prosecution when the airline voluntarily self-reported its violation of campaign finance laws. Another reformer called the US Chamber of Commerce "a conduit for secret money" to influence policy and elections and to lobby for policies that some of the chamber's members do not support, such as the sale and marketing of cigarettes overseas and policies relating to climate change and corporate tax avoidance. According to reports by a reform group based on FEC data, the US Chamber of Commerce spent approximately $140 million on political advertisements between 2010 and 2018.[48] (It spends many times more on lobbying.[49])

While the reformers expressed doubts about the accountability of some of the challengers, none of the challengers betrayed any concerns about whether they were serving the interests of the clients and constituencies they claimed to represent. The closest any of the challengers came to expressing such concern came from a Tea Party sympathizer who had recently turned to other issues. He said of the legal-advocacy groups that claim to represent the Republican base that he would be "very surprised if the rank and file have a strong opinion about campaign finance one way or the other." He indicated that grassroots conservative groups occasionally engage with the issue when called on by the small group of lawyers who orchestrate litigation coalitions. For the actual constituencies the lawyers claim to represent, he explained, "it's not one of their issues either way." He added, "You have your actors, hardcore people that care about their issues, but I don't think social conservatives really care about this stuff. They're more the grassroots people. . . . There are just not a lot of rich social conservatives, and so they don't have a voice in things like most of the big policy fights in DC."

The challengers appeared to be unabashed about—indeed, proud of— their roles in constructing the litigation campaign, serving up test cases, recruiting clients to serve as lead plaintiffs, and assembling litigation coalitions to support the deregulatory effort. One lawyer told me he creates test cases to "move the law." He described his strategy: "I always construct a case so that we have a ground that I . . . we, think will be accepted, that moves the law in the right direction, and it is worthwhile to achieve . . . Some narrow grounds that you could win a case on aren't worth the litigation. So we want to make sure the narrow ruling is one that really the Court ought to accept under the law and is worth achieving. But at the same time, we always build into it the fact that the Court could go big."

He explained that in one case, he declined to make a narrow argument that seemed likely to prevail in the Supreme Court and that might have protected the immediate interests of his client because a narrow ruling was "not worth having." A libertarian recalled how his organization identified a client for a test case; they "talked to quite a few groups until [they] found one that actually said, 'Yes, that's us. We have that problem.'" Another challenger recalled how he recruited a client to challenge a law he thought might be vulnerable under the Court's emerging First Amendment jurisprudence. He explained the legal issue to a prospective client and asked whether he was interested in litigating, but the client initially declined. Several weeks later, according to the lawyer's own account, he again raised the issue with the same prospective client, this time asking: "Doesn't that piss you off that somebody's telling you [that] you can't spend your money how you want? . . . Don't you think you have a right to [do so]?" When the client answered, "Yeah, it does," the lawyer responded, "'Well, . . . I think we can make something happen here. I think we can take this case to the Supreme Court, and I think we can win. Do you want to fight for this?'" The lawyer's description of this exchange was "probably a bit exaggerated," he said, but he emphasized that the way he asked the question made all the difference: "When I pitched it to him, originally, it was about standard of review, and the applicable case law, and how the Court analyzes these things, the way the different precedents [work] . . . and he didn't care. But when I made it about him and his rights, the government taking away something from him, that got him animated."

Several challengers emphatically rejected reformers' claims that they were disserving the interests of the GOP's populist elements. They manifested no qualms about the practical impact of their work. One lawyer who called himself an "outsider" (saying: "It's my nature, my client base") explained that among his fellow travelers "on the Tea Party side" there is "discomfort" with the amount of money in politics. But he said that "the conservative response" is this: "If you want money out of politics, get government out of our lives, and then there's no real impetus for the money to be there in the first place." He called the conflict between those who support campaign finance regulation and those who oppose it "truly a battle of socialism versus the free market." According to this lawyer, campaign finance regulation is a "socialist solution," according to which "government must be in our lives and regulate every corner of it and . . . prevent people from speaking out about the government and regulation in our lives." The same lawyer bristled at my question about whether the Republican base might benefit from supporting campaign finance regulation to gain leverage vis-à-vis wealthy individuals and corporations in struggles over policy and power within the GOP:

> I doubt this will end up in your book, but I have this view. It's that liberals think, "You're stupid, because . . ." Maybe not you, personally, but—"You're not voting the right way because if you were, if you were smart, you'd vote for

them. We have to protect you from these bad ideas so that you vote the right way, which is our way, and so we're going to institute all these protections to make it really hard for you to get bad ideas in your head that will keep you from voting with us, which is the right way to vote." That's the liberal model.

His model was "a little different," he said: "When you walk into the polling booth . . . you're alone, and you cast that vote as an individual citizen, and that's the unit of democracy that matters. So all the money in the world that gets spent on TV and radio is utterly meaningless beyond the fact that it either propenses you to get out and vote—good, we want people to vote—or it gives you information on which to make decisions—good, we want decisions. That is the difference between where I would stand and where the Left is on this issue." This lawyer chalked up reformers' support for campaign finance restrictions to their lack of confidence in the ability of the average voter to sift through the products of election spending to discern the truth and fight corruption through their voting power—essentially the argument made by Winter in his AEI pamphlet almost fifty years earlier.[50]

Another challenger expressed similar confidence about the positions advanced by his advocacy group. He said that he would worry about deregulated campaign finance system only if he believed that all moneyed interests shared a point of view, which he does not:

> In America, there is no moneyed interest. There are people with money, but their interests are so varied, enormously varied and conflicting . . . The nature of their wealth, where it comes from, the activities that are involved and everything, how they end up ultimately politically, is just all over the lot. And so, it is categorically wrong to say that moneyed interests drive the agenda. You see this in liberal talk all the time. "If we just got money out of politics, we could pass a higher minimum wage"—in other words, the liberal wish list. Well, you've got moneyed interests supporting that agenda. You have moneyed interests opposing that agenda . . . It's varied. To say that moneyed interests are lined up on any one side of any equation is simply false.

This lawyer's observations about the varying political commitments of people with money also revealed his understanding about which types of moneyed interests were his allies and the allies of the groups he represents: "We've got the crony capitalists that are in the pocket of the Democrats and the liberals. And they're fighting the Koch brothers, the people that are for free enterprise—not a corporate welfare system, but a free system. . . . And then we've got the trust-fund babies. They're almost all liberal, the hereditary wealth . . . And, of course, they're fighting the people that have gotten money because they started a business and now become wealthy." Although "it's human nature" to want to use campaign finance reform to disadvantage one's rivals, he said, "what overcomes that within the Republican Party" is that conservatives are now "dominating" and "conservatives have come to accept and understand that freedom is necessary." He added, "For me and many conservatives, that is part of our ideology."

This lawyer is correct that the political views of economic elites are not homogeneous. They vary by industry. The technology sector comprises a growing share of the ultra-wealthy, and wealthy individuals in this sector have long given more to Democrats than to Republicans.[51] But there is also evidence that major donors within each party often do not share the policy priorities of the party base on economic issues, and that the wealthy are more likely to get what they want from the political process than the poor when their legislative preferences diverge.[52]

I have no reason to believe that any of the challengers failed in their professional responsibilities as defined in the ethics rules—to abide by their clients' decisions about the goals of the representation, to keep their clients informed, and to avoid conflicts of interest.[53] Some challengers recruited clients, but I have no basis for suggesting that "a significant motive" for doing was "the lawyer's or law firm's pecuniary gain"—a distinction at the heart of the profession's rules on soliciting clients.[54] (I did not gather information about whether and how these lawyers were paid for their work.) Nor do I have any reason to believe that the lead plaintiffs in any of these cases were unsophisticated, vulnerable individuals needing protection from lawyer overreach. I am prepared to believe that the lawyers leading this campaign were faithfully pursuing what they understood to be the instrumental and ideological goals of the groups they represented.

Still, the interviews left me wondering about broader issues about the accountability of lawyers and advocacy groups involved in the litigation campaign. Those questions are most obviously relevant as to organizations claiming to represent constituencies with no direct stake in loosening the regulation of big money in American politics. Some of those constituencies are enormous, diffuse, complex—and sometimes fragmented by internal conflict. How did the lawyers and leaders determine that they had the authority to speak for and create rulings on campaign finance regulation potentially affecting those constituencies? What were the decision-making processes of the organizations they led and represented, and what mechanisms were available to hold the lawyers and leaders accountable? Did they believe that they were obliged to discern and follow the preferences of the members and constituencies they claimed to serve, or did they instead feel justified in identifying a goal and then seeking to rally support behind it? What part, if any, did funders play in setting strategy for the campaign, either directly through their support for particular initiatives or indirectly through lawyers' efforts to anticipate funders' wishes?

Other questions apply to the larger set of lawyers and leaders on the challengers' side of this litigation campaign. How did they think about their roles in generating frames that helped to draw advocacy groups associated with various strands of the Republican coalition into this litigation effort, thereby contributing to the campaign's success?[55] How did they understand their roles in communicating ideas about constitutional meaning to the public, thereby influencing attitudes about the constitutional bounds of legislative action in this area? And what responsibility should they bear for the effects of these rulings on the political process and the health of our democracy?

## Conclusion

The commentary of the interviewed lawyers reveals how these competing teams of lawyers want this momentous litigation campaign, and their parts in advancing or resisting it, to be understood and remembered. The challengers applauded the Court for its willingness to intervene to vindicate constitutional rights, and they expressed confidence about their roles in the process. They portrayed themselves and the justices as modern First Amendment champions—inheritors of a noble law-reform tradition pioneered by NAACP lawyers. In their telling, the Roberts Court's majority has brought campaign finance doctrine into compliance with constitutional law that stands apart from politics.

Reformers portrayed themselves as almost helpless bystanders in a process by which challengers and a partisan Court have dismantled campaign finance regulation in defiance of judicial norms and the will of most voters. Some of them suggested that the Court is not just implementing what some court scholars call "high politics," involving competing values, ideologies, and constitutional theories, but also "low politics," involving struggles over which party will hold power.[56] They scoffed at challengers' attempts to draw a parallel between the campaign to deregulate campaign finance and the NAACP's campaign against racial segregation. They instead characterized it as an example of the political right's success in co-opting strategies once used to advance social justice for purposes antithetical to that goal. Reformers also suggested that some of the challengers had allowed their own professional self-interest or ideological goals to interfere with their duties to clients and the broader constituencies they claimed to serve.

The interviewed lawyers' competing accounts add up to more than the usual posturing of winning and losing advocates. They provide a window into how polarized legal elites today view the Supreme Court and the constitutional doctrine that the conservative justices work with politically aligned advocacy groups to produce. The commentary vividly illustrates how, with respect to one highly consequential constitutional rights campaign, conservatives and liberals have swapped scripts on judicial activism and judicial restraint, reflecting their different positions with respect to the power to make that doctrine. Beyond that, it hints at what can happen when a polarized Court, operating in a polarized political environment, issues rulings that appear to advance the political fortunes of the party that controls the Court. The commentary invites renewed consideration of questions about the responsibilities of those who pursue constitutional rights campaigns that have far-reaching practical and symbolic consequences for people not represented in the litigation. These questions are important, even if those leading the campaigns and the justices who issue the rulings insist that the rights they declare were there in the Constitution all along.

# Continuing Battles

There's never an end to this. There's only a middle.
INTERVIEW WITH LEADING REFORMER

Almost half a century after the Supreme Court's ruling in *Buckley*, battles over regulating money in politics continue unabated. Advocates seek advantage in different arenas of contest, including the courts, agencies, legislatures, and media. At the time of the interviews, some reformers were pursuing legislation that could be reconciled with existing doctrine, while others sought a constitutional amendment to upend *Citizens United*. To increase the odds of succeeding in these strategies, reformers hoped to disrupt the coalition that has supported the deregulatory trends described in this book. Challengers, emboldened by the Roberts Court's rulings, had set their sights on striking down individual contribution limits and disclosure requirements and decimating what remains of McCain-Feingold. Lawyers on both sides of the fight indicated that they were attentive to the interplay between the courts and other policy arenas.

## Reformers' Strategies

Reformers are focusing on what they can now do within existing constraints. There are many more organizations involved on the reform side than there were in the 1970s, and the strategy is more diffuse. "The reform community is a lot more complicated now than it used to be," one longtime reformer told me: "I think back in the '70s, '80s, even well into the '90s, the reform landscape was really kind of dominated by Common Cause . . . and there were a couple of other groups, but they were very, very much kind of minor players . . . Today, there are a lot more groups. The strategy, I think, is a lot more fragmented." The various reform groups are pursuing several angles: new jurisprudential rationales for upholding reforms; legislation that can be defended within the bounds of the current doctrine; efforts to broaden their coalition to improve their prospects of success through legislation and in the courts; and a constitutional amendment to overturn *Citizens United*.

**New Frames and Jurisprudence.**   One priority for reformers is to develop and legitimate a new rationale to help them prevail in future litigation. What's needed, one said, is "a complete revision of our First Amendment and constitutional jurisprudence around money in politics." Another reformer emphasized the importance of somehow persuading courts to accept that "there are issues at stake beyond just corruption."

Reformers recognized that the doctrine would not change anytime soon. One conceded that a new First Amendment jurisprudence would "not . . . happen overnight" given the Court's current membership. Another cautiously predicted that "ultimately there are going to be changes in the law in this area" even though, "as in lots of areas of law, things go back and forth, and it sometimes takes a long time." Only one reformer stated more confidently that the law *would* eventually change: "It's just . . . so flawed, so rejected by the American people . . . That overwhelming rejection regardless of where you are in the political spectrum [means] it just won't stand." He predicted that when change comes, "it's going to be with a broader rationale than came out of the *Buckley* decision."

While many reformers found the *Buckley* framework problematic, most did not advocate abandoning it because they feared that any alternative framework coming from the Roberts Court might be much worse. One said of his organization's mission, "We want to overturn everything going back to *Buckley*," and another stated that his group would "go back to the [Justice] White view of the constitutionality of the expenditure limits in the original Federal Election Campaign Act"—that the Court should uphold limits on expenditures as well as contributions.[1] However, most reformers were circumspect about what might be lost in such a broad assault. A reformer who believed that "*Buckley* got it wrong in trying to treat expenditures differently than contributions" and that both can be regulated consistently with the First Amendment nevertheless asserted that challenging the *Buckley* framework would be dangerous: "The current majority of the Supreme Court may think that *Buckley* got that wrong too, but in the opposite direction."

One long-term strategy for eventually introducing different ideas about constitutional meaning into constitutional doctrine is to persuade lower court judges to entertain and articulate those alternative rationales. A reformer described his organization's plan to "introduce a notion of political equality"— the justification for regulation that the DC Circuit had found sufficiently compelling in *Buckley*—back into the jurisprudence about money in politics. He acknowledged that a court of appeals was unlikely to say, "Oh, we're persuaded; this is the basis on which we're going to overhaul [the law]." Instead, he hoped for "maybe a footnote or perhaps a brief concurrence or even a dissent that mentioned this issue." The goal, he said, is to "inject a broader constitutional value into the conversation—maybe sort of an additional basis for a ruling or something [similar]." The same lawyer delineated how his organization planned to challenge several lower court precedents that they believed were vulnerable "lower-hanging fruit." He explained why he thought that the holding in *SpeechNow.org*—in which the DC Circuit found that limits on contributions to super PACs were unconstitutional—was such a case: "We see that as low hanging because it's a DC Circuit decision that's never been reviewed by the Supreme Court. It would have a huge impact in itself, and . . . [we're] not asking them to overrule any of their own precedent, just a lower court. So, we have ideas both through initiating offensive litigation and also through getting units of government to pass laws which would create a conflict with *SpeechNow*, and then helping to defend them."

Another reformer, however, indicated that his organization would do its best to stay away from the federal courts and especially the Supreme Court. The Roberts Court's campaign finance decisions "aren't well reasoned" and provide no "sound rationale for reversing existing precedents." What that means, he said, is that "we know what we're dealing with; our main goal is to keep campaign finance cases out of the Court."

Reformers have also been active in defending state campaign finance laws, such as Alaska's and Montana's contribution limits.[2] Reformers stressed how problematic it would be if all individual contributions disappeared, or if the Court "did *Randall* with a vengeance on contribution limits" by holding that the threshold on contributions must be very high to be constitutional. One reformer explained that he thinks it's important to defend efforts by states to set contribution limits "at levels that are even close" to amounts that "a normal person" could afford to give.[3] Reformers have also worked to defend state legislation designed to protect state elections from big money influence from out-of-state donors.

**Legislation.** In early 2021, reformers launched an effort to pass additional campaign finance regulations as part of the For the People Act, HR 1/S 1, which has been called "the most sweeping piece of election-reform legislation in decades, if not ever."[4] It was a sprawling bill, with provisions addressing not only campaign finance but also partisan gerrymandering and voting rights. The legislation attracted support from a coalition of activists, advocacy groups, and elected officials, primarily on the Left. It passed in the House along strictly partisan lines, without significant discussion of specific provisions. But it stalled in the Senate, where Republicans uniformly opposed the bill. Its campaign finance provisions included increased disclosure requirements, the extension of current law to reach Internet ads, stricter limits on coordination between candidates and outside groups, small-donor public financing for congressional elections, and a reduction in the number of FEC commissioners from six to five, with no more than two from any one party.

The last of these measures was designed to overcome the paralysis that reformers say has gripped the FEC since 2008. That is when Donald McGahn II joined the commission as Mitch McConnell's pick for a Republican slot following his service from 1999 to 2008 as chief counsel to the National Republican Congressional Committee. From that point forward, the commission has been deadlocked. During the Trump administration, several commission seats went unfilled, so that the commission lacked the quorum necessary to act. Those seats are now occupied, but the impasse between Republican and Democratic commissioners continues.

The legislative fight over HR 1/S 1 reflected dynamics by now familiar to readers. Fred Wertheimer, one of the lawyers for Common Cause in *Buckley* and president of Democracy 21 since its founding, was a principal author of the campaign finance provisions, and Mitch McConnell led the opposition. One reformer noted that "McConnell was at the forefront of challenging [the BCRA]; he was at the forefront of *Citizens United*; he's at the forefront of efforts to prevent new campaign finance legislation from going anywhere." In a speech to an annual event organized by Charles and David Koch in June 2014, McConnell signaled his continuing commitment to the fight. He praised the ability of large donors to spend freely on elections,[5] celebrated how *Citizens United* has "leveled the playing field for corporate speech," and stressed the importance of maintaining the Supreme Court majority on campaign finance issues: "I pray for the health of the five." (He has since won the confirmation of more justices to pray for.) He disparaged those who advocate reform: "They want to use the power of the government to quiet the voices of their critics."[6] In 2019, he characterized an earlier version of HR 1/S 1 as an effort "to grow the federal government's power over Americans' political speech and elections."[7] In 2021 he warned that the legislation's donor disclosure requirements would "authorize federal bureaucrats to poke around in a much broader slice of private citizens' free speech."[8]

In the fall of 2022, President Biden urged Republicans to join Democrats in supporting a narrower bill limited to the disclosure provisions and introduced by Senator Sheldon Whitehouse. It would have required groups that spend on political ads or fund super PACs that do so to disclose donors who give $10,000 or more in an election cycle. Established reform advocacy organizations—the Campaign Legal Center, Democracy 21, and the Brennan Center—supported the bill, while groups that have consistently opposed similar measures—the Heritage Foundation, the US Chamber of Commerce, the Institute for Free Speech, and the ACLU—opposed this one. The bill was defeated on a procedural vote in which every Republican followed Mitch McConnell's lead. On the Senate floor, McConnell said that the measure would "erode the First Amendment" and give "Democrats' friends in the unelected government bureaucracy even more power to police political speech and activism of private citizens."[9]

Interviewed lawyers on both sides of this campaign agreed that Republican legislators fear defying McConnell and other party leaders on the issue. A lawyer who claimed partial credit for galvanizing Republican opposition said that "the last RNC chairman that believed" in any type of campaign finance regulation was Ken Mehlman, who served as RNC chair from 2005 to 2007.[10] The same lawyer noted the vulnerability of moderates who defy the party's current position on campaign finance, observing that Republicans who favor reform are "basically all out of office." Today, he said, "it's really hard to find [a Republican] that actually thinks that we ought to have campaign finance reform" because the GOP has "come to embrace [opposition to campaign finance regulation] over the last several decades in a full-throated way." He noted that even John McCain, who was sufficiently powerful within the party to head the presidential ticket in 2008, had "stopped talking about campaign finance" during his last years in office.

Reformers agreed that the GOP's stance had hardened and that Republicans who failed to fall into line faced consequences. One reformer called the shift away from limited bipartisan support for campaign finance regulation at the time of McCain-Feingold to uniform Republican opposition today as "a case study of the general partisanship and polarization in Washington." He added: "There's just been this general process of leeching out any moderates in the Republican congressional delegation, so it's much, much harder to get any bipartisan traction" now that the Republican establishment has been pushed aside.[11] Indeed, some say that McCain-Feingold, and John McCain himself, were products of a bygone era.[12] One experienced reformer said that an occasional Republican politician would respond to appeals for reform by saying, "Look, I understand the issue. I'm with you . . . ; I'm sympathetic; [but] I can't do anything about it." He explained that while "a Democrat is free to do whatever they want on the issue and is not going to get into any trouble with their party," the same is not true for Republicans: "Some Republicans . . .

express fear. . . . Yes, they're sympathetic, but it's just not something they're willing to go to war over." Another reformer said that while grassroots Republicans "are with the rest of the electorate on this, overwhelmingly supporting" campaign finance reform, that position is "inconsistent with where the Republican leadership [is]," which "may be an indication of how much of a stronghold big-money interests have on that leadership." This lawyer observed that "Mitch McConnell very strongly controls the debate on this question within the Republican caucus in the Senate, and if you want to keep your committee assignment, or you want to get X, Y, or Z done for your constituents, crossing Mitch McConnell on this issue would not be a good idea."

Even if HR 1/S1, or portions of it, were somehow to pass and be signed into law, McConnell would have reason to believe that the federal courts would strike down the campaign finance provisions. One reason for McConnell to feel good about his chances is the favorable constitutional doctrine generated by the litigation campaign described in this book. Another is his continued success in managing the federal judicial appointments process as the Republican leader in the Senate. McConnell blocked Senate action on President Obama's nomination of Merrick Garland to fill a vacancy on the Supreme Court created by Justice Scalia's death in March 2016, saying that the next justice should be chosen by the next president, to be elected in November. That move left the Court shorthanded for more than a year. But after Donald Trump's election, McConnell oversaw Senate confirmation of three new Supreme Court justices—Gorsuch, Kavanaugh, and Barrett. He pushed Barrett's confirmation through the Senate just thirty days after she was nominated by President Trump and a week before the presidential election. Altogether, he oversaw the appointment of almost two hundred federal judges in the Trump administration,[13] and some of those appointees have taken strong stances against any regulation of campaign finance.[14]

Assisting in this transformation of the federal judiciary were former FEC chair and longtime Federalist Society regular Donald McGahn and the Federalist Society's longtime executive vice president and co-chair, Leonard Leo. As the top campaign lawyer for 2016 presidential candidate Donald Trump, McGahn encouraged Trump to publicly commit to nominating only candidates approved by the Federalist Society—a move that may have helped Trump win the election. As Trump's White House counsel from his inauguration until he resigned in October 2018, McGahn worked with McConnell and Leo on the judicial nomination and appointments process. Leo continued to oversee the process after McGahn returned to private practice.[15] Leo is also a key figure in a network of well-resourced nonprofit groups that have mobilized media campaigns and other initiatives to influence judicial nominations.[16] The federal courts are now well stocked with judges who share the perspective of McConnell and the Federalist Society network on campaign finance regulation (and other policy priorities of the primary constituencies of the Republican coalition).

**Broadening the Coalition.** Reformers are trying to bring more groups into their camp. That effort is linked to the "Democracy Initiative," a network whose core groups at its inception were Communication Workers of America, Sierra Club, Greenpeace, and the NAACP. The network has since expanded to include organizations that focus primarily on voting rights, workers' rights, climate justice, and campaign finance reform. One lawyer described the Democracy Initiative as a "deliberate effort to strengthen the movement for reform by understanding that the goals of these diverse groups with respect to having a healthy and participatory democracy are closely aligned, and that by staying siloed and not understanding the intersection and exploiting that intersection, we're basically less powerful than we could be if we were to be acting together."

Reformers also seek to attract support, or at least neutralize opposition from, some of the groups that have previously stood in their way. One lawyer explained that "one of the movement-building efforts" since *Citizens United* has involved bringing "nontraditional partners into the space of campaign finance reform."

*Labor.* Reformers were generally optimistic about winning support from more labor groups, but they identified significant barriers. Several emphasized the pragmatic perspectives that tend to drive union leaders' positions. Union leaders typically assess whether proposed reforms will serve their long-term interests while simultaneously protecting what they already have. One challenger explained that while some progressive advocacy groups have publicly supported legislative-reform proposals to appease their donors while "secretly opposing them," labor has taken a more "realistic" approach; it has "weighed in as necessary to protect its interests." A reformer offered a similar view about the typical stance of unions: "Everybody who's in the system tries to preserve what they've got . . . [Labor unions] tend to be supportive but wary [of] change." Another reformer observed that there is "some pushback" to reform efforts "coming from those in the labor community who think that unions, frankly, should keep the advances that were made, in their view, under *Citizens United*." Another reformer emphasized that "some labor organizations are big money; they have enormous influence on the political process." Summing up the overall position of labor, another reformer said,

"Hopefully, more of the unions will come around on this issue, but I don't view the unions . . . as totally on board yet."

Reformers pointed out that some labor groups have blocked reform at the state level. One said of California public employee unions that "they've got a system that works for them right now . . . and they're resistant to change." Another reformer said that in his blue state, unions had "put the kibosh" on a reform proposal that would have eliminated one of their advantages; "so, if they're doing well in a state, they'll say, 'Hey, we've got a good thing going here.'" Overall, he said, "there are some unions that totally get it and are on our side, and they recognize that in general corporations and individual wealthy donors will always be able to outspend them," but in particular scenarios where they have the advantage, they "don't want to give it up."

Reformers believed that union leaders eventually would find it in their members' interests to support reform. One said, "I think if you can show them that they can adjust to it in a way that won't harm them . . . , they're open to it," because "they recognize that in the long run, they're going to lose." He continued: "They can only hold back the Kochs and the others for so long . . . On an unregulated playing field, they don't have the resources to be able to compete with the other side. And so, I think they're amenable to it, but they just want to make sure that they're not shooting themselves in the foot and disarming themselves and leaving the other side free."

Another reformer asserted that "the more progressive elements of the labor movement" increasingly "are seeing that trying to fight the money game is bringing a knife to a gun fight; they can't match the corporations on money; they never will." He continued, "What they can match is people power, and so, to torture the analogy, what they want is a fist fight because they've got tons more people, and they'll win that all the time; you start bringing machine guns into the mix, and they're in trouble."

Several reformers characterized labor's position on campaign finance regulation as one of gradual acceptance of the need for reform. "I think it's evolving," one said. He explained that Communications Workers of America "has been at the forefront" of that evolution because Larry Cohen, who served as CWA's president from 2005 through 2015, came to realize that campaign finance was an important obstacle to labor's legislative agenda. This lawyer referred to an "eye-opening moment"—when labor failed to win enactment of the Employee Free Choice Act:[17] "They had a majority in the Senate, in the House, and a Democratic president, and this was labor's top priority, and they didn't get it. And they said, 'So why is that?' And so [Cohen] identified the filibuster . . . He identified money in politics, and voting rights, and then redistricting came along later, as key . . . 'democracy blocks.'"[18]

CWA's leadership was able to bring other labor organizations, including AFSCME, into the coalition.[19] There had been "an evolution on the labor side on this issue," another reformer said:

> There was a tendency to see some campaign finance regulations, and in particular restrictions on soft money under McCain-Feingold, as hampering union political activity. I think that over time, and especially in the wake of *Citizens United*, the realization has set in that the amount of financial resources that unions can bring to bear in the political process is nowhere near the equal of what corporations can do with general treasury funds. And so, the stark inequality in that fight, when you open up corporate general treasuries to political activity, I think, it's starting to hit home—that an anti-regulation stance is ultimately harmful to the goals that labor wants to achieve.

Reformers generally agreed that labor unions' positions would continue to change as they saw that they would be at a significant disadvantage in an unregulated campaign finance system. Recent FEC data indicate that election spending by business interests vastly exceeds such spending by organized labor in federal elections.[20]

*The ACLU.*    For many years, the ACLU supported disclosure rules and public financing of campaigns while also opposing any limits on campaign contributions and spending. In 2010, the ACLU's board of directors narrowly voted to accept "reasonable" government limitations on contributions to candidates.[21] Several young reformers told me that they felt hopeful that the ACLU's position on campaign finance would eventually change more fundamentally. One of them attributed the organization's current stance to the experience of its board members, many of whom came of age with a different set of concerns top of mind: "The board is . . . still made up of some of those old-school '60s [activists with] a legacy of the Free Speech Movement" who like to be able to say, " 'We're not just leftists. We're principled First Amendment advocates, and here's the example.' " Another young reformer agreed that "the ACLU has always been a reflection of who's running the organization" and that "the progressive community" is "coming together more and more around money in politics." He added: "I think the ACLU is in constant flux, and so I don't think they're going to stay necessarily where they've been, especially once my generation starts having more of an impact on them." Referring to how the ACLU's stances on other issues, such as hate speech, have changed in recent years, he predicted that "eventually money in politics will get in there too. We just literally have to wait for some of the old guard to disappear." He noted that Public Citizen brought some of the cases establishing protection for commercial speech but changed its stance after seeing how businesses were using First Amendment arguments to shield themselves from liability for false or misleading factual statements directed at consumers.[22] He predicted that a similar change might occur at the ACLU: "Look, Public Citizen was behind the *Virginia Pharmacy* case in 1976,[23] and they've completely reversed on that. They regret having created the commercial speech doctrine, and the ACLU might shift in time as well."

Meanwhile, opponents of campaign finance regulation find the ACLU's position useful in legislative fights. One reformer mentioned how Ted Cruz "brings out the ACLU as an ally with him on why the First Amendment means that you can spend money up to the sky and not have it be limited in any way whatsoever." Another reformer explained that the ACLU's position "makes it harder . . . in terms of getting legislation passed." Recall the conference call described in the book's introduction, in which McConnell's policy advisers strategized about how to defeat the donor disclosure provisions of HR 1/S 1. The research director for Stand Together, a 501(c)(3) organization founded by Charles Koch, expressed dismay that the message of the legislation's supporters—that it "stops billionaires from buying elections"—resonated so powerfully with the public, including conservatives. He explained that conservatives were "actually as supportive as the general public was" when they read a neutral description of the bill: "There's a large, very large chunk of conservatives who are supportive of these types of efforts." Not even characterizing the bill as an attempt to silence conservative voices persuaded participants in focus groups. He asserted that the only "ray of hope" for opponents of these provisions was to emphasize that some groups ordinarily associated with the political left, including the ACLU, opposed increasing donor disclosure requirements. His research found that the most effective message was that a "diverse coalition of groups" opposed the legislation: "When you put that in front of people . . . they're like, 'Oh, conservatives and some liberal groups all oppose this, like, I should maybe think about this more.' You know, there must be bigger implications to this if these groups are all coming together on it."[24]

*Republicans.* The skepticism that was so pervasive in the commentary of Republicans on the challengers' side makes it difficult to imagine support for reform coming from GOP leaders anytime soon. Nor did reformers think it likely that they could recruit a Republican Party base that is so hostile to government and committed to the idea that liberals are foes of American values and the Constitution. They pointed to different visions of reality shaped by geography, social background, and divided media.

Several reformers nevertheless thought it worth trying to draw strands of the Republican coalition into a cross-partisan reform effort. One observed that the challengers' side is "stitched together with rather weak thread," and he predicted that antagonism between the constituencies in this coalition "will just grow." This reformer pointed to "somewhat of a rebellion in places like Kansas, where the Koch brothers started losing support among evangelicals and [others], . . . particularly farmers, on renewables." Another reformer said, "I don't pretend to understand Republican politics anymore, but the populist grassroots wing of it seems anti-corporate, so I don't know how long that marriage can last." A reformer with strong family ties to a rural conservative region said, "People have heard of *Citizens United*, and they do not like it. I think that there are large numbers of people from across the political spectrum who are becoming aware that we have a political system that is not functioning effectively." While they "may have different views about what it would mean for it to function effectively and different views about things like guns and abortion," he explained, "I don't think that very many members of the public think that what the system really needs is larger infusions of corporate cash." Another reformer thought that some elements of the Republican base might be recruitable, as "they start to see that they're not going to win the money battle." He wondered aloud: "Could we approach some of the Tea Partiers—maybe not the national Tea Party groups, which [are] too aligned with the Republican Party," but maybe through a "grassroots, main-street, small-town effort to go after small businesses and multiparty groups." The biggest challenge, he said, was getting them to understand the relationship between campaign finance and the issues they most care about: "Whatever your number one issue is, you're not gonna get to it . . . unless you deal with campaign finance."

One example of infighting within the Republican coalition that inspired such hopes in a few reformers arose in connection with Mitch McConnell's inclusion of a provision in the 2015 omnibus spending bill that would have lifted limits on coordination between campaigns and parties but left in place limits on coordination between campaigns and independent expenditure groups. Some critics, including representatives of Citizens United (the plaintiff in *Citizens United v. FEC*), characterized the measure as a power grab by the Republican establishment.[25] Some Freedom Caucus members objected because they feared that Republican leaders might use that leverage to defeat Tea Party–supported candidates in primaries.[26] Opposition also came from conservative political leaders including Ed Meese, Phyllis Schlafly, Tony Perkins (president of the Family Research Council), Gary Bauer (president of American Values), and Herman Cain. A letter demanding that congressional Republicans fight for "conservative priorities" included this objection to the proposed rider: "Among the priorities being added as riders . . . is a provision by Senate Majority Leader Mitch McConnell that would allow party committees to spend an unfettered amount of money in coordination with candidates. The provision would apply to political parties only, setting up a different standard between the parties and other multi-candidate committees. Political contribution is a form of free speech, which is protected by our Constitution and should not be limited . . . [T]he McConnell rider provides preferential treatment to the Washington establishment and subordinates the voices of those who contribute to other multi-candidate organizations."[27] Opposition to this rider put these conservatives in league with reform groups such as the Campaign Legal Center and Democracy 21.[28]

Even if such incursions on the challengers' litigation coalition might be possible, reformers knew that they could not be the ones to make the pitch to GOP populists. "They're not going to listen to someone like me," one reformer explained, although he thought that an approach might work if it came from "somebody they respect"—namely, "a conservative . . . who believed in campaign finance reform." He acknowledged that "it's real hard in this climate to get that." Richard Painter, ethics counsel to President George W. Bush, offered what he called "an impassioned case for why conscientious Americans, and politically conservative Americans in particular, must respond to the campaign finance problem."[29] He helped to establish Take Back Our Republic, a group that proposed the use of tax credits to fund campaigns. Another cross-partisan reform group, Issue One, was founded in 2014 by former members of Congress, including moderate Republicans such as Richard Lugar, John Danforth, and Chuck Hagel. One reformer thought that the existence of these groups "shows that there is an interest [in reform] among some parts of the Republican Party."

Challengers expressed intense skepticism about strategies to recruit Republicans to the reform side. One conservative firmly rejected the idea that Take Back Our Republic spoke for the interests of conservatives: "They're charlatans; they are getting money from Soros and Open Society Foundation. And it is basically—it's a false flag operation."[30] This lawyer expressed deep mistrust in the group's leader, John Pudner, whom he described as "parad[ing]" like he's a conservative just because he previously worked on Dave Brat's campaign, while "getting all this money from the Left." He also disapproved of the tax break proposal supported by the group: "I'm against tax breaks for political [participation] . . . The government should be a neutral arbiter. I don't like when they start picking sides for things like . . . 'We want to encourage people to do X and Y.' That's where crony capitalism comes in, that's probably my biggest issue, I hate crony capitalism. When you start having the government come in and saying, 'This is a good behavior for you citizens. We're going to juice the tax code to encourage you to do that.' I disagree with that." Another challenger described the Republican founders of Issue One as "just a list of liberals, most of them" or "at best moderates within the party." He added, "Of course, that's one of the reasons we defeated [them]."

Lawyers on both sides emphasized that understanding groups' positions on money in politics requires looking beyond economic interests. It is at least partly about ideology—views about the role of government and elites. One reformer attributed the opposition of Tea Party groups to campaign finance regulation to "competing cross-currents." He explained: "The Tea Party groups hate . . . government, so, if government is establishing laws, that's not what they want. And then they buy this notion of, they're going to restrict your speech just like the gun folks buy the notion they're going to take away your guns . . . Using public money for anything, they don't like. . . . They're anti-government, and campaign finance laws are government, so they can't match the two things. They don't like corporate power being exercised, yet they don't like anything that would do anything about it."

Another reformer agreed that anti-government sentiment made it very difficult to imagine bringing Tea Partiers into the reform camp: "Their language is crony capitalism." He observed that "the Tea Party has high on their list of worries the big business nexus" with government, but they see government as the bigger problem, which "impedes any solution where the answer is government regulation. They'll say, 'We agree that big business is dominating our politics and it's bad because they are getting all these favors and earmarks out of government. And the way to solve that is by shrinking the government, so there are fewer favors to go around; there's less opportunities for pork and waste.'"

Several challengers similarly emphasized the ideological aspect of the fight and insisted that there was no tension and no basis for divisions about campaign finance on the Right. A lawyer who expressed affinity with GOP populists asserted that there is no daylight between the Club for Growth and the base on the issue of campaign finance regulation:

LAWYER: Well, for example, the Club for Growth is an organization of billionaires who are . . . or is an organization to raise money jointly to finance campaigns. There are no Christian groups, or pro-life groups, or homeschooling groups, or grassroots groups on the Right who object to what the Club for Growth is doing and want to put restrictions on their participation or their contributions. So I see that on the Left though. So on the Left, you've got these conflicting views because I think the real conflict on the Left was when they start to think about whether their regulations are going to affect their own participation. So, unions might, at a certain point, feel that the regulations are preventing them from participating to the degree they want, or making the contributions they want to make. And when that arises, and it seems to be significant, then they're opposed to the regulation. But otherwise, they may not be. I don't see that on the right side.

SOUTHWORTH: I just want to make sure I understand you . . . On the Right, you don't see social-conservative groups opposing the Koch brothers' influence. . . .

LAWYER: Right, I don't see that. But what I see more on the Right is the thought, "Gee I wish we could get some of that money from the Kochs." Or "I wish we could get some money from the Club for Growth or . . . for what we need . . . for our views and our positions."

Another challenger who identifies with populist strands on the Right said that he found it hard to imagine circumstances that would lead him to favor any regulation of money in politics: "I can't conceive of that circumstance arising, except for . . . I guess, conceivably, as I think about it, I mean, the more socialistic our country gets, ultimately everybody becomes dependent on the government . . . And that could align all the moneyed interests in favor of one party ultimately . . . I could see the moneyed interests ultimately lining up once the government gets total power. Well, of course now we now have bigger problems than campaign finance, don't we? And I don't think just changing the campaign finance laws will fix that problem."

Several lawyers suggested that attitudes about campaign finance regulation might be shifting among young conservatives. A lawyer associated with Tea Party elements hinted that the mantra that Mitch McConnell has repeated over and over, and that this lawyer had long believed, might no longer be true: "McConnell has a saying . . . that 'Nobody ever won or lost an election . . . on the issue of campaign finance reform.' . . . But I think that's starting to change a little." This lawyer observed that in the 2016 presidential race, the Democratic base was "deeply turned off about Hillary Clinton and her relationship with massive amounts of corporate money," and he suggested that something similar might be percolating on the Right. One reformer claimed that there might be an emerging "generational difference" given that some young conservatives "don't like *Citizens United*." Another reformer told me that he and others were asking themselves, "Could we reach out to younger Republicans, [and] how do you reach out to them?" A key informant in Hochschild's research hinted at this possibility when he identified campaign finance, along with environmental issues and criminal justice reform, as potential crossover issues that could excite some young conservatives and bridge the partisan divide: "Big money escalates our differences. Let's get it out of politics—both sides!"[31]

One young conservative told me that "arcane [campaign finance] rules just don't matter to me anymore." He described what does matter to him:

> What Twitter is doing, that's what matters. What Facebook is doing, what You-Tube is doing, what Google is doing, that's what matters. . . . Look what Twit-ter did yesterday. They went and de-verified a bunch of people, and if you're a libertarian, you have to say, "Look, these are private companies. They have the right to set their terms. They shouldn't be regulated as utilities or anything like that." But a conservative will sit there for years and build up a following, and they can take it away like that. And Facebook can do the same thing. And Twitter is much more up-front about it. They admit their biases. They admit like, "Look, we're left wing." The guy, Jack Dorsey, he's a progressive person, and they don't hide it. Facebook, because Zuckerberg has more political ambi-tions, I think they're a little bit better, but Google is the same way. The head guys have given to Democrat candidates and all of that. . . . Even if you're say-ing things that are deplorable things, bad things, as long as you're not inciting violence, then you should be able to say it without them looking over your shoulder like Big Brother.

Sentiments like these have drawn some conservatives into conversation with progressives around initiatives to use antitrust laws to break up big tech.[32] The suspension of Donald Trump's Facebook and Twitter accounts in the wake of the January 6, 2021, attack on the Capitol has also led some conservatives, including Justice Clarence Thomas, to suggest regulating social media compa-nies as public utilities.[33] Conflicting lower court rulings on whether the First Amendment protects social media platforms' editorial control or ability to remove posts based on its content suggest that this issue may be heading for the Supreme Court.[34] Thomas has expressed concern about "the concentrated control of so much speech in the hands of a few private parties." Such interest in regulating to counteract accumulated private power to control social media content suggests skepticism among some conservatives about market-based free-speech rules, at least as applied to social media platforms.[35] It may also indicate a broader and significant realignment underway in First Amendment politics.[36]

Some reformers argued that business leaders might eventually reject some of the positions that the US Chamber of Commerce has taken on campaign fi-nance since the 1970s. One lawyer defended the chamber's role, asserting that it "has supported First Amendment rights for the business community before the courts and the Supreme Court for decades now," thereby "represent[ing]

the business interests even if business in general is not aware that it's necessary to do so." But several reformers questioned whether the chamber is really
protecting American business interests. One reformer explained why some
major corporations support campaign finance regulation: they are "quite
frank to say that money is being extorted from them" and that they spend
money on political campaigns to avoid being disadvantaged with respect to
their competitors. Another reformer insisted that some business leaders are
concerned about broader societal implications: "It [is] not the monolithic
view of all businesses in the United States that treating corporations as full
persons for purposes of political spending from their corporate treasuries [is]
going to be a good thing for democracy." Another reformer pointed out that
many industry groups, investors, and publicly traded companies supported a
proposed SEC rule that would have required public companies to disclose to
shareholders their use of corporate resources for political activities, although
the chamber opposed it. He also noted that some companies are voluntarily
adopting measures to increase disclosure and accountability because they
"actually understand that it protects [companies] from shakedowns." Business leaders face increasing pressure from investors, consumers, and employees for transparency about their political spending.

   *Democrats.*    Reformers regret that they still lack a major-party champion
truly committed to reform. Explaining why he was doubtful about the prospects for real change, one lawyer offered a skeptical view of both major parties'
leadership: "I think incumbents don't want reform, whether they're Democrats or Republicans. They don't like to change the system under which they've
been elected. . . . Without scandals, you really don't get substantial reform."
Another reformer asked rhetorically, "You want to know why there's no Wall
Street reform, or why nobody went to jail after the meltdown? It's because
Democrats get their same money out of Wall Street as the Republicans do."

   As for the possibility of building a cross-partisan movement to challenge
big money in politics, one reformer doubted that it was possible in this age
of extreme political polarization and siloed media: "I don't know how that
can happen. . . . We're so fragmented in where we get our news. Maybe this
will sound ridiculous in five years, and someone will have figured out how to
curate the news, and we'll go back to having the most trusted man, whatever
Walter Cronkite was. But right now, I honestly don't know how you could
have that. I honestly don't know how you could have a bipartisan groundswell
of people being disgusted with politics and thinking they can fix it."

**Constitutional Amendment.**    Several of the interviewed reformers were active in efforts to amend the Constitution to overturn *Citizens United.* One

proponent of this strategy claimed that the Republican leadership's opposition to such an amendment does not represent the will of the GOP base: "At the grassroots level, Republicans are with the rest of the electorate on this—overwhelming support for an amendment. I do think that that is inconsistent with where the Republican leadership is." The same lawyer thought that even some in the Republican leadership might be persuadable—that "there have been chinks in that armor." He referred to how "Lindsey Graham, in his brief run for president, talked about the need for an amendment."

Some reformers asserted that the constitutional-amendment strategy meshed well with efforts in other arenas. The various approaches are "not necessarily mutually exclusive," one reformer explained: "I mean, you can say both that we should amend the Constitution in order to overrule *Citizens United*, but in the meantime, we should try to do X, Y, and Z in terms of legislative reforms that are consistent with the Court's First Amendment jurisprudence." Another lawyer observed that legal-advocacy strategies are "very elite," while the constitutional amendment push "is a way that ordinary people can get engaged." Describing how the amendment initiative might operate as a lever for change, another reformer observed that

> the Court cares about its own legitimacy almost as a fundamental priority. . . . Judges are not politicians, but they don't adjudicate in a vacuum. And so, I do think that creating a public context where it is an assumed truth that *Citizens United* is a terrible decision is important and plays a role and makes it easier. The Court is always going to need a nonpublic legal justification for moving where it does. They're never going to go, say, "Oh, we're overturning *Citizens United* [because] the public really hated it." That's counter to the Court's mission. But they will start to look for those justifications when it's clear their legitimacy is threatened. We have examples of that throughout history where the Court has done about-faces, and it's partially because they realized their position was unsustainable in the body politic.

"That's why I think that the drive for a constitutional amendment is actually so helpful to our litigation efforts," he explained. "My view is that nothing would change the Court's opinion so fast as if they thought there was an actual present risk of there being an amendment to overturn them. . . . [That's why] I find the agitation and the organizing for an amendment to be extremely helpful context for a judicial thrust."

Several challengers expressed horror about the idea of amending the Constitution to overturn *Citizens United*. This comment was typical: "I view the idea as dangerous. I view it as a . . . largely, as a fundraising mechanism for some liberal organizations, and they never explain what they mean anyway. . . . There are really a lot of amendments that have been proposed in the Senate and the House, and I've . . . read them all and I've yet to find one that I thought was anything at all reasonable." A libertarian called the idea of a constitutional amendment to reverse *Citizens United* "scary."

Not all reformers thought that the constitutional-amendment strategy was a sound one. A reformer who called the constitutional-amendment strategy "a steep mountain to climb" referred to a "split" among reformers "between [those] who think the right response is to go directly at *Citizens United* by trying to get some kind of constitutional amendment to overrule it" and those working on "a more incrementalist approach," pursuing reforms within the *Citizens United* framework. Another reformer explained that he strongly opposed the idea of pursuing such an amendment, especially via a constitutional convention rather than the more arduous route that has been used for the twenty-seven amendments to the Constitution made so far. Under the usual approach, amendments originate in Congress subject to ratification by two-thirds of the states. Under the alternative approach never used before, two-thirds of state legislatures can petition Congress to call a constitutional convention. One reformer called the idea of a constitutional convention to overturn *Citizens United* "really frightening. Nobody knows what would happen then." Recent initiatives by conservatives to force a constitutional convention to amend the Constitution to substantially restrict federal government power illustrates what this reformer likely feared would happen if such a constitutional convention were convened.[37]

## Challengers' Targets

**Contribution Limits.**    The Court's reasoning in *McCutcheon* makes contribution restrictions vulnerable. A prominent opponent of campaign finance regulation predicted that a challenge to contribution limits would be the next big case to reach the Court and believed that his side now had the votes they needed to prevail. A lawyer with ties to national Republican Party leaders told me that his brief in *McCutcheon* was designed to set the stage for eventually overturning all limits on contributions by showing that the distinction drawn in *Buckley* between contributions and expenditures "is not analytically sound." He acknowledged that there "are plenty of anomalies throughout law that are so well established that they are never changed" and that this one might endure too. He was optimistic, however, that the Roberts Court would eventually "revisit that distinction." A lawyer representing more populist elements of the coalition confessed to some ambivalence about challenging contribution limits because "if somebody gives a billion dollars to somebody,

it might influence them . . . And that . . . looks bad." But he also believed
that "corrupt people find a way of being corrupt." Where he came out on the
issue—"not always but usually"—was to "let the voters decide." He continued:
"If a candidate running in Kentucky would get a billion dollars from the tobacco industry, what would they—the people there—say? What would they
think? They would think, 'Great, wonderful. We know that's our guy because
they're for the tobacco industry.' . . . If a candidate got a $1,000 [from the
tobacco industry] in New York City, people would say, 'Well, we can't possibly vote for that guy because he's obviously somebody who agrees with the
tobacco industry, and we're against that.'"

A lawyer for a group that has brought several cases designed to "nibble
at the edges" of contribution limits thought that the Court was "not terribly
interested" in those "little efforts." The question now, he said, is "whether . . .
to just go straight after contribution limits. . . . There's a part of us that says,
should we just bring that case? We'd lose it in the district court. We'd lose it in
the court of appeals because they'd say, well you know *Buckley* is the controlling precedent. You'd have to get to the Supreme Court and see if the Court is
willing to take it." He added, "You don't want to bring that case too early and
lose it." But most challengers appeared to agree with the view expressed by
another lawyer that when such a case reaches the Supreme Court, "contribution limits are going to be gone."

Several reformers agreed with that prediction. One said that he strongly
doubted that reformers could "salvage" federal contribution limits given the
Supreme Court's composition. The Court's ruling in *McCutcheon* was an important step toward "undermining the whole concept of contribution limits,"
leading one reformer to wonder, "Will the Roberts Court drop the other shoe
and get rid of contribution limits altogether?" Another reformer said, "The
fact they came out the way they did in [*McCutcheon*] is one of the reasons
I say that if we get another Scalia on the Court, we may see contribution
limits banned completely." This interview occurred before Justices Gorsuch,
Kavanaugh, and Barrett joined the Court. Another reformer believed that
"where they're headed" is "toward getting rid of everything, both in terms of
soft-money limits and just plain old hard-money contribution limits." Agree-
ing that individual contribution limits are "hanging on by a thread," another
reformer explained what made the situation "really interesting" from his perspective: "I don't know whether this was the whole idea as part of the scheme
or whether it's just developed that way, but what essentially has happened
is by unleashing unlimited independent expenditures and unlimited contributions to independent expenditure committees, you've now essentially
made the candidates' committees, which are subject to contribution limits,

secondary players . . . The consultants, the money, all goes to the supposedly independent committees."

What that means, he said, is that the candidates "do what they can" with the "measly money" they control, but they cannot match the resources of outside groups. "At some point," he continued, "I think there's a legitimate argument that says, 'You know what? The contribution limits on candidates are now harmful because they can no longer compete with the other messages that are out there in their name or by others against them.' And there will be a movement, both legally and politically, I think, to start to undo those limits."

One challenger indicated that the current federal ban on corporate contributions to campaigns should also fall because "analytically, under *Citizens United*, corporations should be able to contribute . . . just like anybody else, because it's not who, it's what." One reformer agreed that the prohibition on corporate contributions is vulnerable. "The way we would lose that case," he explained, is "if the Court says, 'Contribution limits address the dangers of corruption; so, just as with individuals, so too a corporation should be able to make contributions.'" Such a ruling, he thought, "would be very consistent with the tone of *Citizens United*," in that "you just don't differentiate among speakers, and corporations and people should be treated the same." Another reformer called the survival of the corporate contribution ban "tenuous."

Challengers have also prevailed in recent lawsuits testing the constitutionality of state individual contribution limits on the theory that they are too low.[38]

**Disclosure Requirements.**  In *Citizens United*, eight of the nine justices joined in upholding the BCRA's disclosure, disclaimer, and reporting requirements absent evidence of "a reasonable probability of threats, harassment, or reprisal."[39] Justice Kennedy's opinion for the majority emphasized disclosure as the way to deal with the potential problems of enormous sums of money coming into political races. Justice Thomas wrote separately to say that the Court should have invalidated the disclosure requirements.[40]

Several of the interviewed challengers supported disclosure requirements as a legitimate means of addressing potential corruption. One agreed with Justice Scalia's opinion in a case upholding a state disclosure requirement as applied to referendum petitions. Scalia wrote: "Requiring people to stand up in public for their political acts fosters civic courage, without which democracy is doomed. For my part, I do not look forward to a society which, thanks to the Supreme Court, campaigns anonymously (*McIntyre*) and even exercises the direct democracy of initiative and referendum hidden from public scrutiny and protected from the accountability of criticism. This does not resemble the Home of the Brave."[41]

But many challengers raised objections to disclosure requirements. A business advocate explained that conservatives who previously supported disclosure have become more reluctant because they "now see how it's being abused . . . [and] that it's being used as a weapon." A lawyer with ties to Tea Party–affiliated groups asserted that "disclosure is going to be a continuing issue, mainly because the Left isn't looking for transparency, they're looking for a target list. . . . They want to know who gives money to conservative groups, so that they can then target those people and get them to stop funding their political opponents. It's that simple. That's what they want. That's what they've done. All you have to do is look and see what they've done with the Kochs. They love to pillory people who give big money." Other lawyers mentioned the Internal Revenue Service scandal involving increased scrutiny of tax-exempt-status applications from groups with "Tea Party" or "Patriot" in their names as evidence that government could not be trusted with information about donors' identities.[42]

Frames and narratives play a role in current debates over disclosure requirements, just as they have shaped debates about other campaign finance regulations throughout this campaign. Reformers use the term "dark money" to describe political expenditures by groups that do not disclose their donors, while some challengers call such expenditures "anonymous speech." Some challengers also rely on doctrines developed to protect the NAACP from having to disclose its membership lists and donors in Alabama in the 1950s.[43] They argue that campaign finance disclosure requirements subject conservative donors to harassment and intimidation and that existing laws against threats and intimidation provide insufficient protection. (A First Circuit opinion upholding Rhode Island's election-spending disclosure rule found that comparing this requirement to the disclosure order invalidated in the NAACP case was "like equating aardvarks with alligators."[44])

Because tax-exempt 501(c) organizations are not supposed to be political organizations, they generally are not required to disclose their donors. Tax-exempt 501(c)(4) "social welfare" groups are permitted to engage in some political activities without jeopardizing their tax-exempt status, so long as their primary activity is promoting the social welfare.[45] However, the IRS has not offered clear guidance on how much political spending by a social welfare organization constitutes a basis for finding that its primary purpose is not promoting social welfare. In the wake of a controversy over its handling of tax-exempt-status applications in 2013, the agency began a rulemaking process to better define what constitutes permissible political activity by nonprofits. But Republicans in Congress attached an appropriations rider that halted that rulemaking process and prohibited the IRS from revising or issuing new rules on the political spending of 501(c)(4) organizations.

While super PACs are legally required to disclose their donors, they are permitted to accept unlimited amounts from politically engaged nonprofits and shell corporations that do not disclose their donors. Thus, super PACs are often grouped together with politically active nonprofits as part of the "dark money" phenomenon when their funding comes from sources that cannot be traced back to the original donors.

*Citizens United* and *SpeechNow* have contributed substantially to the influence of independent expenditure groups that do not disclose their donors. While these rulings initially gave an advantage to Republican-aligned organizations, groups affiliated with Democratic candidates quickly exploited the opportunities too. Most of the top political spenders among dark-money groups from 2010 through 2018 were aligned with the Republican Party.[46] In the 2018 midterm election, however, dark-money groups supporting Democratic candidates outspent those supporting Republicans by a small margin.[47] In the 2020 federal election cycle, dark-money groups spent well over $1 billion, benefiting Democrats more than Republicans.[48]

Reformers expressed frustration that Republicans have backtracked on the need for disclosure of large donors to politically active groups. One explained:

> The Republican argument in opposition to BCRA was, "We don't need limits on soft money. Everything is fine as long as there is full, timely disclosure." And the Republicans had this tight embrace of disclosure as the one-size-fits-all remedy for all campaign finance ailments. And they kept talking about the virtues of disclosure and just give people full timely accurate information and let the voters decide what they want to do with it. Well, that was the rhetoric then. Now, it's "Whoa, disclosure chills speech. It's a violation of the First Amendment. It's terrible. People are intimidated because when their name is disclosed, they're subject to threats and harassment."

Several reformers complained, in particular, about Mitch McConnell's reversal on the issue. "Although McConnell was saying fifteen years ago, 'All we need is disclosure, and we don't need all these other things,'" one said, "now that we don't have these other things, he says, 'Now we don't need disclosure, either.'" Another reformer attributed Republican leaders' revised position on disclosure to the "hardening" of "partisan lines."

In 2021, some of the challenger groups profiled in this book joined in a constitutional challenge to California's requirement that charitable nonprofits that seek to raise funds in the state disclose their donors' identities to the state's attorney general's office for potential investigation into fraud and other wrongdoing. One of the petitioners was the Americans for Prosperity Foundation, an organization founded by David and Charles Koch with the mission of "educating citizens about economic policy and a return of the federal government to its Constitutional limits."[49] The other petitioner, the Thomas More Law Center, seeks to "preserve America's Judeo-Christian heritage; Defend the religious freedom of Christians; Restore time-honored moral and family values; Protect the sanctity of human life; [and] Promote a strong national defense and a free and sovereign United States of America."[50] Many of the amicus briefs filed in that case argued that government should be prohibited from collecting information about donors to nonprofit groups that engage in advocacy. (Floyd Abrams, who represented Mitch McConnell in *McConnell v. FEC* and *Citizens United*, filed a brief arguing that "the First Amendment is *vindicated* by the identification of large donors to charitable entities that take positions on issues of public importance.")[51] Some groups argued that such disclosure requirements should be subject to the most demanding standard of review—"strict scrutiny."[52]

The Supreme Court ruled 6–3 in favor of the challengers, finding that California's donor disclosure requirement violated the First Amendment right to freedom of association.[53] As in *Federal Election Commission v. Wisconsin Right to Life, Inc.* (2007), the majority opinion noted the variety of organizations on the challengers' side; they "span[ned] the ideological spectrum," with participants ranging "from the American Civil Liberties Union to the Proposition 8 Legal Defense Fund; from the Council on American-Islamic Relations to the Zionist Organization of America; from Feeding America—Eastern Wisconsin to PBS Reno."[54] Justice Roberts wrote that "exacting scrutiny" (not the tougher "strict scrutiny" standard) should apply to such challenges, but Justice Alito's concurrence redefined "exacting scrutiny" to require the government to show that its regulation is "narrowly tailored" to an important governmental interest. If the Court had ruled that some charitable nonprofits were entitled to an as-applied exception to California's donor disclosure requirement because they would face a real threat of harassment if donor information were publicly revealed, the ruling might have been uncontroversial. But the Court ruled instead that California's requirement was facially invalid. In her dissenting opinion, Justice Sotomayor wrote that the ruling "marks reporting and disclosure requirements with a bull's eye."[55] Reformers fear that the decision will make it harder to defend campaign finance disclosure rules and easier for politically active nonprofit groups to exercise influence over elections and elected officials without revealing the identities of the large donors who are pulling the strings.

**Other Targets.**   Reformers also wonder what other restrictions the Roberts Court might be prepared to strike down. In the words of one reformer, "the

question is, . . . 'How far will they go?' and so far, the answer is, 'Pretty far.' "
But challengers have not won every case they have taken to the Roberts Court,
and some opponents of regulation expressed caution about bringing additional test cases. In *Bluman v. FEC* (2012), the Court summarily affirmed a
district court judgment upholding the constitutionality of a prohibition on
campaign finance activity in US elections by foreign individuals, corporations,
and governments.[56] The Court did not explain why the reasoning of *Citizens
United*—that spending on elections cannot corrupt and that the identity of the
speaker should not matter—did not require the Court to hold that a foreign
individual or corporation could spend on American elections. In *Williams-
Yulee v. Florida Bar* (2015), the Court found that Florida's prohibition on the
personal solicitation of campaign funds by a judicial candidate did not violate
the First Amendment, in part because "judges are not politicians."[57] One libertarian said that he "get[s] the sense that [the justices] have a little bit of fatigue
on these issues. I mean, they've taken up a ton of campaign finance cases since
2006. Their decisions have frequently been very unpopular." Another libertarian said that he believed that the Court's ruling in *Williams-Yulee* was a "signal
from the Court" saying, " 'We're not doing campaign finance for the foreseeable future.' . . . I think it was a signal to people like me, 'Don't challenge stuff
anymore, because we're over it.' " Another challenger expressed similar doubts
about whether it would be wise to pursue "an all-out attack on disclosure by
candidates and parties" because "that's kind of baked in the cake" and because
"it would create too much of a backlash."

Such concerns about possible reluctance by the Supreme Court to issue
new controversial campaign finance rulings have not stopped the flow of new
requests for judicial review. The Court has declined some of these requests, including invitations to overturn the federal ban on soft money,[58] but it has taken
up others. In May 2022, in a 6–3 decision that broke along partisan lines, the
Court ruled in favor of Ted Cruz in a constitutional challenge to a provision in
the BCRA that no more than $250,000 in campaign contributions collected af-
ter an election may be used to repay a candidate's loans to his own campaign.[59]
Cruz lent his Senate campaign $260,000 the day before the 2018 general elec-
tion for the purpose of testing the constitutionality of the provision. The majority opinion by Chief Justice Roberts found that the challenged provision
"burdens core political speech without proper justification." The opinion also
reaffirmed the notion that "influence and access" to elected officials by donors
"embody a central feature of democracy." In her dissenting opinion, Justice
Kagan wrote that political contributions made to repay a candidate's loan to
his own campaign after he is already in office "pose a special danger of corruption" because "the candidate has a more-than-usual interest in obtaining

the money (to replenish his personal finances), and is now in a position to give something in return." The ruling, she wrote, "greenlights all the sordid bargains Congress thought right to stop" through the BCRA's prohibition on "personally enrich[ing] those already elected to office." Still, the Court did not go quite as far as some had feared. Mitch McConnell, represented by Donald McGahn and Noel Francisco, who served as solicitor general in the Trump administration, had filed an amicus brief urging the Court to strike down all of what remains of McCain-Feingold: "From the beginning, the [BCRA] was a constitutional train wreck . . . It is time to put the BCRA out to pasture."[60]

## Conclusion

The Roberts Court's campaign finance rulings may not be the last word. Supreme Court decisions, especially controversial ones, are rarely final in any meaningful sense. They sometimes provide an impetus for legislative responses, and they can serve as symbolic catalysts for political mobilization in other arenas.[61] Some critics of the Court see its recent campaign finance decisions as among the reasons to resist the Court's authority to tell us what the Constitution means. They see a political reckoning ahead for a Court that has defied the preferences of most Americans on a host of issues.[62] At least in the short term, however, the rulings limit legislative action and constrain policy debates.[63] Opponents of campaign finance have momentum on their side, and they anticipate more wins now that they have a supermajority of movement conservatives on the Court. In terms of the *Scrabble* game analogy employed by Gordon Silverstein to describe the interplay between legislatures and the courts in the history of campaign finance regulation, reformers are now operating on an extremely tight space on the board. And as they seek to exercise their remaining available moves, they must defend against charges that they are enemies of the First Amendment.

# Big Money Unleashed

What has happened with the campaign finance system is we have allowed economic inequalities to spill over and dominate our political process, so much so that the vast majority of the public believes that our system is rigged . . . And that undermines the faith in our elections but also in our government . . . So, we are in a deep crisis in our democracy today. It's a constitutional crisis, and it's a crisis of whether it's we the people, or we the corporations and big money interests that shall govern in America.

INTERVIEW WITH REFORMER

The sorts of abuses [that] . . . had the country set its hair on fire in the early '70s are just commonplace now, if you look at the extreme amounts of money that both corporations, but particularly wealthy individuals, just are routinely putting into the political process. And the country has become . . . so inured to that . . . On the one hand, I think people are still very, very upset about it, but there's a kind of sense of hopelessness about being able to do anything about it . . . We're at this moment where things that just outraged the public following Watergate now are just being met with a sense of, kind of, futility and, I think, somewhat with a sense of despair.

INTERVIEW WITH REFORMER

Yes, there are some people who try to corrupt the process—no question about it—but I think they're going to do that regardless of the efforts that we make to impose limits on political speech. And I think it's dangerous—it's dangerous medicine—for the federal government, or the state governments, to believe that they're sufficiently insightful to impose limits on public debate.

INTERVIEW WITH CHALLENGER

I think we have more political speech now than we ever did, and if the billionaires have more to say, what else is new? And if you limit them, they're going to go buy a newspaper, and if you limit that, they're going to fund a cause organization. You can't stop it without having the kind of total control that we usually associate with North Korea or places like that.

INTERVIEW WITH CHALLENGER

This book has explored the processes that generated the Roberts Court's momentous campaign finance decisions and the larger political dynamics surrounding them. The justices played central roles in the process, but this account highlights other necessary participants, including the lawyers and organizations that filed the lawsuits, the individuals and institutions that generated legitimacy for the arguments presented in those cases, financial backers, and networks connecting the actors. Current constitutional doctrine governing money in politics is the product of investments made over many decades in actors and activities outside the Supreme Court.

The conservative legal movement provided some of the resources and a favorable environment for this litigation campaign. It spawned most of the groups that participated on the challengers' side, including specialized organizations that took the lead early in the first decade of the 2000s. The Federalist Society cultivated a network of lawyers to advance the goals of the campaign, served as a site for coordinating amicus participation, and provided a sympathetic elite audience for the rulings. Advocacy groups linked to the conservative legal movement policed the judicial nominations process to ensure that justices nominated by Republican presidents would share their perspectives on constitutional meaning.

The story of constitutional development told in this book is consistent with Charles Epp's claim that successful rights litigation requires "an interaction between supportive judges and the support structure for rights-advocacy litigation."[1] Appointments to the federal judiciary by Republican presidents since the 1980s—and especially since the middle of the first decade of the 2000s—made the courts more receptive to arguments against campaign finance regulation. But the major deregulatory rulings of the Roberts Court would not have occurred without strategic organizing by advocates, organizations, and political and financial patrons.

For Epp, the interaction between a sympathetic judiciary and support structures was a partial answer to concerns raised in the Warren Court years about the tension between democracy and rights, and between the powers of democratic majorities and appointed judges. Epp argued that the US rights revolution of the 1960s and 1970s "grew primarily out of pressure from below, not leadership from above."[2] He suggested that judicially created rights generally are the result of processes that reflect broad public approval.

But the pressure that generated the constitutional change described in this book did not come from below—or at least it did not begin that way. It began with wealthy individuals who wanted to use their financial resources to influence elections, and with the lawyers who demonstrated how the First Amendment could facilitate that goal. Patrons thereafter invested in ideas, organizations, and professional networks that would help them fight campaign finance regulation through the courts. They funded the organizations that would lead this effort in the name of ordinary Americans. The lawyers who led the campaign framed it as a battle on behalf of regular people against liberal elites, the mainstream media, academics, and intellectuals, and they used an emerging conservative media ecosystem to disseminate that frame. Those who bankrolled the effort mostly operated in the background.

The campaign benefited from the participation of several old-line liberal interest groups, including the ACLU, whose opposition to campaign finance regulation dates back to the Watergate era. Also helpful to the deregulatory cause was the support of organizations associated with populist elements of the Republican coalition—abortion opponents, religious conservatives, gun-rights advocates, and Tea Party–affiliated groups. Some of these groups received funding from wealthy donors, and some had their own reasons to resist campaign finance regulations that interfered with their ability to engage in election activities. Supporting the broader effort to unleash big money in American politics helped organizations associated with financially weaker constituencies of the Republican coalition win favor with their better-resourced political allies. In addition, they found the messages and doctrines developed to resist campaign finance regulation useful in other policy fights more immediately relevant to them. The breadth of the amicus coalition behind this campaign fortified the challengers' claims that the outcomes they favored were consistent with the preferences of a broad cross section of American voters, even if the heterogeneity of the coalition was more apparent than real, and even if consistent polling belies the claims of broad public support.

The litigation campaign described in this book is part of a larger story of how the Republican coalition has embraced the First Amendment as a vehicle for challenging regulations ranging from health care to securities regulation and antidiscrimination law.[3] Lawyers and advocacy groups have played key roles in these developments, working through the courts to alter what falls into the category of constitutionally protected free speech and association and connecting it to a larger tapestry of ideas about constitutional meaning whose overarching theme is that liberty requires freedom from all government constraint. An increasingly conservative Supreme Court has become more receptive to First Amendment arguments during an era in which conservatives more often are the ones asserting them.[4] The Democratic Party's extended party network is divided on some of the policy issues implicated in the First Amendment's expanded reach, including campaign finance regulation.

This account adds to scholarship that situates the development of First Amendment doctrine in the history of party competition, struggle among interest groups, and opportunistic behavior by clients and lawyers.[5] Frederick Schauer has observed that "a full account of the political economy of the First Amendment" might show that "repeat players and other aggregations of influence are arrayed substantially more on one side of the constitutional right than on the other."[6] Repeat players show up on both sides of campaign finance cases, but opponents of regulation hold the clear advantage in terms of the "aggregations of influence" assembled in these polarized support structures. Moreover, influence exerted in the judicial arena in this litigation campaign has spillover effects in other institutional domains, especially electoral politics, as the litigation outcomes help to translate one species of power and influence—economic might—into durable political power.[7]

This story of how moneyed interests acquired constitutional protection for campaign spending bears some resemblance to what Arjun Appadurai has described as "populism from above" or "the revolt of elites" against the "chains of democracy."[8] Appadurai describes our era as one in which new elites have sought to replace established elites while purporting to act on behalf of "the people." In the US, he says, these new elites—the Koch network, Silicon Valley billionaires, evangelical pastors, leaders of right-wing think tanks, and new media—have tapped into the frustrations of an aggrieved populist base that is impatient with the outcomes and pace of democratic processes. This book shows how new elites enlisted help from advocacy groups associated with populist constituencies to loosen restrictions on their own ability to use money to influence elections and policy, while framing the effort as one about the expressive rights of ordinary Americans. These efforts were tied to strategies by networks of conservative donors to move the GOP to the right.[9]

This account raises issues of accountability that have been persistent themes in a large literature on lawyering for causes of the Left but mostly absent in scholarship on advocacy for causes of the Right. Interviewed challengers portrayed the litigation and the resulting rulings as a heroic effort to advance important constitutional values, much like the NAACP's desegregation campaign on which it was modeled. But reformers described the rulings as the creations of an activist court, assisted by lawyers and leaders who were insufficiently accountable to the broader constituencies affected by the decisions. Reformers claim that these actors have enabled millionaires and billionaires to acquire outsized political clout to advance policies that most Americans oppose.

Enormous investments in armies on opposing sides of this epic battle over law attest to its importance. The consequences are both direct and indirect.[10] The decisions have resulted in court orders prohibiting government from enforcing campaign finance laws. They affect whether individuals and groups comply with existing law, whether civil society groups bring complaints about violations to regulators, and whether regulators respond. The rulings also influence public discourse and perceptions about the constitutional validity of legislative efforts to regulate money in politics.[11] At the same time, they fuel

popular dissatisfaction with the undemocratic and anti-majoritarian consequences of judicial review. In short, the rulings matter in terms of their direct
and indirect impacts, even as they are also part of larger processes of mobilization and countermobilization—moves and countermoves—that indirectly
yet powerfully shape politics and constitutional doctrine over time.[12]

The rulings have inspired opponents of campaign finance regulation to
file new lawsuits to dismantle what remains of restrictions on big money in
politics, and large teams of interest groups and advocates battle one another
in these cases. As reflected in the quotes that begin this chapter, reformers
describe a broken democracy urgently in need of repair, while challengers
emphasize what they say are the threats to freedom associated with reform efforts. These opposing phalanxes of advocacy groups and lawyers direct their
arguments to justices who are themselves divided on this and many other issues. The Court is now split into opposing camps, with all justices appointed
by Democratic presidents prepared to uphold some campaign finance regulations and all Republican appointees much more willing to strike them down.
With Republican appointees imbued with the challengers' perspective now
holding a supermajority, the Court's anti-regulatory stance seems likely to continue for the foreseeable future.[13]

Consistent polling shows that most Americans, including most Republicans, believe that tougher campaign finance rules are necessary.[14] As one interviewed lawyer observed, *Citizens United* has become "a talking point in an
age of inequality" and a "rallying cry" for Americans across party lines. In an
era of highly polarized public opinion on a host of policy issues, differences
between Republicans and Democrats in their support for more restrictions
on campaign finance are relatively narrow.[15] It may be, as David Primo and
Jeff Milyo claim, that voters' desire for campaign finance reform is based on
ignorance about how money operates in politics.[16] But these polling results
suggest a disparity between the uniform opposition to regulation by conservative and libertarian organizations participating in the litigation campaign
and the policy preferences of some of the people they claim to represent. This
public sentiment also presents a possible impediment to the long-term vi-
ability of the rulings and a possible opening to build new alliances around the
issue. To achieve durable change on such a politically high-salience area of
constitutional doctrine, opponents of regulation may need more buy-in from
a broader segment of the public.

The consensus about campaign finance regulation among conservative
legal elites, megadonors, and lawyers for rank-and-file Republican-aligned
groups remains mostly intact, but doubts displayed by some of the interviewed
lawyers hint at how that consensus might crumble and new alignments might

form. As explored in previous chapters, some challengers conveyed ambivalence about their organizations' positions on campaign finance regulation
and the consequences of the Court's rulings, just as some reformers acknowledged concerns about the unanticipated consequences of reform legislation.
Several reformers expressed hope that groups aligned with populist elements
of the GOP might eventually join them in efforts to address the outsized political and policy influence of economic elites.

Any such realignment of interest groups would require overcoming polarized and "calcified" views on the issue.[17] It would also require different
emissaries than the lawyers who now lead reform efforts. One prominent reformer acknowledged that any effort to persuade organizations connected to
the Republican base to join in some version of campaign finance reform would
need to come from "somebody they respect," while another reformer admit-
ted that he and his colleagues "are not the right messengers to those folks." The
profiles of the lawyers involved on the reform side of these cases, as explored
in chapters 1 and 4, suggest that the "wrong messenger" problem is deep.[18]
Any serious effort to bring populist elements of the Left and Right together
around campaign finance reform would require overcoming the narrative of
the litigation campaign that appears to have some basis in fact—that reformers are primarily coastal elites who lack deep connections to the working-class
communities whose interests they seek to represent.

Tensions within the coalition behind the litigation campaign described in
this book—especially between the Republican Party establishment and the
party's insurgent populist elements—roiled in the immediate aftermath of
the 2020 presidential election, in episodes in which key figures in this book
played prominent roles. James Bopp, who brought most of the campaign finance test cases decided by the Roberts Court, also filed four lawsuits on
behalf of True the Vote, which alleged that massive voter fraud had affected
the outcome of the 2020 presidential election. Bopp dropped the lawsuits following a series of adverse rulings in other cases challenging the election results.[19] Cleta Mitchell, who represented the NRA in the *McConnell* litigation
and several Tea Party groups in *Citizens United*, was on the phone call with
Georgia's secretary of state, Brad Raffensperger, when Trump asked him to
"find" enough votes to overturn Joe Biden's victory.[20] William Olson, counsel
to the Free Speech Coalition, Gun Owners of America, and other conservative groups in many of these challenges, urged President Trump to fire acting
attorney general Jeffrey Rosen if he did not agree to use the Justice Department to challenge the election in court.[21] John Eastman, who filed an amicus brief on behalf of the Center for Constitutional Jurisprudence in *Citizens
United*, was the key purveyor of the bogus legal theory that Donald Trump

used to pressure Mike Pence to stop the certification of the Electoral College vote.[22]

The GOP and its candidates lost some of their most reliable megadonors amid this political turmoil. Sheldon Adelson, who with his wife Miriam contributed over $170 million to outside spending groups aligned with Republicans in the 2020 election cycle,[23] died in January 2021. The Koch donor network signaled that it intends to operate more independently of the Republican Party going forward,[24] and other major donors indicated similar intentions.[25] Some corporate PACs and trade associations temporarily suspended contributions to Republican members of Congress who voted against certifying President-elect Joe Biden's election victory, but contributions from those sources quickly rebounded.[26] Mitch McConnell's comments in early 2021 about corporations that protested Georgia's new voting restrictions reflected the quandary he faced as insurgents within the party attempted to exert control. He warned corporate America to "stay out of politics," but he then immediately clarified his position: "I'm not talking about political contributions."[27] In the 2022 election cycle, business PAC contributions exceeded those made in the 2018 midterm election cycle.[28] The Republican ecosystem has also acquired a host of new megadonors who jockey among themselves to shape the future of the party while operating mostly outside the formal party structure and with little disclosure.[29]

Some legal liberals see in First Amendment jurisprudence a deeply inegalitarian tendency that has become more pronounced during the Roberts Court era.[30] Critics argue that free-speech doctrine now operates much like the early twentieth century's Fourteenth Amendment jurisprudence, enabling economically powerful actors to thwart regulation to protect their advantages.[31] Liberal critics also worry about how arguments about First Amendment rights of expressive freedom are being used to undermine antidiscrimination laws and to defeat economic regulations.[32] Justice Kagan has accused the Court's majority of "weaponizing the First Amendment, in a way that unleashes judges, now and in the future, to intervene in economic and regulatory policy," giving "black-robed rulers" vast license to "overrid[e] citizens' choices."[33] Judges are the ones actually striking down these laws, but this account shows that lawyers, advocacy organizations, and patrons have served as essential partners in some of that work.[34]

Several core assumptions of current campaign finance doctrine have become increasingly difficult to defend. One of those premises is that unregulated election spending promotes a robust marketplace of ideas and indirectly contributes to the health of our democracy. According to this theory, unrestricted campaign money facilitates open public debate and political competition, thereby promoting democratic deliberation and the search for truth. A related premise is that a free flow of information, from whatever source, serves the interests of listeners and voters in the unregulated marketplace of ideas.[35] This concept, first introduced into campaign finance doctrine in *Bellotti* and later used to justify broader corporate speech rights in *Citizens United* and its progeny, is now so well embedded that litigants and the Court no longer bother to explain how this unregulated flow actually serves voters.[36] The doctrine has become unmoored from its roots in ideas about democratic self-governance and largely agnostic about the identity and motivations of "speakers." The Supreme Court has long found disclosure laws constitutional in the context of campaign finance, as a means to help voters evaluate the reliability of the sources of messages and hold funders and politicians accountable.[37] But there is now reason to doubt that the Court's new conservative supermajority will hold that line.[38]

Whatever the merits of these laissez-fair market-of-ideas and "free flow of information" metaphors at the time they took hold in campaign finance doctrine in the 1970s, their limitations are apparent today. The web and social media have made it easier and less expensive than ever for politicians and their supporters to communicate with voters and organize for political action. But overwhelming amounts of information now vie for voters' attention, and not all communications that win exposure reflect the earned choices of consumers of content or bear any relationship to truth. Some of that exposure flows instead from economic power to drive people's attention and from the increasingly sophisticated operations of attention merchants who use machine learning and data analytics to exploit the psychological weaknesses of target audiences.[39] The economics of "cheap speech" via the Internet has contributed to the rise of fake news propagated by unidentified domestic and foreign sources for their own financial and political purposes and amplified through opaque algorithms.[40] These developments leave voters more vulnerable to manipulation through data-targeted election-related content, some of it false and misleading. Much of this content is designed to confuse and divide people. Richard Hasen argues convincingly that "the marketplace of ideas is experiencing market failure" and that misinformation and disinformation about politics and elections, much of it from anonymous sources, pose a grave threat to American democracy.[41] The Court's First Amendment jurisprudence did not create these problems, but it could make them more difficult to address.[42]

In debates about how to make elected officials more responsive to the concerns of the general electorate and less beholden to the interests of moneyed interests, many emphasize the need to change First Amendment doctrine to better protect democracy. Others say that the focus on modifying the Court's campaign finance jurisprudence is misguided. They argue that effort is better spent on other strategies, such as building civic associations and strengthening the organizational capacity of ordinary Americans.[43] Some favor strategies designed to rein in the Court, thereby preventing it from playing the role that Mitch McConnell praised in the book's opening episode when he observed that "the court system over the years . . . has kept us restrained" from regulating big money in politics.[44] Campaign finance is just one of many issues on which the Supreme Court's recent rulings are seriously out of step with public opinion, leading to a growing chorus of calls for court reform.[45]

This much is clear: those who hope to loosen current constitutional constraints on the regulation of money in American politics will need to focus on matters beyond who sits on the Supreme Court. The process that generated existing law on campaign finance involved many decades of investment in legal theories, institutions, networks, coalition-building, and messaging. It also took serious work to connect the goal of campaign finance deregulation to larger themes that reconcile and prioritize the claims of disparate groups within the Republican political alliance while still maintaining partial support from some liberal interest groups. If the doctrine now tilts too far toward a libertarian conception of the First Amendment that views free speech as an entirely negative right against government constraint, and if it rests on a flawed conception of responsive democracy that prioritizes responsiveness to major donors over accountability to the people, achieving a better balance will depend upon substantial long-term investments like the ones that got us here. It will be necessary to inspire Americans to demand change and find common cause across difference. And it will require close attention to how discourse—including talk about the meaning of the Constitution—reflects and shapes how people understand what they are fighting for and where they can find allies.

*Acknowledgments*

This book has taken many years to complete, and I have accumulated many debts along the way.

This book would not have been possible without the willingness of so many lawyers to take time from their busy schedules to speak with me. They provided invaluable information about the history of this campaign, strategic considerations, and various participants' understanding of the stakes.

Colleagues at UC Irvine helped me launch this project and shape its development. Rick Hasen provided especially valuable advice at the initial stages and many helpful recommendations thereafter. Other UCI faculty who commented on portions of the manuscript at various stages include Sameer Ashar, Mario Barnes, Josh Blank, Alex Camacho, Joe DiMento, Catherine Fisk, Bryant Garth, Howard Gillman, Jonathan Glater, Stephen Lee, Jack Lerner, Ji Li, Elizabeth Loftus, Carrie Menkel-Meadow, Keramet Reiter, Michael Robinson-Dorn, Ezra Ross, Ji Seon Song, Carroll Seron, Shauhin Talesh, Benjamin van Rooij, Henry Weinstein, Chris Whytock, and Dean Austen Parrish. Emily Taylor Poppe, Rachel Moran, Bryant Garth, and Swethaa Ballakrishnen offered especially detailed comments on several chapters.

At a 2019 UC Irvine Law conference on lawyers and constitutional change, Ken Kersch, Jane Schacter, Lawrence Baum, Sandy Levinson, Neal Devins, Mark Graber, Scott Cummings, Mary Ziegler, Gordon Silverstein, Chris Schmidt, Leah Litman, Amanda Hollis-Brusky, and Paul Baumgardner sharpened my thinking about the role of discourse and frames. Participants too numerous to name at other conferences—the New Legal Realism Tenth Anniversary Conference, Law and Society Association annual meetings, the Legal Ethics Schmooze, International Legal Ethics Conferences at Melbourne and UCLA Law Schools, the International Working Group for the Comparative

Study of the Legal Professions, and the Midwest Political Science Association Annual meeting—gave me useful comments on other parts of the manuscript. Beth Mertz, Chris Schmidt, and anonymous reviewers of an article based on some of this research and published in *Law and Social Inquiry* helped me clarify what eventually became the book's thesis.

In the nadir of my writing wilderness experience while on sabbatical during the pandemic, a workshop of generous colleagues—Rick Abel, Swethaa Ballakrishnen, Ben Barton, Scott Cummings, Catherine Fisk, Bryant Garth, Rick Hasen, Amanda Hollis-Brusky, and Carroll Seron—helped me find my way. Others who read and commented on the entire manuscript or on particular chapters include Mary Ziegler, Calvin TerBeek, Nina Varsava, Ken Kersch, Susan Carle, John Weissenbach, Amy Weissenbach, Ben Weissenbach, and Amy Barry.

Terrific research assistants—Aaron Benmark, Thomas Eisweirth, Aleksander Danielyan, Timothy Duong, Grace Park, Christine Wendell, Amy Abshier, and Brooke Bolender—gathered data and supplied other crucial assistance. Zack Watson helped me generate the analyses and charts used in chapter 6. Kenneth Armstrong, Cameron Dekens, and Evelyn Oates proofread the manuscript. UCI Law's superb librarians—Diana Sahar, Christine Tsou, Jeff Latta, and Matt Flyntz—located obscure sources. My extraordinary faculty assistant, Naomi Aguilar, organized other aspects of my work life while I toiled on this book.

Calvin TerBeek shared archival materials uncovered through his own dissertation research, and Nicholas Confessore provided documents from Libertarian Party archives housed at the University of Virginia and Stanford—materials that otherwise would have been unavailable to me during the pandemic.

I am indebted to the Law and Society series editors at the University of Chicago Press—Lynn Mather, Chuck Epp, and John Conley—and Senior Editor Sara Doskow for responding to this book proposal enthusiastically and moving it forward expeditiously. Outside reviewers offered excellent suggestions for improving the manuscript. In the final stages of this process, the book benefited from the efforts of many at the University of Chicago Press. I am particularly grateful to copy editor Jessica Wilson and production editor Stephen Twilley.

My sister, Amy Barry, provided perspective and welcome diversion.

Most of all, I am grateful to my husband, John Weissenbach, and my children, Amy and Ben. They sustain and inspire me. I could not be more fortunate in love.

# *Appendix*

This book draws heavily from my in-person, semi-structured, confidential interviews with fifty-two lawyers from July 2015 through November 2017. I sought primarily to interview lawyers who represented key parties and amici in one or more of three major rulings by the Roberts Court: *Citizens United v. FEC, Arizona Free Enterprise Club v. Bennett*, and *McCutcheon v. FEC*. Wherever possible, I interviewed the counsel of record, but in several instances, when that lawyer was unavailable, I interviewed another lawyer listed on the brief. Forty-four of the interviewed lawyers represented parties or amici in one or more of those rulings. Thirty of these lawyers participated in *Citizens United v. FEC*, twenty-six in *Arizona Free Enterprise Club v. Bennett*, and twenty-three in *McCutcheon v. Federal Election Commission*. Altogether, I interviewed lawyers on sixty-eight of the 122 briefs filed in those three cases. Five of the remaining interviewed lawyers worked on at least one other major Supreme Court case involving a challenge to campaign finance regulation, and three worked on major lower court cases, including *SpeechNow.org v. FEC* and *American Tradition Partnership, Inc. v. Bullock*. The interviewed lawyers represented all major constituencies active in the litigation: political parties and candidates, sponsors and opponents of legislation, other elected and appointed government officials, business and trade groups, labor unions, think tanks, advocacy organizations, and scholars. I cannot say more about the parties and amici represented by these lawyers without jeopardizing the confidentiality commitment I made to these lawyers.

Twelve of the lawyers I hoped to interview did not respond to my request—six on the challengers' side, four on the reformers' side, and two on neither side (meaning that the brief took a qualified position indicating that it sided with neither party). But with respect to four of the briefs filed by those lawyers, I was able to interview another lawyer on the same brief. Scheduling problems prevented me from interviewing four lawyers who indicated that they were willing to meet with me. Only one lawyer—a challenger who had filed an amicus brief on behalf of several libertarian groups in *Citizens United*—explicitly declined my request.

The interviews focused primarily on how and why the lawyers participated in these cases; their views about the holdings and reasoning and the cases' broader stakes and consequences; the lawyers' strategies, including work outside the courts; cooperation and coordination among parties and amici; the alignment of parties and constituencies; their perceptions about their influence on the Court; and the future of political and legal struggles over campaign finance regulation. The interviews lasted from thirty minutes to more than two and a half hours, and they were recorded, transcribed, and coded. To encourage lawyers to speak candidly, I assured them that I would not identify them or attribute quotations from the interviews without their permission.

For the word count analyses in chapter 6, my research assistant and I removed the "front matter" from the opinions: the headnotes (summaries of the legal issues addressed) and lawyer names and positions. We coded each opinion according to whether it favored upholding or invalidating the challenged restriction. We cleaned and coded the party and amicus briefs in the same cases and categorized them as challenging the regulation, supporting the regulation, or taking neither side. My research assistant then generated word frequency and word combination data for the opinions and briefs, lemmatizing the data to catch all forms of key words.

I also gathered biographies of the lawyers who filed party and amicus briefs in *Citizens United v. FEC*, *Arizona Free Enterprise Club v. Bennett*, and *McCutcheon v. FEC*. Table 4.1 summarizes the characteristics of the full set of lawyers who participated on party and amicus briefs in these cases.

# Notes

## Introduction

1. Mayer 2021.

2. Hulse 2021.

3. Jones 2018. Compare Primo and Milyo 2020, 158 (asserting that "Americans believe that corruption has infected nearly all aspects of the political process" but that this cynical perspective is based on the message they receive from the media, politicians, reform groups, and scholars).

4. See Nilsen 2019 (on how Sanders railed against the influence of millionaires and billionaires in his 2016 and 2020 presidential campaigns); Johnson 2022 (describing a letter from Sanders to the Democratic National Committee complaining of a "billionaire-funded effort to crush the candidacies of a number of progressive women of color who are running for Congress" in 2022).

5. In his 2016 presidential campaign and again in the lead-up to the 2020 race, Trump emphasized his independence from big money, his ability to self-finance and to attract small donations, and his effort to combat corruption in Washington ("we're draining the swamp") (Watson 2019). In a 2016 interview with Jake Tapper on "State of the Union," Trump said that when "somebody gives them money, not anything wrong, just psychologically, when they go to that person, they're going to do it. They owe them" (LoBianco 2016).

6. Brenan 2019.

7. There were cases before *Buckley* in which the Supreme Court ruled on different types of constitutional objections to campaign finance regulations. For more on this history, see Mutch 1988, 1–52.

8. Buckley v. Valeo, 424 U.S. 1, 49–50 (1976).

9. Citizens United v. Federal Election Commission, 558 U.S. 310 (2010).

10. See, e.g., Chemerinsky 2010, 197; Hasen 2016a, 108; Mutch 2014, 175.

11. But see Williams-Yulee v. Florida Bar, 575 U.S. 433 (2015) (holding that a state prohibition on the personal solicitation of campaign funds by a judicial candidate did not violate the First Amendment because "judges are not politicians" [1662]); Bluman v. FEC, 565 U.S. 1104 (2012) (summarily affirming a district court judgment upholding the constitutionality of the prohibition on campaign finance activity in US elections by foreign individuals, corporations, and governments).

12. Both Gorsuch and Kavanaugh signaled deep skepticism about campaign finance regulation before joining the Court. See Riddle v. Hickenlooper, 742 F.3d 922 (10th Cir. 2014)

(Gorsuch's concurrence suggested that limits on campaign contributions should be subject to strict scrutiny); Emily's List v. FEC, 581 F.3d 1 (D.C. Cir. 2009) (Kavanaugh's opinion for the DC Circuit Court of Appeals found that several FEC regulations that governed how non-connected PACs should allocate their political spending between federal and nonfederal elections violated the First Amendment and exceeded the FEC's authority); Bluman v. FEC, 800 F. Supp. 2d 281 (D.D.C. 2011), aff'd, 132 S. Ct. 1087 (2011) (Kavanaugh's opinion upheld a ban on foreign national spending money in connection with elections but defined the challenged ban as applying only to "express advocacy"). Barrett appears likely to follow in the footsteps of Antonin Scalia, the justice for whom she clerked, and to resist most campaign finance regulations except disclosure requirements. See Tushnet 2020a (predicting that, with Barrett's confirmation, "efforts to rein in campaign finance will almost certainly be held unconstitutional").

13. See, e.g., Hasen 2016a; Mutch 2014.

14. Batchis 2016.

15. Mutch 1988; Mutch 2014.

16. Silverstein 2009, 152–74.

17. Hollis-Brusky 2015, 61–89.

18. Winkler 2018b, 324–76; Gerken and Newland 2016; Coyle 2013, 220–52.

19. Collins and Skover 2014.

20. Ziegler 2022.

21. Batchis 2016, 56.

22. Arizona Free Enterprise Club's Freedom PAC v. Bennett, 564 U.S. 721 (2011).

23. McCutcheon v. Federal Election Commission, 572 U.S. 185 (2014).

24. See, for example Bethel 1999 ("Campaign finance laws are abridgments of political speech . . . Now, reformers want even more restrictions"); Patch 2011 (applauding Mitch Mc-Connell for "standing up for free speech against skewed polls and goo-goo talking points manufactured by campaign finance 'reformers'"); McConnell 1999 ("Under the guise of 'reform,' . . . free speech utilitarians are seeking to regulate and diminish the ability of citizens to discuss issues of public concern and political figures inextricably linked to these issues"); Smith 2016, 327 (disputing whether the self-described "reformers" deserved the label but using that term in quotation marks, along with "advocates of greater regulation" and "regulatory advocates," to describe the same actors); Spakovsky 2012 ("The unprecedented attacks on political speech by "reform" groups and mainstream media outlets have been unrelenting in the last three decades").

## Chapter One

1. Justices John Roberts, Antonin Scalia, Clarence Thomas, and Samuel Alito joined in the majority opinion by Anthony Kennedy. Justices John Paul Stevens, Ruth Bader Ginsburg, Stephen Breyer, and Sonia Sotomayor dissented.

2. See Mutch 1988, 1–52; Hasen 2016b, 289–94.

3. See, e.g., Mutch 2014, 139–85.

4. See, e.g., Roe v. Wade, 410 U.S. 113 (1973) (abortion); Furman v. Georgia, 408 U.S. 238 (1972) (the death penalty).

5. See Hasen 2016b, 303 (finding that conference notes from a meeting held two days after the oral argument show that the justices "did not all have definite opinions about the constitutionality of the core contribution and spending provisions of [the challenged legislation]").

6. Austin v. Michigan Chamber of Commerce, 494 U.S. 652 (1990).

7. 494 U.S. at 658–59.

8. 494 U.S. at 680.

9. 494 U.S. at 679.

10. 494 U.S. at 680, 681, 694.

11. Mutch 2014, 160.

12. Mutch 2014, 160–61.

13. Mutch 2014, 160–61.

14. In the years since *Austin*, Justices Marshall, White, and Blackmun had retired, and David Souter, Ruth Bader Ginsburg, and Stephen Breyer had joined the Court.

15. McConnell v. FEC, 540 U.S. 93 (2003).

16. 540 U.S. at 95–96.

17. 540 U.S. at 340 (Kennedy, J., dissenting).

18. BeVier 2007.

19. Gerken 2011.

20. 558 U.S. at 372.

21. 558 U.S. at 343.

22. 558 U.S. at 393–94.

23. 558 U.S. at 396.

24. The dissent took strong issue with the Court's critique of identity-based distinctions:

The basic premise underlying the Court's ruling is its iteration, and constant reiteration, of the proposition that the First Amendment bars regulatory distinctions based on a speaker's identity, including its "identity" as a corporation. . . . The conceit that corporations must be treated identically to natural persons in the political sphere is not only inaccurate but also inadequate to justify the Court's disposition of this case. 558 U.S. 310, 394.

25. 558 U.S. at 425.

26. 558 U.S. at 428.

27. 558 U.S. at 479.

28. 558 U.S. at 414.

29. 558 U.S. at 414. The challenged restriction did not prevent corporations from using segregated funds established by the corporation for political purposes and did not prevent the corporation's stockholders and their families, or the corporation's personnel, from pooling their resources to finance electioneering communications.

30. Post 2014, 4.

31. Post 2014, 4.

32. Post 2014, 4. Post characterized the opposing views this way: "For challengers, regulation is necessary to preserve the integrity of the Republic; for opponents, regulation threatens the freedom of speech necessary for democratic self-governance" (2014, 3).

33. Devins and Baum 2019.

34. Balkin 2020b, 116–17.

35. See, e.g., Bronner 1989. Kalman (2017) traces the origins of "battles royal" over Supreme Court vacancies to the late 1960s.

36. Balkin 2015; Graber 2013.

37. Devins and Baum 2019; Baum 2006.

38. Rubin's vase is an ambiguous figure that can appear as either a vase or as two faces directly opposite one another. Ludwig Wittgenstein used a duck-rabbit image in *Philosophical Investigations* (1953) to illustrate "change of aspect." Escher's woodcuts illustrate a similar perceptual phenomenon. See *Sky and Water I*, woodcut, 1938.

39. Kersch 2006, 295.

40. See Balkin and Levinson 2001, 1068; Gillman 2002, 521–22; McMahon 2011.

41. See, e.g., Dahl 1957; Shapiro 1990; Whittington 2005; Graber 2004; Gillman and Clayton 1999; Tushnet 2005; Balkin 2020b.

42. Balkin and Levinson 2001; Gillman 2006; Teles 2008, 11–12.

43. Balkin and Levinson 2006; Gillman 2006.

44. Epp 1998, 2–5.

45. See Teles 2008; Hollis-Brusky 2011; Hollis-Brusky and Wilson 2020.

46. Teles 2008; Hollis-Brusky 2011, 2015; Southworth 2008, 2017, 2018; Decker 2016; Hollis-Brusky and Wilson 2020.

47. Richard Nixon's victory over George McGovern in the 1972 presidential election gave conservatives four appointments, but the Court's changed composition did not immediately deliver significant change in constitutional law (see Blasi 1983; Schwartz 1998). McMahon (2011, 7) suggests that Nixon's "policy toward the judiciary was geared less toward constructing a thoroughly conservative Supreme Court and more toward tempering judicial liberalism as a means of dismantling the New Deal Democratic coalition."

48. Teles 2008; Southworth 2008.

49. Teles 2008, 6–9.

50. For more on this conceptualization of political parties as "extended party" networks, see Desmarais, La Raja, and Kowal 2015; Masket 2009; Herrnson 2009.

51. See Caldeira and Wright 1998; Shapiro 1990.

52. This is similar to an argument by Stephan Stohler (2019, 6) that shifting understandings of constitutional texts are "best understood as developing within a deliberative partnership between judges and their aligned political parties or elected coalition as they work across governing institutions to elaborate evolving legal positions."

53. Schmidt 2008; Noel 2012; Stohler 2019.

54. Caldeira and Wright 1988; Epstein and Kobylka 1992; Kearney and Merrill 2000; Collins 2004; Hazelton and Hinkle 2022.

55. Balkin 2015, 14–15.

56. Balkin 2015, 16.

57. McMahon 2011, 11.

58. Epp 1998, 18; Kearney and Merrill 2000, 745.

59. McGuire 1995; Johnson, Wahlbeck, and Spriggs 2006; Shapiro and Sweet 2002.

60. Mertz 1996, 235–36.

61. Baird 2007.

62. Devins and Baum 2019; Baum 2006.

63. Siegel 2008; Cole 2016a.

64. NeJaime 2013b; Ziegler 2013; Cole 2016a; Southworth 2008, ch. 7.

65. For example, lawyers teamed up with citizen activists to expand gun rights and to advance marriage equality (Cole 2016a).

66. Since litigating parties face limits on the length of their briefs, amicus briefs can be useful in filling gaps, elaborating key points, and addressing counterarguments.

67. See, generally, Batchis 2016.

68. See, e.g., Sorrell v. IMS Health, Inc., 564 U.S. 552 (2011) (finding that a statute that prohibited the sale of information about medication prescriptions was unconstitutional because it restricted the speech rights of data miners); Janus v. AFSCME, 138 S. Ct. 2448 (2018) (holding that a statute that required public employee unions to pay a fee for the services they received from unions violated the First Amendment).

69. Brown 2002; Lewis 2017. A recent example of the latter type of challenge is Kennedy v. Bremerton School District, 597 U.S. _ (2022) (holding that a Washington state public school district violated the free speech and free exercise rights of a Christian high school football coach who was suspended for refusing to stop praying with players on the field after games).

70. See, e.g., Masterpiece Cakeshop, Ltd. v. Colorado Civil Rights Commission, 584 U.S. _ (2018); 303 Creative LLC v. Elenis, 600 U.S. __ (2023).

71. Batchis 2016; Winkler 2018b; Kessler 2016.

72. For a discussion of how political parties use abstract appeals, including constitutional ideals, as part of a competitive strategy to win elections by building coalitions of support, see Schmidt 2008, 2011. Schmidt calls this phenomenon "coordinative discourse."

73. Schauer 2004, 1790.

74. The "elite" category included law schools ranked in the top seven in the 2017 *US News and World Report* rankings; the "prestige" category included those ranked 8–20; and the "regional" category included those ranked 21–50. Seventeen of the twenty-six interviewed reformers attended Harvard, Yale, Stanford, Chicago, Michigan, NYU, or Columbia, while just six of the challengers attended those schools.

75. The gender composition of the group of interviewed lawyers skewed slightly more heavily male than the larger pool of lawyers involved in these cases, probably reflecting my selection criteria: I sought wherever possible to interview the counsel of record, typically the most senior lawyer involved on the brief, because I was interested in speaking with the lawyers who were most knowledgeable about strategic choices made in connection with this campaign. The underrepresentation of women in counsel of record roles in my research is consistent with their underrepresentation in the top ranks of most sectors of the legal profession.

76. For lists of denominations fitting the evangelical Protestant and mainline Protestant categories, see Pew 2015.

77. Scheingold and Sarat 2004, 3–11.

78. One reformer explained that private-sector election law experts often resist campaign finance regulation, not on policy or ideological grounds, but rather because

> they want to have as few rules apply to their clients as possible. So, their motivation is much different than [the motivation of] the political strategy folks, who are trying to craft messages that resonate with the general public to gain votes on election day. And there's a disconnect there. There's some slippage between the political messaging folks, who know that campaign finance reform is wildly popular, [and] the lawyers who show up at the FEC. Every law that's on the books is another headache for an election lawyer representing a political spender or a political committee, and they just don't want to have to get dragged in front of the FEC and potentially pay a fine for breaking a law. So they'd rather the law not exist . . . They have a job to do, which is keep their clients out of the newspapers and out of trouble with campaign finance regulators. And the fewer rules, the easier it is to do that.

But several election law experts acknowledged that they sometimes benefit from new regulations, as they find lucrative work helping clients navigate the changed legal context. One such lawyer explained that any legal change—whether through legislation imposing restrictions or judicial rulings striking them down—"sends people scrambling" and directs "a lot of work to the practitioners." Another election lawyer observed that reform efforts "provide me and a group of twelve lawyers here [in DC] a very healthy livelihood."

## Chapter Two

1. Common Cause is a government watchdog group founded in 1970 by John Gardner, former secretary of health, education, and welfare under President Lyndon Johnson.

2. The 1971 FECA replaced the Federal Corrupt Practices Act of 1925. It strengthened disclosure requirements and imposed limits on broadcast expenditures while also repealing contribution and expenditure limits. For more on the 1971 FECA and the 1974 amendments, see Mutch 2014, 129–38.

3. United States Senate 1974, 508–09.

4. The Senate Watergate Report documented illegal corporate contributions to the Committee to Reelect the President of over $780,000, including by American Airlines, Ashland Oil, Minnesota Mining and Manufacturing (known as 3M), Gulf Oil, Northrop, Phillips Petroleum, Goodyear, and American Ship Building Co. In their Senate testimony, corporate executives from these companies explained that they made these contributions with the understanding that they were necessary to ensure that their companies' calls would be returned and in response to the implicit threat that if they failed to contribute, they would not be prejudiced in their dealings with the administration. United States Senate 1974, 445–92.

5. See Teles 2008; Decker 2016; Lewis 2017.

6. Teles 2008.

7. Many conservatives were disappointed that the Court did not move sharply to the right after the end of Earl Warren's service as chief justice. Republican presidents made a string of appointments between 1969 and 1991 and moved the Court to the right on some issues. But the Court's rulings on civil rights and civil liberties remained relatively moderate. See Devins and Baum 2019, 88–102.

8. Epp 1998.

9. Horowitz 1980.

10. Duxbury 1995, 330–419; Dezalay and Garth 2002, 276–77; Baumgardner 2022.

11. Brown 2002; den Dulk 2008, 56–79; Lewis 2017; Hollis-Brusky and Wilson 2020.

12. Epstein 1985; Southworth 2005.

13. The memo prepared for the Scaife Foundation by Michael Horowitz explained that liberal public interest lawyers had largely succeeded in "isolat[ing] their conservative counterparts as hyphenated 'public-interest' pretenders"—as organizations "largely oriented to and indeed dominated by business interests, a description which is unhappily not wide of the mark for many such firms." Horowitz predicted that the conservative public interest movement would "make no substantial mark on the American legal profession or American life as long as it is seen as and is in fact the adjunct of a business community possessed of sufficient resources to afford its own legal representation" (Horowitz 1980, 1–2).

14. Horowitz 1980, 85–86.

15. Horowitz 1980, 5 ("It is the premise of this report that the principal yardstick by which conservative public interest law firms must be measured is the caliber, enthusiasm and initiative

of its young lawyer-employees and volunteers, and that real impact on public policy decisions and the law can only come if such talent and enthusiasm can be generated"); 54 ("Only when the staffs at conservative public interest law firms are comprised of law review editors, former law clerks and, in no small part, of alumni of national law schools, will the movement be in a position to initiate and participate in real dialogue and in a truly national competition as to which legal policies and ideologies are truly 'in the public interest'").

16. Horowitz 1980.

17. Southworth 2005, 1255–63; Teles 2008, 220–64.

18. Southworth 2005, 1252–55; Teles 2008, 58–79.

19. Kersch 2019, 365 (as more conservatives joined the bench, conservatives' commitment to judicial deference to majorities "began to wane").

20. Teles 2008, 221; Decker 2016.

21. Southworth 2008, 124–49.

22. Gordon 2017, 362 (originalism "promotes fusionism by means of nostalgia—reconciling disparate elements of the conservative coalition by evoking an imagined past of libertarian economics in solidary Christian community—'traditional values' and 'free markets' together at last"); Post and Siegel 2006, 548 ("claims about fidelity to originalist interpretive methodology became a vehicle for widespread and sustained mobilization of conservatives").

23. Gordon 2017, 366; Cole 2022.

24. See, e.g., Cole 2022.

25. See, e.g., Gordon 2017, 361–81; Greene 2021, 79–82; Siegel 2022, 47–50; Tushnet 2020b, 19–43.

26. See Bork 1971, 6–7; Scalia 1989, 863–64.

27. Teles 2009.

28. Balkin 2020b, 102–08; Keck 2004, 282; Whittington 2004, 604.

29. Barnett 2004; Ginsburg 1995; Epstein 2006.

30. For more on the "many varieties of originalism," see Balkin 2020a.

31. See, e.g., Wilkinson 2012.

32. See, e.g., Barnett 1999.

33. Neily 2013; Barnett 2015.

34. Bork 1971, 22. The idea that the Constitution had a fixed meaning at odds with the vision of progressives long predates the version of originalism that is now a touchstone of the Republican Party (Gillman 1997; TerBeek 2021). But originalism as we understand it today, as an interpretive theory embraced by conservative legal elites, entered legal academic debates in connection with the Warren Court's voting rights decisions. Bork argued that "the rigid one person, one vote requirement" in the Warren Court's legislative reapportionment rulings "runs counter to the text of the fourteenth amendment, the history surrounding its adoption and ratification and the political practice of Americans from colonial times up to the day the Court invented the new formula" (Bork 1971, 18). Even earlier, law review articles by Alfred Avins used claims about the framers' intent to argue for the constitutionality of literacy tests to disqualify voters (TerBeek 2021).

35. Strauss 2010, 52–53; Levy 1985.

36. See Rabban 1983; Post 2000; Neuborne 2015. It was not until the early 1990s, in connection with government efforts to suppress opposition to the First World War, that judges began to articulate views that gave life to the First Amendment. Those views remained minority views into the 1950s and 1960s, but eventually became majority holdings. The Court has since then expanded the categories of "speakers" and "speech."

37. Brief of Amicus Curiae of Center for Constitutional Jurisprudence in Support of Appellant, 2009 WL 2359478.

38. See, e.g., Teachout 2014; Lessig 2011, 245–47; Natelson 2003, 48. Brief of the Brennan Center for Justice at NYU School of Law as Amicus Curiae in Support of Appellee (in *Citizens United*), 2013 WL 3874429; Brief of the League of Women Voters of the United States and Constitutional Accountability Center as Amici Curiae in Support of Appellee, 2009 WL 2365227 (in *Citizens United*); Brief of Constitutional Scholars as Amicus Curiae in Support of Respondents (in *Arizona Free Enterprise Club v. Bennett*), 2011 WL 661706; Brief of Amicus Curiae of Professor Lawrence Lessig in Support of Appellee (in *McCutcheon*), 2013 WL 3874388; McCutcheon v. Federal Election Commission, 572 U.S. at 236–47 (Breyer, J., dissenting) (asserting that the framers enacted the First Amendment to facilitate the connection between the people and their representatives and to make democracy responsive to the people).

39. Justice Stevens made this argument in his dissenting opinion in *Citizens United*, giving reasons why "the Constitution would have been understood" by the framers "to permit reasonable restrictions on corporate electioneering" (558 U.S. at 425–32 [Stevens, J., dissenting]).

40. Southworth 2008, 138–39; Teles 2008, 141–42.

41. In the George H. W. Bush administration, Lee Liberman, one of the Federalist Society's student founders, served as deputy counsel to the president and worked on judicial nominations.

42. See Federalist Society n.d.b. For more on the immense resources of Leo's network of nonprofits, see Vogel and Goldmacher 2022b.

43. The organization's first and only executive director, Eugene Meyer, is the son of Frank Meyer, who in the 1950s tried to unite libertarians and traditionalists around "fusionism," a synthesis of ideas about freedom and moral authority (Nash 1996, 321–22; Gottfried 1993, 16–17). Under Eugene Meyer's leadership, the Federalist Society has pursued a consensus among conservative and libertarian lawyers much like the fusionism that Eugene's father sought among conservative intellectuals decades earlier (see Southworth 2008, 124–48). The organization seeks to cultivate a sense of shared identity among the lawyers for these different constituencies by promoting conversation about the organization's stated purpose of "reordering priorities within the legal system to place a premium on individual liberty, traditional values, and the rule of law" (Federalist Society n.d.a).

44. Federalist Society n.d.a.

45. For more on the importance of amicus coordination, see Collins, Corley, and Hamner 2014; Ebner and Conrad 2015; Hazelton and Hinkle 2022.

46. Hollis-Brusky 2015, 23–27; Southworth 2008, 130–48.

47. Teles 2008, 161.

48. Southworth 2008, 130–47; Teles 2008, 152–62.

49. See, e.g., Scalia 1989. For a discussion of Scalia's inconsistent application of the originalist methods he championed, see Hasen 2018.

50. Silverstein 2009, 164–66.

51. I am indebted to Robert Mutch for exploring the significance of these publications in his first book on the history of campaign finance law (see Mutch 1988, 56–64).

52. Winter 1971.

53. Winter 1971, 60–61.

54. Winter 1971, 60.

55. Winter 1971, 51–52.

56. Winter 1971, 57–58.

57. Winter 1971, 62.

58. Redish 1971, 910. Redish was an associate at Proskauer, Rose, Goetz, and Mendelsohn when he published the article. He joined the Northwestern Law School faculty in 1973.

59. Redish 1971, 907 (citing Meiklejohn 1961).

60. Redish 1971, 908.

61. New York Times v. Sullivan, 376 U.S. 254 (1964).

62. Red Lion Broadcasting v. FCC, 395 U.S. 367 (1969). The fairness doctrine required licensed radio and television broadcasters to present fair and balanced coverage of controversial issues by devoting equal time to opposing viewpoints. In 1987, the Federal Communications Commission formally repealed the fairness doctrine.

63. Mills v. Alabama, 384 U.S. 214 (1966).

64. Redish 1971, 910.

65. Redish 1971, 910.

66. Redish 1971, 911.

67. Winter and Bolton 1973, 3.

68. Winter and Bolton 1973, 12.

69. Winter and Bolton 1973, 14 (quoting Abrams v. United States, 250 U.S. 616, 630 [1919] [Holmes, J., dissenting]).

70. Winter and Bolton 1973, 18.

71. Winter and Bolton 1973, 19.

72. Winter expanded on these arguments in his decisions as a Second Circuit Court of Appeals judge. In *Randall v. Sorrell*, for example, he dissented from a panel's decision upholding Vermont's limits on campaign contributions and expenditures (382 F.3d 91 (2d Cir. 2004)). The Supreme Court thereafter struck down the statute (see Randall v. Sorrell, 548 U.S. 230 (2006)).

73. "Political Reforms" 1973, 1396 ("Financing a candidate to one's heart's content is presumably among the activities that the First Amendment protects. Free speech has some limitations, but the evidence disclosed to date is not convincing on the point that giving more than $3,000 to a candidate is like crying 'fire' in a crowded theater"); "Public Financing: Booby Trap for Conservatives" 1974 (quoting extensively from a report that Winter wrote for the Senate Watergate committee spelling out his First Amendment objections to legislative proposals); Phillips 1974 ("Regulations and ceilings on contributions and expenditures are unjust restrictions on free expression"); "Free Speech and Spending" 1975, 980 ("The First Amendment has become a ball of silly putty in recent years. People whose blood freezes at the thought of not being able to publish government secrets in New York newspapers, whose hearts fail when pornographers are prevented from pandering their wares, who faint at the suggestion that such non-verbal acts as flag-burning and blood-pouring are not speech and hence are not entitled to First Amendment protection—have no doubt about the constitutionality of a law that restricts candidates from spending their own money to get out their messages, which prevents citizens from contributing to candidates and even from taking out advertisements in newspapers on behalf of candidates of their choice"); Kilpatrick 1975 ("[Senators James L. Buckley and Eugene McCarthy] make an odd couple. Philosophically opposed on most issues, they are united in their conviction that the new law tramples upon 1st Amendment freedoms. I think they are right").

74. Brief of the Appellants, 1975 WL 173792.

75. Friedman 1987; BeVier 1987; Cooper 1987.

76. BeVier 1987, 11.

77. BeVier 1987, 13.

78. Cooper 1987, 18–19. BeVier and Cooper thereafter continued to resist campaign finance regulation—BeVier as a constitutional scholar and Cooper as an advocate for parties before the Court. BeVier's articles are frequently cited in briefs filed by challengers—for example, by Mitch McConnell in *McConnell v. FEC*, by the Pacific Legal Foundation in *FEC v. Beaumont* and *Citizens United*, by Citizens United and Gun Owners of America et al. in *FEC v. Wisconsin Right to Life*, by the Center for Competitive Politics in *Davis*, and by the Cato Institute in *McCutcheon*. The Cato Institute's brief in *Citizens United* cited Cooper's 1987 article. After leaving the Reagan Justice Department, Cooper developed a highly successful appellate litigation practice based in DC, and he has represented parties in some of the Court's most significant campaign finance cases, including *McConnell v. FEC* (2003), *FEC v. Wisconsin Right to Life* (2007), and *Citizens United* (2010) (representing the NRA).

79. See United States v. National Committee for Impeachment, 469 F.2d 1135 (2d Cir. 1972).

80. American Civil Liberties Union v. Jennings, 366 F. Supp. 1041 (D.D.C.1973), *vacated sub nom.*, Staats v. American Civil Liberties Union, 422 U.S. 1030 (1975).

81. The "Valeo" in the case name was Secretary of the Senate Francis Valeo. For more on the history of the case, see Mutch 1988, 53–82.

82. Kabaservice 2004, 132–35.

83. Silverstein 2009, 165.

84. Schauer 2004, 1773.

85. Schauer 2015; Neuborne 2015; Lakier 2020b.

86. Buckley v. Valeo, 519 F.2d 821, 842 (D.C. Cir. 1975).

87. 519 F.2d at 841.

88. 519 F.2d at 821. Judges Bazelon, Tamm, Wilkey, and MacKinnon filed partially dissenting opinions.

89. Brief for the Attorney General as Appellee and for the United States as Amicus Curiae, 1975 WL 412237.

90. Brief for the Attorney General and the Federal Election Commission, 1975 WL 171459.

91. Brief for the Attorney General and the Federal Election Commission, 1975 WL 171459.

92. Memorandum from Frank H. Easterbrook to the solicitor general, October 14, 1975 (calling this defense of the spending limit "only the most formal laying on of hands"). The same internal memo also complained about the attorney general's statement in the brief that the case "has nothing to do with freedom of the press, which is left wholly unfettered." Easterbrook continued:

> After all, what is "the press" but those who own the printing presses? Why is that a source of supplemental rights to speak? Indeed, what is ownership of a printing press but accumulated wealth? The brief goes on for pages about the evils of wealth, but would allow Kay Graham [publisher of the *Washington Post*] to speak as much as she wants because her wealth is invested in printing presses rather than in oil refineries. Why?

93. Brief for Appellees Center for Public Financing of Elections, Common Cause, League of Women Voters of the United States et al., 1975 WL 171457.

94. Brief of Amicus Curiae of the Socialist Labor Party in Support of the Appellants Appeal of the Judgments of the United States District Court of the District of Columbia and the United States Court of Appeals for the District of Columbia, 1975 WL 184942.

95. Hasen 2016b, 303–04. According to conference notes, Brennan found the political equality justification for the spending limits compelling, but he nevertheless joined in the part of the opinion that invalidated the spending limits. Hasen has suggested that Brennan "may have sacrificed expressing his views on this question" to further "his desire for as much unanimity as possible when the Court announced its decision" (2016b, 303–304). William Rehnquist, the most conservative jurist on the Court at the time, joined in upholding the limitations on contributions.

96. The *Buckley* Court also found that the method for constituting the FEC violated the appointments clause of the US Constitution (article II, section 2, clause 2), but Congress revised the FEC's appointments procedure soon after the ruling.

97. Buckley v. Valeo, 424 U.S. at 48–49.

98. 424 U.S. at 262 (White, J., dissenting).

99. The phrase "money is speech" first arose during the oral argument in *Buckley*, during Justice Potter Stewart's exchange with the deputy solicitor general, who insisted that large contributions were "not speech." Stewart—who ultimately wrote the part of the decision striking down the spending limitations—responded, "We are talking about speech, money is speech, and speech is money, whether it is buying television or radio time or newspaper advertising, or even buying pencils and paper and microphones" (transcript of Oral Argument, *Buckley v. Valeo*, November 10, 1975, part 1, 1:20:04, https://www.oyez.org/cases/1975/75–-436).

100. 424 U.S. at 17, 25.

101. Undated memorandum from Brice M. Clagett to the plaintiffs in *Buckley v. Valeo*, housed at the University of Virginia's Albert and Shirley Small Special Collections Library in Charlottesville (indicating an outstanding balance of unpaid fees of $18,905.52).

102. In one letter, Koch explained that he had previously supported the Republican Party "but abandoned them in disgust when I found that in spite of their free enterprise rhetoric, they were not better allies in the fight for free enterprise than the Democratic Party." The letter cited President Ford's signing of the Energy Policy and Conservation Act in December 1975 after maintaining he was for oil deregulation as "one of many demonstrations of the bankruptcy of the Republican alternative to Democratic interventionism." He called "Ford's and Nixon's reversals" on wage and price controls "additional examples of selling out by those who claimed to be 'friends of free enterprise'" (Charles G. Koch to "Rocky Mountain Oilman," December 23, 1975, Special Collections, University of Virginia Library, Charlottesville, Virginia).

103. Koch 1974.

104. In one letter to Koch, Crane explained that the Libertarian Party was prepared to request an advisory opinion from the FEC but would prefer to avoid this step because "asking for an advisory opinion from the FEC is a little like telling a child not to put beans in his ear" (Edward Crane to Charles Koch, September 24, 1975, Special Collections, University of Virginia Library, Charlottesville, Virginia).

105. Edward H. Crane III to Charles Koch, February 3, 1976, Special Collections, University of Virginia Library, Charlottesville, Virginia. Upon receiving this letter, Koch immediately sent Crane checks totaling $25,000 from himself, his brother David, and his mother. See Edward H. Crane III to Brice M. Clagett, February 19, 1976, Special Collections, University of Virginia Library, Charlottesville, Virginia.

106. Charles Koch provided most of the money for the founding of the Cato Institute and continued to raise money for it through the early 1990s. But a later rupture in Koch's relationship with Crane led Koch to drastically cut back his support. The Koch brothers sued for control of Cato in 2012. See Mayer 2012.

107. David H. Koch to Libertarian Party delegates, August 22, 1979, Special Collections, University of Virginia Library, Charlottesville, Virginia. The statement also proclaimed that "we exist under a system of restrictive election laws which were passed in order to restrict our growth and preserve the two party monopoly."

108. Clark statement, September 6, 1979, Special Collections, University of Virginia Library, Charlottesville, Virginia.

109. David H. Koch to Libertarian Party delegates, August 22, 1979, Special Collections, University of Virginia Library, Charlottesville, Virginia.

110. Mayer 2016, 57–58.

111. Page, Seawright, and Lacombe 2019, 47, 72–74.

112. 1907 Mass. Acts ch. 581 § 3, 4; 1943 Mass. Acts ch. 273, § 1.

113. Motion of the Chamber of Commerce of the United States of America for Leave to File a Brief Amicus Curiae and Brief Amicus Curiae in Support of Appellants, 1977 WL 189653.

114. Motion of New England Council for Leave to File Brief as Amicus Curiae, 1977 WL 189659 ("Corporations have the same speech rights as natural persons"); Motion for Leave to File Brief as Amicus Curiae and Brief of Amicus Curiae Pacific Legal Foundation in Support of Appellants, 1977 WL 189658 ("The right of both national and local corporate businesses to inform the Massachusetts public of their perspective on important issues is jeopardized by this ill-conceived attempt to isolate the business sector of the American system from the political process"); Motion for Leave to File Brief as Amici Curiae and Brief of Amici Curiae Northeastern Legal Foundation and Mid-America Legal Foundation in Support of Appellants, 1977 WL 189654 (any restriction on the speech rights of corporations would interfere with the need for "a free flow of information, regardless of the character of the speaker").

115. Brief of the State of Montana, Amicus Curiae, 1977 WL 189656. For many years, the Supreme Court took the position that commercial speech—communication facilitating commercial transactions—was not protected by the First Amendment. But in a series of decisions beginning in the 1970s, it struck down laws affecting commercial advertising, finding that the First Amendment protects the right to receive information as well as the right to speak. Commercial speech currently does not receive as much protection as political and artistic expression, but some of the Court's recent rulings seem to call that differential treatment into question. See, e.g., Sorrell v. IMS Health, Inc., 564 U.S. 552 (2011) (invalidating a state law prohibiting the sale of pharmacy data as an impermissible restriction on free speech); Reed v. Town of Gilbert, 576 U.S. 155 (2015) (finding that speech is content-based and subject to heightened review if a regulation "applies to particular speech because of the topic discussed or the idea or message expressed").

116. American Tradition Partnership v. Bullock, 567 U.S. 516 (2012).

117. First National Bank of Boston v. Bellotti, 435 U.S. 765 (1978).

118. Winkler 2018b, 314–20.

119. Winkler 2018b, 312–15 (explaining that Powell's private papers indicate that he identified the issue in the case as the "1st Amend. rts of corps").

120. See Motion of New England Council for Leave to File Brief as Amicus Curiae and Brief of Amicus Curiae the New England Council in Support of Appellants, 1977 WL 189659 ("Corporations have the same first amendment rights as natural persons").

121. 435 U.S. at 775–76 ("The Constitution often protects interests broader than those of the party seeking their vindication. The First Amendment, in particular, serves significant societal interests. The proper question . . . is not whether corporations 'have' First Amendment rights and, if so, whether they are coextensive with those of natural persons. Instead, the question must

be whether [Massachusetts's law] abridges expression that the First Amendment was meant to protect").

122. See Brief of the Chamber of Commerce of the United States of America, 1977 WL 189653 (emphasizing the value to society in having "all points of view, including those of incorporated enterprises, be presented to the public on this important matter"); Motion for Leave to File Brief as Amici Curiae and Brief of Amici Curiae Northeastern Legal Foundation and Mid-America Legal Foundation in Support of Appellants, 1977 WL 189654 (citing cases indicating that the Court "recognized that the First Amendment serves to protect both the speaker's right to speak and the listener's right to hear"); Motion for Leave to File Brief as Amicus Curiae and Brief of Amicus Curiae Pacific Legal Foundation in Support of Appellants, 1977 WL 189658 ("Free speech limitations, such as those imposed by the Massachusetts statute, not only curtail the rights of the plaintiffs who wish to be heard but also limit the public's right to receive information; a right which has been accorded the strongest legal protection").

123. Virginia State Board of Pharmacy v. Virginia Citizens Consumer Council, Inc., 425 U.S. 748 (1976).

124. 435 U.S. at 783.

125. 435 U.S. at 787 n. 26.

126. Appellants' Reply Brief, 1977 WL 189651 ("In order to rule in favor of the Appellants, this Court need not decide whether the Constitution forbids limitations on corporate expenditures or contributions *relative to candidates and political parties*.") In a subsequent case, the Supreme Court upheld a requirement that corporations must use a separate segregated fund to make political contributions and expenditures and solicit contributions to the fund only from their "members." FEC v. National Right to Work Committee, 459 U.S. 197 (1982).

127. See Winkler (2018b, 310–23) using the papers of justices who have retired or died to piece together the story of Justice Powell's efforts to persuade the Court to issue a broad declaration of corporate speech rights and the compromise that resulted—a more limited ruling about the rights of listeners. Winkler credits Powell's law clerk with the idea of emphasizing the rights of listeners rather than the rights of speakers, citing her bench memo to Powell about the case (2018b, 318–19). But the briefs, filed several months before Powell's clerk submitted the bench memo, may have inspired this suggestion.

128. Powell 1971, 2–8.

129. Powell 1971, 8.

130. Powell 1971, 7.

131. US Chamber of Commerce Litigation Center 2022.

132. See Katz 2015.

133. Lewis 2017, 36–37.

134. 424 U.S. at 44 n. 52. The Court distinguished issue advocacy from communications "containing express words of advocacy of election or defeat [for a candidate], such as 'vote for,' 'elect,' 'support,' 'cast your ballot for,' 'Smith for Congress,' 'vote against,' 'defeat,' 'reject.'" Subsequent lower court decisions interpreted this language to mean that communications that did not contain these words were not express advocacy and therefore could not be regulated. Campaign consultants quickly became adept at drafting campaign ads that avoided such "magic words" identified with express advocacy (Hasen 2003, 250).

135. See Brief for the Appellee, 1986 WL 727495. The challengers also received amicus curiae support from the Reporters Committee for Freedom of the Press, the ACLU and Civil Liberties Union of Massachusetts, the National Rifle Association, the Homebuilders Association of

Massachusetts (represented by the Northeastern Legal Foundation), the Catholic League for Religious and Civil Rights, and the US Chamber of Commerce.

136. Brief for the Appellee, 1986 WL 727495.

137. Federal Election Commission v. Massachusetts Citizens for Life, 479 U.S. at 259.

138. Austin v. Michigan Chamber of Commerce, 494 U.S. 652 (1990).

139. Brief for Amici Curiae National Organization for Women, Greenpeace Action, National Abortion Rights Action League, National Right to Work Committee, Planned Parenthood Federation of America, and the Fund for the Feminist Majority in Support of Appellee, 1989 WL 1126845.

140. Brief for Common Cause as Amicus Curiae in Support of Appellants, 1989 WL 1126837.

141. Brief of the Federal Election Commission as Amicus Curiae in Support of the Appellants, 1989 WL 1126834.

142. 494 U.S. at 658–59.

143. Baird 2007, 55–58.

144. Hasen 2012, 779–80, 785–86.

145. Hasen 2012.

### Chapter Three

1. John Cheves, reporter for the *Lexington Herald-Leader*, quoted in McEvers 2019.

2. The local scheme, he wrote, did not go nearly far enough in "controlling . . . the many corrupt—or potentially corrupt—campaign practices involving the raising and spending of money for electioneering." The column called for greater limits on self-funding by candidates and on contributions from persons other than the candidate, disclosure of sources of all contributions over $50, and an effective enforcement authority ("without effective enforcement, the ordinance . . . could become a farce." The column indicated that McConnell's concern about the corrupting influence of unregulated money in politics extended well beyond his local scene; it urged reconsideration of "the place of the private financial contributions in the political process" and called public funding, at least for presidential elections, "an idea whose time has come" (McConnell 1973).

3. Dyche 2009, 28.

4. McConnell 2016, 92.

5. McConnell 2016, 90–91.

6. McConnell 2016, 112.

7. Mayer 2010.

8. In 1998, for example, McConnell helped to defeat a bill sponsored by John McCain to regulate the tobacco industry. The *Wall Street Journal* reported that on the day of the vote, McConnell told his Republican colleagues that the tobacco industry would support the reelection of anyone who opposed the bill.

9. Connolly and Neal 1997.

10. McConnell 1994.

11. McConnell 2016, 94.

12. McConnell 2016, 114.

13. Sonka 2014.

14. Bush 2002.

15. McConnell 2016, 150 ("The day after McCain-Feingold passed the Senate, I announced that I had put together a powerful coalition—including groups as varied as the NRA and the

ACLU—and a top-notch legal team, who'd be taking the case to court . . . We were prepared to take our case all the way to the Supreme Court, and in fact, I had been ready with a legal team since the early 1990s").

16. Briffault 2009, 211; Lichtblau and Confessore 2015.

17. Brief for Intervenor-Defendants Senator John McCain, Senator Russell Feingold, Representative Christopher Shays, Representative Martin Meehan, Senator Olympia Snowe, and Senator James Jeffords, 2003 WL 21999280; Brief of the Honorable Fred Thompson as Amicus Curiae in Support of Defendants-Appellees, 2003 WL 21846015; Brief of Amici Curiae Bipartisan Former Members of the United States Congress in Support of Appellees, 2003 WL 21840772.

18. The 1992 Republican Party platform pledged support for "eliminat[ing] political action committees supported by corporations, unions, or trade associations," but it condemned "the Democrats' shameless plots to make taxpayers foot the bills for their campaigns" through public financing, and it vowed to oppose "arbitrary spending limits—cynical devices which hobble challengers to keep politicians in office." The 1996 platform indicated that the GOP would "eliminate made-in-Washington schemes to rig the election process under the guise of campaign reform," while also asserting that "true reform is indeed needed: ending taxpayer subsidies for campaigns, strengthening party structures to guard against rogue operations, requiring full and immediate disclosure of all contributions, and cracking down on the indirect support, or 'soft money,' by which special interest groups underwrite their favored candidates." The 2000 GOP platform pledged to "stop the abuses of corporate and labor 'soft' money contributions to political parties" and to "require full and timely disclosure on the Internet of all campaign contributions—so the media and public can immediately know who is giving how much to whom." The 2004 platform similarly declared that Republicans supported "enhanced financial disclosure requirements for political campaigns . . . in order to bring about more transparency and accountability in the political system."

19. Republican Party Platforms 2008; 2012.

20. Republican Party Platforms 2016.

21. Republican National Committee 2020.

22. See Persily, Bauer, and Ginsberg 2018; Mann and Corrado 2014.

23. Mutch 2014, 165–69.

24. The 2008 Democratic Party platform stated, "We support campaign finance reform to reduce the influence of moneyed special interests, including public financing of campaigns combined with free television and radio time. . . . As a national party, we will not take any contributions from Political Action Committees during this election." The 2012 platform included this language:

> Our political system is under assault by those who believe that special interests should be able to buy whatever they want in our society, including our government. Our opponents have applauded the Supreme Court's decision in *Citizens United* and welcomed the new flow of special interest money with open arms. In stark contrast, we believe we must take immediate action to curb the influence of lobbyists and special interests on our political institutions. President Obama signed an executive order to establish unprecedented ethics rules so that those who leave the executive branch may not lobby this administration and officials may not accept gifts from lobbyists. We support campaign finance reform, by constitutional amendment if necessary. We support legislation to close loopholes and require greater disclosure of campaign spending. President Obama and the national Democratic Party do not accept contributions from federal

lobbyists this cycle. We support requiring groups trying to influence elections to reveal their donors so the public will know who's funding the political ads it sees. President Obama and the Democrats are fighting to reduce the influence of money in politics and holding Congress to higher conflict-of-interest standards.

The 2016 platform said:

Democrats believe we must fight to preserve the essence of the longest standing democracy in the world: a government that represents the American people, not just a handful of powerful and wealthy special interests. We will fight for real campaign finance reform now. Big money is drowning out the voices of everyday Americans, and we must have the necessary tools to fight back and safeguard our electoral and political integrity. Democrats support a constitutional amendment to overturn the Supreme Court's decisions in *Citizens United* and *Buckley v. Valeo*. We need to end secret, unaccountable money in politics by requiring, through executive order or legislation, significantly more disclosure and transparency—by outside groups, federal contractors, and public corporations to their shareholders. We need to amplify the voices of the American people through a small donor matching public financing system. We need to overhaul and strengthen the Federal Election Commission so that there is real enforcement of campaign finance laws. And we need to fight to eliminate super PACs and outside spending abuses. Our vision for American democracy is a nation in which all people, regardless of their income, can participate in the political process and can run for office without needing to depend on large contributions from the wealthy and the powerful.

The 2020 platform stated:

Democrats believe that the interests and voices of the American people should determine our elections. Money is not speech, and corporations are not people. Democrats will fight to pass a Constitutional amendment that will go beyond merely overturning *Citizens United* and related decisions like *Buckley v. Valeo* by eliminating all private financing from federal elections. In the meantime, Democrats will work with Congress on legislation to strengthen the public funding system by matching small-dollar donations for all federal candidates, crack down on foreign nationals who try to influence elections, and ensure that super PACs are wholly independent of campaigns and political parties. We will bring an end to "dark money" by requiring full disclosure of contributors to any group that advocates for or against candidates, and bar 501(c)(4) organizations from spending money on elections. Democrats will ban corporate PACs from donating to candidates and bar lobbyists from donating, fundraising, or bundling for anyone they lobby.

25. See, e.g., Brief of the Democratic National Committee as Amicus Curiae in Support of Appellee, 2009 WL 2365226 (defending restrictions on corporate campaign spending in *Citizens United*); Brief of the Democratic National Committee as Amicus Curiae Supporting Respondents, 2006 WL 325181 (defending Vermont's candidate expenditure limits in *Randall v. Sorrell* [2006]).

26. Edsall 2019.

27. Bonica and Rosenthal 2016.

28. See Broockman, Ferenstein, and Malhotra 2019 (showing that tech entrepreneurs lean Democratic and share Democratic leanings on social issues [e.g., same-sex marriage, gun con-

trol, the death penalty], taxation, health care, and programs targeted toward the poor, but "do not share conventional Democratic views on the regulation of product and labor markets"); Page and Gilens 2017, 163–65 ("For Democrats, reliance on wealthy campaign donors has dampened any liberal drift on economic policy").

29. In the 2018 cycle, 38 percent of all business PAC contributions—including corporate PACs and PACs affiliated with industry trade associations—went to Democrats and 66 percent went to Republicans. In the 2020 cycle, 43 percent went to Democrats and 57 percent went to Republicans (Huggins 2022, citing data compiled by *OpenSecrets*).

30. Grossmann and Hopkins 2016.

31. See Schauer 2004 (referring to the First Amendment's "magnetism" and describing the many forces exerting outward pressure on the boundaries of the First Amendment and the dearth of interest groups pushing to restrict those boundaries).

32. McConnell 1996.

33. Bopp 1996.

34. Smith 1997a.

35. Bader 1997; Volokh 1999; Caso 1999.

36. Walpin 1997; Stettin 1998.

37. Troy 1998.

38. McConnell 1999.

39. See, e.g., Faucher v. Federal Election Commission, 743 F. Supp. 64 (D. Me. 1990); Maine Right to Life v. FEC, 914 F. Supp. 8 (D. Me. 1996); New Hampshire Right to Life PAC v. Gardner, 99 F.3d 8 (1st Cir. 1996); West Virginians for Life v. Smith, 919 F. Supp. 954 (S.D. W. Va. 1996); Right to Life of Dutchess County v. Federal Election Commission, 6 F. Supp. 2d 248 (S.D.N.Y. 1998); Arkansas Right to Life Political Action Committee v. Butler, 146 F.3d 558 (8th Cir. 1998); Klepper v. Christian Coalition, 259 A.D.2d 926 (N.Y. App. Div. 1999).

40. McIntyre v. Ohio Elections Commission, 514 U.S. 334 (1995).

41. Smith 1994.

42. Smith 1996, 1051.

43. Smith 2001.

44. Lichtblau 2010.

45. See, e.g., BeVier 1985; 1994; 1997; 1999.

46. See, e.g., Smith 2004; BeVier 2002; 2004; Cooper and Shaffer 2004.

47. See sources reviewed in Hollis-Brusky 2015, 61–89.

48. See, e.g., Smith 1997b; Simpson 2007; Simpson and Sherman 2011.

49. Smith 2016, 313–57.

50. See Brennan Center n.d. Neuborne served as national director of the ACLU from 1981 to 1986. In his book on the First Amendment, Neuborne describes how he came to believe that the ACLU's position on campaign finance was misguided (2015, 62–74).

51. Smith 2016, 327.

52. See, e.g., James Madison Center for Free Speech n.d.

53. Institute for Free Speech n.d.

54. Altman 2015.

55. Institute for Justice 2001 ("Charles Koch provided the initial seed funding that made it possible to launch the Institute in 1991. David Koch has been a generous benefactor each year of IJ's first decade").

56. See Institute for Justice n.d.a.

57. Institute for Justice n.d.c.

58. Institute for Justice n.d.b.

59. For more on the NAACP's strategy, see Tushnet 2005. For an account of civil rights legal strategies, including test case litigation, that preceded NAACP initiatives beginning in the 1920s and 1930s, see Carle 2013.

60. Smith 2016, 333.

61. Smith 2016, 334.

62. Mencimer 2011.

63. James Arthur Pope took over his family's discount conglomerate and family foundation after graduating from Duke Law School in 1981. He served in the state legislature in North Carolina but was badly defeated in his race for lieutenant governor in 1992. He has been a major financial ally in efforts spearheaded by conservative political strategist Ed Gillespie to accomplish a Republican takeover of state legislatures (Mayer 2011, describing Pope's role in the REDMAP project).

64. Bose 2020.

65. Amway's business model, in which salesmen were treated as independent business owners and compensated based on their own sales and sales by distributors they recruited, resulted in numerous disputes with the Internal Revenue Service and Federal Trade Commission, which alleged that the company essentially operated as an illegal pyramid scheme.

66. DeVos 1997.

67. Southworth 2017. Donors Trust Inc. later became a major funder of these groups.

68. Stevens and Dolmetsch 2013.

69. *OpenSecrets* 2020b (showing that he gave over $65 million to outside groups in the 2020 election cycle).

70. Joyce Foundation n.d.

71. Pew Charitable Trusts n.d.

72. In 2005, the Pew Charitable Trusts came under scrutiny for its role in funding efforts in 2002 to ensure passage of the Bipartisan Campaign Reform Act. See Philanthropy News Digest 2005.

73. Ford Foundation n.d. (describing as its primary goals "to reduce poverty and injustice, strengthen democratic values, promote international cooperation, and advance human achievement").

74. Open Society Foundations n.d. ("We therefore work to build vibrant and inclusive societies, grounded in respect for human rights and the rule of law, whose governments are accountable and open to the participation of all people").

75. Bruhl and Feldman 2017. Franze and Anderson (2018) found that amici filed on average between nine and fourteen briefs per argued case in the seven terms preceding 2017–2018.

76. Balkin 2001, 1444–45.

77. Abrams 2013, 7.

78. Hollis-Brusky and Wilson 2020, 51–52 (quoting from a "Proposed School of Law Feasibility Study" prepared by Titus for Pat Robertson and the board of trustees of Christian Broadcasting Network University, later renamed Regent University).

79. William J. Olson, P.C., Attorneys at Law n.d.

80. See https://www.linkedin.com/in/william-olson-925235b.

81. Sekulow is also a key figure in long-standing efforts to integrate various strands of the conservative coalition. In 2003, the year *McConnell* was decided, C. Boyden Gray, an establishment

icon who served as White House counsel to President George H. W. Bush, formed the Committee for Justice to unite the conservative coalition around the goal of confirming President George W. Bush's judicial nominations. Sekulow was one of the lawyers whom Gray recruited to help with the effort. Other prominent lawyers associated with the Committee for Justice during its first few years included Leonard Leo, then executive vice president of the Federalist Society, and Edwin A. Meese III of the Heritage Foundation.

82. Cato and IJ joined in asking the Supreme Court to invalidate the BCRA but also to reconsider *Buckley's* holding that limitations on campaign contributions and disclosure requirements were constitutional (Brief Amici Curiae the Cato Institute and the Institute for Justice in Support of Appellants, 2003 WL 21649638).

83. The last of these reform groups was founded in 2002 by former FEC chairman Trevor Potter, who also served as general counsel to John McCain's 2000 and 2008 presidential campaigns and as deputy general counsel to George H. W. Bush's 1988 presidential campaign. Potter is perhaps better known to the public as the lawyer for Stephen Colbert's super PAC, "Americans for a Better Tomorrow, Tomorrow." In a series of segments in 2011 and 2012 on the television comedy show *The Colbert Report*, Stephen Colbert, as a mock conservative pundit, interviewed former FEC commissioner Trevor Potter to review the basics of setting up a PAC, a super PAC (Americans for a Better Tomorrow, Tomorrow, Inc.), and a 501(c)(4) (Colbert super PAC Shhh!) to which donations could be given anonymously. These segments also explored laws designed to prevent coordination between candidates and supposedly independent groups.

84. Brief of Amici Curiae, Former Leaders of the American Civil Liberties Union, in Support of Appellees/Cross-Appellants Federal Election Commission, et al., 2003 WL 21845108.

85. Brief of Amici Curiae Committee for Economic Development, Warren E. Buffett, Edward A. Kangas, Jerome Kohlberg, Paul Volcker, and Sixteen Other Business Leaders in Support of Appellees, 2003 WL 21841439.

86. McConnell v. FEC, 540 U.S. 93 (2003).

87. 540 U.S. at 96 (quoting Federal Election Commission v. Colorado Republican Federal Campaign Committee, 533 U.S. 431, 444 [2001]).

88. Robert Bork called Miers's nomination a "disaster" and "a slap in the face to the conservatives who've been building up a conservative legal movement for the last 20 years" (Cannon 2005). Religious conservatives initially defended Miers against those objections, arguing that they reflected an elitism common within the legal establishment. But Christian right leaders later concluded that Miers had not taken sufficiently clear positions on abortion, gay rights, and religious expression in public life (Scheiber 2005).

89. One exception for Justice Roberts came in Williams-Yulee v. Florida Bar, 575 U.S. 433 (2015). That decision found that a restriction on personal solicitation of campaign contributions by judicial candidates was necessary to preserve public confidence in the integrity of the judiciary.

### Chapter Four

1. The Supreme Court essentially agreed with Judge Ralph Winter's dissenting opinion in the DC Circuit Court of Appeals decision below. *Landell v. Sorrell*, 382 F.3d 91 (2d Cir. 2004) (Winter J., dissenting).

2. Federal Election Commission v. Wisconsin Right to Life, 551 U.S. 449 (2007).

3. Davis v. Federal Election Commission, 554 U.S. 724 (2008).

4. SpeechNow.org v. FEC, 599 F.3d 686, 694 (D.C. Cir. 2010) (finding that *Citizens United* held "as a matter of law that independent expenditures do not corrupt or create the appearance of *quid pro quo* corruption," so that "contributions to groups that make only independent expenditures also cannot corrupt or create the appearance of corruption").

5. American Tradition Partnership Inc. v. Bullock, 567 U.S. 516 (2012).

6. It was founded in 1988 by Floyd Brown, who is perhaps best known for creating the famous "Willie Horton" ad attacking 1988 Democratic presidential nominee Michael Dukakis in his race against George H. W. Bush. During Bill Clinton's first presidential campaign, Brown established a 1-900 number to enable people to hear segments of recorded phone conversations between Bill Clinton and Gennifer Flowers (Cockerman 2007).

7. Citizens United n.d.c. Bossie took a brief leave of absence in 2016 to serve as deputy campaign manager of Donald Trump's presidential campaign and then to lead the transition team before returning to the organization.

8. Citizens United n.d.a.

9. Titles in its collection include *Occupy Unmasked, Battle for America, America at Risk, Border War: The Battle of Illegal Immigration, ACLU: At War with America, Broken Promises: The United Nations at 60, The Gift of Life*, and *Fire from the Heartland* (Citizens United n.d.b).

10. The First Amendment reads in relevant part: "Congress shall make no law respecting an establishment of religion, or prohibiting the free exercise thereof; or abridging the freedom of speech, or of the press."

11. See Gerken and Newland 2016, 368–75. The Court granted the Internet heightened constitutional protection in cases such as Reno v. ACLU, 521 U.S. 844 (1997), which held that the federal Communications Decency Act was an unconstitutional restriction on free speech.

12. Mencimer 2008.

13. See Palazzolo 2008.

14. Still, Olson's brief criticized the definition of corruption adopted in some of the Court's previous rulings and questioned the soundness of the BCRA's distinction between different types of media—its regulation of broadcast advertising but not other forms of communication (Brief for the Appellants, 2009 WL 61467). The Court eventually took up these arguments.

15. Transcript of Oral Argument at 26–31.

16. Toobin 2012.

17. Toobin 2012.

18. Brief for Appellant, 2009 WL 61467 (quoting Justice Roberts's opinion in Wisconsin Right to Life II, 127 S. Ct. at 266).

19. Memorandum in Support of Plaintiff's Summary Judgment Motion, Citizens United v. Federal Election Commission, No. 07–2240 (D.D.C. May 16, 2008).

20. See, e.g., Amicus Curiae Brief of the American Civil Rights Union in Support of Appellant Citizens United, 2009 WL 132718 ("The movie is the cinematic equivalent of a book presenting a biography of a leading political figure, with both factual analysis and opinion. The author may openly express a political ideology or viewpoint, but that does not reduce constitutional protection for the book"); Brief of Amicus Curiae the Cato Institute in Support of Appellant, 2009 WL 106650 (arguing that the First Amendment protects contributors' freedom of anonymous expressive association and quoting the Court's decision in Talley v. California, 362 U.S. 60, 64 [1960] ["Anonymous pamphlets, leaflets, brochures, and even books have played an important role in the progress of mankind. Persecuted groups and sects from time to time throughout history have been able to criticize oppressive practices and laws either anonymously or not at

all"]); Brief of the Foundation for Free Expression as Amicus Curiae Supporting Petitioner, 2009 WL 97752 ("Although current law extends only to broadcast media, if it is applied to an informational documentary so dissimilar to the 'virtual torrent' of TV ads that concerned Congress, the potential exists to enact laws that regulate television shows, books, magazines, and newspaper editorials—in short, the entire press").

21. This lawyer was referring to an opinion by Justice Roberts, on behalf of the majority, announcing that "enough is enough" before finding that an ad could be regulated only if it "is susceptible of no reasonable interpretation other than as an appeal to vote for or against a specific candidate" (551 U.S. at 479).

22. The challenged section of the BCRA applied only to broadcast, cable, and satellite communications, but the book-banning exchange in the first round of argument had raised the specter that the statutory scheme of which it was a part might be construed to reach books.

23. Transcript of Oral Argument at 65–66, Citizens United v. Federal Elections Commission, 558 U.S. 310 (2010), September 9, 2009, 2009 WL 6325467 (U.S.) (oral argument).

24. Transcript of Oral Argument at 66.

25. Amici on the FEC's side generally insisted that the Court should not roll back longstanding restrictions on corporate campaign expenditures. The Committee for Economic Development, a 501(c)(3) organization of two hundred senior corporate executives and university leaders, argued that "a decision striking down the ban on corporate electioneering expenditures would severely harm corporate interests" by "expos[ing] corporations to corrupt shakedowns for political money." Other amici focused primarily on defending the constitutionality of the BCRA's disclosure and reporting provisions and similar state statutes. The Hachette Book Group, Inc. and Harper Collins brief addressed the deputy solicitor general's response to a question during oral argument about whether books downloaded on a Kindle could be regulated by the FEC; it asserted that books were clearly exempted from BCRA section 203 and therefore that there was no reason for the Court to overrule *Austin* or *McConnell* to guarantee the constitutional protection of electoral speech in books. A brief filed by twenty-six states urged the Court to resolve the case without overruling *Austin*; it argued that the states have a strong interest in regulating corporate campaign electioneering to protect the integrity of the political process. The Independent Sector, a nonprofit organization that advocates for charities and foundations, asked the Court to rule for Citizens United under the MCFL exception.

26. This reference is to United States v. International Union United Automobile Workers, 352 U.S. 567 (1957), a case establishing congressional power to regulate political expenditures by labor unions.

27. 558 U.S. at 340, 354.

28. See, e.g., Brief Amicus Curiae of the Institute for Justice in Support of Appellant on Supplemental Question, 2009 WL 2365219 ("*Austin* and *McConnell* allow discrimination against speech based on . . . the identity of the speaker"); Brief of the Michigan Chamber of Commerce as Amicus Curiae in Support of Appellant and Reversal of Austin v. Michigan Chamber of Commerce on Supplemental Question, 2009 WL 2359476 (arguing that "there is no compelling state interest justifying the discrimination against corporations and suppression of their political speech").

29. McConnell v. FEC, 540 U.S. at 297 (opinion of Kennedy, J.)

30. 558 U.S. at 360.

31. 558 U.S. at 469.

32. 558 U.S. at 469.

33. 558 U.S. at 447–48:

Corruption can take many forms. Bribery may be the paradigm case. But the difference between selling a vote and selling access is a matter of degree, not kind. And selling access is not qualitatively different from giving special preference to those who spend money on one's behalf. Corruption operates along a spectrum, and the majority's apparent belief that *quid pro quo* arrangements can be neatly demarcated from other improper influences does not accord with the theory or reality of politics. It certainly does not accord with the record Congress developed in passing BCRA, a record that stands as a remarkable testament to the energy and ingenuity with which corporations, unions, lobbyists, and politicians may go about scratching each other's backs—and which amply supported Congress' determination to target a limited set of especially destructive practices.

34. Childress 2012; Brissenden 2012.

35. See, e.g., "The Court's Blow to Democracy" 2010 ("With a single, disastrous 5-to-4 ruling, the Supreme Court has thrust politics back to the robber-baron era of the 19th century. Disingenuously waving the flag of the First Amendment, the court's conservative majority has paved the way for corporations to use their vast treasuries to overwhelm elections and intimidate elected officials into doing their bidding"); "Corporate Money in Politics" 2010 ("The Supreme Court's ruling in the *Citizens United* campaign finance case opened a dangerous pathway for corporations to spend money in direct support of—or in opposition to—candidates for federal office").

36. One explained, "We weren't that concerned that Chevron and Exxon and McDonald's and Wendy's and Pepsi and Coke were going to jump into elections and spend a bunch of money . . . We didn't think that would happen because generally businesses don't want their names explicitly associated with partisan politics because it alienates huge sections of their consumer base." Another reformer explained that individual business owners, or business executives coordinating through PACs, now typically handle political spending that serves their interests: "Corporations themselves, I don't think, have poured a great deal of money in, but they don't have to. . . . It's the rich guys that own them." But he predicted that corporations would get more directly into the game if managers believed that the strategy would be effective: "There's a slight inhibition now, and the inhibition now is because General Motors doesn't want to sell Democratic cars and Ford doesn't want to sell Republican cars. . . . But there will come settings in which the stakes are such that they won't hold back." Another reformer agreed that most corporations avoid direct spending in elections because "it still seems sort of skeevy." But this "wave has yet to crash," he believed: "I don't think we have the full ramifications of *Citizens United* yet—I think it's on the horizon still."

37. Federal Election Commission v. Wisconsin Right to Life, Inc., 551 U.S. 449 (2007).

38. This lawyer also referred to an article coauthored by the chief justice of the Delaware Supreme Court, which argues that the holding of *Citizens United* is at war with conservative corporate governance theory. That theory assumes that corporate managers should focus solely on maximizing profit while leaving it to government regulation to set the rules of the game. Allowing corporate wealth to target who gets elected to regulate corporate conduct undermines conservative corporate governance theory's reliance on regulation as the answer to the risk that corporations will impose negative externalities on society. See Strine and Walter 2015.

39. Buckley v. Valeo, 424 U.S. at 58–59, 107–108 (1976) (per curiam).

40. Reply Brief of Petitioners Arizona Free Enterprise Club's Freedom Club PAC, et al., 2011 WL 970340.

41. W. Maurer 2011.

42. Keller 2008.

43. See Koslov 2011.

44. See, e.g., Brief of Amici Curiae Campaign Legal Center, Democracy 21, League of Women Voters of the United States, League of Women Voters of Arizona, Public Citizen, Citizens for Responsibility and Ethics in Washington, New Jersey Appleseed Public Interest Law Center and Sierra Club in Support of Respondents, 2011 WL 686401; Brief of Amicus Curiae Center for Governmental Studies in Support of Respondents, 2011 WL 639368.

45. See, e.g., Brief for Amici Curiae Anthony Corrado, Thomas Mann and Norman Ornstein in Support of Respondents, 2011 WL 661708; Professors of Constitutional and Election Law in Support of Respondents, 2011 WL 686402.

46. Arizona Free Enterprise Club's Freedom PAC v. Bennett, 564 U.S. 721, 749 (2011).

47. 564 U.S. at 784.

48. 564 U.S. at 761.

49. 564 U.S. at 763.

50. B. Maurer 2011.

51. Koslov 2011.

52. Randall v. Sorrell, 548 U.S. 230 (2006).

53. Buckley v. Valeo, 424 U.S. at 38; McConnell v. FEC, 540 U.S. at 138 n. 40, 152–53 n. 48 (approving Buckley's holding on aggregate limits).

54. Najvar and Backer 2013.

55. The following organizations filed amicus briefs supporting the challenge: the Cato Institute, Institute for Justice, Center for Competitive Politics, Downsize DC Foundation, Free Speech Coalition (and Free Speech Defense and Education Fund), Gun Owners Foundation, Gun Owners of America, Inc., English First Foundation, English First, Lincoln Institute for Research and Education, Abraham Lincoln Foundation for Public Policy, Institute on the Constitution, American Civil Rights Union, Cause of Action Institute, Wisconsin Institute for Law and Liberty, Committee for Justice, Tea Party Leadership Fund, National Defense PAC, Combat Veterans for Congress PAC, Conservative Melting Pot, Freedom Defense Fund, US Justice Foundation, Western Center for Journalism, Libertarian National Committee, Constitution Party National Committee, and Thomas Jefferson Center for Protection of Free Expression.

56. Organizations that filed or joined amicus briefs in support of the FEC's position were the Campaign Legal Center, Asian American Legal Defense and Education Fund, Common Cause, League of Women Voters, Public Campaign, US PIRG, Brennan Center for Justice, Americans for Campaign Reform, AARP, Asian Americans Advancing Justice, Citizens for Responsibility and Ethics in Washington, Progressives United, Communication Workers of America, Greenpeace, NAACP, Sierra Club, American Federation of Teachers, National Education Association, AFSCME, Service Employees International Union, Main Street Alliance, OurTime.org, People for the American Way Foundation, Rock the Vote, and Working Families Organization. Also filing briefs in support of the FEC's position were a group of Democratic members of the US House of Representatives, as well as Harvard Law professor Lawrence Lessig.

57. Reply Brief for Appellant Shaun McCutcheon, 2013 WL 4495142. The Supreme Court has ruled that government regulation of First Amendment rights must be "narrowly tailored," which means that laws must be written precisely to minimize burdens on protected liberties.

58. McCutcheon v. Federal Election Commission, 572 U.S. at 227.

59. 572 U.S. 185.

60. 572 U.S. at 191.

61. 572 U.S. at 192 (quoting *Citizens United*, 558 U.S. at 360).

62. 572 U.S. at 192 (quoting *Citizens United*, 558 U.S. at 360).

63. McCutcheon v. Federal Election Commission, 572 U.S. at 260–61 (2012) (Breyer, J., dissenting).

64. For descriptions of the various contribution limits as of 2023, see Federal Election Commission n.d.a.

65. Kumar 2020.

66. Muller 2021.

67. A lawyer who identified himself as "an Elizabeth Warren Democrat" observed that Republicans have more billionaire supporters than Democratic candidates do, but that was not his biggest concern: "We have our billionaires; they have their billionaires." The larger problem, he said, is that the opinions and priorities of big donors aligned with both major parties differ from the policy preferences of average American voters, especially on economic issues.

68. For more detail on foundation grants to organizations that filed briefs in *Citizens United* and *McCutcheon*, see Southworth 2017, 13–16.

69. The careers of some of these advocates have benefitted from their willingness to argue either side of the issue, even though they have become more associated with one side than the other as the Court and the profession have become more politically divided. Ted Olson, for example was solicitor general when the Supreme Court decided *McConnell* in favor of the FEC, but he thereafter argued on behalf of Citizens United to overturn parts of *McConnell*. While serving as deputy solicitor general and solicitor general, Paul Clement represented the FEC in McConnell v. FEC, 540 U.S. 93 (2003) and Federal Election Commission v. Beaumont, 539 U.S. 146 (2003). (One reformer believed that Clement's success in *Beaumont* "was one of the things that started his rise within the ranks of Supreme Court advocates.") But after returning to private practice, he represented plaintiffs in a First Amendment challenge to Vermont's contribution limits in Randall v. Sorrell, 548 U.S. 230 (2006) and to Alaska's campaign finance law in Thompson v. Hebdon, 589 U.S. _ (2019). He has also handled high-profile cases challenging other types of government regulations, including McDonald v. Chicago, 561 U.S. 742 (2010), which found that Washington, DC's handgun ban violated the Second Amendment; Hobby Lobby v. Burwell, 573 U.S. 682 (2013), which invalidated regulations imposing a contraception mandate under the Affordable Care Act; and Epic Systems Corp. v. Lewis, 584 U.S. _ (2018), which upheld the enforceability of arbitration agreements containing class- and collective-action waivers despite contrary protections under federal and state labor law; and New York State Rifle & Pistol Ass'n v. Bruen, 597 U.S. _ (2022), which struck down a New York law requiring applicants for an unrestricted license to carry a concealed firearm in public to demonstrate a special need for self-defense.

70. For more on the importance of these factors, see Nelson and Epstein 2022; McGuire 1995.

71. Olson disappointed many conservatives by arguing in favor of overturning California's Proposition 8, banning same-sex marriages in Hollingsworth v. Perry, 558 U.S. 183 (2010), and against the Trump administration's rescission of the Deferred Action for Childhood Arrivals

(DACA) in US Dept. of Homeland Security v. Regents of the University of California, 591 U.S. _ (2020).

72. Bopp served as co-chair of the Society's Free Speech and Election Law Practice from its founding in 1996 until 2005. Allison Hayward, another past chair of the practice group, filed a brief on behalf of several campaign finance scholars in *Citizens United* and for IFS in the Arizona case. Other lawyers who participated in these cases and have been active in the practice group include Anthony Caso (Center for Constitutional Jurisprudence); Reid Alan Cox, Stephen Hoersting, and Brad Smith (IFS); William Maurer and Steve Simpson (IJ); Hans von Spakovsky (Heritage Foundation); and Stephen Klein and Benjamin Barr (Wyoming Liberty Group). Ted Olson was one of the speakers at the first Federalist Society symposium (along with Robert Bork) at Yale Law School in 1982 and has been active ever since. Curt Levey, who filed a brief on behalf of the Committee for Justice in *McCutcheon*, is on the Executive Committee of the Federalist Society's Civil Rights Practice Group. Ilya Shapiro, who filed briefs on behalf of the Cato Institute in all three cases, is a regular lecturer at Federalist Society events. Charles Cooper, counsel for the NRA in *Citizens United*, has been a frequent speaker at the Federalist Society's national conventions and a regular contributor to its publications since the 1980s. Edwin Meese III, on the brief for the Center for Constitutional Jurisprudence in *Citizens United*, is on the Federalist Society's board of directors. Cleta Mitchell, counsel for the American Justice Partnership and Let Freedom Ring in *Citizens United*, has served on Free Speech and Election Law Practice Group panels and as a frequent speaker at Federalist Society city chapter meetings. Other lawyers who participated in these cases on the challengers' side and also served as speakers at Federalist Society events include Paul Avelar and Nicholas Dranias.

73. Federalist Society 2015, 44.

74. As shown in table 4.1, 87 percent of lawyers on the FEC's side in *Citizens United* attended law schools in the top twenty in the *US News and World Report* rankings (the "elite" and "prestige" categories combined), as compared to half the lawyers on briefs on Citizens United's side. One-third of lawyers on Citizens United's side attended local law schools, defined as schools ranked below fifty in *US News*, while just 2 percent of lawyers for the FEC's side attended those schools. These differences were even more pronounced in *Arizona Free Enterprise Club* and *McCutcheon*, probably because the ACLU and several other civil liberties groups that tend to attract lawyers with especially elite credentials and were on the challenger's side in *Citizens United* did not participate in those cases. In the *Arizona* case, 75 percent of the lawyers on the defenders' side had attended top-twenty law schools, while that was true of just 22 percent of the lawyers on the challengers' side. In *McCutcheon*, 94 percent of the lawyers on the government's side attended top-twenty law schools versus 49 percent of lawyers on the challengers' side.

75. Lichtblau 2010.


## Chapter Five

1. Mutch 2014, 165–69, 171.

2. Epstein and Kobylka 1992; Kearney and Merrill 2000; Collins 2004.

3. Brief for Intervenor Defendants Senator John McCain et al., 2003 WL 21999280; Brief of Amici Curiae Representatives Castle and Price et al., 2003 WL 21845700; Brief of Amicus Curiae Bipartisan Former Members of the United States Congress in Support of Appellees, 2003 WL 21840772; Brief of the Honorable Fred Thompson as Amicus Curiae in Support of Defendants-Appellees, 2003 WL 21846015.

4. Supplemental Brief of Amici Curiae Senator John McCain et al., 2009 WL 2365214. John McCain became a reformer after the "Keating Five" scandal made news in the late 1980s and tarnished his reputation. The scandal involved large campaign contributions made by Charles Keating Jr., head of Lincoln Savings and Loan, to five senators who helped to scuttle an investigation by the Federal Home Loan Bank Board into the thrift's operations. Lincoln eventually collapsed, at great cost to taxpayers.

5. Brief of Amicus Curiae National Rifle Association in Support of Appellant, 2009 WL 147861.

6. See, e.g., Brief of Amicus Curiae Alliance Defense Fund in Support of Appellant, 2009 WL 132716.

7. Brief of Amicus Curiae Chamber of Commerce of the United States of America in Support of Appellant, 2009 WL 154011; Brief of the Michigan Chamber of Commerce as Amicus Curiae in Support of Appellant and Reversal of Austin v. Michigan Chamber of Commerce on Supplemental Question, 2009 WL 2359476.

8. See Brief of Amicus Curiae National Rifle Association in Support of Appellant on Supplemental Question, 2009 WL 2359481, p. 3 (arguing that the Court "should overrule *Austin* and *McConnell v. FEC*, 540 U.S. 93 (2003), at least to the extent they stand for the arresting proposition that government may bar nonprofit advocacy corporations from using individual donations to fund political speech . . . Alternatively, this Court should overrule *Austin* in whole and *McConnell* in part, holding that all corporations (for-profit and nonprofit alike) are no less entitled under the First Amendment than are other speakers to air their independent political speech to the public, including around election time").

9. Among the organizations taking this position were the Center for Constitutional Jurisprudence, Alliance Defense Fund, Fidelis Center for Law and Policy, CatholicVote.com, American Justice Partnership, Let Freedom Ring, Wyoming Liberty Group, and the Goldwater Institute. Also supporting this position was a coalition of conservative organizations that included the National Center for Public Policy Research, DownsizeDC.org, Gun Owners of America, National Right to Work Committee, National Taxpayers Union, US Border Control, and English First. Other organizations represented on this brief included Free Speech Defense and Education Fund, Inc.; American Values; Concerned Women for America; Conservative Legal Defense and Education Fund; Downsize DC Foundation; English First Foundation; Gun Owners Foundation; Institute on the Constitution; Lincoln Institute for Research and Education; National Center for Public Policy Research; US Border Control Foundation; United States Constitutional Rights Legal Defense Fund, Inc.; Free Speech Coalition, Inc.; Abraham Lincoln Foundation for Public Policy Research, Inc.; and Americans for the Preservation of Liberty.

10. Motion for Leave to File Brief as Amicus Curiae and Brief of Amicus Curiae Pacific Legal Foundation in Support of Appellants, 1977 WL 189658.

11. Brief Amicus Curiae of Pacific Legal Foundation in Support of Appellant on Supplemental Question, 2009 WL 2349017.

12. Brief Amicus Curiae of Pacific Legal Foundation in Support of Appellants on Supplemental Question, 2009 WL 2349017.

13. Supplemental Brief for Amicus Cato Institute in Support of Appellant, 2009 WL 2365223 (arguing that *Austin* and *McConnell* "were fundamentally erroneous and untrue to the core principles of the First Amendment" and therefore that the policies supporting the observance of precedents were "at their nadir" in this case); Brief Amicus Curiae of the Institute for Justice

in Support of Appellant on Supplemental Question, 2009 WL 2365219 (asserting that *"Austin* and *McConnell* Allow Discrimination Against Speech Based on Its Content and the Identity of the Speaker").

14. See, e.g., Brief for the Appellant, 2009 WL 61467 ("Whatever the continuing vitality of *Austin*, its rationales clearly do not support a ban on speech that, like *Hillary*, is funded predominantly by individuals. *MCFL* held that a voluntary membership organization committed to a political purpose does not lose its First Amendment rights simply by taking the corporate form. Although the "resources in the treasury of a *business corporation* . . . are not an indication of popular support for the corporation's political ideas," nonprofit advocacy groups that take the corporate form "do not pose that danger of corruption" because they are "formed to disseminate political ideas, not to amass capital" (citing Federal Election Commission v. Massachusetts Citizens for Life, 479 U.S. at 258–59 [emphasis added]).

15. As explored in chapter 2, in an influential critique of conservative public interest organizations delivered in a report for the Scaife Foundation, Michael Horowitz argued that most of the existing organizations had failed to meet "the great need for vibrant, intellectually respectable conservative law/action centers." The Institute for Justice was one of the "second-generation" public interest organizations established thereafter to respond to concerns raised by Horowitz and others. See Southworth 2005, 1252–58.

16. See, e.g., Maine Right to Life Committee v. FEC, 98 F.3d 1 (1st Cir. 1996); FEC v. Christian Action Network, Inc., 110 F.3d 1049 (4th Cir. 1997); Right to Life of Dutchess County v. FEC, 6 F. Supp.2d 248 (S.D.N.Y. 1998); Vermont Right to Life v. Sorrell, 875 F. Supp. 2d 376 (D. Vt. 1998); Federal Election Commission v. Christian Coalition, 52 F. Supp. 2d 45 (1999).

17. Carney 1997.

18. Doe v. Reed, 561 U.S. 186 (2010).

19. Kirkpatrick 2010.

20. 479 U.S. 238 (1986).

21. Federal Election Commission v. Wisconsin Right to Life, Inc., 551 U.S. 449 (2007).

22. Wisconsin Right to Life was a not-for-profit corporation that accepted contributions by for-profit corporations, but the Court found that unless its ads could not reasonably be interpreted as anything other than appeals to support or defeat a candidate, they were eligible for an "as applied" exception to the McCain-Feingold limits on issue ads close to an election.

23. Davis v. Federal Election Commission, 554 U.S. 724 (2008).

24. Federal Election Commission v. Beaumont, 539 U.S. 146 (2003).

25. Ziegler 2022.

26. See Beaumont v. Federal Election Commission, 137 F. Supp. 648 (E.D. N.C. 2000); Beaumont v. FEC, 278 F.3d 261 (4th Cir. 2002).

27. Respondent's Brief, 2003 WL 301151.

28. FEC v. Beaumont, 539 U.S. 146, 147 (2003).

29. 539 U.S. at 160.

30. 539 U.S. at 160.

31. The "soft money" restrictions were designed to ban unlimited contributions from individuals, labor unions, and corporations to party committees that were purportedly for "party building" but in practice often were used to help specific campaigns. The electioneering provisions were designed to address what were often dubbed "sham" issue ads—ads that effectively operated as direct support for a candidate. The electioneering provisions prohibited an organization from using its corporate treasury to fund advertisements run within thirty days of

the election, but they permitted an organization to pay for the ads through the organization's political action committee.

32. Brief of Plaintiffs-Appellants/Cross-Appellees National Right to Life Committee et al., 2003 WL 21999398. The Court upheld the BCRA's limitations on corporate electioneering against a facial challenge in Wisconsin Right to Life, Inc. v. Federal Election Commission (WRTL I), 546 U.S. 410 (2006), but in Federal Election Commission v. Wisconsin Right to Life (WRTL II), 551 U.S. 449 (2007), the Court found that those limitations were unconstitutional as applied to Wisconsin Right to Life's ads.

33. 551 U.S. 449 (2007).

34. Reply Brief for Appellant, 2006 WL 26087; Brief Opposing Motion to Dismiss or Affirm, 2005 WL 1827796; Brief for Appellee, 2007 WL 868545.

35. Brief of Amicus Curiae Chamber of Commerce of the United States of America in Support of Appellee, 2007 U.S. S. Ct. Briefs Lexis 272 ("The corporate form of certain nonprofit organizations is disregarded for purposes of the restriction at issue in this case. . . . Like the vast majority of corporations, WRTL is not an *MCFL* corporation").

36. Federal Election Commission v. National Rifle Association, 254 F.2d 173 (D.C. Cir. 2001).

37. See Marcus and Baker 1998; Lewis 1996; Niekirk 1996.

38. Ziegler 2022, 149.

39. Ziegler (2022, 86, 129) identifies several antiabortion activists who disagreed with the NRLC's emphasis on campaign finance, such as Harold Cassidy, founder of the National Foundation for Life.

40. See Ziegler 2022, 91.

41. Grunwald 1999 (citing a letter signed by fifteen antiabortion House members complaining that the NRLC was "confusing a commitment to protecting the unborn with extraneous issues that do not involve the sanctity of life").

42. Dobbs v. Jackson Women's Health Organization, Slip Opinion, no. 19–1392, June 24, 2022, p. 6.

43. See, e.g., Karol 2009, 56–101.

44. Lewis 2017, 51–52.

45. Carney 1997 (indicating that the NRLC received $650,000 from the RNC in the 1995–1996 election cycle); Cooper 2003 (citing an affidavit filed in federal court by the NRLC's executive director in 2002 indicating that the organization had received donations from parties or committees); Grunwald 1999 (reporting that the NRLC received a $650,000 donation from the Republican National Committee three weeks before the 1996–1997 election).

46. Grunwald 1999.

47. Kleefeld 2009. The pledge stated:

(1)  We support smaller government, smaller national debt, lower deficits and lower taxes by opposing bills like Obama's "stimulus" bill;

(2)  We support market-based health care reform and oppose Obama-style government run healthcare;

(3)  We support market-based energy reforms by opposing cap and trade legislation;

(4)  We support workers' right to secret ballot by opposing card check;

(5)  We support legal immigration and assimilation into American society by opposing amnesty for illegal immigrants;

(6)  We support victory in Iraq and Afghanistan by supporting military-recommended troop surges;

(7)   We support containment of Iran and North Korea, particularly effective action to eliminate their nuclear weapons threat;

(8)   We support retention of the Defense of Marriage Act;

(9)   We support protecting the lives of vulnerable persons by opposing health care rationing and denial of health care and government funding of abortion; and

(10)  We support the right to keep and bear arms by opposing government restrictions on gun ownership.

The resolution concluded that any candidates who disagreed with three out of ten of these propositions, "as identified by the voting record, public statements and/or signed questionnaire of the candidate," would be ineligible for the national party's endorsement or financial support.

48. Martin 2010.

49. Kabaservice 2012.

50. Wilson 2013, 15–16 (discussing how abortion politics upset "the traditional alignment of ideology and interpretation of the First Amendment").

51. Brown 2002.

52. Wilson 2013, 15–17, 35–36.

53. National Institute of Family and Life Advocates v. Becerra, 585 U.S. _ (2018).

54. Hobby Lobby v. Burwell, 573 U.S. 682 (2014).

55. See, e.g., Masterpiece Cakeshop, Ltd. v. Colorado Civil Rights Commission, 584 U.S. _ (2018). For discussion of the leadup to this line of cases, see Brown 2002, 58–77.

56. See, e.g., Espinoza v. Montana Department of Revenue, 591 U.S. _ (2020); Carson v. Makin, 596 U.S. _ (2022).

57. See, e.g., Federal Election Commission v. NRA, 553 F. Supp. 1331 (D.D.C. 1983) (FEC action against NRA for alleged violation of the Federal Election Campaign Act of 1971).

58. Brief for the National Rifle Association of America as Amicus Curiae, 1986 WL 727486.

59. 528 U.S. 377 (2000) (holding that *Buckley*'s ruling that limits on campaign contributions in federal elections are constitutional also applied to state limits on campaign contributions in state elections).

60. Federal Election Commission v. National Rifle Association, 254 F.2d 173 (D.C. Cir. 2001).

61. Brief of Amicus Curiae National Rifle Association in Support of Appellant, 2009 WL 147861. The brief noted that the BCRA's principal sponsors had included an exemption (the "Snowe-Jeffords" exception) from the electioneering ban for 501(c)(4) organizations, so long as their funds came solely from individual contributions and were maintained separately from corporate contributions. But an amendment by the late Senator Wellstone ("Wellstone Amendment") eliminated that exemption for groups such as the NRA, Sierra Club, and similar advocacy groups. The NRA's brief urged the Court to "hold that, whatever *Austin*'s vitality and application may be with respect to for-profit corporations, *Austin*'s anti-distortion rationale supplies no justification for regulating *amicus*, Citizens United, and their nonprofit brethren along the lines of the Wellstone Amendment, which cannot be constitutionally applied to them. Instead, the original Snowe-Jeffords exception is the less restrictive—and therefore constitutionally compelled—alternative by which to pursue any operative regulatory interest associated with *Austin*."

62. Brief of Amicus Curiae National Rifle Association in Support of Appellant on Supplemental Question, 2009 WL 2359481.

63. Houston 1976 (quoting Viguerie saying that "gun enthusiasts are one of the great untapped money markets for the new right"); Lacombe 2021, 156.

64. *OpenSecrets* n.d.b.

65. The FEC defines independent expenditures as expenditures "for a communication, such as a website, newspaper, TV or direct mail advertisement that expressly advocates the election or defeat of a clearly identified candidate; and [that] is not made in consultation or cooperation with, or at the request or suggestion of a candidate, candidate's committee, party committee or their agents" (Federal Election Commission n.d.b.). Independent expenditures are not treated as contributions and are not subject to limits.

66. See Lacombe 2021, 5 (asserting that "financially focused arguments cannot fully—or even mostly—explain the NRA's influence in American politics" and that is instead "*ideational* resources: the identity and ideology it cultivates among its members" that explain its political power).

67. Lacombe 2021, 31.

68. Lacombe 2021, 26.

69. *OpenSecrets* 2016.

70. Maguire 2017.

71. Nass 2020.

72. The NRA became the subject of an investigation by the New York state attorney general into various allegations, including that the organization created shell corporations to hide its contributions to several campaigns. It was also accused of using shell corporations to illegally coordinate campaign spending with seven federal candidates. After the FEC declined to act on these complaints, a gun control group, Giffords, and the Campaign Legal Center sued the FEC. See *Giffords v. FEC*, case 1:19-cv-01192-EGS, filed April 24, 2019, https://www.fec.gov/resources/cms -content/documents/giffords_giffords_complaint.pdf. In August 2019, the FEC voted to block an investigation into allegations that Russians illegally donated to the NRA in an effort to bolster Donald Trump's presidential election prospects (Seipel 2019).

73. Pallasch 2010.

74. Heritage Foundation 2009 (in this video of the rant, Santelli says, "We're thinking of having a Chicago tea party in July. All you capitalists that want to show up in Lake Michigan, I'm gonna start organizing").

75. Skocpol and Williamson 2014, 64–68.

76. Gervais and Morris 2018, 14–30.

77. The 1992 Republican Party Platform contained language on guns, abortion, and immigration. On guns, it stated: "Republicans defend the constitutional right to keep and bear arms. We call for stiff mandatory sentences for those who use firearms in a crime. We note that those who seek to disarm citizens in their homes are the same liberals who tried to disarm our Nation during the Cold War and are today seeking to cut our national defense below safe levels. We applaud congressional Republicans for overturning the District of Columbia's law blaming firearm manufacturers for street crime." It also included a plank on abortion: "We believe the unborn child has a fundamental individual right to life which cannot be infringed. We therefore reaffirm our support for a human life amendment to the Constitution, and we endorse legislation to make clear that the Fourteenth Amendment's protections apply to unborn children. We oppose using public revenues for abortion and will not fund organizations which advocate it. We commend those who provide alternatives to abortion by meeting the needs of mothers and offering adoption services. We reaffirm our support for appointment of judges who respect traditional

family values and the sanctity of innocent human life." A plank on immigration included this language: "Illegal immigration . . . undermines the integrity of border communities and already crowded urban neighborhoods. . . . [W]e will increase the size of the Border Patrol in order to meet the increasing need to stop illegal immigration and we will equip the Border Patrol with the tools, technologies, and structures necessary to secure the border."

78. Republican Party Platform 1972 (expressing a commitment to "safeguard the right of responsible citizens to collect, own and use firearms for legitimate purposes, including hunting, target shooting and self-defense").

79. See, for example, new provisions in the 2000 Republican Party platform on guns: "Although we support background checks to ensure that guns do not fall into the hands of criminals, we oppose federal licensing of law-abiding gun owners and national gun registration as a violation of the Second Amendment and an invasion of privacy of honest citizens"; in the 2004 platform: "Republicans and President Bush strongly support an individual right to own guns, which is explicitly protected by the Constitution's Second Amendment" and "We oppose federal licensing of law-abiding gun owners and national gun registration as a violation of the Second Amendment and an invasion of privacy of honest citizens"; in the 2008 platform: "Gun ownership is responsible citizenship, enabling Americans to defend themselves, their property, and communities" and "We recognize that gun control only affects and penalizes law-abiding citizens, and that such proposals are ineffective at reducing violent crime"; in the 2012 platform: "We condemn frivolous lawsuits against gun manufacturers and oppose federal licensing or registration of law-abiding gun owners" and "We oppose legislation that is intended to restrict our Second Amendment rights by limiting the capacity of clips or magazines or otherwise restoring the ill-considered Clinton gun ban"; in the 2016 platform: "Lawful gun ownership enables Americans to exercise their God-given right of self-defense for the safety of their homes, their loved ones, and their communities," "We salute the Republican Congress for defending the right to keep and bear arms by preventing the President from installing a new liberal majority on the Supreme Court. The confirmation to the Court of additional anti-gun justices would eviscerate the Second Amendment's fundamental protections," and "We oppose ill-conceived laws that would restrict magazine capacity or ban the sale of the most popular and common modern rifle." The RNC did not adopt a new platform for 2020 because of the reduced size and scope of the 2020 Republican National Convention in Charlotte, North Carolina, but it did adopt a resolution indicating that "had the Platform Committee been able to convene in 2020, [the RNC] would have undoubtedly unanimously agreed to reassert the Party's strong support for President Donald Trump and his Administration" (Republican National Committee 2020).

80. See, e.g., Karol 2009; Bean and Teles 2015. David Karol (2009) describes parties as coalitions of "policy demanders" who come together to win elections and further their individual policy agendas. The role of politicians in his account is primarily to balance and coordinate these demands.

81. Bean and Teles 2015, 20.

82. Cohen et al. 2008, 6, 30–32; Bawn et al. 2012, 573.

83. LoGiurato 2014.

84. Iyengar, Sood, and Lelkes 2012; Iyengar, Lelkes, et al. 2019.

85. Iyengar, Lelkes, et al. 2019; Mason 2018.

86. Abramowitz and Webster 2018; Klein 2020; Drutman 2020b.

87. Finkel et al. 2020

88. Cramer 2016.

89. Hochschild 2016.

90. Gervais and Morris 2018, 245.

91. Bawn et al. 2012, 590 (distinguishing this conception of ideology from the more common understanding of it as "the product of value-based reasoning" and arguing that "thinking about ideology in this way draws our attention to the strategic construction of ideology as an important area of research").

92. Bean and Teles 2015, 3.

93. Brief of Amici Curiae the Wyoming Liberty Group and the Goldwater Institute in Support of Appellant, 2009 WL 1261928.

94. Brief of Amici Curiae the Wyoming Liberty Group and the Goldwater Institute Scharf-Norton Center for Constitutional Litigation in Support of Appellant on Supplemental Question, 2009 WL 2365217. The website for Benjamin Barr, counsel of record for the Wyoming Liberty Group in *Citizens United*, offers this pitch: "If you are being censored, whether by the government's heavy hand or clever red tape, or being sued by someone who's just trying to shut you up, please be in touch" (Barr and Klein PLLC n.d.).

95. Amicus Curiae Brief of the American Civil Liberties Union in Support of Appellant on Supplemental Question, 2009 WL 2365203.

96. See United States v. National Committee for Impeachment, 469 F.2d 1135 (2d Cir. 1972).

97. American Civil Liberties Union v. Jennings, 366 F. Supp. 1041 (D.D.C.1973), vacated sub nom.; Staats v. American Civil Liberties Union, 422 U.S. 1030 (1975).

98. One interviewed lawyer described the ACLU's support for public funding as a way to "counteract the economic inequality" and part of the organization's "three-part theme"—i.e., "no limits, full but targeted disclosure, and broad and even-handed public funding." He called this "the best First Amendment friendly approach."

99. Amicus Curiae Brief of the American Civil Liberties Union in Support of Appellant on Supplemental Question, 2009 WL 2365203.

100. See, for example, Walker 1999; Cose 2020; Weinrib 2016.

101. Weinrib 2016, 202.

102. Weinrib 2016, 326–27.

103. Weinrib 2016, 2.

104. Cose 2020, 136–40, 275.

105. Walker 1999, 197–214; Cose 2020, 182–97, 251, 255–56.

106. Tinker v. Des Moines, 393 U.S. 503 (1967).

107. See National Socialist Party of America v. Skokie, 432 U.S. 43 (1977). The ACLU continues to cite that episode as evidence of the organization's "unwavering commitment to principle" (American Civil Liberties Union n.d.a.).

108. Walker 1999, 339.

109. Supplemental Brief of Former Officials of the American Civil Liberties Union as Amici Curiae on Behalf of Neither Party, 2009 WL 2365208 (arguing that the Court should find that *Hillary* did not fall within the statutory coverage of the BCRA or that the de minimis nature of its for-profit corporate funding and voluntary nature of the movie's contemplated distribution mechanism precluded the FEC from applying the electioneering provision in this case).

110. See American Civil Liberties Union n.d.b.

111. Brief of the American Federation of Labor and Congress of Industrial Organizations as Amicus Curiae in Support of Appellant, 2009 WL 2365216.

112. Brief of the American Federation of Labor and Congress of Industrial Organizations as Amicus Curiae in Support of Appellant, 2009 WL 2365216.

113. Brief of AFL-CIO Appellants/Cross-Appellees, 2003 WL 22002431 (arguing that the BCRA's prohibitions on using the union's treasury funds for electioneering communications "pose[d] an immediate, direct and substantial threat to the AFL-CIO's historic role in advocating for progressive social legislation, influencing other government actions affecting workers and their families, and educating union members and the general public about these issues").

114. Kersch 2006, 274.

115. The government filed similar charges against the Seafarers International Union, which led the AFL-CIO to accuse the Nixon administration of seeking to limit unions' involvement in politics (Stetson 1971).

116. Pipefitters v. United States, 407 U.S. 385 (1972). Justice Lewis Powell wrote a dissent, joined by Justice Burger, arguing that the Pipefitters' PAC was a scheme to make illegal union contributions. He asserted that a truly separate fund would "be managed by a separate nonprofit entity, with independent trustees not subservient to the union or corporate sponsor, who engage independent auditors" (448n). He also wrote that allowing this arrangement to continue would undermine the Tillman and Taft-Hartley Acts, which were designed to "restrict and minimize the influence corporations and unions might exert on elections" (445).

117. Mutch 2014, 122.

118. 117 Cong. Rec. H43379, 43391 (daily ed. November 30, 1971).

119. Mitchell 2001 (quoting Gold).

120. For a summary of this history, see American Federation of Labor v. FEC, 177 F. Supp. 2d 48 (D.D.C. 2001), a case in which the AFL-CIO and the DNC sued to prevent the disclosure of documents relating to the investigation.

121. AFL-CIO 2012.

122. AFL-CIO 2012. But, as one lawyer noted, politicians and interest groups can express support for a constitutional amendment while knowing that it will never succeed: "I think it's very easy to say, 'Let's overturn *Citizens United* with a constitutional amendment,' because you know there's *not* going to be a constitutional amendment."

123. Mark Janus v. American Federation of State, County, and Municipal Employees, Council 31, et al., 585 U.S. _ (2018).

124. Goelzhauser and Vouvalis 2015, 99–116 (finding that increased coalition heterogeneity is associated with an increase in the probability of the Supreme Court granting review and suggesting that ideologically heterogeneous amicus coalitions may be perceived to send more credible signals about case importance); Lynch 2004, 61 (quoting a former Supreme Court clerk who observed that amicus briefs filed by ideologically diverse interests may "convince you that they have a good argument").

125. Collins 2004, 812.

126. Goelzhauser and Vouvalis 2015, 99–116.

127. Collins 2004, 813.

128. 551 U.S. 449. The penultimate paragraph stated:

These cases are about political speech. The importance of the cases to speech and debate on public policy issues is reflected in the number of diverse organizations that have joined in supporting WRTL before this Court: the American Civil Liberties Union, the National Rifle Association, the American Federation of Labor and Congress of

Industrial Organizations, the Chamber of Commerce of the United States of America, Focus on the Family, the Coalition of Public Charities, the Cato Institute, and many others. (551 U.S. at 481.)

129. Citizens United v. Federal Election Commission, 558 U.S. at 393 ("We have had two rounds of briefing in this case, two oral arguments, and 54 *amicus* briefs to help us carry out our obligation to decide the necessary constitutional questions according to law").

130. 558 U.S. at 393.

131. 558 U.S. at 363 ("*Austin* abandoned First Amendment principles . . . by relying on language in some of our precedents that traces back to the *Automobile Workers* Court's flawed historical account of campaign finance laws, see Brief for Campaign Finance Scholars as *Amici Curiae*").

132. 558 U.S. at 334 ("Campaign finance regulations now impose 'unique and complex rules' on '71 distinct entities.' Brief for Seven Former Chairmen of FEC et al. as *Amici Curiae* 11–12. These entities are subject to separate rules for 33 different types of political speech. *Id.*, at 14–15, n. 10. The FEC has adopted 568 pages of regulations, 1,278 pages of explanations and justifications for those regulations, and 1,771 advisory opinions since 1975. See *id.*, at 6, n. 7").

133. 558 U.S. at 354 (citing Supplemental Brief for Chamber of Commerce of the United States as *Amicus Curiae* 1, 3: "96% of the 3 million businesses that belong to the U.S. Chamber of Commerce have fewer than 100 employees").

134. Appellant's Brief, 2009 WL 61467 ("This Court has identified only one compelling interest that is even conceivably sufficient to justify governmental restrictions on political speech: preventing quid pro quo corruption and the appearance of such corruption in the electoral process"); Brief of Amicus Curiae Chamber of Commerce of the United States of America in Support of Appellant, 2009 WL 154011 ("independent speech is not a plausible vehicle for quid pro quo corruption").

135. See Gerken 2012; Briffault 2008.

136. See, e.g., 144 Cong. Rec. S997 (February 25, 1998) (quoting Mitch McConnell saying, "The Snowe-Jeffords amendment, while I'm sure it is well-intentioned, isn't consistent with the First Amendment. The American Civil Liberties Union, America's experts on the First Amendment, say that it falls short of the free speech requirements of the U.S. Supreme Court in First Amendment").

137. This lawyer contrasted the commitments of this small group of "ideologically interested" lawyers with Ted Olson's professional orientation ("more of a hired gun" but also "a brilliant lawyer").

138. Organizations represented by lawyers with Federalist Society ties included Citizens United, several business groups (US Chamber of Commerce and Michigan Chamber of Commerce), the National Rifle Association, the Center for Competitive Politics, the Center for Constitutional Jurisprudence, several conservative religious organizations (Alliance Defending Freedom, CatholicVote.com, and Fidelis Center for Law and Policy), libertarian groups (Cato, Institute for Justice, Pacific Legal Foundation, Goldwater Institute, Wyoming Liberty Group, American Justice Partnership, and Let Freedom Ring), the Committee for Truth in Politics, the ACLU, and AFL-CIO.

## Chapter Six

1. Post 2014, 4.
2. McConnell 2016, 91–92.

3. See, e.g., Snow and Benford 1992; Snow et al. 1986; Entman 2004; Gamson and Modigliani 1989.

4. See Epstein, Roth, and Baumer 2014; Nisbet and Huge 2006.

5. Polletta 2000; McCann 1994; Silverstein 1996.

6. Stohler 2019, 231–32. For more on how ideas can help build political coalitions, see Noel 2013.

7. Pedriana 2006; McCann 1994; NeJaime 2011; Haltom and McCann 2004.

8. Ziegler 2010; NeJaime 2013b; Hunter 2017.

9. Edelman 1988, 37.

10. Kersch 2014, 1088.

11. Kersch 2019, xi.

12. Kersch 2019, 1095.

13. TerBeek n.d.b.

14. Batchis 2016.

15. Edelman, Leachman, and McAdam 2010, 671 (discussing lawyers' involvement in this type of "ideational mobilization, or framing"). Wilson (2016, 62) discusses "the importance of lawyers, as they set the ways the courts can interact with abortion politics by first framing and then appealing cases and by making the arguments that ultimately influence judicial rulings."

16. Edelman, Leachman, and McAdam 2010, 673.

17. Mertz 2007; Winter 2001, xii (exploring the social constructs that "animate thinking and decision making among lawyers, judges, and laypersons alike").

18. Epstein and Kobylka 1992; Wedeking 2010; Corley 2008.

19. Silverstein 2009, 73–75.

20. McCann 1999, 87.

21. Abrams v. United States, 250 U.S. 616, 630 (1919) (Holmes, J., dissenting) ("When men have realized that time has upset many fighting faiths, they may come to believe even more than they believe the very foundations of their own conduct that the ultimate good desired is better reached by free trade in ideas—that the best test of truth is the power of the thought to get itself accepted in the competition of the market.").

22. United States v. Rumely, 345 U.S. 41 (1953) (Douglas, J., concurring) ("Like publishers of newspapers, magazines, or books, this publisher bids for the minds of men in the marketplace of ideas").

23. This metaphor for free speech largely displaced an earlier one in which the free flow of ideas, like the unimpeded flow of a streaming fountain, leads to progress toward truth (Winter 2001, 266–73). But, as explored in chapter 8, this metaphor continues to operate in arguments justifying the extension of speech protections to corporations, typically articulated as an interest in the free flow of *information*.

24. See Winter 1971, 18–19, 20; Redish 1971, 910 (asserting that the "thrust of [the Supreme Court's ruling in *Mills v. Alabama*] is that the ideological marketplace of the political campaign must remain uninhibited").

25. Citizens United v. Federal Election Commission, 558 U.S. at 340 (2010).

26. 558 U.S. at 438.

27. 558 U.S. at 340.

28. See Rosenberger v. Rector and Visitors of the University of Virginia, 515 U.S. 819 (1995) (holding that the university's denial of funding to a student publication due to the religious content of its message amounted to impermissible viewpoint discrimination).

29. 558 U.S. at 424–25.

30. Arizona Free Enterprise Club v. Bennett, 564 U.S. 721, 750 (2011).

31. 564 U.S. at 785 (Kagan, J., dissenting).

32. Pozen, Talley, and Nyarko 2019.

33. See Haltom and McCann 2004, 14–15 (on the compatibility of the notion of strategic use of legal narratives with individual actors' actual belief in those narratives).

34. Mutch 2014, 160–61.

35. I added "chill" to Mutch's list; it appeared just four times in *Buckley* but nineteen times in *Citizens United*. My research assistant generated word frequency and word combination data for the opinions and briefs using MAXQDA software and lemmatizing the data to catch all forms of the key words. The appendix describes this process in more detail.

36. In this analysis, I coded each separate opinion—whether concurring, dissenting, partially concurring, or partially dissenting—according to whether it favored upholding or invalidating the challenged restriction.

37. Brief of Amici Curiae the Wyoming Liberty Group and the Goldwater Institute Scharf-Norton Center for Constitutional Litigation in Support of Appellant on Supplemental Question, 2009 WL 2365217.

38. Brief for Petitioners, 2011 WL 141226.

39. Buckley v. Valeo, 424 U.S. at 48–49.

40. This topic seems like a promising area for use of computational text-analysis techniques pioneered by others. See, e.g., Varsava 2018; Varsava 2020; Pozen, Talley, and Nyarko 2019; McCammon and Beeson-Lynch 2021; Collins, Corley, and Hamner 2015.

41. For a broader discussion of how actors in the judicial arena are constrained by the "fundamental categories in which thinking can take place," see Wuthnow 1989, 13.

42. This phrase refers to remarks by Kellyanne Conway, US counsel to former president Donald Trump, during an interview on January 22, 2017. She defended then–White House press secretary Sean Spicer's false statement about the number of people attending Trump's presidential inauguration. When asked why Spicer would advance a provable falsehood, Conway responded that Spicer had provided "alternative facts."

43. Super PACs spent more than $2.1 billion in the 2020 election cycle. See *OpenSecrets* 2020a.

44. These two comments by interviewees were typical expressions of this perspective:

The view I take is all the regulations should be removed and all that should be required is public reporting. As long as there's public reporting . . . then it's up to the voters to decide. Okay, so you have a candidate, and he takes money from the tobacco industry, or he takes money from the oil industry, or he takes money from the crypto-Marxist groups, or he takes money from foreign countries, alright, so you just report it. . . . You know where he gets his money. It's up to you to decide. It's not up to the government to say, "You can't take money to present your views to the public."

If someone wants to come in and spend a billion dollars, give a billion dollars to a candidate because they want that candidate to win, so long as you disclose it, so long as you say, so-and-so wrote a check to this candidate for a billion dollars, then they should be able to do that. Others would say, "Well, no, that's unfair to someone who doesn't have access to that guy, and oh, by the way, that candidate now is in the pocket of this guy, of this billionaire." But you know what? Then make that a political issue . . .

These comments echoed Winter and Bolton's argument in the 1970s that "if campaign financing really 'distorts' legislative or executive behavior, candidates can raise its effect as an issue and the voters can respond at election time" (Winter and Bolton 1973, 12).

45. Bork 1971, 22. Twenty years later, Bork wrote an op-ed in which he strongly criticized the Michigan campaign finance law that the Court upheld in *Austin v. Michigan Chamber of Commerce* (Bork 1990a, arguing that prohibition on corporate efforts to influence political campaigns was "flatly inconsistent with the idea, central to the First Amendment, that the right to speak is especially important when ideas expressed are not shared, or are even hated, by the majority").

46. One lawyer described the Roberts Court's ruling in *Citizens United* as affirmation that "government cannot screw with the marketplace of ideas when it comes to political participation." Elaborating on why he was unconcerned about the influence of money in politics, another lawyer explained, "This is how the free market of ideas works. All the money in the world isn't going to buy [a candidate] a single vote." Instead, he said, campaign spending "is going to let him get his ideas out there, but at the end of the day, people are going to decide—'Well, I like his ideas, I'm glad I got the opportunity to hear him, and I think I will vote for him after all' or 'I'm not going to vote for him.'"

47. For example, a libertarian asserted that Oprah Winfrey's endorsement of Barack Obama for president in 2008 "probably got him a million additional votes in the Democratic presidential primary, which no amount of money could buy." He was sure that if Winfrey wanted to speak with Obama or his staff about an issue that was important to her, she would have enjoyed special access and influence, but "we don't try to stop her from having that kind of impact." Another challenger questioned reformers' motives in directing their regulatory efforts at money rather than other types of resources:

> There's a ton of ways to influence elections that have nothing to do with the expenditure of money or giving a candidate money, and [reformers] don't want to limit any of those. Why is that? It's very curious to me. . . . Why [are] the reforms that liberals are proposing after *Citizens United* directed only at corporations and not at labor unions? Is it because labor unions spend all their money electing Democrats and liberals? I think so. . . . So, they don't want to limit the mainstream media. . . . They don't want to limit celebrities. Is that because they're all liberal? Probably. They don't want to limit community organizers, people who can mobilize volunteers. Is that because the principal organizations that have a lot of members are liberal? Probably. So, there's a lot of influencers out there that they want to just give a complete pass for, and even explicitly exempt.

This lawyer said that reformers are simply seeking "partisan advantage."

48. As evidence of the Republican establishment's intent to silence grassroots activists and Freedom Caucus members, this lawyer cited Mark Meadows's temporary loss of his subcommittee chairmanship after he defied the Republican leadership on a procedural vote on trade legislation, and Ken Buck's threatened ouster from his position as freshman class president following his refusal to back a trade measure.

49. 572 U.S. at 191 (access and influence by donors "embody a central feature of democracy— that constituents support candidates who share their beliefs and interests, and candidates who are elected can be expected to be responsive to those concerns").

50. 572 U.S. at 192 (quoting *Citizens United*, 558 U.S. at 360).

51. Smith 1995 (citing Ansberry 1995, noting spending on chips in excess of $4.5 billion).

52. See Ellis 1997.

53. "Politics and Potato Chips" 1997. The first example I could find in the public record of McConnell's use of this factoid appeared in the Congressional Record in November 1995: "Professor Bradley Smith, in a work released by the Cato Institute, recently observed that Sony is spending more to promote Michael Jackson's latest album than the 1994 Republic Senate nominee in California spent . . . [I]n the last congressional cycle, we spent on congressional campaigns what Americans spend in one year on bubble gum, and about half what they spend on . . . potato chips" (141 Cong. Rec. S 16722 [November 7, 1995]).

54. See, e.g., Bipartisan Campaign Reform Act Of 1997-Cloture Motion, 143 Cong. Rec. S 10501 (October 8, 1997):

> Further, Mr. President, there was an op-ed piece in the *Washington Times* by Peggy Ellis of the Cato Institute entitled "10 Big Lies About Campaign Finance Reform. . . ." I ask unanimous consent that it be printed in the Record. "Lie No. 9: Obscene amounts of money are spent in political campaigns. Congressional candidates spent approximately $740 million in 1996. This is only slightly higher than the approximately $700 million spent in 1994. It's a lot of money—but not when compared to what we spend as a society in other areas. . . . As a society, we spend more on potato chips, Barbie dolls, yogurt and a host of other commodities than we do on politics. While many of us may like Barbie dolls and potato chips more than we like politics, only politics has control over every aspect of our lives."

See also Bipartisan Campaign Reform Act Of 1997-Cloture Motion, 143 Cong. Rec. S 10719 (October 9, 1997) ("millions of Americans gave $2.6 billion to 476 congressional campaigns and still had enough left over to spend $4.6 billion on potato chips"); 147 Cong. Rec. S 3233 (April 2, 2001) ("Now, Mr. President, the theory of this bill, the underlying theory, is that there is too much money in politics, in spite of the fact that last year Americans spent more on potato chips than they did on politics"); Dreisbach 2019 (quoting from various archived audio recordings of McConnell's speeches: "Americans spent more on potato chips than they did on politics. Spent about what the American public spent in one year on bubble gum . . . Spend on bubble gum . . . Bubble gum . . . Bottle of water. Bottle of water. Cosmetics. Yogurt. Alcoholic beverages, Kibbles 'n Bits ads—so when we talk about spending, we talk about it compared to what?").

55. Winter and Bolton 1973, 19.

56. BeVier 1987, 13.

57. See Issacharoff and Karlan 1999, 1708 (arguing that "political money, like water, has to go somewhere. It never really disappears into thin air" and calling this notion the "hydraulic principle"); see also McConnell v. FEC, 540 U.S. at 224 (2003) ("Money, like water, will always find an outlet").

58. Joshua Wilson (2013) found such variation among lawyers involved in antiabortion activism: "As one might predict, the interviewees that tended to use the strongest movement-style rhetoric were also those that are most clearly seen as classic 'cause lawyers'" (p. 135). In previous research, I found similar variation in the professional identities and rhetoric of lawyers working for causes associated with the political right (Southworth 2008, 66–88, 179–81).

59. Silverstein 2009, 66–70 (discussing how lawyers are constrained by their need to appeal to precedent and to path dependent doctrine).

60. Shelby County v. Holder, 570 U.S. 529 (2013).

61. Scholars have made this argument. See, e.g., Post 2014; Neuborne 2015; Hellman 2016; Abu El-Haj 2017.

62. See discussion in chapter 2.

63. See Nixon v. Shrink Missouri Government PAC, 120 S. Ct. 897, 910 (2000) (Justice Stevens, concurring) ("Money is property; it is not speech . . . These property rights are not entitled to the same protection as the right to say what one pleases").

64. Perry and Powe 2004; Graber 2004, 168 ("The contemporary Republican and Democratic Parties champion very different constitutional approaches and visions").

65. Fishkin and Pozen 2018, 965.

66. See Batchis 2016, 67 ("Coopting the arguments of one's adversaries is a political strategy with a rich pedigree; and there can be little doubt that raising the 'liberal' First Amendment flag was a shrewd move by conservatives eager to give liberals a dose of their own medicine. Whether or not reliance on the First Amendment represented a political calculation or a genuine turn among conservatives toward free-speech values, it was clear that freedom of speech was becoming a conservative rallying cry against the perceived tactics of the left—tactics that ostensibly sought to diminish white male traditionalism in favor of multicultural relativism").

67. Pozen, Talley, and Nyarko 2019.

68. Pozen, Talley, and Nyarko 2019, 5.

69. See Layman, Carsey, and Horowitz 2006; McCarty, Poole, and Rosenthal 2006; Theriault 2008.

70. Pozen, Talley, and Nyarko 2019, 5, 67 (discussing how "conservatives in recent Congresses have developed an especially coherent constitutional vocabulary, with which they have come to 'own' not only the terms associated with originalism and the Framers but also terms associated with textual provisions such as the First Amendment" and documenting "the explosive growth of constitutional polarization").

71. Southworth 2018, 1727 (suggesting that we now have a "two-sided legal establishment serving polarized elites").

72. Southworth 2018.

73. See table 1.1.

74. Bing committed suicide in 2020. Before his death, he contributed millions to the Democratic Party and its candidates (Ramzy and Adams 2020).

75. 424 U.S. at 19 n. 18.

76. For scholarship questioning the metaphor's seeming presumption that truth will win out in an unregulated marketplace, see Joo 2014; Piety 2007; Barron 1967; Hasen 2022.

77. See DC Fandom n.d.

78. Lochner v. New York, 198 U.S. 45 (1905); Hammer v. Dagenhart, 247 U.S. 251 (1918); Coppage v. Kansas, 236 U.S. 1 (1915); Adair v. United States, 208 U.S 161 (1908).

79. For scholarship making this argument, see Rabban 1996, 952–53; Sunstein 1995; Kuhner 2014; Shanor 2016; Kessler 2016.

80. Wedeking 2010, 620.

81. Silverstein 2009, 174.

82. See Lessig 2011; Teachout 2014.

83. See Post 2014.

84. Constitutional scholars have raised similar concerns. See, e.g., Karlan 2014.

85. See Devins and Baum 2019; Pozen, Talley, and Nyarko 2019.

86. On the gap such efforts would address, see Kersch 2014, 1104 ("In recent years, conservatives have been highly successful in telling [stories instituting and justifying new constitutional rules]" while liberals have done a poor job of showing how an activist liberal government "would fulfill—as opposed to simply not transgress—foundational constitutional aims").

## Chapter Seven

1. See, e.g., Glazer 1975; Bickel 1962; Bickel 1975; Horowitz 1977; Ely 1980.

2. See, e.g., Bickel 1975; Bork 1990b; Ely 1973.

3. See, e.g., Rowley 1992, 12; Breger 1985; Powell 1971.

4. Balkin 2020b, 93 (quoting Levinson 2002).

5. Roberts 2005.

6. Article II, section I (providing that the president must be at least thirty-five years old).

7. Whittington 2019, 291.

8. For summaries of this literature, see Balkin and Levinson 2006; 2001.

9. Baum 2006, 60–72, 97–103.

10. Whittington 2019, 291.

11. See, generally, Fallon 2018.

12. See Devins and Baum 2019, 107.

13. Senate voting on judicial nominees, especially Supreme Court nominees, has become more partisan as explicit considerations of ideology have become the norm in Senate voting on judicial nominees. See Devins and Baum 2019, 107–09.

14. Tushnet 2020b, 45 (noting that justices who rule in ways that help the party with which they are aligned "may not have consciously intended to sustain that order . . . Sometimes, sustaining that order was a happy by-product of constitutional philosophies that were themselves well integrated into the very same order"); Devins and Baum 2019, 45 (emphasizing that "any influence of social and political elites does not necessarily stem from deliberate choices by the Justices. To the extent that Justices act in ways that might draw favorable reactions from relevant elites, they are likely to do so unconsciously . . . [E]lite opinion may influence Justices' choices by shaping their preferences"). Tushnet has observed with respect to the Supreme Court's recent campaign finance rulings that the justices "might consciously or *unconsciously* view decisions striking down campaign finance restrictions as helping to preserve the Republican-dominated constitutional order" (Tushnet 2020b, 51; emphasis added).

15. Tushnet 2020b; Balkin 2020b. These theories about cycles of "judicial time" and "constitutional time" draw on the work of Stephen Skowronek, who has shown how American political history has featured successive governing regimes dominated practically and ideologically by successive parties (see Skowronek 2011).

16. Balkin 2020b, 97–111.

17. Gillman 2001, 7.

18. One reformer recalled his reaction upon learning of this development: "Wow, this is a really aggressive Court, really wanting to decide some issues the plaintiffs had not even squarely presented below—and that the FEC and other parties in the case had not had the opportunity to develop any facts around." Another referred to these developments as evidence of the Supreme Court's "very striking activist concern" with trimming back the reach of campaign finance laws.

19. 558 U.S. at 426 (Stevens, J., dissenting) (internal citations omitted). Justice Kennedy's opinion for the majority did not rely on originalist methodology, but the concurrence by Justice Scalia, joined in part by Justices Alito and Thomas, asserted that the majority's result was consistent with originalism. Scalia's concurrence conceded that the framers mistrusted corporations, chartered them only on the condition that they serve public purposes, and restricted their powers. But Scalia insisted that the framers would have viewed modern corporations differently and would have granted them speech rights. 558 U.S. at 353 (Scalia, J., concurring). As Robert

Gordon has observed, this kind of speculation about how the founders' attitudes might have changed with changing circumstances seems to leave "anything resembling strict originalism far behind." Gordon 2017, 371.

20. Citizens United v. Federal Election Commission, 558 U.S. at 414 (Stevens, J., dissenting).

21. In *McCutcheon*, Justice Roberts relied on Edmund Burke to explain "the need to preserve authority for the Government to combat corruption, without at the same time compromising the political responsiveness at the heart of the democratic process." 572 U.S. at 227: "As Edmund Burke explained in his famous speech to the electors of Bristol, a representative owes constituents the exercise of his 'mature judgment,' but judgment informed by 'the strictest union, the closest correspondence, and the most unreserved communication with his constituents.' Constituents have the right to support candidates who share their views and concerns. Representatives are not to follow constituent orders, but can be expected to be cognizant of and responsive to those concerns. Such responsiveness is key to the very concept of self-governance through elected officials"). One reformer found it "interesting" that the Court quoted Burke's address to the Electors of Bristol to support a claim about how representatives should feel beholden to their supporters without acknowledging an important difference in context: "[Burke] was talking about voters and constituents; he wasn't talking about donors, but the Court conflated all of that and said, basically, that there's nothing wrong with an office holder feeling beholden to large donors—that's politics." He called this erroneous interpretation of Burke's speech "really dangerous" and "really significant."

22. See, e.g., Rowley 1992, 12; Breger 1985.

23. But in *NAACP v. Button*, the Warren Court found that the activities of the NAACP and its lawyers were "a form of political expression" protected by the First Amendment (NAACP v. Button, 371 U.S. 415, 429 [1963]). The Court distinguished the challenged law from existing laws against barratry (stirring up lawsuits), reasoning that the NAACP's efforts involved no financial stakes and served public rather than private interests.

24. See Brown 2002, 8–9; Fournier 1994; Whitehead 1983, 126.

25. Powell 1971.

26. Bell 1976. He also raised questions about whether financial contributors to civil rights advocacy organizations had influenced litigation strategy, and about the ethical implications of permitting funders to play any such role (Bell 1976., 489–92). Bell emphasized how psychological motivations, such as the gratification of winning big cases and pursuing ideological goals, can tempt lawyers who participate in litigation campaigns to disregard clients' preferences. He famously claimed that "idealism, though perhaps rarer than greed, is harder to control," and he called on civil rights lawyers "to realize that the special status accorded them by the courts and the bar demands in return an extraordinary display of ethical sensitivity and self-restraint." (1976, 504–05). See also Brown-Nagin 2005; 2011 (describing the history of civil rights activism in Atlanta and the clash between grassroots and elite lawyers over goals and tactics).

27. See, e.g., McMunigal 1996 (questioning whether Sarah Weddington, the lawyer who brought the lawsuit that resulted in the Supreme Court's ruling in *Roe v. Wade*, was justified in pursuing a broad strategy designed to advance the cause of reproductive choice when a narrower strategy might have led to a speedier ruling and increased her client's likelihood of obtaining the abortion she desperately wanted); Hunter 2017, 1700 (noting that "a small group, most lawyers, determined that marriage would become the priority issue of the LGBT rights movement").

28. See, e.g., Scheingold 1974 (arguing that activist lawyers tend to embrace a simplistic "myth of rights" view of social change rather than a more realistic "politics of rights" orientation,

according to which judicial rulings are merely political assets to be used strategically in other arenas); McCann 1986, 204 ("because reform activists are often attracted to public life at least in part by the desire for status and prestige, they tend to be drawn to more dramatic symbolic events such as test-case victories to reaffirm their noble stature before an admiring mass public"); Rosenberg 1991 (asserting that courts serve as "fly-paper" for social reformers who succumb to the "lure of litigation" at the expense of more promising alternative paths); Albiston 2011, 74–76 (highlighting disparities between the goals of those who seek to change legal doctrine and the typically more ambitious political goals of other social-movement actors); Brown-Nagin 2005, 1439 (arguing that "social movements—defined as politically insurgent and participatory campaigns for relief from socioeconomic crisis or the redistribution of social, political, and economic capital—are generally incompatible with constitutional litigation").

29. See, e.g., Cummings 2017; Ashar 2017.

30. See Cummings 2022; Carle and Cummings 2018, 457.

31. See Luban 1988; Cummings 2020, 478–83; Hunter 2017, 1701.

32. See American Bar Association n.d., Model Rules of Professional Conduct, rules 1.2, 1.4.

33. See American Bar Association n.d., Model Rules of Professional Conduct, rule 1.7. If such a conflict exists, the lawyer may, in some circumstances, proceed with the representation, but only if she reasonably believes that she can "provide competent and diligent representation to each affected client" and each affected client gives informed consent ( rule 1.7 [b]). A "personal interest of the lawyer" presumably includes the lawyer's interest in advancing ideological goals.

34. See American Bar Association n.d., Model Rules of Professional Conduct, rule 5.4 (c). See also rule 1.8(f) (providing that a lawyer shall not accept compensation for representing a client from anyone other than the client unless the client gives informed consent and there is no interference with the lawyer's independence or professional judgment or with the client-lawyer relationship).

35. See American Bar Association n.d., Model Rules of Professional Conduct, rule 1.13 (a) (providing that "a lawyer employed or retained by an organization represents the organization acting through its duly authorized constituents").

36. Cummings 2012; Cummings 2020; Carle and Cummings 2018; Southworth 1999.

37. Garth 1982; Rubenstein 1997.

38. Carle and Cummings 2018.

39. But see Rosenblum 2021, 186–89 (applying a race and power-conscious analysis to argue that it was ethically problematic for Edward Blum to recruit plaintiffs for a litigation campaign to attack affirmative action, but that the Becket Fund's cause-driven litigation on behalf of religious minorities was "a closer case"); Hunter 2017, 1702–03 (offering metrics for assessing issues of accountability of law-oriented cause efforts on both the political left and right).

40. Decker 2016; Southworth 2018; Teles 2008.

41. See James Madison Center for Free Speech n.d. (a mission statement indicating that the organization "was founded to protect the First Amendment right of all citizens to free political expression in our democratic Republic. Its purpose is to support litigation and public education activities in order to defend the rights of political expression and association by citizens and citizen groups as guaranteed by the First Amendment of the United States Constitution").

42. In arguing that social conservatives in general, and abortion opponents in particular, should support campaign finance reform, reformers are reprising arguments made by proponents of the BCRA around the time of its enactment. John McCain, an abortion opponent, wrote an open letter to the National Conference of Catholic Bishops asking it to endorse reform.

He accused Bopp's group, the National Right to Life Committee, of caring more about political power than the pro-life cause. See Mitchell 1998.

43. Bopp was a member of the RNC from 2006 to 2012 and served as its vice-chair from 2008 to 2012.

44. Mitchell 1998.

45. Americans for Prosperity (AFP) is a free-market group that was founded along with FreedomWorks in 2004, when Citizens for a Sound Economy, an organization funded primarily by David and Charles Koch, dissolved. AFP has been a major spender in elections on behalf of conservative candidates, and it has also played a significant role in funding the rise and early activities of some Tea Party groups (Skocpol and Williamson 2014; Mayer 2016). IRS forms indicate that some of AFP's major foundation contributors are also major funders of the groups most active in litigation against campaign finance regulation: the Richard and Helen DeVos Foundation; the John William Pope Foundation; the Lynde and Harry Bradley Foundation; the David H. Koch Charitable Trust; the Mercer Family Foundation, and the Searle Freedom Trust.

Crossroads GPS is a spinoff of American Crossroads, a super PAC founded in 2010 by former RNC chair Ed Gillespie and Republican political strategist Karl Rove. In the 2012 election cycle, American Crossroads spent about $105 million, and Crossroads GPS spent $70.8 million to promote Republican candidates. Crossroads GPS also contributed to other 501(c)s, including $26.4 million to Americans for Tax Reform, Grover Norquist's group, which calls on lawmakers to pledge that they will not raise taxes or eliminate deductions during their time in office. Critics of the organization argued that Crossroads GPS should not qualify as a 501(c)(4) social welfare organization because it was engaged primarily in election-related activities. But in November 2015, following a well-publicized scandal in which the IRS's regulatory arm targeted Tea Party groups for special investigation regarding whether they deserved 501(c)(4) designation, the IRS granted Crossroads GPS 501(c)(4) status.

At the time of this interview, the president of Crossroads GPS was Steven Law, who previously served as Mitch McConnell's chief of staff and worked for Elaine Chao, McConnell's wife, when she was Secretary of Labor in the George W. Bush administration. Bobby Burchfield, who represented the RNC in *McConnell v. FEC* and Mitch McConnell in *McCutcheon v. FEC*, was the chairman of Crossroads GPS.

46. Several of the interviewed lawyers also commented about the confusion that resulted in *McConnell* as Justice Scalia grappled with the contrasting positions of the two Larry Golds who had come before the Court on behalf of the AFL-CIO:

QUESTION: Are you Laurence Gold?
MR. GOLD: I am Laurence Gold. We're not related.
QUESTION: Not the Laurence Gold I expected.
MR. GOLD: I'm also instructed by your rules not to introduce myself.

(Transcript of Oral Argument at 135–36, McConnell v. FEC, 540 U.S. 93 [2003] [no. 02–1674])

47. Supplemental Brief of the Committee for Economic Development as Amicus Curiae in Support of Appellee, 2009 WL 2365230.

48. Beckel 2018, 6; 2019.

49. *OpenSecrets* 2021.

50. For an argument that reformers generally have paid too little attention to the roles of voters in the process by which economic elites "get enough of the people to support their interests" by voting for candidates who are captured by elites, see Reese 2018.

51. Broockman, Ferenstein, and Malhotra 2019.

52. Bartels 2008; Gilens 2012. But see Lax, Phillips, and Zelizer 2019 (a study of Senate roll-call votes from 2001 to 2015 found that in intraparty disagreements between the wealthy and poor, politicians reliably side with wealthy co-partisans over poor co-partisans, but that this affluent influence is limited by partisanship; when co-partisan opinion conflicts with rich opinion, senators of both parties tend to side overwhelmingly with their co-partisans over the rich).

53. See American Bar Association n.d., Model Rules of Professional Conduct, rule 1.2 (on the allocation of authority between client and lawyer), rule 1.4 (on communication with the client), and rule 1.7 (conflicts of interest).

54. See American Bar Association n.d., Model Rules of Profession Conduct, rule 7.3 (b): "A lawyer shall not solicit professional employment by live person-to-person contact when a significant motive for the lawyer's doing so is the lawyer's or law firm's pecuniary gain . . ."

Whether this criterion should be the basis for distinguishing between permissible and impermissible solicitation is another matter. In two companion cases—*In re Primus*, 436 U.S. 412 (1978) and Ohralik v. Ohio State Bar Ass'n, 436 U.S. 447 (1978)—the Supreme Court effectively approved ethics rules banning in-person solicitation of business by lawyers for pecuniary gain while also finding that lawyer solicitation of clients to advance personal political beliefs was a form of expression and association protected by the First and Fourteenth Amendments. In his concurrence, Justice Thurgood Marshall argued that prohibitions on soliciting clients for pecuniary gain impeded the flow of information about legal services to people who lack knowledge about lawyers and discriminated against attorneys in small firms and solo practices. He argued in favor of limiting the reach of solicitation bans to circumstances "presenting substantial dangers of harm to society or the client independent of the solicitation itself" (436 U.S. 447, 474 [1978] [Marshall, J., concurring in part and in the judgments]).

55. See chapter 6.

56. Gillman 2001, 7; Balkin and Levinson 2001, 1062–1063.

## Chapter Eight

1. This lawyer was referring to Justice White's partial concurrence and partial dissent in Buckley v. Valeo, 424 U.S. at 259 ("I am . . . in agreement with the Court's judgment upholding the limitations on contributions. I dissent, however, from the Court's view that the expenditure limitations . . . violate the First Amendment").

2. See, for example, Lair v. Motl, 189 F.Supp.3d 1024 (D. Mont. 2016), in which the plaintiff alleged that Montana's contribution limits were unconstitutionally low. After extensive back and forth between the federal district court and the US Court of Appeals for the Ninth Circuit, the Ninth Circuit upheld the limits (Lair v. Motl, 873 F.3d 1170 (9th Cir. 2017)). The Supreme Court denied the challenger's petition for certiorari (Lair v. Mangan, 139 S. Ct. 916 (2019)).

3. A federal trial court and US Court of Appeals for the Ninth Circuit upheld Alaska's $500 individual-to-candidate contribution limit, but on remand from the Supreme Court, the Ninth Circuit struck it down (Thompson v. Hebdon, 7 F.4th 811 (9th Cir. 2021)).

4. Packer 2021.

5. Windsor 2014 (quoting McConnell: "We now have, I think, the most free and open system we've had in modern times. The Supreme Court allowed all of you to participate in the process in a variety of ways. You can give to the candidate of your choice. You can give to Americans for Prosperity, or something else, a variety of ways to push back against the party of government").

6. Sonka 2014.

7. McConnell 2019.

8. McFadden 2021.

9. McConnell 2022.

10. Mehlman advocated for regulating the campaign activities of "527s," groups organized under section 527 of the Internal Revenue Code, but an RNC resolution repudiated his position.

11. On the expulsion of moderates from the Republican Party, see Kabaservice 2012.

12. See Drutman 2020a, 85–93 (describing the collapse of a "four-party" system consisting of liberal Democrats and conservative Democrats, and liberal Republicans and conservative Republicans, each representing distinct and meaningful voting factions); Kabaservice 2012, 381 (describing McCain, not as a moderate, but rather as a conservative Republican who nevertheless dared to occasionally cross the Republican leaders, as he did to support campaign finance reform and Obamacare).

13. Gramlich 2021.

14. See, for example, Fifth Circuit Judge James Ho's dissent, joined by Judge Edith Jones, in Zimmerman v. City of Austin, 888 F.3d 163 (5th Cir. 2018). Ho indicated that he would have invalidated a campaign finance law that capped the amount that donors could give in city-council elections and, indeed, that he thought that all contribution limits were suspect. The opinion stated that "if there's too much money in politics, it's because there's too much government. The size and scope of government makes such spending essential."

15. At the Federalist Society's 2017 annual conference, McGahn gave a speech in which he described with evident relish how he had teased Federalist Society vice president Jonathan Bunch about Trump's plans regarding judicial selection. He recounted how he had initially told Bunch that Trump would appoint "mainstream folks" who would "get through the Senate and will make us feel good that we put some pragmatic folks on the bench," before revealing that the actual plan was to nominate "the kind of people that make some people nervous" because "I know Leader McConnell's going to get it done" (McGahn 2017).

16. O'Harrow and Boburg 2019. See also Southworth 2008, 133 (noting that Leo's multifaceted credentials and experience enable him to work with all constituencies of the conservative alliance and quoting a lawyer who identified Leo as one of the "great figures in the movement—a great organizer").

17. The legislation would have amended the National Labor Relations Act to: (1) require employers to recognize unions based on card checks; (2) impose mandatory mediation and arbitration in first contract negotiations; and (3) substantially increase penalties imposed on employers for labor law violations during organizing campaigns and first contract efforts.

18. See Cohen 2013 ("If we don't fix these democracy blocks, our bargaining will never go forward").

19. Cohen 2013.

20. OpenSecrets n.d.a.

21. Abrams, Glasser, and Gora 2010.

22. See, for example, Brief for Public Citizen, Inc. as Amicus Curiae in Support of Appellees and Affirmance, Chamber of Commerce of the United States v. Acosta, 2017 WL 2992768 (5th Cir.) ("Public Citizen has become increasingly concerned that corporate and commercial interests are promoting stringent applications of commercial speech doctrine to stifle legitimate economic regulatory measures and protections for consumers").

23. Chapter 2 discusses the significance of this case to the development of campaign finance doctrine.

24. Mayer 2021.

25. Palmer and Parti 2014.

26. Swan 2015.

27. Conservative Action Project 2015.

28. Riders that did make it into the final bill included one preventing the IRS from issuing new regulations governing the campaign activities of 501(c)(4) groups and another prohibiting the Securities and Exchange Commission from requiring corporations to disclose their campaign finance activities.

29. Painter 2016, xiii.

30. Data available through the Foundation Center reveal no contributions to this organization by George Soros and his groups. However, they do show that from 2015 through 2018 it received large foundation grants from two foundations based on fortunes made in Silicon Valley: $1.9 million from the William and Flora Hewlett Foundation and $1.85 million from the Democracy Fund, Inc., established by the founder of eBay (*Foundation Directory On-Line* 2022).

31. Hochschild 2016, 233 (quoting Mike Schaff, Tea Party advocate).

32. See Crane 2018; Bowles 2019; De Rugy 2022.

33. See Biden v. Knight First Amendment Institute at Columbia University, 593 U.S. _ (2021) (Justice Thomas, concurring, suggesting the possibility of regulating digital platforms as common carriers or places of public accommodation).

34. NetChoice, LLC v. Att'y Gen. of Fla., 34 F.4th 1196 (11th Cir. 2022); NetChoice, LLC v. Paxton, No. 21–51178 (5th Cir. 2022).

35. For a discussion of this feature of contemporary free speech law—that it construes the constitutional right as a "strong but limited negative autonomy right" that "guarantees freedom from intentional government interference with an individual's autonomy, but one that provides almost no protection whatsoever against private interference and constraint"—see Lakier 2020a.

36. See doueck and Lakier 2022.

37. See Panetta and Griffiths 2022.

38. See, e.g., Thompson v. Hebdon, 7 F. 4th 811 (9th Cir. 2021) (striking down Alaska's $500 individual contribution limit).

39. Citizens United v. Federal Election Commission, 558 U.S. at 366–67.

40. 558 U.S. at 480–85 (Thomas, J., dissenting).

41. Doe v. Reed, 561 U.S. 186, 228 (2010) (Scalia, J., concurring).

42. Cochrane 2017. The inspector general's report of cases between 2004 and 2013 found that the IRS had targeted not only conservative groups but also liberal organizations whose names included terms such as "progressive," "green energy," "medical marijuana," and "occupy" (US Treasury Inspector General for Tax Administration 2017).

43. NAACP v. Alabama ex rel. Patterson, 357 U.S. 449 (1958) (based on "an uncontroverted showing that on past occasions revelation of the identity of its rank-and-file members has exposed these members to economic reprisal, loss of employment, threat of physical coercion, and other manifestations of public hostility").

44. Gaspee Project v. Mederos, 13 F. 4th 79, 94 (1st Cir. 2021).

45. See IRS n.d.b. The same is true for groups organized to qualify for other types of tax-exempt status, such as labor organizations (501[c][5]) and trade associations and business leagues (501[c][6]) (see IRS n.d.a.).

46. See Beckel 2019; 2018.

47. That shift reflected a large influx of money to Majority Forward, a Democratic Party–aligned group that spent about $46 million on the 2018 midterm election. It may also have been partly attributable to the disappearance of several dark-money groups that had previously supported conservatives, including Crossroads GPS, whose leaders moved to a nonprofit called One Nation, which spends millions on political ads but does not report the spending to the FEC because the ads do not explicitly urge viewers to vote for or against candidates.

48. Massoglia and Evers-Hillstrom 2021; Vogel and Goldmacher 2022a (compiling data showing that fifteen of the most politically active nonprofit organizations that generally align with the Democratic Party spent more than $1.5 billion in 2020, compared to roughly $900 million spent by a comparable sample of fifteen of the most politically active groups aligned with the Republican Party).

49. Americans for Prosperity Foundation n.d.

50. Thomas More Law Center n.d.

51. Brief of the Floyd Abrams Institute for Freedom of Expression at Yale Law School as Amicus Curiae in Support of Neither Party, 2021 WL 827027.

52. See, e.g., Amicus Brief of the American Center for Law and Justice in Support of Petitioners, 2021 WL 827034; Brief Amicus Curiae of Goldwater Institute and Rio Grande Foundation in Support of Petitioners, 2021 WL 780733; Brief Amici Curiae of Concerned Women for America, the Congressional Prayer Caucus Foundation, Americans United for Life, the National Legal Foundation, the Pacific Justice Institute, Young Americans for Liberty, the Family Foundation, the Illinois Family Institute, and International Conference of Evangelical Chaplain Endorsers in Support of the Petitioners, 2021 WL 827018.

53. Americans for Prosperity Foundation v. Bonta, 594 U.S. _ (2021).

54. Americans for Prosperity Foundation v. Bonta, 141 S. Ct. 2373, 2388 (2021).

55. 141 S. Ct. 2373, 2392.

56. Bluman v. FEC, 565 U.S. 1104 (2012).

57. Williams-Yulee v. Florida Bar, 135 S. Ct. 1656, 1662 (2015).

58. See Republican Party of La. v. FEC, 219 F. Supp. 3d 86 (D.D.C. 2016), summarily aff'd, 137 S. Ct. 2178 (2017).

59. Federal Election Commission v. Ted Cruz for Senate, 596 U.S. _ (2022).

60. Brief of Senator Mitch McConnell as Amicus Curiae in Support of Appellees, 2021 WL 6144107.

61. Rosenberg 1991; Klarman 2001; Post and Siegel 2007; Silverstein 2009; Miller and Barnes 2004; Keck 2014.

62. See, e.g., Fishkin and Forbath 2022, 435–41. For other, similar arguments suggesting that Americans should not cede so much authority to the Court to tell us what the Constitution means, see Kramer 2004, 247–48; Tushnet 2020b, 243–57.

63. Kersch 2014, 185–88 (noting that constitutional change is a long-term, slow, incremental process that requires overcoming path dependence and entrenchment mechanisms).

## Conclusion

1. Epp 1998, 197.

2. Epp 1998, 2.

3. See, e.g., Sorrell v. IMS Health Inc., 564 U.S. 552 (2011); Nat'l Ass'n of Mfrs. v. SEC, 800 F. 3d 518 (D.C. Cir. 2015); Masterpiece Cakeshop, Ltd. v. Colo. C.R. Comm'n, 138 S. Ct. 1719 (2018).

4. Devins and Baum 2019, 44–45.

5. See, e.g., Balkin and Levinson 2001; Kersch 2004; 2006; Schauer 2004; 2015.

6. Schauer 2004, 1798 n. 154.

7. See Hertel-Fernandez 2019, 72; Huq 2022, 55.

8. Appadurai 2020. Other scholars have described a similar phenomenon as "plutocratic populism" (Hacker and Pierson 2020, 5; Tushnet and Bugaric 2021, 131).

9. See Skocpol and Hertel-Fernandez 2016.

10. For more on this distinction between direct and indirect effects, or between "special effects" and "general effects," see Handler, Hollingsworth, and Erlanger 1978, 209. See also Galanter 1983, 124–27 (on the "radiating effects of courts").

11. See Galanter 1983 (emphasizing the influence of courts on social practices); McCann 1994 (focusing on the effects of litigation on public discourse and the perceptions of activists).

12. For a general discussion of how "the Supreme Court matters in American politics" and considering two linked dimensions of its influence—its impact on the terms of strategic interaction of political actors in society and the "constitutive" power of its rulings—see McCann 1999. See also Galanter 1983 (noting that "courts not only resolve disputes, they prevent them, mobilize them, displace them, transform them").

13. See Baumgardner and TerBeek 2022, 149.

14. See Jones 2018 (finding that 71 percent of Republicans and Republican-leaning independents and 85 percent of Democrats and Democratic-leaning independents say that there should be limits on campaign spending); Brenan 2019 (finding that 20 percent of Americans are satisfied with the nation's campaign finance laws: 15 percent of Democrats and Democratic-leaning independents and 26 percent of Republicans/Republican-leaning independents); Confessore and Thee-Brenan 2015 (finding that "Americans of both parties fundamentally reject the regime of untrammeled money in elections made possible by the Supreme Court's Citizens United ruling and other court decisions and now favor a sweeping overhaul of how political campaigns are financed").

15. See Jones 2018 (documenting a 14 percent difference between Republicans and Republican-leaning independents and Democrats and Democratic-leaning independents in support for limits on campaign spending); Brenan 2019 (finding an 11 percent difference).

16. Primo and Milyo 2020.

17. See Sides, Tausanovitch, and Vavreck 2022 (on America's "calcified politics").

18. Steven Teles has observed that "legal liberals are very strong in the elite circles of the legal profession and continue to be well networked in Washington, but they are weak in grassroots mobilizations, and their elite organizations have few thick connections to mass organizations" (2008, 278, citing Skocpol 2003).

19. Durkee 2020. Bopp also defended True the Vote against fraud allegations by a contributor who gave the organization $2.5 million to stop the certification of the election (Jaramillo 2022). In other litigation that made headlines, Bopp challenged Covid-19 vaccine requirements to attend Indiana University. The Seventh Circuit rejected the challenge to the vaccine mandate, and Justice Barrett denied a petition to have the case heard by the US Supreme Court (Klaassen v. Trustees of the University of Indiana, No. 21–2326, August 2, 2021). Bopp also defended House Republicans Madison Cawthorn and Marjorie Taylor Green against challenges to their eligibility for reelection in 2022 based on arguments that their behavior at the rally that preceded the US Capitol riot in January 2021 constituted "insurrection or rebellion" against the United States (Coyle 2022).

20. Kranish and Hamburger 2021. After her law firm, Foley and Lardner, indicated publicly that it was "concerned" about her role in Trump's attempt to subvert the election, Mitchell

resigned (Durkee 2021). She then became senior legal fellow at the Conservative Partnership Institute, chairing the organization's Election Integrity Network.

21. Olson 2020.

22. Eastman 2020. At the January 6th "Stop the Steal" rally on the National Mall, Eastman appeared alongside Trump and Rudy Giuliani, claiming that fraudulent votes generated by voting machines had changed the election outcome and insisting that if Pence did not set aside or postpone the final counting of the electoral votes, he was unworthy of his office (2021).

23. Miller 2020.

24. Severns 2021.

25. Vogel, Goldmacher, and Mac 2022.

26. McFadden 2021; Day 2021.

27. Snodgrass 2021.

28. Huggins 2022.

29. Arnsdorf 2021; Vogel, Goldmacher, and Mac 2022.

30. Kessler and Pozen 2018, 1961.

31. See, e.g., Kessler and Pozen 2018; Shanor 2016; Kessler 2016; Fishkin and Forbath 2022, 433–41. Mark Tushnet made this argument almost forty years ago: "The first amendment has replaced the due process clause as the primary guarantor of the privileged" (1984, 1387).

32. See, e.g., Bagenstos 2014; Tebbe 2015.

33. Janus v. AFSCME, 138 S. Ct. at 2501 (Kagan, J., dissenting).

34. See Kessler and Pozen 2018, 1970 (describing advocacy groups that have assisted in extending First Amendment protection to new areas as "the First Amendment-industrial complex").

35. See First National Bank of Boston v. Bellotti, 435 U.S. 765 (1978); Citizens United v. FEC, 558 U.S. 310 (2010).

36. See Weiland 2017, 1451–52 (arguing that the "free flow" metaphor "evinces an indifference to the actors who set the flow in motion, their intent, and the consequences of the flow . . . 'Flow' does not invite questions of agency, equity, or fairness but instead shuts them down by suggesting that answering them is neither important nor possible").

37. See Buckley v. Valeo, 424 U.S. at 64–74 (1976) (upholding financial disclosure obligations under 1974 FECA); Citizens United v. FEC, 558 U.S. 310, 365–370 (2010) (upholding the BCRA's disclaimer and disclosure provisions).

38. Hasen 2022, 85.

39. Wu 2020; Parsons 2020.

40. Hasen 2017–2018; Hasen 2022; Pozen 2020.

41. Hasen 2022, 23.

42. Hasen 2022; Tokaji 2020; Wu 2020.

43. See, e.g., Abu El-Haj 2016; 2019; 2022; Andrias 2016; Rahman 2017; Abu El-Haj and Kuo 2022.

44. Hulse 2021.

45. See, e.g., Kramer 2020; Calabresi 2020; Epps and Sitaraman 2019; 2021; Fishkin and Forbath 2022; Huq 2022; Lemley 2022. For a review of prominent reform proposals evaluated by a commission convened by President Biden, see Presidential Commission on the Supreme Court of the United States 2021.

# Bibliography

Abramowitz, Alan I., and Steven W. Webster. 2018. "Negative Partisanship: Why Americans Dislike Parties but Behave Like Rabid Partisans." *Advances in Political Psychology* 39: 119–35.

Abrams, Floyd. 2013. *Friend of the Court: On the Front Lines with the First Amendment*. New Haven, CT: Yale University Press.

Abrams, Floyd, Ira Glasser, and Joel Gora. 2010. "The ACLU Approves Limits on Speech." *Wall Street Journal*, April 30.

Abu El-Haj, Tabatha. 2016. "Beyond Campaign Finance Reform." *Boston College Law Review* 57: 1127–85.

Abu El-Haj, Tabatha. 2017. "'Live Free or Die'—Liberty and the First Amendment." *Ohio State Law Journal* 78: 917–45.

Abu El-Haj, Tabatha. 2019. "Making and Unmaking Citizens: Law and the Shaping of Civic Capacity." *University of Michigan Journal of Law Reform* 53: 63–137.

Abu El-Haj, Tabatha. 2022. "How the Liberal First Amendment Under-Protects Democracy." *Minnesota Law Review* 107: 102–72.

Abu El-Haj, Tabatha, and Didi Kuo. 2022. "Associational Party-Building: A Path to Rebuilding Democracy." *Columbia Law Review Forum* 122: 127–76.

AFL-CIO. 2012. "Executive Council Statement: Restoring Democracy." March 14. https://aflcio.org/about/leadership/statements/restoring-democracy.

Albiston, Catherine. 2011. "The Dark Side of Litigation as a Social Movement Strategy." *Iowa Law Review* 96: 61–77.

Albiston, Catherine. 2018. "Democracy, Civil Society, and Public Interest Law." *Wisconsin Law Review*: 187–212.

Altman, Alex. 2015. "Meet the Man Who Invented the Super PAC." *Time*, May 13.

American Bar Association. n.d. "Model Rules of Professional Conduct—Table of Contents." ABA. Accessed February 10, 2023. https://www.americanbar.org/groups/professional_responsibility/publications/model_rules_of_professional_conduct/model_rules_of_professional_conduct_table_of_contents/.

American Civil Liberties Union. n.d.a. "ACLU History: Taking a Stand for Free Speech in Skokie." Accessed February 7, 2023. https://www.aclu.org/other/aclu-history-taking-stand-free-speech-skokie.

American Civil Liberties Union. n.d.b. "Free Speech: Campaign Finance Reform." Accessed February 7, 2023. https://www.aclu.org/issues/free-speech/campaign-finance-reform.

Americans for Prosperity Foundation. n.d. "Mission." *GuideStar*. Accessed March 25, 2022. https://www.guidestar.org/profile/52-1527294.

Andrias, Kate. 2016. "Confronting Power in Public Law." *Harvard Law Review Forum* 130, no.1: F1.

Ansberry, Clare. 1995. "The Best Beef Jerky Has Characteristics Few Can Appreciate." *Wall Street Journal*, April 4.

Appadurai, Arjun. 2020. "We Are Witnessing the Revolt of the Elites." *Wire*, April 22.

Arnsdorf, Isaac. 2021. "Trump Spawned a New Group of Mega-Donors Who Now Hold Sway Over the GOP's Future." *ProPublica*, March 6.

Ashar, Sameer M. 2017. "Movement Lawyers in the Fight for Immigrant Rights." *UCLA Law Review* 64: 1464–507.

Bader, Hans F. 1997. "Free Speech and Hostile Environment 'Harassment.'" *Free Speech and Election Law Practice Group Newsletter* 1, no. 2.

Bagenstos, Samuel R. 2014. "The Unrelenting Libertarian Challenge to Public Accommodations Law." *Stanford Law Review* 66: 1–33.

Baird, Vanessa A. 2007. *Answering the Call of the Court: How Justices and Litigants Set the Supreme Court Agenda*. Charlottesville: University of Virginia Press.

Balkin, Jack M. 2001. "Bush v. Gore and the Boundary Between Law and Politics." *Yale Law Journal* 110: 1407–58.

Balkin, Jack M. 2011. *Constitutional Redemption*. Cambridge, MA: Harvard University Press.

Balkin, Jack M. 2015. "Constitutional Interpretation and Change in the United States: The Official and the Unofficial." *Jus Politicum*, April 18.

Balkin, Jack M. 2019. "Why Liberals and Conservatives Flipped on Judicial Restraint: Judicial Review in the Cycles of Constitutional Time." *Texas Law Review* 98: 215–64.

Balkin, Jack M. 2020a. "Lawyers and Historians Argue about the Constitution." *Constitutional Commentary* 35: 345–400.

Balkin, Jack M. 2020b. *The Cycles of Constitutional Time*. New York: Oxford Unversity Press.

Balkin, Jack M., and Sanford Levinson. 2001. "Understanding the Constitutional Revolution." *Virginia Law Review* 87: 1045–109.

Balkin, Jack M., and Sanford Levinson. 2006. "The Processes of Constitutional Change: From Partisan Entrenchment to the National Surveillance State." *Fordham Law Review* 75: 489–535.

Barnett, Randy E. 1999. "An Originalism for Nonoriginalists." *Loyola Law Review* 45: 611–54.

Barnett, Randy E. 2004. *Restoring the Lost Constitution: The Presumption of Liberty*. Princeton, NJ: Princeton University Press.

Barnett, Randy E. 2015. "Opinion: Ed Whelan v. George Will on 'Judicial Restraint.'" *Volokh Conspiracy*, October 23.

Barr and Klein PLLC. n.d. "Uncompromising Advocates." Accessed May 4, 2022. https://barrklein.com.

Barron, Jerome. 1967. "Access to the Press—A New First Amendment Right." *Harvard Law Review* 80: 1641–78.

Bartels, Larry M. 2008. *Unequal Democracy: The Political Economy of the New Gilded Age*. New York: Russell Sage.

Batchis, Wayne. 2016. *The Right's First Amendment: The Politics of Free Speech and the Return of Conservative Libertarianism*. Stanford, CA: Stanford University Press.

Baum, Lawrence. 2006. *Judges and Their Audiences: A Perspective on Judicial Behavior*. Princeton, NJ: Princeton University Press.

Baumgardner, Paul. 2022. "Moving to the Right? How the Conservative Movement Has Shaped American Legal Education." *Annual Review of Law and Social Science* 18: 249–61.

Baumgardner, Paul, and Calvin TerBeek. 2022. "The U.S. Supreme Court is Not a Dahlian Court." *Studies in American Political Development*: 148–150.

Bawn, Kathleen, David Karol, Seth Masket, Hans Noel, and John Zaller. 2012. "A Theory of Political Parties: Groups, Policy Demands and Nominations in American Politics." *Perspectives in Politics* 10: 571–97.

Bean, Lydia, and Steve Teles. 2015. "Spreading the Gospel of Climate Change: An Evangelical Battleground." *New America* (November).

Beckel, Michael. 2018. *Dark Money Illuminated*. Washington, DC: Issue One. https://www.issue one.org/wp-content/uploads/2018/09/Dark-Money-Illuminated-Report.pdf.

Beckel, Michael. 2019. *In 2018 Midterms, Liberal Dark Money Groups Outspent Conservative Ones for First Time since Citizens United*. Washington, DC: Issue One. https://www.issueone.org /wp-content/uploads/2019/01/Post-CU-Dark-Money-Mini-Report.pdf.

Bell, Derrick A. 1976. "Serving Two Masters: Integration Ideals and Client Interests in School Desegregation Litigation." *Yale Law Journal* 85: 470–519.

Bensinger, Ken. 2023. "DeSantis, Aiming at a Favorite Foil, Wants to Roll Back Press Freedom." *New York Times*, February 10.

Berger, Raoul. 1977. *Government by Judiciary*. Cambridge, MA: Harvard University Press.

Bethel, Tom. 1999. "The Money Chase." *American Spectator* (November): 18–19.

BeVier, Lillian R. 1985. "Money and Politics: A Perspective on the First Amendment and Campaign Finance Reform." *California Law Review* 73: 1045–90.

BeVier, Lillian R. 1987. "Hands Off the Political Process." *Harvard Journal of Law and Public Policy* 10: 11–14.

BeVier, Lillian R. 1994. "Campaign Finance Reform: Specious Arguments, Intractable Dilemmas." *Columbia Law Review* 94: 1258–80.

BeVier, Lillian R. 1997. "Campaign Finance 'Reform' Proposals: A First Amendment Analysis." *Cato Policy Analysis* 282.

BeVier, Lillian R. 1999. "The Issue of Issue Advocacy: An Economic, Political, and Constitutional Analysis." *Virginia Law Review* 85: 1761–92.

BeVier, Lillian R. 2002. "Campaign Finance Regulation: Less, Please." *Arizona State Law Journal* 34: 1115–21.

BeVier, Lillian R. 2004. "*McConnell v. FEC*: Not Senator Buckley's First Amendment." *2003 Supreme Court Review*: 163–95.

BeVier, Lillian R. 2007. "First Amendment Basics Redux: Buckley v. Valeo to FEC v. Wisconsin Right to Life." *Cato Supreme Court Review* 77: 112–13.

Bickel, Alexander. 1962. *The Least Dangerous Branch: The Supreme Court at the Bar of Politics*. New Haven, CT: Yale University Press.

Bickel, Alexander. 1975. *The Morality of Consent*. New Haven, CT: Yale University Press.

Black, Ryan C., Matthew K. Hall, Ryan Owens, and Evan M. Ringsmuth. 2016. "The Role of Emotional Language in Briefs Before the U.S. Supreme Court." *Journal of Law and Courts* 4: 377–407.

Blasi, Vincent, ed. 1983. *The Burger Court: The Counter-Revolution That Wasn't*. New Haven, CT: Yale University Press.

Bonica, Adam, and Howard Rosenthal. 2016. "Rising Economic Inequality and Campaign Contributions from Very Wealthy Americans." *Scholars Strategy Network*, November 28. https://scholars.org/contribution/rising-economic-inequality-and-campaign-contributions -very-wealthy-americans.

Bopp, James. 1996. "The FEC's Assault on the First Amendment." *Free Speech and Election Law Practice Group Newsletter* (Fall).

Bork, Robert. 1971. "Neutral Principles and Some First Amendment Problems." *Indiana Law Journal* 47: 1–35.

Bork, Robert H. 1990a. "An End to Political Judging?" *National Review*, December 31: 30.

Bork, Robert H. 1990b. *The Tempting of America: The Political Seduction of the Law*. New York: Free Press.

Bose, Debanjali. 2020. "Meet Robert Mercer, the Conservative Billionaire Who Was a Mega-Donor for Trump during the 2016 Campaign but is Notably Absent in 2020." *Business Insider*, July 25.

Bowles, Nellie. 2019. "Fighting Big Tech Makes for Some Uncomfortable Bedfellows." *New York Times*, July 15.

Bradham, Bre, Andre Tartar, and Hayley Warren. 2020. "American Politicians Who Vote Against Climate Get More Corporate Cash." *Bloomberg Green*, October 23.

Breger, Marshall J. 1985. "Accountability and the Adjudication of the Public Interest." *Harvard Journal of Law and Public Policy*: 349–54.

Brenan, Megan. 2019. "Americans Most Satisfied with Nation's Military, Security." *Gallup*, January 28.

Brenan, Megan. 2020. "Support for Stricter U.S. Gun Laws at Lowest Level since 2016." *Gallup*, November 16.

Brennan Center for Justice. n.d. "History." Accessed February 3, 2023. https://www.brennancen ter.org/about/history/.

Briffault, Richard. 2008. "Lobbying and Campaign Finance: Separate and Together." *Stanford Law and Policy Review*: 105–29.

Briffault, Richard. 2009. "Life of the Parties? Money, Politics, and Campaign Finance Reform." *Election Law Journal* 8: 207–18.

Brissenden, Michael, rep. 2012. "What Price Democracy and Freedom?" *7:30 Report*. Aired July 2, 2012, on Australian Broadcasting Corporation.

Bronner, Ethan. 1989. *Battle for Justice: How the Bork Nomination Shook America*. New York: W. W. Norton.

Broockman, David E., Gregory Ferenstein, and Neil Malhotra. 2019. "Predispositions and the Political Behavior of American Economic Elites: Evidence from Technology Entrepreneurs." *American Journal of Political Science* 63: 212–33.

Brown, Steven P. 2002. *Trumping Religion: The New Christian Right, the Free Speech Clause, and the Courts*. Tuscaloosa: University of Alabama Press.

Brown-Nagin, Tomiko. 2005. "Elites, Social Movements, and the Law: The Case of Affirmative Action." *Columbia Law Review* 105, no. 5: 1436–528.

Brown-Nagin, Tomiko. 2011. *Courage to Dissent: Atlanta and the Long History of the Civil Rights Movement*. New York: Oxford University Press.

Bruhl, Aaron-Andrew P., and Adam Feldman. 2017. "Separating the Amicus Wheat from Chaff." *Georgetown Law Journal Online* 106: 135.

Bush, George W. 2002. "President Signs Campaign Finance Reform Act: Statement by the President." Washington, DC: White House Office of the Press Secretary, March 27. https://georgewbush-whitehouse.archives.gov/news/releases/2002/03/20020327.html.

Calabresi, Steven. 2020. "Give Justices Term Limits." *New York Times*, October 27.

Caldeira, Gregory A., and John R. Wright. 1988. "Organized Interests and Agenda Setting in the U.S. Supreme Court." *American Political Science Review* 82: 1109–27.

Caldeira, Gregory A., and John R. Wright. 1998. "Lobbying for Justice: Organized Interests, Supreme Court Nominations, and the United States Senate." *American Journal of Political Science* 42, no. 2: 499–523.

Cannon, Carl. 2005. "What Was It about Miers and the Intellectuals?" *National Journal*, November 12: A1.

Carle, Susan D. 2013. *Defining the Struggle: National Organizing for Racial Justice, 1880–1915.* New York: Oxford University Press.

Carle, Susan D., and Scott L. Cummings. 2018. "A Reflection on the Ethics of Movement Lawyering." *Georgetown Journal of Legal Ethics* 31: 447–74.

Carney, Eliza Newlin. 1997. "Abortion Foes Fight the 'Speech Police.'" *National Journal*, November 22.

Carter, Terry. 2018. "The Executive Branch Pushes the Boundaries of the Separation of Powers." *ABA Journal*, April 1.

Caso, Anthony. 1999. "Supreme Court Preview: Compelled Financing of Expressive Activities." *Free Speech and Election Law Practice Group Newsletter* 3, no. 1.

Chemerinsky, Erwin. 2010. *The Conservative Assault on the Constitution.* New York: Simon and Schuster.

Childress, Sarah. 2012. "James Bopp: What Citizens United Means for Campaign Finance." *Frontline*, July 2.

Citizens United. n.d.a. "Fulfilling Our Mission." Accessed October 24, 2020. http://www.citizensunited.org/fulfilling-our-mission.aspx.

Citizens United. n.d.b. "Citizens United Online Store." Accessed October 24, 2020. https://secure.donationreport.com/productlist.html?key=1QSEBUQ9MLSW.

Citizens United. n.d.c. "Who We Are: David N. Bossie." Accessed October 24, 2020. http://www.citizensunited.org/about-david-bossie.aspx.

Coates, John C. IV. 2015. "Corporate Speech and the First Amendment: History, Data, and Some Implications." *Constitutional Commentary* 30: 223–75.

Cochrane, Emily. 2017. "Justice Department Settles with Tea Party Groups after I.R.S. Scrutiny." *New York Times*, October 26.

Cockerman, Sean. 2007. "The Man behind Willie Horton Ads Has New Target: Hillary Clinton." *McClatchy Newspapers*, July 14.

Cogan, Marin. 2015. "The Trade Vote Reignited the War within the House G.O.P." *Intelligencer*, June 26.

Cohen, Larry. 2013. "Remarks to the 74th CWA Convention." Remarks as prepared for delivery to the 74th Communications Workers of America convention, Pittsburgh, PA, April 22. https://cwa-union.org/pages/president_larry_cohens_remarks_to_the_74th_cwa_convention.

Cohen, Marin, David Karol, Hans Noel, and John Zaller. 2008. *The Party Decides: Presidential Nominations before and after Reform*. Chicago: University of Chicago Press.

Cole, David. 2016a. *Engines of Liberty: The Power of Citizen Activists to Make Constitutional Law*. New York: Basic Books.

Cole, David. 2016b. "How to Reverse Citizens United: What Campaign-Finance Reformers Can Learn from the NRA." *Atlantic* (April).

Cole, David. 2022. "Originalism's Charade." *New York Review of Books*, November 24.

Collins, Paul. 2004. "Friends of the Court: Examining the Influence of Amicus Curiae Participation in U.S Supreme Court Litigation." *Law and Society Review* 38: 807–29.

Collins, Paul M., Pamela C. Corley, and Jesse Hamner. 2014. "Me Too? An Investigation of Repetition in U.S. Supreme Court Amicus Briefs." *Judicature*: 228–34.

Collins, Paul M., Pamela Corley, and Jesse Hamner. 2015. "The Influence of Amicus Curiae Briefs on U.S. Supreme Court Opinion Content." *Law and Society Review* 49, no. 4: 917–44.

Collins, Ronald K. L., and David M. Skover. 2014. *When Money Speaks: The McCutcheon Decision, Campaign Finance Law, and the First Amendment*. Oak Park, IL: Top Five Books LLC.

Confessore, Nicholas, and Megan Thee-Brenan. 2015. "Poll Shows Americans Favor an Overhaul of Campaign Financing." *New York Times*, June 2: A18.

Connolly, Ceci, and Terry M. Neal. 1997. "McConnell Leads Way to 'Soft Money' Record." *Washington Post*, October 5: A6.

Conservative Action Project. 2015. *Memo for the Movement: Stop Funding Bad Policies*. Washington, DC: Conservative Action Project, December 4. https://assets.documentcloud.org/documents/2640350/Continuing-Resolution-Post-Rel-12-4-15.pdf.

Cooper, Charles. 1987. "The First Amendment, Original Intent, and the Political Process." *Harvard Journal of Law and Public Policy* 10: 15–20.

Cooper, Charles, and Derek L. Shaffer. 2004. "What Congress 'Shall Make' the Court Will Take: How McConnell v. FEC Betrays the First Amendment in Upholding Incumbency Protection under the Banner of 'Campaign Finance Reform.'" *Election Law Journal* 3: 223–28.

Cooper, Cynthia L. 2003. "Republican Party Donates to Right to Life." *Women'sENews*, March 18.

Corley, Pamela C. 2008. "The Supreme Court and Opinion Content: The Influence of Parties' Briefs." *Political Science Quarterly* 6: 468–78.

"Corporate Money in Politics." 2010. Editorial. *Washington Post*, May 9. http://www.washingtonpost.com/wp-dyn/content/article/2010/05/08/AR2010050803134_pf.html.

Cose, Ellis. 2020. *Democracy If We Can Keep It: The ACLU's 100-Year Fight for Rights in America*. New York: New Press.

"The Court's Blow to Democracy." 2010. Editorial. *New York Times*, January 21. http://www.nytimes.com/2010/01/22/opinion/22fri1.html.

Coyle, Marcia. 2013. *The Roberts Court: The Struggle for the Constitution*. New York: Simon and Schuster.

Coyle, Marcia. 2022. "GOP Veteran Lawyer James Bopp Jr. Takes Marjorie Taylor Greene Appeal to 11th Circuit." *National Law Journal*, April 29.

Cramer, Katherine J. 2016. *The Politics of Resentment: Rural Consciousness in Wisconsin and the Rise of Scott Walker*. Chicago: University of Chicago Press.

Crane, Daniel A. 2018. "Antitrust's Unconventional Politics." *Virginia Law Review Online* 104: 118–55.

Cummings, Scott L. 2012. "The Accountability Problem in Public Interest Practice: Old Paradigms and New Directions." In *Lawyers in Practice: Ethical Decision Making in Context*, edited by Leslie C. Levin and Lynn Mather, 340–64. Chicago: University of Chicago Press.

Cummings, Scott L. 2017. "Movement Lawyering." *University of Illinois Law Review*: 1645–732.

Cummings, Scott L. 2020. *An Equal Place: Lawyers in the Struggle for Los Angeles*. New York: Oxford University Press.

Cummings, Scott L. 2022. *Lawyers and Movements*. New York: Oxford University Press.

Dahl, Robert. 1957. "Decision-Making in a Democracy: The Supreme Court as National Policy-Maker." *Journal of Public Law* 6, no. 2: 279.

Day, Chad. 2021. "More Coprporate PACs Resume Political Donations to Republicans Who Rejected Election Results." *Wall Street Journal*, July 16.

DC Fandom. n.d. "Htrae." Accessed February 9, 2023. https://dc.fandom.com/wiki/Htrae.

De Rugy, Veronique. 2022. "Both Democracts and Republicans Want to Break Up Big Tech. Consumers Would Pay the Price." *Reason*, July 21.

Decker, Jefferson. 2016. *The Other Rights Revolution: Conservative Lawyers and the Remaking of American Government*. New York: Oxford University Press.

Democratic Party Platforms. 2008. "Democratic Party Platform of 2008." Posted online by Gerhard Peters and John T. Woolley, *American Presidency Project*. https://www.presidency.ucsb.edu/node/278858.

Democratic Party Platforms. 2012. "Democratic Party Platform of 2012." Posted online by Gerhard Peters and John T. Woolley, *American Presidency Project*. https://www.presidency.ucsb.edu/node/302346.

Democratic Party Platforms. 2016. "Democratic Party Platform of 2016." Posted online by Gerhard Peters and John T. Woolley, *American Presidency Project*. https://www.presidency.ucsb.edu/node/318309.

den Dulk, Kevin R. 2008. "Purpose-Driven Lawyers: Evangelical Cause Lawyering and the Culture War." In *The Cultural Lives of Cause Lawyers*, edited by Austin Sarat and Stuart Scheingold, 56–79. New York: Cambridge University Press.

Desmarais, Bruce A., Raymond J. La Raja, and Michael S. Kowal. 2015. "The Fates of Challengers in U.S. House Elecctions: The Role of Extended Party Networks in Supporting Candidates and Shaping Electoral Outcomes." *American Journal of Political Science* 59, no. 1: 194–211.

Devins, Neal, and Lawrence Baum. 2019. *The Company They Keep: How Partisan Divisions Came to the Supreme Court*. New York: Oxford University Press.

DeVos, Betsy. 1997. "Soft Money Is Good: 'Hard-Earned American Dollars that Big Brother Has Yet to Find a Way to Control.'" *Roll Call*, September 6.

Dezalay, Yves, and Bryant Garth. 2002. *The Internationalization of the Palace Wars: Lawyers, Economists, and the Contest to Transform Latin American States*. Chicago: University of Chicago Press.

Dezalay, Yves, and Bryant G. Garth. 2011. *Lawyers and the Rule of Law in an Era of Globalization*. New York: Routledge.

douek, evelyn, and Genevieve Lakier. 2022. "First Amendment Politics Gets Weird: Public and Private Platform Reform and the Breakdown of the Laissez-Faire Free Speech Consensus." *University of Chicago Law Review Online*, June 6. https://lawreviewblog.uchicago.edu/2022/06/06/douek-lakier-first-amendment/.

Dreisbach, Tom. 2019. "Mitch McConnell Has Long Argued for More Money in Politics." *All Things Considered*, aired August 1 on NPR. Radio broadcast, 8:17. https://www.npr.org/2019 /08/01/747368694/mitch-mcconnell-has-long-argued-for-more-money-in-politics.

Drutman, Lee. 2020a. *Breaking the Two-Party Doom Loop*. New York: Oxford University Press.

Drutman, Lee. 2020b. "How Hatred Came to Dominate American Politics." *FiveThirtyEight*, October 5.

Durkee, Alison. 2020. "G.O.P. Suddenly Drops Election Lawsuits in Four Battleground States amid Recent Court Failures." *Forbes*, November 16.

Durkee, Alison. 2021. "Trump Attorney Cleta Mitchell Resigns from Law Firm after Participating in President's Georgia Phone Call." *Forbes*, January 5.

Duxbury, Neil. 1995. *Patterns of American Jurisprudence*. New York: Oxford University Press.

Dyche, John D. 2009. *Republican Leader: A Political Biography of Senator Mitch McConnell*. Wilmington, DE: ISI Books.

Eastman, John. 2020. Memorandum. Posted at "Read: Trump Lawyer's Memo on Six-Step Plan for Pence to Overturn Election." *CNN*, September 21, 2021. https://www.cnn.com/2021/09/21 /politics/read-eastman-memo/index.html.

Eastman, John. 2021. Remarks. Rally on Electoral College Vote Certification, Washington, DC, January 6. Posted to C-SPAN, March 24, 2021. MP4 video, 3:14. https://www.c-span.org /video/?c4953961/user-clip-john-eastman-january-6-rally/.

Ebner, Lawrence S., and Robin S. Conrad. 2015. "Making Strategic Use of Amicus Briefs." *For the Defense* (October): 75–78.

Edelman, Lauren B., Gwendolyn Leachman, and Doug McAdam. 2010. "On Law, Organizations, and Social Movements." *Annual Review of Law and Social Science* 6: 653–85.

Edelman, Murray. 1988. *Constructing the Political Spectacle*. Chicago: University of Chicago Press.

Edsall, Thomas B. 2019. "The Changing Shape of the Parties Is Changing Where They Get Their Money." *New York Times*, September 18.

Eggen, Dan. 2012. "To Shield Donors, Chamber Gets More Political." *Washington Post*, May 31: A13.

Ellis, Peggy. 1997. "Ten Big Lies about Campaign Finance Reform." *Commentary*, October 9.

Ely, John Hart. 1973. "The Wages of Crying Wolf." *Yale Law Journal* 82: 920–49.

Ely, John Hart. 1980. *Democracy and Distrust*. Cambridge, MA: Harvard University Press.

Entman, Robert M. 2004. *Projections of Power: Framing News, Public Opinion, and U.S. Foreign Policy*. Chicago: University of Chicago Press.

Epp, Charles R. 1998. *The Rights Revolution: Lawyers, Activists, and Supreme Courts in Comparative Perspective*. Chicago: University of Chicago Press.

Epps, Daniel, and Ganesh Sitaraman. 2019. "How to Save the Supreme Court." *Yale Law Journal* 129: 148.

Epps, Daniel, and Ganesh Sitaraman. 2021. "The Future of Supreme Court Reform." *Harvard Law Review Forum* 134: 398.

Epstein, Dmitry, Merrill C. Roth, and Eric P. S. Baumer. 2014. "It's the Definition, Stupid! Framing of Online Privacy in the Internet Governance Forum Debates." *Journal of Information Policy* 4: 144–72.

Epstein, Lee. 1985. *Conservatives in Court*. Knoxville: University of Tennessee Press.

Epstein, Lee, and Joseph F. Kobylka. 1992. *The Supreme Court and Legal Change: Abortion and the Death Penalty*. Chapel Hill: University of North Carolina Press.

Epstein, Lee, Jeffrey A. Segal, Harold J. Spaeth, and Thomas G. Walker. 2012. *The Supreme Court Compendium*. 5th ed. Thousand Oaks, CA: CQ Press.

Epstein, Richard A. 2006. *How Progressives Rewrote the Constitution*. Washington, DC: Cato Institute.

Escher, M. C. 1938. *Sky and Water I*. Woodcut. Accession no. 1974.28.10, Cornelius Van S. Roosevelt Collection, National Gallery, Landover, MD. https://www.nga.gov/collection/art-object-page.54215.html.

Fallon, Richard H. 2018. *Law and Legitimacy in the Supreme Court*. Cambridge, MA: Harvard University Press.

Federal Election Commission. n.d.a. "Contribution Limits for 2023–2024." Accessed February 6, 2023. https://www.fec.gov/help-candidates-and-committees/candidate-taking-receipts/contribution-limits/.

Federal Election Commission. n.d.b. "Making Independent Expenditures." Accessed March 29, 2023. https://www.fec.gov/help-candidates-and-committees/making-independent-expenditures/.

Federalist Society. n.d.a. "About Us: Our Purpose." Accessed June 25, 2021. https://fedsoc.org/about-us.

Federalist Society. n.d.b. "Leonard A. Leo." Accessed September 3, 2022. https://fedsoc.org/contributors/leonard-leo.

Federalist Society. 2015. *2014 Annual Report*. Washington, DC: Federalist Society, June 22. https://fedsoc.org/commentary/publications/2014-annual-report.

Finkel, Eli J., Christopher A. Bail, Mina Cikara, Peter H. Ditto, Shanto Iyengar, Samara Klar, and Lilliana Mason. 2020. "Political Sectarianism in America." *Science* 370: 533–36.

Fishkin, Joseph, and William E. Forbath. 2022. *The Anti-Oligarchy Constitution*. Cambridge, MA: Harvard University Press.

Fishkin, Joseph, and David A. Pozen. 2018. "Asymmetric Constitutional Hardball." *Columbia Law Review* 118: 915–82.

Ford Foundation. n.d. "About Ford." Accessed February 4, 2023. https://www.fordfoundation.org/about/about-ford/.

*Foundation Directory On-Line*. 2022. Prod. Foundation Center. https://fconline.foundationcenter.org/fdo-search/member-index/.

Fournier, Keith. 1994. *A House Divided? Evangelicals and Catholics Together*. Colorado Springs, CO: NavPress.

Franze, Anthony J., and R. Reeves Anderson. 2018. "Supreme Court Amicus Curiae Review: 'Friends of the Court' Roared Back in 2017–2018 Term." *National Law Journal*, October 16.

"Free Speech and Spending." 1975. Editorial. *National Review*, September 12.

Friedman, Milton. 1987. "Free Markets and Free Speech." *Harvard Journal of Law and Public Policy* 10: 1–9.

Frymer, Paul. 2008. "Law and American Political Development." *Law and Social Inquiry* 33: 779–98.

Galanter, Marc. 1983. "The Radiating Effects of Courts." In *Empirical Theories of Courts*, edited by Keith O. Boyum and Lynn M. Mather, 117–42. New York: Longman.

Gamson, William A., and Andre Modigliani. 1989. "Media Discourse and Public Opinion on Nuclear Power: A Constructionist Approach." *American Journal of Sociology* 95: 1–37.

Garth, Bryant. 1982. "Conflict and Dissent in Class Actions." *Northwestern Law Review* 77: 492–535.

Gerken, Heather. 2012. "Keynote Address: Lobbying as the New Campaign Finance." *Georgia State University Law Review* 27, no. 4: 1147–60.

Gerken, Heather K. 2011. "Campaign Finance and the Doctrinal Death Match." *Balkinization*, June 27.

Gerken, Heather K., and Erica J. Newland. 2016. "The Citizens United Trilogy: The Myth, the True Tale, and the Story Still to Come." In *Election Law Stories*, edited by Joshua A. Douglas and Eugene D. Mazo, 359–404. St. Paul, MN: Foundation Press.

Gervais, Bryan T., and Irwin L. Morris. 2018. *Reactionary Republicanism: How the Tea Party in the House Paved the Way for Trump's Victory*. New York: Oxford University Press.

Gilens, Martin. 2012. *Affluence and Influence: Economic Inequality and Political Power in America*. Princeton, NJ: Princeton University Press.

Gillman, Howard. 1997. "The Collapse of Constitutional Originalism and the Rise of the Notion of the 'Living Constitution' in the Course of American State-Building." *Studies in American Political Development* 11: 191–247.

Gillman, Howard. 2001. *The Votes That Counted: How the Court Decided the 2000 Presidential Election*. Chicago: University of Chicago Press.

Gillman, Howard. 2002. "How Political Parties Can Use the Courts to Advance Their Agendas: Federal Courts in the United States, 1875–1891." *American Political Science Review* 96, no. 3: 511–24.

Gillman, Howard. 2006. "Party Politics and Constitutional Change: The Political Origins of Liberal Judicial Activism." In *The Supreme Court and American Political Development*, edited by Ronald Kahn and Ken I. Kersch, 138–68. Lawrence: University Press of Kansas.

Gillman, Howard, and Cornell Clayton. 1999. *The Supreme Court in American Politics*. Edited by Howard Gillman and Cornell Clayton. Lawrence: University Press of Kansas.

Ginsburg, Douglas H. 1995. "Delegation Running Riot." *Regulation* (Winter): 83.

Glazer, Nathan. 1975. "Toward an Imperial Judiciary." *Public Interest* 45: 104–23.

Goelzhauser, Greg, and Nicole Vouvalis. 2015. "Amicus Coalition Heterogeneity and Signaling Credibility in Supreme Court Agenda Setting." *Publius: The Journal of Federalism* 40: 99–116.

Gold, Matea. 2014. "How National Tea Party Groups Missed the David Brat Boat." *Washington Post*, June 10.

Gordon, Robert W. 2012. " 'Critical Legal Histories Revisited': A Response." *Law and Social Inquiry* 37: 200–13.

Gordon, Robert W. 2017. *Taming the Past: Essays on Law in History and History in Law*. Cambridge: Cambridge University Press.

Gottfried, Paul. 1993. *The Conservative Movement*. New York: MacMillan.

Graber, Mark A. 2004. "Judicial Supremacy and the Structure of Partisan Conflict." *Indiana Law Review* 50: 141–80.

Graber, Mark A. 2013. "The Coming Constitutional Yo-Yo? Elite Opinion, Polarization, and the Direction of Judicial Decision Making." *Howard Law Journal* 56, no. 3: 661–719.

Gramlich, John. 2021. "How Trump Compares with Other Recent Presidents in Appointing Federal Judges." Pew Research Center, January 13. https://www.pewresearch.org/fact-tank/2021/01/13/how-trump-compares-with-other-recent-presidents-in-appointing-federal-judges/.

Greene, Jamal. 2021. *How Rights Went Wrong: Why Our Obsession with Rights Is Tearing America Apart*. New York: Houghton Mifflin Harcourt.

Grossman, Matt, and David A. Hopkins. 2016. *Asymmetric Politics: Ideological Republicans and Group Interest Democrats*. New York: Oxford University Press.

Grunwald, Michael. 1999. "Campaign Finance Issue Divides Abortion Foes." *Washington Post*, September 14.

Hacker, Jacob S., and Paul Pierson. 2020. *Let Them Eat Tweets: How the Right Rules in an Age of Extreme Inequality*. New York: Liveright.

Haltom, William, and Michael McCann. 2004. *Distorting the Law: Politics, Media, and the Litigation Crisis*. Chicago: University of Chicago Press.

Handler, Joel F., Ellen Jane Hollingsworth, and Howard S. Erlanger. 1978. *Lawyers and the Pursuit of Legal Rights*. New York: Academic Press.

Harris Interactive. 2008. "Does the Second Amendment Provide a Right to Bear Arms? U.S. Adults Think So." June 3.

Hasen, Richard L. 2003. "The Untold Drafting History of Buckley v. Valeo." *Election Law Journal* 2: 241.

Hasen, Richard. 2012. "Anticipatory Overrulings, Invitations, Time Bombs, and Inadvertence: How Supreme Court Justices Move the Law." *Emory Law Journal* 61: 779–99.

Hasen, Richard L. 2016a. *Plutocrats United: Campaign Money, the Supreme Court, and the Distortion of American Elections*. New Haven, CT: Yale University Press.

Hasen, Richard L. 2016b. "The Nine Lives of Buckley v. Valeo." In *Election Law Stories*, edited by Joshua A. Douglas and Eugene D. Mazo, 287–312. St. Paul, MN: Foundation Press.

Hasen, Richard L. 2017–2018. "Cheap Speech and What It Has Done (to American Democracy)." *First Amendment Law Review* 16: 200–33.

Hasen, Richard L. 2018. *The Justice of Contradictions: Antonin Scalia and the Politics of Disruption*. New Haven, CT: Yale University Press.

Hasen, Richard L. 2019. "Polarization of the Judiciary." *Annual Review of Political Science* 22, no. 1: 261–76.

Hasen, Richard L. 2022. *Cheap Speech: How Disinformation Poisons Our Politics—and How to Cure It*. New Haven, CT: Yale University Press.

Hayward, Allison. 1997. "Election Law Observer." *Free Speech and Election Law Practice Newsletter* (Fall).

Hazelton, Morgan L. W., and Rachael K. Hinkle. 2022. *Persuading the Supreme Court: The Significance of Briefs in Judicial Decision-Making*. Lawrence: University Press of Kansas.

Hegland, Kenney. 1971. "Beyond Enthusiasm and Commitment." *Arizona Law Review* 13: 805–17.

Hellman, Deborah. 2016. "Resurrecting the Neglected Liberty of Self-Government." *University of Pennsylvania Law Review Online* 164: 233–39.

Heritage Foundation. 2009. "CNBC's Rick Santelli's Chicago Tea Party." Posted February 20. YouTube video, 4:36. https://www.youtube.com/watch?v=zp-Jw-5Kx8k.

Herrnson, Paul S. 2009. "The Roles of Party Organizations, Party-Connected Committees, and Party Allies in Elections." *Journal of Politics* 71: 1207–24.

Hertel-Fernandez, Alexander. 2019. "Asymmetric Partisan Polarization, Labor Policy, and Cross-State Political Power-Building." *Annals of the American Academy of Political and Social Science* 685, no. 1: 64–79.

Heyman, Steven J. 2014. "The Conservative-Libertarian Turn in First Amendment Jurisprudence." *West Virginia Law Review* 117: 231–343.

Hochschild, Arlie. 2016. *Strangers in Their Own Land: Anger and Mourning on the American Right*. New York: New Press.

Hollis-Brusky, Amanda. 2011. "Support Structures and Constitutional Change: Teles, Southworth, and the Conservative Legal Movement." *Law and Social Inquiry* 36: 516–36.

Hollis-Brusky, Amanda. 2015. *Ideas with Consequences: The Federalist Society and the Conservative Counterrevolution*. New York: Oxford University Press.

Hollis-Brusky, Amanda, and Joshua Wilson. 2020. *Separate but Faithful: The Christian Right's Radical Struggle to Transform Law and Legal Culture*. New York: Oxford University Press.

Horowitz, Donald L. 1977. *The Courts and Social Policy*. Washington, DC: Brookings Institute.

Horowitz, Michael. 1980. *The Public Interest Law Movement: An Analysis with Special Reference to the Role and Practices of Conservative Public Interest Law Firms*. Unpublished manuscript on file with author.

Houston, Paul. 1976. "Gun Lobby Seeks Millions to Fight Its Foes at Polls." *Los Angeles Times*, April 25: A1.

Huggins, Katherine. 2022. "Senators' Bills Aim to Ban Corporate PACs Following Record-Breaking Business PAC Giving in 2020." *OpenSecrets*, March 28. https://www.opensecrets.org/news/2022/03/ban-corporate-pacs-act/.

Hulse, Carl. 2021. "Yet Again, Mitch McConnell Digs In against Campaign Law Changes." *New York Times*, April 7.

Hunter, Nan. 2017. "Varieties of Constitutional Experience: Democracy and the Marriage Equality Campaign." *UCLA Law Review* 64: 1662–726.

Huq, Aziz Z. 2022. "The Supreme Court and the Dynamics of Democratic Backsliding." *Annals of the American Academy of Political and Social Science* 699, no. 1: 50–65.

Hur, Krystal. 2021. "Small Donors Ruled 2020; Will That Change Post-Trump?" *OpenSecrets*, February 3.

Institute for Free Speech. n.d. "About Us: Our Mission." Accessed February 23, 2022. https://www.ifs.org/about-us/.

Institute for Justice. n.d.a. "About Us." Accessed January 27, 2021. https://ij.org/about-us/.

Institute for Justice. n.d.b. "First Amendment." Accessed February 3, 2023. https://ij.org/issues/first-amendment/.

Institute for Justice. n.d.c. "Political Speech: IJ Defends the First Amendment from Political Censorship." Accessed February 23, 2022. http://ij.org/issues/first-amendment/political-speech/.

Institute for Justice. 2001. "IJ Thanks Its Cornerstone Supporters." November. https://web.archive.org/web/20150222184415/http://www.ij.org/charles-a-david-koch-2.

IRS. n.d.a. "Requirements for Exemption." Accessed February 10, 2023. https://www.irs.gov/charities-non-profits/other-non-profits/requirements-for-exemption.

IRS. n.d.b. "Social Welfare Organizations." Accessed February 10, 2023. https://www.irs.gov/charities-non-profits/other-non-profits/social-welfare-organizations.

Issacharoff, Samuel, and Pamela S. Karlan. 1999. "The Hydraulics of Campaign Finance Reform." *Texas Law Review* 77: 1705–38.

Iyengar, Shanto, Yphtach Lelkes, Neil Malhotra, and Sean J. Westwood. 2019. "The Origins and Consequences of Affective Polarization in the United States." *Annual Review of Political Science* 22: 129–46.

Iyengar, Shanto, Gaurav Sood, and Yphtach Lelkes. 2012. "Affect, Not Ideology: A Social Identity Perspective on Polarization." *Public Opinion Quarterly* 76, no. 3: 405–31.

James Madison Center for Free Speech. n.d. "Mission Statement of the James Madison Center for Free Speech: The Threat to Free Political Speech." Accessed February 23, 2022. https://www.jamesmadisoncenter.org/about/mission.html.

Jaramillo, Cassandra. 2022. "True the Vote Raised Millions to Combat Voter Fraud—But No One Really Knows Where the Money Went." *Mother Jones*, June 8.

Johnson, Jake. 2022. "Bernie Sanders Calls Out DNC after Billionaires Use Super PACs to Try to 'Buy Democratic Primaries.'" *Salon*, May 17.

Johnson, Timothy R., Paul J. Wahlbeck, and James F. Spriggs. 2006. "The Influence of Oral Arguments on the U.S. Supreme Court." *American Political Science Review* 100: 99–113.

Jones, Bradley. 2018. *Most Americans Want to Limit Campaign Spending, Say Big Donors Have Greater Political Influence*. Washington, DC: Pew Research Center, May 8. https://www.pew research.org/fact-tank/2018/05/08/most-americans-want-to-limit-campaign-spending -say-big-donors-have-greater-political-influence/.

Jones, Jeffrey M. 2022. "Confidence in U.S. Supreme Court Sinks to Historic Low." *Gallup*, June 23.

Joo, Thomas W. 2014. "The Worst Test of Truth: The 'Marketplace of Ideas' as Faulty Metaphor." *Tulane Law Review* 89: 383–433.

Joyce Foundation. n.d. "About Us." Accessed April 17, 2021. http://www.joycefdn.org/who-we-are /about-us.

Kabaservice, Geoffrey. 2004. *The Guardians: Kingman Brewster, His Circle, and the Rise of the Liberal Establishment*. New York: Henry Holt and Company LLC.

Kabaservice, Geoffrey. 2012. *Rule and Ruin: The Downfall of Moderation and the Destruction of the Republican Party, from Eisenhower to the Tea Party*. New York: Oxford University Press.

Kalman, Laura. 1996. *The Strange Career of Legal Liberalism*. New Haven, CT: Yale University Press.

Kalman, Laura. 2017. *The Long Reach of the Sixties: LBJ, Nixon, and the Making of the Contemporary Supreme Court*. New York: Oxford University Press.

Karlan, Pamela S. 2014. "Citizens Deflected: Electoral Integrity and Political Reform." In *Citizens Divided: Campaign Finance Reform and the Constitution*, edited by Robert C. Post, 141–51. Cambridge, MA: Harvard University Press.

Karol, David. 2009. *Party Position Change in American Politics: Coalition Management*. New York: Cambridge University Press.

Katz, Alyssa. 2015. *The Influence Machine: The U.S. Chamber of Commerce and the Corporate Capture of American Life*. New York: Random House.

Kearney, Joseph D., and Thomas W. Merrill. 2000. "The Influence of Amicus Briefs in the Supreme Court." *University of Pennsylvania Law Review* 148: 743–855.

Keck, Thomas M. 2004. *The Most Activist Supreme Court in History*. Chicago: University of Chicago Press.

Keck, Thomas M. 2014. *Judicial Politics in Polarized Times*. Chicago: University of Chicago Press.

Keller, Tim. 2008. "Freeing Speech from Government Control." *Law and Liberty*, February 1.

Kersch, Ken I. 2004. *Constructing Civil Liberties: Discontinuities in the Development of American Constitutional Law*. New York: Cambridge University Press.

Kersch, Ken I. 2006. "How Conduct Became Speech and Speech Became Conduct: A Political Development Case Study in Labor Law and the Freedom of Speech." *University of Pennsylvania Journal of Constitutional Law* 8: 255–97.

Kersch, Ken I. 2014. "The Talking Cure: How Constitutional Argument Drives Constitutional Development." *Boston University Law Review* 94: 1083–108.

Kersch, Ken I. 2019. *Conservatives and the Constitution: Imagining Constitutional Restoration in the Heyday of American Liberalism*. New York: Cambridge University Press.

Kessler, Jeremy K. 2016. "The Early Years of First Amendment Lochnerism." *Columbia Law Review* 116: 1915–2004.

Kessler, Jeremy, and David Pozen. 2018. "The Search for the Egalitarian First Amendment." *Columbia Law Review* 118: 1953–2010.

Kilpatrick, James J. 1975. "Campaign Reform Act Violates 1st Amendment." *Human Events*, January 4.

Kirkpatrick, David D. 2010. "A Quest to End Spending Rules for Campaigns." *New York Times*, January 24.

Klarman, Michael J. 2001. "Bush v. Gore through the Lens of Constitutional History." *California Law Review* 89: 1721–65.

Klarman, Michael J. 2006. *From Jim Crow to Civil Rights: The Supreme Court and the Struggle for Racial Equality.* New York: Oxford University Press.

Kleefeld, Eric. 2009. "A Purity Test for the G.O.P.?" *Talking Points Memo*, November 23.

Klein, Ezra. 2020. *Why We're Polarized.* New York: Avid Reader Press.

Koch, Charles. 1974. "Anti-Capitalism and Business." Speech to the board of directors at the annual meeting of the Institute for Humane Studies, Dallas, TX, April 27.

Koslov, Keith, dir. 2011. *Freedom Watch with Judge Napolitano.* Episode dated June 27. Aired on Fox Business Network LLD. https://www.imdb.com/title/tt6660232/.

Kramer, Larry D. 2020. "Pack the Courts." *New York Times*, October 27.

Kramer, Larry D. 2004. *The People Themselves: Popular Constitutionalism and Judicial Review.* New York: Oxford University Press.

Kranish, Michael, and Tom Hamburger. 2021. "Cleta Mitchell, a Key Figure in President's Phone Call, Was an Early Backer of Trump's Election Fraud Claims." *Washington Post*, January 4.

Kuhner, Timothy K. 2014. *Capitalism v. Democracy: Money in Politics and the Free Market Constitution.* Stanford, CA: Stanford Law Books.

Kumar, Anita. 2020. "Trump Readies Thousands of Attorneys for Election Fight." *Politico*, September 27.

Lacombe, Matthew J. 2021. *Firepower: How the NRA Turned Gun Owners into a Political Force.* Princeton, NJ: Princeton University Press.

Lakier, Genevieve. 2020a. "The First Amendment's Real Lochner Problem." *University of Chicago Law Review* 87: 1241–342.

Lakier, Genevieve. 2020b. "The Problem Isn't the Use of Analogies but the Analogies Courts Use." In *The Perilous Public Square: Structural Threats to Free Expression Today*, edited by David E. Pozen, 150–55. New York: Columbia University Press.

Lax, Jeffrey R., Justin Phillips, and Adam Zelizer. 2019. "The Party of the Purse? Unequal Representation in the U.S. Senate." *American Political Science Review* 113, no. 4: 917–40.

Layman, Geoffrey, Thomas Carsey, and Juliana Horowitz. 2006. "Party Polarization in American Politics." *Annual Review of Political Science* 9: 83–110.

Lemley, Mark A. 2022. "The Imperial Supreme Court." *Harvard Law Review Forum* 136: 97–118.

Lessig, Lawrence. 2011. *Republic Lost: How Money Corrupts Congress—and a Plan to Stop It.* New York: Twelve.

Levinson, Sanford. 2002. "The Warren Court Has Left the Building: Some Comments on Contemporary Discussions of Equality." *University of Chicago Legal Forum* 2002, no. 1: article 7.

Levy, Leonard W. 1985. *Emergence of a Free Press.* New York: Oxford University Press.

Lewis, Andrew R. 2017. *The Rights Turn in Conservative Christian Politics: How Abortion Transformed the Culture Wars.* New York: Cambridge University Press.

Lewis, Neil A. 1996. "Clinton Apologizes over Use of F.B.I. to Get G.O.P. Files." *New York Times*, June 10.

Lichtblau, Eric. 2010. "Long Battle by Foes of Campaign Finance Rules Shifts Landscape." *New York Times*, October 15.

Lichtblau, Eric, and Nicholas Confessore. 2015. "Life of the Parties? Money, Politics, and Campaign Finance Reform." *New York Times*, May 30: A1.

Lipton, Eric, and Alexander Burns. 2018. "The True Source of the N.R.A.'s Clout: Mobilization, Not Donations." *New York Times*, February 24.

LoBianco, Tom. 2016. "Trump and Sanders Using Anger against Big Money to Build Their Movements." *CNN Politics*, January 20.

LoGiurato, Brett. 2014. "It's Official: The G.O.P. Civil War is Over." *Business Insider*, May 22.

Luban, David. 1988. *Lawyers and Justice: An Ethical Study*. Princeton, NJ: Princeton University Press.

Lynch, Kelly J. 2004. "Best Friends? Supreme Court Law Clerks on Effective Amicus Curiae Briefs." *Journal of Law and Politics* 20: 33–75.

Mack, Kenneth W. 2005. "Rethinking Civil Rights: Lawyers and Politics in the Era Before Brown." *Yale Law Journal* 256–354.

Maguire, Robert. 2017. "Audit Shows NRA Spending Surged $100 Million amidst Pro-Trump Push in 2016." *OpenSecrets*, November 15.

Mann, Thomas E., and Anthony Corrado. 2014. *Party Polarization and Campaign Finance*. Washington, DC: Brookings Institute.

Marcus, Ruth, and Peter Baker. 1998. "Clinton 'Thwarted' Probe, Starr to Say." *Washington Post*, November 19.

Martin, Jonathan. 2010. "Republicans Reject 'Purity Test.'" *Politico*, January 29.

Masket, Seth E. 2009. *No Middle Ground: How Informal Party Organizations Control Nominations and Polarize Legislatures*. Ann Arbor: University of Michigan Press.

Mason, Lilliana. 2018. *Uncivil Disagreement: How Politics Became Our Identity*. Chicago: University of Chicago Press.

Massoglia, Anna, and Karl Evers-Hillstrom. 2021. "'Dark Money' Topped $1 Billion in 2020, Largely Boosting Democrats." *OpenSecrets*, March 17. https://www.opensecrets.org/news/2021/03/one-billion-dark-money-2020-electioncycle.

Maurer, Bill. 2011. "IJ Scores a Major Free Speech Victory." Institute for Justice, July 29. https://ij.org/ll/ij-scores-a-major-free-speech-victory-liberty-law/.

Maurer, William R. 2011. "IJ's Challenge to Arizona's 'Clean Elections' Goes to the U.S. Supreme Court." *Law and Liberty*, February 1.

Mayer, Jane. 2010. "How Mitch McConnell Became Trump's Enabler-in-Chief." *New Yorker*, April 20.

Mayer, Jane. 2011. "State for Sale." *New Yorker*, October 3.

Mayer, Jane. 2012. "The Kochs vs. Cato." *New Yorker*, March 1.

Mayer, Jane. 2016. *Dark Money: The Hidden History of the Billionaires Behind the Rise of the Radical Right*. New York: Doubleday.

Mayer, Jane. 2021. "Inside the Koch-Backed Effort to Block the Largest Election Reform Bill in Half a Century." *New Yorker*, March 29.

McCammon, Holly J., and Cathryn Beeson-Lynch. 2021. "Fighting Words: Pro-Choice Cause Lawyering, Legal-Framing Innovations, and Hostile Political-Legal Contexts." *Law and Social Inquiry* 36, no. 3: 599–634.

McCann, Michael. 1994. *Rights at Work: Pay Equity Reform and the Politics of Legal Mobilization*. Chicago: University of Chicago Press.

McCann, Michael. 1996. "Causal Versus Constitutive Explanations (or, On the Difficulty of Being So Positive . . .)." *Law and Social Inquiry* 21, no. 2: 457–82.

McCann, Michael. 1999. "How the Supreme Court Matters in American Politics: New Institutionalist Perspectives." In *The Supreme Court in American Politics*, edited by Howard Gillman and Cornell Clayton, 63–97. Lawrence: University Press of Kansas.

McCann, Michael W. 1986. *Taking Reform Seriously: Perspectives on Public Interest Liberalism*. Ithaca, NY: Cornell University Press.

McCarty, Nolan, and Eric Schickler. 2018. "On the Theory of Parties." *Annual Review of Political Science* 21: 175–93.

McCarty, Nolan, Keith T. Poole, and Howard Rosenthal. 2006. *Polarized America: The Dance of Ideology and Unequal Riches*. Cambridge, MA: MIT Press.

McConnell, Mitch. 1973. "Election Ordinance Is, in Part, Reaction to Past Excesses." *Louisville Courier-Journal*, December 15.

McConnell, Mitch. 1994. "Why We Are Stopping Campaign Finance Reform." *Heritage Lectures*, Heritage Foundation, September 21.

McConnell, Mitch. 1996. "Campaign Finance 'Reform': A View from Capitol Hill." *Free Speech and Election Law Practice Group Newsletter* (Fall).

McConnell, Mitch. 1999. "It's a Matter of Principle." *Free Speech and Election Law Practice Group Newsletter* 3, no. 1.

McConnell, Mitch. 2016. *The Long Game: A Memoir*. New York: Sentinel.

McConnell, Mitch. 2019. "Behold the Democrat Politician Protection Act." *Washington Post*, January 17.

McConnell, Mitch. 2022. "Democrats' Plan to Receive Less Criticism: Target the First Amendment." *Republican Leader, Newsroom/Remarks*, September 21. https://www.republicanleader.senate.gov/newsroom/remarks/democrats-plan-to-receive-less-criticism-target-the-first-amendment.

McEvers, Kelly. 2019. "Mitch Part 2: Money, Money, Money." June 6. In *Embedded*, produced by Tom Dreisbach. Podcast, MP3 audio, 34:32. https://www.npr.org/transcripts/729736263.

McFadden, Alyce. n.d. "McConnell and His Allies Lead Opposition to S1." *OpenSecrets*, May 13.

McFadden, Alyce. 2021. "A Look at the Companies Freezing PAC Contributions after Capitol Riot." *OpenSecrets*, January 13.

McGahn, Donald. 2017. Keynote remarks. Federalist Society National Lawyers Convention, Washington, DC, November 17. Posted to C-SPAN. https://www.c-span.org/video/?437462-8/2017-national-lawyers-convention-white-house-counsel-mcgahn.

McGuire, Kevin T. 1995. "Repeat Players in the Supreme Court: The Role of Experienced Lawyers in Litigation Success." *Journal of Politics* 57: 187–96.

McGuire, Kevin T. 1999. "The Supreme Court Bar and Institutional Relationships." In *The Supreme Court in American Politics*, edited by Howard Gillman and Cornell Clayton, 115–32. Lawrence: University Press of Kansas.

McMahon, Kevin J. 2011. *Nixon's Court: His Challenge to Judicial Liberalism and Its Political Consequences*. Chicago: University of Chicago Press.

McMunigal, Kevin C. 1996. "Of Causes and Clients: Two Tales of Roe v. Wade." *Hastings Law Journal* 47: 779–819.

Meiklejohn, Alexander. 1961. "The First Amendment Is an Absolute." *Supreme Court Review* 1961: 245–66.

Mencimer, Stephanie. 2008. "Hillary's Hero: Judge Royce Lamberth." *Mother Jones*, January 13.

Mencimer, Stephanie. 2011. "The Man behind Citizens United Is Just Getting Started." *Mother Jones* (May/June).

Mertz, Elizabeth. 1996. "Recontextualization as Socialization: Text and Pragmatics in the Law School Classroom." In *Natural Histories of Discourse*, edited by Michael Silverstein and Greg Urban, 229–49. Chicago: University of Chicago Press.

Mertz, Elizabeth. 2007. *The Language of Law School: Learning to "Think Like a Lawyer"*. New York: Oxford University Press.

Miller, Eliana. 2020. "Adelsons Give Big to G.O.P. Super PACS, Setting New Donation Record." *OpenSecrets*, October 21.

Miller, Mark C., and Jeb Barnes. 2004. *Making Policy, Making Law: An Interbranch Perspective*. Washington, DC: Georgetown University Press.

Millhiser, Ian. 2022. "The Supreme Court Just Made it Much Easier to Bribe a Member of Congress." *Vox*, May 16.

Mitchell, Allison. 1998. "Foes of Abortion Split over Campaign Finance Bill." *New York Times*, March 26: A21.

Mitchell, Allison. 2001. "A.F.L.-C.I.O. Will Oppose Some Limits in Finance Bill." *New York Times*, February 17.

Muller, Derek T. 2021. "Reducing Election Litigation." *Fordham Law Review* 90, no. 2: 561–82.

Mutch, Robert E. 1988. *Campaigns, Congress, and Courts: The Making of Federal Campaign Finance Law*. New York: Praeger.

Mutch, Robert E. 2014. *Buying the Vote: A History of Campaign Finance Reform*. New York: Oxford University Press.

Najvar, Jerad, and Dan Backer. 2013. "McCutcheon v. FEC: Why It Matters." *Daily Caller*, October 14.

Nash, George H. 1996. *The Conservative Intellectual Movement in America since 1945*. Wilmington, DE: Intercollegiate Studies Institute.

Nass, Daniel. 2020. "How Much Is the NRA Spending to Reelect Donald Trump?" *Trace*, August 31.

Natelson, Robert. 2003. "The General Welfare Clause and the Public Trust: An Essay on Original Understanding." *University of Kansas Law Review* 52: 1–56.

Neily, Clark M. 2013. *Terms of Engagement: How Our Courts Should Enforce the Constitution's Promise of Limited Government*. New York: Encounter.

NeJaime, Douglas. 2011. "Winning through Losing." *Iowa Law Review* 96: 941–1012.

NeJaime, Douglas. 2013a. "Constitutional Change, Courts, and Social Movements." *Michigan Law Review* 111: 877–902.

NeJaime, Douglas. 2013b. "Framing (In)Equality for Same-Sex Couples." *UCLA Law Review Discourse* 60: 184–99.

Nelson, Michael J., and Lee Epstein. 2022. "Human Capital in Court: The Role of Attorney Experience in US Supreme Court Litigation." *Journal of Law and Courts* 10, no. 1: 61–85.

Neuborne, Burt. 2015. *Madison's Music: On Reading the First Amendment*. New York: New Press.

Niekirk, William. 1996. "Clinton Admits FBI Files Acquired." *Chicago Tribune*, June 10.

Nilsen, Ella. 2019. "Bernie Sanders Takes Aim at the DNC with His New Anti-Corruption Plan." *Vox*, October 7.

Nisbet, Matthew C., and Mike Huge. 2006. "Attention Cycles and Frames in the Plant Biotechnology

Debate: Managing Power and Participation through the Press/Policy Connection." *Harvard International Journal of Press/Politics* 11, no. 2: 3–40.

Noel, Hans. 2012. "The Coalition Merchants: The Ideological Roots of the Civil Rights Realignment." *Journal of Politics* 74, no. 1: 156–73.

Noel, Hans. 2013. *Political Ideologies and Political Parties in America*. Cambridge: Cambridge University Press.

O'Harrow, Robert Jr., and Shawn Boburg. 2019. "A Conservative Activist's Behind-the-Scenes Campaign to Remake the Nation's Courts." *Washington Post*, May 21.

Olson, William J. 2020. "Preserving Constitutional Order." Memorandum to President Donald Trump. Vienna, VA: William J. Olson, P.C., Attorneys at Law, December 28. https://int.nyt .com/data/documenttools/olson-memo-trump-election/e59dca011b5db8c5/full.pdf.

Open Society Foundations. n.d. "Who We Are." Accessed April 17, 2021. https://www.opensoci etyfoundations.org/who-we-are.

*OpenSecrets.* n.d.a. "Business-Labor-Ideology Split in PAC & Individual Donations to Candidates, Parties, Super PACs and Outside Spending Groups." Accessed March 2, 2022. https:// www.opensecrets.org/elections-overview/business-labor-ideology-split.

*OpenSecrets.* n.d.b. "National Rifle Assn: Totals." Accessed February 7, 2023. https://www .opensecrets.org/orgs/totals.php?id=D000000082&cycle=2020.

*OpenSecrets.* 2016. "National Rifle Assn Outside Spending Summary 2016." https://www.opense crets.org/outsidespending/detail.php?cmte=National+Rifle+Assn&cycle=2016.

*OpenSecrets.* 2020a. "2020 Outside Spending, by Super PAC." https://www.opensecrets.org/out side-spending/super_pacs/2020?chrt=2022&disp=O&type=S.

*OpenSecrets.* 2020b. "2020 Top Donors to Outside Spending Groups." https://www.opensecrets .org/outside-spending/top_donors/2020?chrt=2022&disp=O&type=V.

*OpenSecrets.* 2021. "Client Profile: US Chamber of Commerce." https://www.opensecrets.org /federal-lobbying/clients/summary?cycle=2021&id=D000019798.

Packer, George. 2021. "The Man Who Waited 50 Years for This Moment." *Atlantic*, April 8.

Page, Benjamin I., Larry M. Bartels, and Jason Seawright. 2013. "Democracy and the Policy Preferences of Wealthy Americans." *Perspectives on Politics* 11: 51–73.

Page, Benjamin I., and Martin Gilens. 2017. *Democracy in America?* Chicago: University of Chicago Press.

Page, Benjamin I., Jason Seawright, and Matthew J. Lacombe. 2019. *Billionaires and Stealth Politics*. Chicago: University of Chicago Press.

Painter, Richard W. 2016. *Taxation Only with Representation: The Conservative Conscience and Campaign Finance Reform*. Auburn, AL: Take Back Our Republic Press.

Palazzolo, Joe. 2008. "Anti-Hillary Movie Smacks of Campaign Ad, Judges Say." *BLT: The Blog of LegalTimes*, January 10. https://legaltimes.typepad.com/blt/2008/01/anti-hillary-mo.html.

Pallasch, Abdon. 2010. "'Best 5 Minutes of My Life': His '09 CNBC Rant against Mortgage Bailouts for 'Losers' Ignited the Tea Party Movement." *Chicago Sun-Times*, September 19: A4.

Palmer, Anna, and Tarini Parti. 2014. "Tea Party Fumes over Campaign Finance Plan: Activists See High Dollar Limits as a Power Grab by the G.O.P. Establishment." *Politico*, December 11.

Panetta, Grace, and Brent Griffiths. 2022. "Republicans' Next Big Play Is to 'Scare the Hell Out of Washington' by Rewriting the Constitution." *Business Insider*, July 31.

Parsons, G. Michael. 2020. "Fighting for Attention: Democracy, Free Speech, and the Marketplace of Ideas." *Minnesota Law Review* 104: 2157–56.

Patch, Jeff. 2011. "McConnell Recounts Campaign Finance Fight at CPAC." *Institute for Free*

*Speech* (blog), February 10. https://www.ifs.org/blog/mcconnell-recounts-campaign-finance -fight-at-cpac/.

Pedriana, Nicholas. 2006. "From Protective to Equal Treatment: Legal Framing Processes and Transformation of the Women's Movement in the 1960s." *American Journal of Sociology* 111: 1718–61.

Perry, H. W., and L. A. Powe. 2004. "The Political Battle for the Constitution." *Constitutional Commentary* 21: 641–96.

Persily, Nathaniel, Robert F. Bauer, and Benjamin L. Ginsberg. 2018. *Campaign Finance in the United States: Assessing an Era of Fundamental Change.* Stanford, CA: Stanford Cyber Policy Center, January.

Pew Charitable Trusts. n.d. "Mission and Values." Accessed April 17, 2021. https://www.pewtrusts .org/en/about/mission-and-values.

Pew Research Center. 2015. *America's Changing Religious Landscape.* Washington, DC: Pew Research Center, May 12. https://www.pewresearch.org/religion/2015/05/12/americas-chang ing-religious-landscape/.

Pew Research Center. 2018. *The Public, the Political System and American Democracy.* Washington, DC: Pew Research Center, April 26. https://www.pewresearch.org/politics/2018/04/26 /the-public-the-political-system-and-american-democracy/.

Philanthropy News Digest. 2005. "Pew Trusts, Other Foundations Criticized for Influencing Passage of Campaign-Finance Legislation." July 6. https://philanthropynewsdigest.org/news /pew-trusts-other-foundations-criticized-for-influencing-passage-of-campaign-finance -legislation.

Phillips, Howard. 1974. " 'Campaign Reform' Should be Challenged in Court." *Human Events,* November 2.

Piety, Tamara R. 2007. "Market Failure in the Marketplace of Ideas: Commercial Speech and the Problem That Won't Go Away." *Loyola Law Review* 41: 181–82.

Piety, Tamara R. 2013. *Brandishing the First Amendment: Commercial Expression in America.* Ann Arbor: University of Michigan Press.

Pildes, Richard H. 2019. "Small-Donor-Based Campaign-Finance Reform and Political Polarization." *Yale Law Journal Forum* 129 (November 18). https://www.yalelawjournal.org/forum /small-donor-based-campaign-finance-reform-and-political-polarization.

Pildes, Richard H. 2022. "Democracies in the Age of Fragmentation." *California Law Review* 110: 2051–68.

"Political Reforms." 1973. Editorial. *National Review,* December 21.

"Politics and Potato Chips." 1997. Letter. *Washington Post,* October 11.

Polletta, Francesca. 2000. "The Structural Context of Novel Rights Claims: Southern Civil Rights Organizing, 1961–1966." *Law and Society Review* 34: 367–406.

Post, Robert C. 2000. "Reconciling Theory and Doctrine in First Amendment Jurisprudence." *California Law Review* 88: 2355–74.

Post, Robert C. 2014. *Citizens Divided: Campaign Finance Reform and the Constitution.* Cambridge, MA: Harvard University Press.

Post, Robert C., and Reva Siegel. 2006. "Originalism as a Political Practice: The Right's Living Constitution." *Fordham Law Review* 75: 545–74.

Post, Robert C., and Reva Siegel. 2007. "Roe Rage: Democratic Constitutionalism and Backlash." *Harvard Civil Rights-Civil Liberties Law Review*: 373–433.

Powell, Lewis. 1971. "Confidential Memorandum: Attack on American Free Enterprise System." *Washington Report Supplement,* August 23.

Pozen, David. 2020. "Straining (Analogies) to Make Sense of the First Amendment in Cyberspace." In *The Perilous Public Square: Structural Threats to Free Expression Today*, edited by David Pozen, 113–77. New York: Columbia University Press.

Pozen, David E., Eric L. Talley, and Julian Nyarko. 2019. "A Computational Analysis of Constitutional Polarization." *Cornell Law Review* 105: 1–84.

Presidential Commission on the Supreme Court of the United States. 2021. *Draft Final Report*. Washington, DC: December 2021. https://www.whitehouse.gov/wp-content/uploads /2021/12/SCOTUS-Report-Final.pdf.

Primo, David M., and Jeffrey D. Milyo. 2020. *Campaign Finance and American Democracy: What the Public Really Thinks and Why It Matters*. Chicago: University of Chicago Press.

"Public Financing: Booby Trap for Conservatives." 1974. Editorial. *Human Events*, April 20.

Rabban, David. 1996. "Free Speech in Progressive Social Thought." *Texas Law Review* 74: 951–1038.

Rabban, David M. 1983. "The Emergence of Modern First Amendment Doctrine." *University of Chicago Law Review* 50: 1205–351.

Rahman, K. Sabeel. 2017. *Democracy against Domination*. New York: Oxford University Press.

Ramzy, Austin, and Rachel Adams. 2020. "Steve Bing, Hollywood Producer and Financier, Is Dead at 55." *New York Times*, June 23.

Redish, Martin H. 1971. "Campaign Spending Laws and the First Amendment." *New York University Law Review* 46: 900–35.

Reese, Elizabeth A. 2018. "The Inexplicable Absence of the Voters in the Campaign Finance Debate." *Houston Law Review* 56: 123–52.

Republican National Committee. 2020. "Resolution Regarding the Republican Party Platform, as Adopted by the Republican National Committee." Washington, DC: Republican National Committee, August 22. https://wehco.media.clients.ellingtoncms.com/news/documents/2020 /08/24/GOP_resolution.pdf.

Republican Party Platforms. 1972. "Republican Party Platform of 1972." Posted online by Gerhard Peters and John T. Woolley, *American Presidency Project*. https://www.presidency.ucsb.edu /node/273411.

Republican Party Platforms. 1992. "Republican Party Platform of 1992." Posted online by Gerhard Peters and John T. Woolley, *American Presidency Project*. https://www.presidency.ucsb .edu/node/273439.

Republican Party Platforms. 1996. "Republican Party Platform of 1996." Posted online by Gerhard Peters and John T. Woolley, *American Presidency Project*. https://www.presidency.ucsb .edu/node/273441.

Republican Party Platforms. 2000. "Republican Party Platform of 2000." Posted online by Gerhard Peters and John T. Woolley, *American Presidency Project*. https://www.presidency.ucsb .edu/node/273446.

Republican Party Platforms. 2004. "Republican Party Platform of 2004." Posted online by Gerhard Peters and John T. Woolley, *American Presidency Project*. https://www.presidency.ucsb .edu/node/273450.

Republican Party Platforms. 2008. "Republican Party Platform of 2008." Posted online by Gerhard Peters and John T. Woolley, *American Presidency Project*. https://www.presidency.ucsb .edu/node/278999.

Republican Party Platforms. 2012. "Republican Party Platform of 2012." Posted online by Gerhard Peters and John T. Woolley, *American Presidency Project*. https://www.presidency.ucsb .edu/node/302338.

Republican Party Platforms. 2016. "Republican Party Platform of 2016." Posted online by Gerhard Peters and John T. Woolley, *American Presidency Project.* https://www.presidency.ucsb.edu/node/318311.

Roberts, John G. 2005. "Confirmation Hearing on the Nomination of John G. Roberts, Jr. to be Chief Justice of the United States." In *Hearings before the Committee on the Judiciary, United States Senate, 109th Congress,* 55–56. Washington, DC: US Government Printing Office. Excerpted online at https://www.uscourts.gov/educational-resources/educational-activities/chief-justice-roberts-statement-nomination-process.

Rosenberg, Gerald N. 1991. *The Hollow Hope: Can Courts Bring About Social Change?* Chicago: University of Chicago Press.

Rosenblum, Noah A. 2021. "Power-Conscious Professional Responsibility: Justice Black's Unpublished Dissent and a Lost Alternative Approach to the Ethics of Cause Lawyering." *Georgetown Journal of Legal Ethics* 34: 125–90.

Rowley, Charles K. 1992. *The Right to Justice: The Political Economy of Legal Services in the United States.* Brookfield, VT: Edward Elgar.

Rubenstein, William B. 1997. "Divided We Litigate: Addressing Disputes among Group Members and Lawyers in Civil Rights Campaigns." *Yale Law Journal* 106: 1623–81.

Scalia, Antonin. 1989. "Originalism—The Lesser Evil." *University of Cincinnati Law Review* 57: 849–65.

Scalia, Antonin. 1997. *A Matter of Interpretation.* Princeton, NJ: Princeton University Press.

Schauer, Frederick. 2004. "The Boundaries of the First Amendment: A Preliminary Exploration of Constitutional Salience." *Harvard Law Review* 117: 1765–809.

Schauer, Frederick. 2015. "The Politics and Incentives of First Amendment Coverage." *William and Mary Law Review* 56: 1613–35.

Scheiber, Noam. 2005. "Merit Scholars." *New Republic,* October 17.

Scheingold, Stuart A. 1974. *The Politics of Rights: Lawyers, Public Policy, and Political Change.* Ann Arbor: University of Michigan Press.

Scheingold, Stuart A., and Austin Sarat. 2004. *Something to Believe In: Politics, Professionalism, and Cause Lawyering.* Stanford, CA: Stanford University Press.

Schmidt, Christopher W. 2018. *The Sit-Ins: Protest and Legal Change in the Civil Rights Era.* Chicago: University of Chicago Press.

Schmidt, Vivien A. 2008. "Discursive Institutionalism: The Explanatory Power of Ideas and Discourse." *Annual Review of Political Science* 11: 303–26.

Schmidt, Vivien A. 2011. "Reconciling Ideas and Institutions through Discursive Institutionalism." *Ideas and Politics in Social Science Research* 1: 76–95.

Schwartz, Herman, ed. 1998. *The Burger Court: Counter-Revolution or Confirmation?* New York: Oxford University Press.

Seipel, Brooke. 2019. "Wyden Blasts FEC Republicans for Blocking Probe into NRA over Possible Russia Donations." *Hill,* August 16.

Severns, Maggie. 2021. "Koch Network Pledges to 'Weigh Heavy' Lawmakers' Actions in Riots." *Politico,* January 13.

Shanor, Amanda. 2016. "The New Lochner." *Wisconsin Law Review* 133: 133–80.

Shanor, Amanda. 2022. "The Tragedy of Democratic Constitutionalism." *UCLA Law Review* 68: 1302–91.

Shapiro, Ilya, and Nicholas Mosvick. 2010–2011. "Stare Decisis after Citizens United: When Should Courts Overturn Precedent." *Nexus Journal of Law and Public Policy* 16: 121–35.

Shapiro, Martin. 1990. "Interest Groups and Supreme Court Appointments." *Northwestern University Law Review* 84, nos. 3–4: 935–61.

Shapiro, Martin, and Alec Sweet. 2002. *On Law, Politics, and Judicialization*. New York: Oxford University Press.

Sherfinsky, David. 2020. "'Diminished' NRA at Crossroads ahead of 2020 Election." *Washington Post*, January 5.

Shiffman, John. 2014. "Chamber of Commerce Forms Its Own Elite Law Team." *Reuters*, December 8.

Sides, John, Chris Tausanovitch, and Lynn Vavreck. 2022. *The Bitter End: The 2020 Presidential Campaign and the Challenge to American Democracy*. Princeton, NJ: Princeton University Press.

Siegel, Reva. 2008. "Dead or Alive: Originalism as Popular Constitutionalism in Heller." *Harvard Law Review* 122: 190–245.

Siegel, Reva. 2022. "The Politics of Constitutional Memory." *Georgetown Journal of Law and Policy* 20: 19–58.

Silverstein, Gordon. 2009. *Law's Allure: How Law Shapes, Constrains, Saves, and Kills Politics*. New York: Cambridge University Press.

Silverstein, Helena. 1996. *Unleashing Rights: Law, Meaning, and the Animal Rights Movement*. Ann Arbor: University of Michigan Press.

Silverstein, Helena, and Michael McCann. 1998. "Rethinking Law's 'Allurements': A Relational Analysis of Social Movement Lawyers in the United States." In *Cause Lawyering: Political and Professional Commitments*, edited by Austin Sarat and Stuart A. Scheingold, 261–92. New York: Oxford University Press.

Simon, William H. 1994. "The Dark Secret of Progressive Lawyering: A Comment on Poverty Law Scholarship in the Post-Modern, Post-Reagan Era." *University of Miami Law Review* 48: 1099–1114.

Simpson, Stephen. 2007. "If You Wanna Speak, You Better Have a Lawyer." *National Review Online*, March 27.

Simpson, Stephen, and Paul Sherman. 2011. "Stephen Colbert's Free Speech Problem." *Wall Street Journal*, May 9.

Skocpol, Theda. 2003. *Diminished Democracy: From Membership to Management in American Civil Life*. Norman: University of Oklahoma Press.

Skocpol, Theda, and Alexander Hertel-Fernandez. 2016. "The Koch Network and Republican Party Extremism." *Perspectives on Politics* 14, no. 3: 681–99.

Skocpol, Theda, and Vanessa Williamson. 2014. *The Tea Party and the Remaking of Republican Conservatism*. New York: Oxford Unversity Press.

Skowronek, Stephen. 2011. *Presidential Leadership in Political Time: Reprise and Reappraisal*. 2nd ed. Lawrence: University Press of Kansas.

Smith, Bradley A. 1994. "Congress Shall Make No Law." *Washington Times*, December 29: A19.

Smith, Bradley A. 1995. *Cato Institute Policy Analysis No. 238: Campaign Finance Regulation: Faulty Assumptions and Undemocratic Consequences*. Washington, DC: Cato Institute, September 13.

Smith, Bradley A. 1996. "Faulty Assumptions and Undemocratic Consequences of Campaign Finance Reform." *Yale Law Journal* 105: 1049–91.

Smith, Bradley A. 1997a. "Should 'Committing Politics' Be a Crime? The Case for Deregulating Campaign Finance." *Free Speech and Election Law Practice Newsletter* (Fall).

Smith, Bradley A. 1997b. "Why Campaign Finance Reform Never Works." *Wall Street Journal*, March 19: A19.

Smith, Bradley A. 1998. "Soft Money, Hard Realities: The Constitutional Prohibition on a Soft Money Ban." *Notre Dame Journal of Legislation* 24: 179–200.

Smith, Bradley A. 2001. *Unfree Speech: The Folly of Campaign Finance Reform.* Princeton, NJ: Princeton University Press.

Smith, Bradley A. 2003. "Searching for Corruption in All the Wrong Places." *Cato Supreme Court Review*: 187–222.

Smith, Bradley A. 2004. "McConnell v. FEC: Ideology Trumps Reality." *Election Law Journal* 3: 345–53.

Smith, Bradley A. 2007. "The John Roberts Salvage Company: After McConnell, A New Court Looks to Repair the Constitution." *Ohio State Law Journal* 68: 891–924.

Smith, Bradley A. 2016. "Politics, Money, and Corruption: The Story of McConnell v. Federal Election Commission." In *Election Law Stories*, edited by Joshua A. Douglas and Eugene D. Mazo, 313–57. St. Paul, MN: Foundation Press.

Smith, Bradley A., and Jason Robert Owen. 2007. "Boundary-Based Media Restrictions in Boundless Broadcast Media Markets: McConnell v. FEC's Underinclusive Overbreadth Analysis." *Stanford Law and Policy Review* 18: 240–65.

Snodgrass, Erin. 2021. "McConnell Says the Quiet Part Out Loud, Tells Corporate America to 'Stay Out of Politics,' but Clarifies He's 'Not Talking about Political Contributions.' " *Business Insider*, April 7.

Snow, David A., and Robert D. Benford. 1992. "Master Frames and Cycles of Protest." In *Frontiers in Social Movement Theory*, edited by Aldon D. Morris and Carol McClurg Mueller, 133–55. New Haven, CT: Yale University Press.

Snow, David A., E. Burke Rochford Jr., Steven K. Worden, and Robert D. Benford. 1986. "Frame Alignment Processes, Micro-Mobilization, and Movement Participation." *American Sociological Review* 51, no, 4: 464–81.

Sonka, Joe. 2014. "Leaked Audio of McConnell's Speech before Billionaires Reveals His Greatest Hopes and Fears." *Louisville Future*, August 27.

Southworth, Ann. 1999. "Collective Representation for the Disadvantaged: Variations in Problems of Accountability." *Fordham Law Review* 5: 2449–73.

Southworth, Ann. 2000. "The Rights Revolution and Support Structures for Rights Advocacy." *Law and Society Review* 34, no. 4: 1203–20.

Southworth, Ann. 2005. "Conservative Lawyers and the Contest over the Meaning of 'Public Interest Law.' " *UCLA Law Review* 52: 1223–78.

Southworth, Ann. 2008. *Lawyers of the Right: Professionalizing the Conservative Coalition.* Chicago: University of Chicago Press.

Southworth, Ann. 2017. "Elements of the Support Structure for Campaign Finance Litigation in the Roberts Court." *Law and Social Inquiry* 43: 319–59.

Southworth, Ann. 2018. "Lawyers and the Conservative Counterrevolution." *Law and Social Inquiry* 43: 1698–728.

Spakovsky, Hans von. 2012. "Free Speech for Me, but Not for Thee." *Heritage Foundation*, March 13.

Stetson, Damon. 1971. "Head of I.L.G.W.U. Sees Threat to Union's Role." *New York Times*, May 14.

Stettin, Brian. 1998. "Cities Are Finding Ways to Sweep Gangs Off the Streets." *Free Speech and Election Law Practice Group Newsletter* 2, no. 2.

Stevens, Charles, and Chris Dolmetsch. 2013. "Robert W. Wilson Leaps to His Death at 87, Hedge-Fund Founder and Philanthropist." *Washington Post*, December 25: B1.

Stohler, Stephan. 2019. *Reconstructing Rights: Courts, Parties, and Equality Rights in India, South Africa, and the United States*. New York: Cambridge University Press.

Strauss, David A. 2010. *The Living Constitution*. New York: Oxford University Press.

Strine, Leo E., and Nicholas Walter. 2015. "Conservative Collision Course? The Tension between Conservative Corporate Law Theory and Citizens United." *Cornell Law Review* 100: 335–90.

Strine, Leo E., and Nicholas Walter. 2016. "Originalist or Original: The Difficulties of Reconciling Citizens United with Corporate Law History." *Notre Dame Law Review* 91: 878–934.

Sunstein, Cass R. 1995. *Democracy and the Problem of Free Speech*. New York: Free Press.

Swan, Jonathan. 2015. "Backlash Grows over McConnell's Campaign Spending Measure." *Hill*, December 5.

Teachout, Zephyr. 2014. *Corruption in America: From Benjamin Franklin's Snuff Box to Citizens United*. Cambridge, MA: Harvard University Press.

Tebbe, Nelson. 2015. "Religion and Marriage Equality Statutes." *Harvard Law and Policy Review* 9: 25–61.

Teles, Steven M. 2008. *The Rise of the Conservative Legal Movement*. Princeton, NJ: Princeton University Press.

Teles, Steven M. 2009. "Transformative Bureaucracy: Reagan's Lawyers and the Dynamics of Political Investment." *Studies in American Political Development* 23: 61–83.

Teles, Steven M. 2016. "How the Progressives Became the Tea Party's Mortal Enemy." In *The Progressives' Century: Political Reform, Constitutional Government, and the Modern American State*, edited by Stephen Skowronek, Stephen Engel and Bruce Ackerman, 453–77. New Haven, CT: Yale University Press.

TerBeek, Calvin. n.d.a. "From Critique to Command: Brown v. Board of Education and the Political Development of Constitutional Originalism and the Republican Party, 1954–1971." Unpublished manuscript.

TerBeek, Calvin. n.d.b. "The Enemy Was Always the Establishment: Constitutional Conservatism Takes Its Contemporary Form in the Shadow of the Administrative State, 1974–1980." Unpublished manuscript on file with author.

TerBeek, Calvin. 2021. " 'Clocks Must Always Be Turned Back': Brown v. Board of Education and the Racial Origins of Constitutional Originalism." *American Political Science Review* 115: 821–34.

Theriault, Sean. 2008. *Party Polarization in Congress*. New York: Cambridge University Press.

Thomas More Law Center. n.d. "Battle Ready to Defend America." Accessed March 25, 2022. https://www.thomasmore.org.

Tokaji, Daniel P. 2020. "Truth, Democracy, and the Limits of Law." *St. Louis University Law Journal* 64: 579–94.

Toobin, Jeffrey. 2012. "Money Unlimited: How Chief Justice John Roberts Orchestrated the Citizens United Decision." *New Yorker*, May 14.

Torres-Spelliscy, Ciara. 2019. "Trump's Judicial Picks Are Gutting Campaign Finance Law." *Law360*, September 12.

Troy, Daniel E. 1998. "Taking Commercial Speech Seriously." *Free Speech and Election Law Practice Group Newsletter* 2, no. 1.

Tushnet, Mark. 1984. "An Essay on Rights." *Texas Law Review*: 1363–403.

Tushnet, Mark V. 2005. *The NAACP's Legal Strategy Against Segregated Education, 1925–1950*. Durham: University of North Carolina Press.

Tushnet, Mark V. 2006. "The Supreme Court and the National Political Order: Collaboration and Confrontation." In *The Supreme Court and American Political Development*, by Ronald Kahn and Ken Kersch, 117–37. Lawrence: University Press of Kansas.

Tushnet, Mark V. 2020a. "Over Time, She Will Swing the Court to the Right." *Politico*, September 26.

Tushnet, Mark V. 2020b. *Taking Back the Constitution: Activist Judges and the Next Age of American Law*. New Haven, CT: Yale University Press.

Tushnet, Mark V., and Bojan Bugaric. 2021. *Power to the People: Constitutionalism in an Age of Populism*. New York: Oxford University Press.

United States Senate. 1974. *Final Report of the Senate Committee on Presidential Campaign Activities*. Report no. 93–981. Washington, DC: United States Senate, June, https://www.senate.gov/about/resources/pdf/watergate-final-report-1974.pdf.

US Chamber of Commerce Litigation Center. 2022. "What We Do." March. https://www.chamberlitigation.com/what-we-do.

US Treasury Inspector General for Tax Administration. 2017. *Review of Selected Criteria Used to Identify Tax-Exempt Applications for Review*. Ref. no. 2017-10-054. Washington, DC: US Department of the Treasury, September 28. https://www.oversight.gov/sites/default/files/oig-reports/201710054fr.pdf.

Varsava, Nina. 2018. "Elements of Judicial Style: A Quantitative Guide to Neil Gorsuch's Opinion Writing." *New York University Law Review* 93: 75–112.

Varsava, Nina. 2020. "Computational Legal Analysis, Digital Humanities, and Textual Analysis." In *Computational Legal Studies: The Promise and Challenge of Data-Driven Research*, edited by Ryan Whalen, 29–52. Northampton, MA: Edward Elgar Publishing.

Viebeck, Elise. 2015. "Mark Meadows' House of Cards Moment." *Washington Post*, June 25.

Vogel, Kenneth P., and Shane Goldmacher. 2022a. "Democrats Decried Dark Money. Then They Won with It in 2020." *New York Times*, August 21.

Vogel, Kenneth P., and Shane Goldmacher. 2022b. "An Unusual $1.6 Billion Donation Bolsters Conservatives." *New York Times*, August 22.

Vogel, Kenneth P., Shane Goldmacher, and Ryan Mac. 2022. "Dissatisfied with Their Party, Wealthy Republican Donors Form Secret Coalitions." *New York Times*, April 6.

Volokh, Eugene. 1995. "Cheap Speech and What It Will Do." *Yale Law Journal* 104: 1805–50.

Volokh, Eugene. 1999. "Is Criticizing Affirmative Action Illegal in Chicago?" *Free Speech and Election Law Practice Group Newsletter* 3, no. 2 (Summer).

Walker, Samuel. 1999. *In Defense of American Liberties: A History of the ACLU*. Carbondale: Southern Illinois Press.

Walpin, Gerald. 1997. "A Scholarly and Courageous Treaty on the Victory of Obscenity over Morality." *Free Speech and Election Law Practice Group Newsletter* 1, no. 3.

Watson, Kathryn. 2019. "Trump Says He's Draining the Swamp as He Fills His Cabinet with Ex-Lobbyists." *CBS News*, June 20.

Wedeking, Justin. 2010. "Supreme Court Litigants and Strategic Framing." *American Journal of Political Science* 54: 617–31.

Weiland, Morgan N. 2017. "Expanding the Periphery and Threatening the Core: The Ascendant Libertarian Speech Tradition." *Stanford Law Review*: 1389–472.

Weinrib, Laura. 2016. *The Taming of Free Speech: America's Civil Liberties Compromise*. Cambridge, MA: Harvard University Press.

Weinrib, Laura. 2021. "Breaking the Cycle: Rot and Recrudescence in American Constitutional History." *Boston University Law Review* 101: 1857–78.

Wheeler, Lydia. 2021. "Kagan Accuses Supreme Court Majority of Weaponizing the First Amendment." *Hill*, April 15.

Whitehead, John W. 1983. *The Stealing of America*. Westchester, IL: Crossway Books.

Whittington, Keith. 2005. " 'Interpose Your Friendly Hand': Political Supports for the Exercise of Judicial Review by the United States Supreme Court." *American Political Science Review* 99, no. 4: 583–96.

Whittington, Keith E. 2004. "The New Originalism." *Georgetown Journal of Law and Public Policy* 2: 500–613.

Whittington, Keith E. 2019. *Repugnant Laws: Judicial Review of Acts of Congress from the Founding to the Present*. Lawrence: University Press of Kansas.

Wilkinson, J. Harvey. 2012. "The Lost Arts of Judicial Restraint." *Green Bag 2d*: 16.

William J. Olson, P.C., Attorneys at Law. n.d. "Areas of Practice." Accessed May 2, 2022. http://www.lawandfreedom.com/wordpress/areas-of-practice/.

Wilson, Joshua. 2013. *The Street Politics of Abortion: Speech, Violence, and America's Culture Wars*. Stanford, CA: Stanford Law Books.

Wilson, Joshua. 2016. *The New States of Abortion Politics*. Stanford, CA: Stanford Briefs.

Windsor, Lauren. 2014. "Caught on Tape: What Mitch McConnell Complained About to a Roomful of Billionaires (Exclusive)." *Nation*, August 26.

Winkler, Adam. 2013. *Gun Fight: The Battle Over the Right to Bear Arms in America*. New York: Norton.

Winkler, Adam. 2018a. "Is the Second Amendment Becoming Irrelevant?" *Indiana Law Journal* 93: 253–77.

Winkler, Adam. 2018b. *We the Corporations: How American Business Won Their Civil Rights*. New York: Liveright.

Winter, Ralph K. 1974. "Watergate and the Law: Political Campaigns and Presidential Power." Washington, DC: American Enterprise Institute.

Winter, Ralph K., and John R. Bolton. 1973. *Campaign Finance and Political Freedom*. Washington, DC: American Enterprise Institute.

Winter, Ralph K., Jr. 1971. "Money, Politics, and the First Amendment." In *Campaign Finances: Two Views of the Political and Constitutional Implications*, by Ralph K. Winter and Howard R. Penniman, 44–71. Washington, DC: American Enterprise Institute.

Winter, Steven L. 2001. *A Clearing in the Forest: Law, Life, and Mind*. Chicago: University of Chicago Press.

Wittgenstein, Ludwig. 1953. *Philosophical Investigations*. Oxford: Basil Blackwell.

Wu, Tim. 2020. "Is the First Amendment Obsolete?" In *The Perilous Public Square: Structural Threats to Free Expression Today*, edited by David E. Posen, 15–43. New York: Columbia University Press.

Wuthnow, Robert. 1989. *Communities of Discourse: Ideology and Social Structure in the Reformation, the Enlightenment, and European Socialism*. Cambridge, MA: Harvard University Press.

Ziegler, Mary. 2010. "Framing Change: Cause Lawyering, Constitutional Decisions, and Social Change." *Marquette Law Review* 94: 263–310.

Ziegler, Mary. 2013. "Grassroots Originalism: Rethinking the Politics of Judicial Philosophy." *University of Louisville Law Review* 51: 201–38.

Ziegler, Mary. 2022. *Dollars for Life: The Anti-Abortion Movement and the Fall of the Republican Establishment*. New Haven, CT: Yale University Press.

# Index

The Chicago Series in Law and Society

EDITED BY JOHN M. CONLEY, CHARLES EPP, AND LYNN MATHER

*Series titles, continued from front matter*

www.ingramcontent.com/pod-product-compliance
Lightning Source LLC
Chambersburg PA
CBHW022139020426
42334CB00015B/967